Herbert R. Reginbogin

Faces of Neutrality

Herbert R. Reginbogin

Faces of Neutrality

A Comparative Analysis
of the Neutrality of Switzerland
and other Neutral Nations
during WW II

With a Foreword by
Detlev F. Vagts, HLS

LIT

Editor: Working Group Lived History, Bern, Switzerland

This book was first published in 2006 under the Title DER VERGLEICH by Arbeitskreis Gelebte Geschichte, Switzerland

Translated by Ulrike Seeberger and Jane Britten

Copy edited by Thomas Ryan

∞ ™ The paper used in this publication meets the minimum requirements of American National Standard for Information Sciences – Permanence of Paper for Printed Library Materials ANSI/NISO Z.39.48-1992

Bibliographic information published by the Deutsche Nationalbibliothek
The Deutsche Nationalbibliothek lists this publication in the Deutsche Nationalbibliografie; detailed bibliographic data are available in the Internet at http://dnb.d-nb.de.

ISBN 978-3-8258-1914-9

A catalogue record for this book is available from the British Library

© LIT VERLAG Dr. W. Hopf Berlin 2009

Distribution:
In Germany and Switzerland: LIT Verlag Fresnostr. 2, D-48159 Münster
Tel. +49 (0) 2 51/620 32 - 22, Fax +49 (0) 2 51/922 60 99, e-Mail: vertrieb@lit-verlag.de

In Austria: Medienlogistik Pichler-ÖBZ GmbH & Co KG
IZ-NÖ, Süd, Straße 1, Objekt 34, A-2355 Wiener Neudorf
Tel. +43 (0) 2236/63 535-290, +43 (0) 2236/63 535 - 243, mlo@medien-logistik.at

Distributed in the UK by: Global Book Marketing, 99B Wallis Rd, London, E9 5LN
Phone: +44 (0) 20 8533 5800 – Fax: +44 (0) 1600 775 663
http://www.centralbooks.co.uk/html

Distributed in North America by:

Transaction Publishers
New Brunswick (U.S.A.) and London (U.K.)

Transaction Publishers
Rutgers University
35 Berrue Circle
Piscataway, NJ 08854

Phone: +1 (732) 445 - 2280
Fax: + 1 (732) 445 - 3138
for orders (U. S. only):
toll free (888) 999 - 6778
e-mail: orders@transactionpub.com

TABLE OF CONTENTS

FOREWORD

Interest in the United States in the actions of neutral states during World War II has been erratic. For several years after 1945 there was interest in the doings of Franco's Spain, a country regarded here as more a co-belligerent of Germany than a true neutral. Spain's incorporation in NATO and the death of Franco set aside those attitudes. In the 1980s here came a flurry of interest in the behavior of Switzerland, centered on the management by Swiss banks of the accounts of individuals fleeing Nazi persecution. Excitement ran high, to a large extent because the media conveyed a sense that secrets were being uncovered. I recall a conference in 1988 at the Cardozo Law School that had the moral fervor of a revival meeting in an Evangelical church. Holocaust survivors were called upon to testify about their grievances. Politicians offered their support to the claimants. I found it hard to get a word of caution or nuance into the proceedings. The result was the generation of public attitudes in the United States quite hostile to Switzerland. Even at home in the Alps the general upshot was negative, particularly among younger people who had no direct experience of the wartime situation. The latter wave of excitement died down with the settlement. The leading figures in the furor – Alphonse d'Amato, Alan Hevesi, Rabbi Israel Singer and Stuart Eizenstat have gone from their public positions and prominence.

I was also an observer of the negotiations that led to a settlement of the claims against German companies for having employed slave and forced labor during World War II. The often horrifying facts about this were quite well known, in part because of the post-war Nuremberg trials of the Krupp, Farben and Flick managers. German scholars, sometimes with the active support of the corporations in question, had brought out further details. The German firms did not attempt to deny what they had done. As a result the media showed little interest in the matter, mainly reporting the status of the bidding rounds that led to a settlement. Almost the only item that provoked newspaper coverage interest was the discovery that some American firms such as IBM, Ford and General Motors had used slave labor or provided the Nazi system with important items of equipment.

We are thus in a period of calm that should be hospitable to this volume which benefits from the detachment afforded by the time distance and from the work done by scholars and journalists in the interim. Rather than focus solely on Switzerland or any other country it first surveys Swiss policy, starting with a review of the ways in which the economic positions of Switzerland and other states was shaped by the great depression of the 1930s and national responses to it. It then reviews the posture of other European neutrals (Part 2) and in a separate Part 3 deals with the behavior of the United States itself. Finally Part 4 undertakes a comparison of the performances of those nations. It is comprehensive but not exhaustive since it would take several bookshelves to hold a complete study of all aspects of neutral behavior. The list consists at its core of Portugal, Spain,

Sweden Switzerland and Turkey with Ireland on the periphery. For brief periods, Denmark, Norway, The Netherlands and Belgium to the West and Hungary, Rumania, Greece, Bulgaria and Yugoslavia to the East were neutrals before the German army came. France stood in a peculiar position; it was a defeated and occupied state but still regarded itself as neutral. These are the actors treated in his book. Outside of Europe, the United States was a neutral until the Japanese (December 7th 1941) and German (December 10th 1941) declarations of war and some of its activities arguably went beyond what neutral rights permit. The Soviet Union was a neutral until the German invasion of 1941 and contributed generously to the Nazi war economy.

While Professor Reginbogin approaches neutrality issues more from the perspective of an historian, I tend to analyze these questions from an international lawyer's point of view as in my prior writings on the topic of Switzerland. [International Law and World War II, 91 Am. J Int'l L. 467 (1997), and Neutrality Law in World War II, 20 Cardozo Law Review. (1998).] The standards for neutral behavior were, from a legal point of view, set forth in two conventions arrived at in the Hague in 1907, one dealing with neutrality during warfare on land and the other with neutrality during warfare at sea. Neither of these conventions has been revised since 1945 as was the prisoner of war convention. The two conventions also afforded neutrals and their nationals some protections vis-à-vis the warring powers. The 1929 Geneva Convention on the treatment of prisoners of war was important to Switzerland as it served as the supervising power with respect to the treatment of prisoners by the Allies and the Axis. There was at that time no international agreement imposing duties on states to be open in the admission of refugees. It was only in 1950 that the Protocol on the Status of Refugees with its obligation not to turn back ("refouler") persons fleeing from persecution took effect. Of course, these legal rules did not settle moral questions. For example, was it right to stand aside from the war when the powers on one side were engaged in such murderous activities as to render them outlaws? Should the neutrals have been more generous in welcoming those fleeing the Holocaust? One notes that the Hague conventions on neutrality have not been revised since 1907. The current status of their provisions is unclear. It was believed that with the advent of the United Nations and its prohibitions on armed attacks that there would be no more "war." If the Security Council took forceful action to restore peace a member of the UN could not be neutral. Nonetheless, parties arguing about the rules during the long war between Iran and Iraq sometimes drew upon the old Hague rules.

It is possible then to line up the mandates of the Hague rules and to inquire as to how well each neutral state performed in that category. The following pages undertake this project and guide the reader to those pages in the text which deal with it.

First, a neutral shall not fight. This is the essence of neutrality. Neutrality is not violated by a nation if some of its citizens slip individually into the army of a belligerent. Some Americans, for example served in the Royal Air Force during World War II. Spain went well beyond that by furnishing a regular army division to fight alongside the German army on the eastern front. The United States navy gave support to Great Britain in is struggle with the Nazi submarine fleet in the North Atlantic in a manner the Germans regarded as highly un-neutral.

Second, a neutral shall prevent its land, water and air space from being utilized for operations by the contending armies. Correspondingly the combatants shall refrain from such operations. Troops and aircraft that trespass on neutral soil should be interned. The problematic performer in this regard was Sweden which felt compelled to allow German forces to cross its territories from Denmark to Norway and from Norway to Finland. Spain also tolerated the use of its ports by Nazi submarines; sometimes they took aboard new crewmen who had transited across Spain. Switzerland permitted the use of its railroads not only to transport goods but also the wounded back to Germany. However, these transits were not forbidden. It probably violated the rules in favor of the Allies when it allowed British troops to move from Italy toward home through the Swiss railroad system when the war with Japan was still in progress. Its air force strove to drive off both German and Allied incursions into its air space. American bombers headed for Germany inadvertently caused significant casualties in Switzerland (for which the United States paid). Sweden also suffered losses from British and Soviet bombers. Portugal leaned towards the Allied side by permitting the use of the Azores by its longstanding friends in the British navy.

The question of neutral trading is more complicated. In general neutrals may trade with warring parties, even in goods of military significance. There are however certain limitations on this right, such as inhibitions on sales by governments or sales terms that are discriminatory. In fact the exercise of that right during World War II was strongly influenced by geography. From 1940 to 1944 Switzerland was completely surrounded by Germany and Italy. It had to do business with Germany in order to survive since it could not support itself without substantial imports of fuel and food. And it could not purchase supplies unless it could produce goods to be exported to pay for them. Sweden was in a rather similar situation. Some of Sweden's exports to Germany, in particular that of iron ore, were more important to the German war effort than what Switzerland offered. Spain and Turkey were not so constrained. The United States both before and after its own entry into the war supplied Britain with desperately needed supplies. American firms in Germany, Ford and General Motors (Opel) produced motor vehicles for the German army and IBM provided machines to keep track of the persecuted.

The warring parties put pressure on the neutrals to curtail their trade with the other side. The British used a "navicert" system to assure themselves that goods going to a neutral state would not be transshipped to the enemy. Firms dealing with the enemy could find themselves on a blacklist that cut them off from transactions with the allies. Belligerent states, particularly the United States, engaged in preemptive buying of such scarce commodities as chrome and tungsten in order to deny access to the Germans. Switzerland had to enter into delicate trilateral negotiations to assure that it received the minimum necessities of supplies. It is a matter for economic historians rather than lawyers to make a judgment as to how much the German war effort was aided by Swiss supplies of small arms and hydroelectric power or Swedish iron ore and ball bearings.

Financial transactions, the chief focus of interest in the case of Switzerland, were not regulated by the Conventions. The handling of the bank accounts of persecuted persons was governed only by Swiss commercial law, including its injunctions of confidentiality. The inquiry into these transactions following the class action in the New York federal court was about as thorough as it could be and involved the expenditure of millions of dollars in accounting fees plus widespread publications of long lists of the names of holders of unclaimed accounts. The outcome disappointed enthusiasts by not finding the massive treasures they had expected. The panels that were set up to scrutinize claims for abandoned accounts felt themselves under great pressure to be liberal in allowing claims and assessing their amounts. Much less conspicuously other countries, including the United States, Great Britain and Israel discovered that their banks also had unclaimed accounts.

Dealings in gold brought from Germany were indirectly affected in another Hague Convention. The Regulations annexed to the 1907 Convention respecting the Laws and Customs of War on Land proscribe looting of private property by an occupying power but they do permit the taking of property, including financial assets, of the state. Presumably knowingly receiving property that was illegally seized by the Nazis would also violate international law. It is not clear whether the gold reserves held by the central banks of such occupied countries as Czechoslovakia were strictly state property. It is also not clear who in Switzerland knew or should have known about the circumstances under which the gold came into Nazi hands. Gold also came from Germany to other neutrals – Spain, Portugal and Sweden for example – often to pay for raw materials and other warlike supplies. Swiss traders, most conspicuously art dealers, did traffic in property that had been taken by force or pressure from racially and politically persecuted persons in Germany and the territories it occupied. Much of the art in question ended up in other countries and some of it has recently been the subject of litigation by heirs of the original owners.

Each of the neutral countries had to cope with an influx of refugees and responded in different ways. The critical focus was on Switzerland's handling of the flight of Jews in the fall of 1942 as it became apparent that the Nazi regime was deporting to the extermination camps the Jewish population of France. It is clear that some were turned back at the border. From a humanitarian perspective the rejection of any refugees in such a terrible plight is repugnant and the episode caused tribulation in Swiss media and public opinion starting at the time of the exclusion. The book and movie "The Boat is full" gave widespread circulation to the problem. It is not clear, however, how many were turned back; among the complications is the fact that some who were rejected at one border crossing encountered a more sympathetic reception when they tried elsewhere. It should be noted that Switzerland did receive a total of some 300,000 refugees of one category or another. A particularly large influx came with the fall of the Mussolini regime in Italy and the invasion by German forces. Feeding and housing these numbers placed a very substantial burden on the Swiss economy. No other neutral power had to cope with such numbers. Some refugees made it to Spain over the arduous and dangerous passes through the Pyrenees and were not sent back by Franco's government. Quite a few refugees transited through Portugal on their way to the Americas – Paul Henried and Ingrid Bergman symbolized those refugees. The Turkish government, reluctant to harbor refugees, did facilitate their transit to Palestine. Sweden is famous for having received the Jewish émigrés that came by fishing boats from Denmark when the Danish resistance learned of the Nazi plans for deportation.

Neutrality is not irreconcilable with efforts to terminate hostilities and to ameliorate the human consequences of war. Switzerland, through the International Commission of the Red Cross, played an important role as the supervisor of prisoner of war camps. In part because of Red Cross inspections the survival rate of American and British POWs in Germany was high. What has aroused criticism was the refusal to go beyond the mandate of the 1929 Geneva Convention on prisoners of war to try to protect civilian detainees. Would such an effort have had any utility, given Nazi attitudes? Would it have jeopardized its prisoner of war activities? Note that the Geneva Convention (IV) Relative to Protection of Civilian Persons in Time of War of 1949 does extend the Red Cross mandate to the protection of civilian detainees in occupied territory.

Diplomatic representatives of the neutral powers did make efforts, with modest success, to protect persecuted Jews. The most famous of these was the Swedish emissary Raoul Wallenberg, who disappeared into Soviet hands when the Red arm moved into Budapest. But there were also Spanish, Swiss and other neutral consuls who provided visas, identity cards and other life-saving materials

Given the intensity of popular feelings there was no chance that World War II could have been settled by mediation, unlike the Russo-Japanese War (1905) that the American president brought to settlement. However, Swiss intermediation did finally bring about a surrender of the German armies in Italy a few days before the final capitulation and Swiss diplomatic communications provided a channel through which the Japanese could surrender.

The reader can find much more detail about these issues in the volume at hand. In particular questions about the number of refugees turned away and the number allowed into Switzerland, the amounts involved in the gold transactions and arms exports are all given careful attention in the light of recent research.

Detlev F. Vagts,
Harvard Law School

Preface

The decision to embark upon a comparative research study of neutral Switzerland and other neutral countries during World War II began with an international groundswell of popular theories of the late 1990s that European neutral countries as part of the Nazis' 'New Order' should take some responsibility for one of the bloodiest conflicts in history. Among neutral countries, Switzerland was pilloried as a major offender, while other neutrals including the USA – neutral until the end of 1941 – were not subjected to the same criticism.

American public policy changed dramatically from a neutral, non- belligerent nation following the attack on Pearl Harbor by the Japanese on December 7th 1941. Strong contours of nationalism appeared as a result of these events and in time as the war progressed moral self righteousness was clearly observable. The USA exerted pressure on all neutral countries to curtail any commercial or political relationships with America's enemies. By the end of the war America's policy of isolationism and neutrality had become a public policy of the past. As America endorsed the ideals of the United Nations Charter, it supported a foreign policy which would henceforth be more and more held accountable for both legal and moral justifications.

Swiss leadership was accused of having collaborated with Nazi Germany in breach of neutrality. The heroic image of free Swiss citizens courageously defending their homeland against Hitler's Fascist armies was considered illusionary by a generation of scholars whose perspectives of Swiss history and ideals for human rights spilled over into the Holocaust Era. Many people within the academic and political community wished to dismantle the national myth of the Swiss people because they believed that this alpine country was spared the horrors of the German military onslaught because it collaborated with the Nazis in support of Germany's goals. Many attempts were made to strip Switzerland's image of political neutrality and respectable mixed financial services, idyllic alpine mountain landscapes and ingenious watchmakers by portraying the country as having an unsavoury war record. They criticized the older generation for their patriotic memories of the wartime period, with its celebration of Swiss armed neutrality, vigilant resistance to Nazism and upholding the ideals of humanitarianism. However, such criticism was perceived as unfounded, ideological, prejudicial and even injurious to the men who served their country and are known today as the Generation of Active Military Servicemen (Aktivdienstgeneration) in Switzerland.

Beginning in 1996 a series of class action lawsuits representing millions of Holocaust victims from around the world were filed by New York attorneys in American courts on the behalf of Jewish plaintiffs against the three largest Swiss banks claiming hundreds of millions of dollars in damages and restitution for failing to return monies that had been deposited by Holocaust victims. [1] Even still today there are various voices in the United States and abroad that indeed claim that Switzerland was a collaborator to Nazi Germany. Dozens of law firms battled for several months in several countries about offenses committed during the Holocaust. [2]

In 1996 and 1997 the noted historian Gerhard L. Weinberg before the Committee on Banking and Financial Services of the House of Representatives of the United States went as far as to say, "the position of the Swiss Government at the time and in the immediate post-war years was always that looting is legal" and that "priority number one of the Swiss banks was to make as much money as possible... and to do so regardless of the legalities, moralities and decency or anything else." [3]

The subsequent litigation and debate surrounding the handling of stolen Holocaust assets led to several other law suits and prompted 24 governments to form national commissions endowed with the responsibility to document and verify how Holocaust assets were handled within their countries. The commission with the broadest mandate was the Independent Commission of Experts Switzerland – Second World War (ICE) more generally known as the Bergier Commission, after its chairman Jean François Bergier.

The Bergier Commission was given an extremely broad mandate lasting several years and extending into several areas of research to assess Switzerland's role during the period of 1933-1945. The object of the commission was "to shed light upon certain controversial or insufficiently analyzed aspects of this history, aspects in which it appeared that Switzerland, that is to say its political authorities and economic decision-makers, had perhaps been derelict in assuming their responsibilities." [4] The Commission criticized Switzerland for being too obliging in areas such as clearing credits and financial links (gold transactions). It tried to force Switzerland to concede blame not only because of its extensive financial links, but because of its refugee policy. The country was said to have contributed to the Holocaust when the Swiss "... handed over apprehended refugees directly to their persecutors, assisting the National Socialists in achieving their goals." [5]

In response to American claims about bringing Switzerland and neutral Europeans to a reluctant acknowledgement of their wartime pasts, the United States has not until now held itself up to the same harsh light of history. The Presidential

---

[1] William S. Slaney, U.S. and Allied Efforts to Recover and Restore Gold and Other Assets Stolen or Hidden by Germany During World War II. Preliminary Study. Coordinated by Stuart E. Eizenstat. Undersecretary of Commerce and International Trade. (Washington, D.C., May, 1997) available at http://www.state.gov/www/regions/eur/rpt_9806_ng_links.html *See also,* Michael J. Bazyler, Holocaust Justice. The Battle for Restitution in America's Courts. (New York, 2003), pp. 1-58.

[2] See Michael R. Marrus, "Some Measures of Justice: The Holocaust Era Restitution Campaign of the 1990s," (an upcoming publication)

[3] Hearings before the Committee on Banking and Financial Services, House of Representatives, December 11, 1996 and June 25, 1997.

[4] *See* Jean-Francois Bergier, Introductory Address, ICE Press Conference, (Mar. 22, 2002), *available at http://www.uek.ch/en/index.htm*

[5] Unabhängige Expertenkommission Schweiz – Zweiter Weltkrieg (UEK), Die Schweiz, der Nationalsozialismus und der Zweite Weltkrieg: Schlussbericht. (Zurich, 2001), p. 172

Advisory Commission on Holocaust Assets (PCHA) under President Clinton's administration failed in its effort to assess United States dealings in Holocaust-era assets and to get to the bottom of American responsibilities. According to two prominent international legal experts on the Holocaust Michael J. Bazyler and Amber J. Fitzgerald, "there seems to be a double standard at play. The demands made by the United States towards European governments and corporations to honestly confront and document their wartime financial dealings and other activities are not being registered in the United States itself."[6] The United States did not embark on having a commission compare the international context of their findings with other commissions from other countries as well as examining very closely some of America's major financial institutions and corporate businesses between 1933-1945, which were not deterred by pogroms and mishandling of civilians to continue cultivating an intertwining set of amicable relations with their future enemies before it was forced to become a belligerent country.[7]

In the realm of high-stakes American litigation, historical interpretations were utilized by lawyers for the plaintiffs, seeking what they understood as belated justice for the Holocaust "by fitting an unfathomable historic catastrophe more than half a century old into menacing legal threats and fierce accusations."[8] And so as history was enlisted by both the Swiss and their opponents, in the great struggle that unfolded in the United States, history became ever more distorted and prejudicial.

Subsequently, this book provides a more accurate account about the international context of trade, finance, humanitarian services, refugee policies, as well as international law of the times based on a comparative analysis of neutral Switzerland and neutral countries of World War II including the USA. It is my hope that this book might make a modest contribution to understand the weight of past events during an era of humanity's most horrible self imposed affliction. A more meticulous understanding of the forces at work in the years between the wars and its impact on ordinary people is needed to explain the attitudes and activities of perpetrators, collaborators and victims of World War II. Notably comparisons drawn in this book between the actions of Switzerland and those of other neutral states during World War II is but an excerpt of a much more complex dimension of world history. The research conducted in writing this book illustrates how Swiss policies conformed to the rules of international law and how the principles of neutrality were practiced in those terrible and trying times. It is ironic that many in America who had urged that the lex Americana defined in the 1990's continue to be applied, live in a new millennium with America laying claims to hegemony and some abandonment of its commitment to upholding the rule of law in their pursuit of fighting the 'Global War on Terror'.[9]

---

[6]   Michael J. Bazyler and Amber J. Fitzgerald, "Trading with the Enemy: Holocaust Restitution, The United States Government, and American Industry", in: Brookings Journal of International Law. Vol. 28:3, 2004, available at www.brooklaw.edu/students/journals/bjil/bjil28iii_bazyler.pdf

[7]   Walther Hofer and Herbert R. Reginbogin, Hitler, der Westen und die Schweiz. (Zurich, 2001)

[8]   See Michael R. Marrus, "Some Measures of Justice: The Holocaust Era Restitution Campaign of the 1990s,". (an upcoming publication)

[9]   Ibid.

At this time I would like to take the opportunity of thanking many people who assisted me in carrying out this research although it is impossible to mention everyone. My thanks go to the staff of the library at Basel University, the United States National Archives in College Park, Maryland, whereby Dr. Greg Bradsher was tremendously helpful. Also Patrick Halbeisen of the Swiss National Bank and Dr. Robert Vogler, Senior Political Analyst of the UBS Public Policy, who helped in so many different ways. I am also deeply grateful to Oliver Pluess of the Swiss Economic Archive at the University of Basel for his continuous support and assistance in acquiring literature difficult to locate in a professional and competent manner. Also, many thanks to my student assistant, Munevver Ebedi, and colleagues, Prof. K.M. George,

Prof. Christian Lekon, and Prof. Walther Hofer for their valuable support and suggestions. In addition I am grateful to Ms. Ulrike Seeberger and Ms. Jane Britten for translating the original German version of the book and to Thomas Ryan for his efforts to copy editing the text for American readers. Thanks go to Beatrice Gyssler who tanslated the original Greek text of Thucydides' quotation into English.

My special gratitude goes to the 'Members of the Working Group for Lived History in Bern' known as the AGG and other generous sponsors who made it possible to publish this book. My thanks go to Georg Gyssler, who spent countless hours organizing and editing the publication of the book while providing essential remarks and suggestions.

I dedicate this book to my wife, Karin. Without her critically reading, commenting and editing of the manuscript, this book would have never been completed.

INTRODUCTION

> As far as the facts that have been passed down of the war are concerned, I did not deem it appropriate to write on the basis of hearsay from anyone who happened to be near, nor as I did myself imagine, but on the basis of what I and others had experienced, having proceeded with the greatest possible accuracy in every detail.
>
> But it was found to be laborious, since those present at a single event did not relate the same thing about the same event, either due to partiality or due to the memory each one might be holding.
>
> *Thucydides – Early 5th century BC*

As the capitalist world came to a halt around the turn of the 1930s through a world economic crisis, acts of aggressive expansionist power-politics conducted by totalitarian regimes in Germany, Italy, and Japan increased dramatically creating a global political climate in which eventually the world stood by and saw how millions of people were brutally mistreated.

After World War II many judicial and political issues remained unsettled until after the end of the Cold War. This was about the unfinished business of that global conflict. There were the unresolved Holocaust-related issues like compensation for slave and forced laborers in German industry, looted Jewish art hanging in European museums and in private collections, and permissive prosecution of Nazi war criminals and their collaborators living in the West. But it was the role Switzerland and its banks played during the war which became the first most prominently known judicial and political issue following the end of the Cold War.

What role did Switzerland play during World War II? Did Switzerland collaborate with Germany in support of the Holocaust? Never before in its history has Switzerland been the target of such massive attacks, and never before has it been more necessary to provide an accurate comparative analysis about the international context of Switzerland's role during World War II.

History is full of national idols and mythologies and each generation attempts to critically examine them in light of newly discovered records or other forms of questions. Many national mythologies have been dismantled through critical evaluation of history such as the French resistance and collaboration with Nazi Germany and a better understanding for events in general. However, there is a strong wish within the academic and political community to dismantle the national psyche of the Swiss people. They believe that this alpine country was spared the horrors of the German military onslaught because it collaborated with the Nazis in support of Germany's goals. Many attempts have been made to strip Switzerland of its image of a mixed financial integrity and political neutrality, alpine landscapes and ingenious watchmakers by portraying the country as having an unsavory war record by blending out the international context of world events. The list of accusations is not long, but the allegations are severe indeed: financing the National Socialist war economy and seizing assets belonging to victims killed by Hitler's henchmen in concentration camps or elsewhere, turning back refugees at the border and so supporting genocide, and finally the blame of prolonging the Second World War.

In recent years, a series of works have appeared by different authors condemning Switzerland for its conduct during the war. Books like Tom Bower's, *Blood Money: The Swiss, the Nazis and the Looted Billions* or Jean Ziegler with, *The Swiss, the Gold and the Dead,* and Adam LeBor with *Hitler's Secret Bankers: The Myth of Swiss Neutrality during the Holocaust* have contributed in disseminating a much distorted image of Switzerland throughout the world by highlighting some of *"Switzerland's shady dealings in the war."* [10]

As early as 1970 a multi-volume pioneering work by Edgar Bonjour portrayed Switzerland's foreign relations during World War II. [11] His research resulted in the publication of subsequent studies about the most important events of Switzerland's diplomatic and military history without fully addressing the causes for such events. He was able to gain access to unpublished government records which portrayed Switzerland as a country enormously pressured by pro-Nazi sympathizers and followers of the New European Order – i.e. from the so-called Fifth Column and from those willing to concede defeat.

After Bonjour's work was published, Daniel Bourgeois, in *Le Troisième Reich et la Suisse 1933-1941,* also started taking a closer look at the question of neutrality in the context of the economic and financial relations between Switzerland and Nazi Germany. [12] Linus von Castelmur ventured to look across the fence and admitted that while economic and financial concessions were made while being hermetically sealed off by the Axis powers, these allowances did not violate Switzerland's prerogatives or obligations as a neutral country. Accordingly, these concessions played but a secondary role during the course of events in the Second World War. [13]

But these earlier works were by no means the last word. A young generation of researchers, who do not have first-hand experience of war, descended on documents which meanwhile had been declassified by the respective governments of the United States of America, Great Britain and France. Questions began to surface about different aspects of Switzerland's role during World War II and the heroic image of Switzerland was starting to show cracks.

---

[10] Cf. Tom Bower, Blood Money: The Swiss, the Nazis and the Looted Billions. (London, 1997), Jean Ziegler, The Swiss, the Gold and the Dead. (New York, 1998) and Adam LeBor, Hitler's Secret Bankers: The Myth of Swiss Neutrality during the Holocaust. (London, 2000).

[11] Edgar Bonjour, Geschichte der Schweizerischen Neutralität. Vier Jahrhunderte eidgenössischer Aussenpolitik. 9 Vols (Basle, 1967-1976).

[12] Daniel Bourgeois, Le Troisième Reich et la Suisse, 1933-1941. (Neuchâtel, 1974).

[13] Linus von Castelmur, Schweizerisch-Allierte Finanzbeziehungen im Übergang vom Zweiten Weltkrieg zum Kalten Krieg: Die deutschen Guthaben in der Schweiz zwischen Zwangsliquidierung und Freigabe (1945-1952). (Zürich, 1992), p. 11.

New information concerning the relations between Switzerland and Germany, the USA and Britain permitted an insight into Switzerland's delicate geopolitical position which required constant maneuvering between opposing demands made by the Axis and the Allies in view of the constant but latent threat of a German invasion. The recent findings were disseminated in a flood of relevant publications. Works such as Klaus Urner's *Die Schweiz muss noch geschluckt werden! Hitlers Aktionspläne gegen die Schweiz (Zurich, 1990) [Let's swallow Switzerland, Hitler's plans against the Swiss Confederation, 2001 Lexington Books, USA]* revealed German plans after the capitulation of France in the summer of 1940 to prevent Swiss goods from reaching Britain.

A book by Georg Kreis explored General Guisan's arrangement with the French to fight side by side against Nazi Germany in the event of a German attack on Switzerland.[14] Marco Durrer, in his 1984 work *Die schweizerisch-amerikanischen Finanzbeziehungen im Zweiten Weltkrieg. Von der Blockierung der schweizerischen Guthaben in den USA über die Safehaven-Politik zum Washington Abkommen (1941-1946) (Bern und Stuttgart, 1984) [Swiss-American Financial Relations during World War II: From blocking Swiss assets in the USA via the Safehaven Policy to the Washington Agreement (1941-1946])*, came to the conclusion that the blocking of Swiss assets held in the United States by the American government was *de facto* a decisive step towards abandoning Switzerland to Germany.[15]

Like Durrer and von Castelmur, Marc Perrenoud also reached the conclusion that the USA was able to exert considerable financial pressure on Switzerland – because of Swiss investments in the USA – to block Swiss banks from giving financial support to Germany. All three historians made restrained (and disputed) arguments concerning moral issues relating to the Swiss stance during World War II.[16]

But soon afterwards the tone began to change. While Philippe Marguerat[17] interpreted Swiss purchases of gold as absolutely legal and in conformity with the guidelines of neutrality, the first revisionist attacks emerged in a critical study, *"Raubgold aus Deutschland" [Looted Gold from Germany]*, by the publicist and film- maker Werner Rings who portrayed Switzerland as a "revolving door for gold".[18] However, he provided no clear evidence about the level of knowledge that the Swiss National Bank's (SNB) directorate had about the moral context of the gold purchases. Jakob Tanner, on the other hand, in a work published in 1986,

---

[14] Georg Kreis, Auf den Spuren von La Charité. Die schweizerische Armeeführung im Spannungsfeld des deutsch-französischen Gegensatzes 1936-1941. (Basel, 1976).

[15] Marco Durrer, Die schweizerisch-amerikanischen Finanzbeziehungen im Zweiten Weltkrieg. Von der Blockierung der schweizerischen Guthaben in den USA über die "Safehaven"-Politik zum Washington Abkommen 1941-1946. (Berne and Stuttgart, 1984), p. 46.

[16] Marc Perrenoud, "Banques et diplomatie suisse à la fin de la Deuxième Guerre mondiale. Politique de neutralité et relations financières internationales," in: Studien und Quellen. 13/14 (Berne, 1987/88), pp. 3-128.

[17] Philippe Marguerat, "La Suisse et la Neutralité dans le domaine économique pendant la seconde guerre mondiale 1940 – fin 1944," in: Louis-Edouard Roulet and Roland Blaettler (ed.), Les Etats neutres européens et la seconde guerre mondiale. (Neuchâtel, 1985), pp. 55-67.

[18] Werner Rings, Raubgold aus Deutschland. Die "Golddrehscheibe" Schweiz im Zweiten Weltkrieg. (Zurich, 1985), p. 189

analyzed the economic links between gold and capital flows by detailing how the Swiss Federation with a so-called gold sterilization meshed with the SNB's money supply and foreign-exchange currency operations. [19]

Based on continuing declassified records, a revisionist school of thought expanded. Its representatives ruthlessly dismantled the long-established traditional image of Switzerland as a victim of circumstances, and accused the Swiss leadership of that time of having collaborated with Nazi Germany in breach of Swiss neutrality. The heroic image – free Swiss citizens courageously defending their homeland against Hitler's Fascist armies – had indeed taken root in the population's minds in the post-war years. But the new revisionist criticism even attacked former members of the armed services. It criticized the older generation for their pride in Swiss defense and reproached them for holding on to the patriotic stereotypes of the Commander-in-Chief of Swiss armed forces General Guisan or the strategically located fortress in the Alps known as the Réduit. Such criticism was perceived as unfounded, ideological, prejudicial and even injurious to the men who served their country and are known today as the Generation of Active Military Servicemen (Aktivdienstgeneration) in Switzerland. [20]

In the late 1990s, the urge to point a finger at others led to a groundswell of popular theories that neutral countries had contributed to prolonging one of the bloodiest conflicts in history. [21] Among neutral countries, Switzerland was pilloried as the prime offender. The country was portrayed as Germany's main financer and stock broker and thereby was supposed to have handled vast amounts of gold and hard currency on behalf of the Nazis. [22] Historian Gerhard L. Weinberg wrote "the position of the Swiss Government at the time and in the immediate post-war years was always that looting is legal" and that "priority number one of the Swiss banks was to make as much money as possible... and to do so regardless of the legalities, moralities and decency or anything else." [23] However, Weinberg did not see fit to mention that as late as June 1940 the then neutral USA saw no need – in terms of legality, morality or common decency – to check the origin of American gold imports to ascertain whether such imports included gold stolen from Holland and Belgium, countries which had been attacked by Germany. [24] In fact, Dexter White, head of the Division of Monetary Research at the United States Treasury

---

[19] Jakob Tanner, Bundeshaushalt, Währung und Kriegswirtschaft. Eine finanz-soziologische Analyse der Schweiz zwischen 1938 und 1953. (Zurich, 1986), p. 298.

[20] Linus von Castelmur, Schweizerisch-Alliierte Finanzbeziehungen im Übergang vom Zweiten Weltkrieg zum Kalten Krieg: Die deutschen Guthaben in der Schweiz zwischen Zwangsliquidierung und Freigabe (1945-1952). (Zurich, 1992), p. 11.

[21] William S. Slaney, U.S. and Allied Efforts to Recover and Restore Gold and Other Assets Stolen or Hidden by Germany During World War II. Preliminary Study. Coordinated by Stuart E. Eizenstat. Undersecretary of Commerce and International Trade. (Washington, D.C., May, 1997) http://www.state.gov/www/regions/eur/rpt_9806_ng_links.html With reference to the Eizenstat Report (1997).

[22] Greg J. Rickmann, Swiss Banks and Jewish Souls. (New Brunswick and London, 1999); Tom Bower, Blind Eye to Murder: Britain, America and the Purging of Nazi Germany – A Pledge Betrayed. (London, 1981).

[23] Hearings before the Committee on Banking and Financial Services, House of Representatives, December 11, 1996 and June 25, 1997.

[24] Ibid., cf. pp. 40-43 – USA not interested in the origin of the gold.

Department, had nothing but contempt for this kind of suggestion. His attitude is apparent in a note he wrote six months later recording his "adamant opposition to give even serious consideration to proposals coming from those who know little of the subject that we stop purchasing gold, or that we stop buying the gold of any particular country, for this or for that or for any particular reason." [25]

Although it seems excessive to denounce one small country for prolonging World War II, some historical crusaders soon felt called upon to enlighten the world on what they saw as the reprehensible role of the Swiss economy in World War II. Their moral outrage was prompted by the fact that Switzerland supplied arms not only to the Allied powers but also to Germany. This fact was sufficient for the authors to come to the knife-sharp conclusion that Swiss arms supplied to Germany caused a prolongation of World War II. Their fact finding, however, overlooked that the Swiss supply of arms to Germany amounted to just 1% of the entire German production of armaments.

The revisionist camp consisted of a group of scholars who accused Switzerland of putting reasons of state before moral principles, and that it was only because of this fact that Switzerland escaped a German invasion. Historians such as Daniel Bourgeois, Werner Rings, Markus Heiniger, Hans Ulrich Jost and Jakob Tanner voiced the opinion that it was primarily financial connections and the country's flourishing foreign trade that forestalled a German invasion and not the courage, persistence and creativity of the Swiss. Jakob Tanner based his allegations on Swiss arms deliveries to Germany, deliveries which were worked out by a permanent Economics Delegation to Germany named by the Swiss Federal Council (Bundesrat). The necessary credits for these deliveries, according to Tanner, were thereby guaranteed by the Swiss government.

Revisionist Swiss historians also tried to force Switzerland to concede blame not only because of its extensive financial links, but because of its refugee policy. The country was said to have contributed to the Holocaust when the Swiss "…handed over apprehended refugees directly to their persecutors, assisting the National Socialists in achieving their goals." [26] Some of these historians also joined with foreign colleagues in a commission established by the Swiss government and led by Jean-François Bergier, a specialist in medieval economic history, which achieved considerable international attention. In its final report published in 2002, the Bergier Commission put Switzerland on trial for being too obliging in areas such as refugee policy, clearing credits and financial links (gold transactions). Swiss historian Thomas Maissen, who teaches in Heidelberg, portrays that members of the Bergier Commission in fact had the aim of reinterpreting Switzerland's most recent history and managed to achieve their goal. [27]

---

[25] H. D. White, "The Future of Gold", March 1, 1940 Princeton University, Seely Mudd Manuscript Library, Harry Dexter White Collection, Box 4, Section III, and corrected memos in Box 3, with last corrected version dated December 20, 1940.

[26] Unabhängige Expertenkommission Schweiz – Zweiter Weltkrieg (UEK), Die Schweiz, der Nationalsozialismus und der Zweite Weltkrieg: Schlussbericht. (Zurich, 2001), p. 172, hereafter referred to as the Bergier Report.

[27] Thomas Maissen, Verweigerte Erinnerung: Nachrichtenlose Vermögen und Schweizer Weltkriegsdebatte 1989-2004. (Zurich, 2005), pp. 515-519.

Today there is another group of historians of international renown who grew up with their country's neutrality. Their studies contradict the conclusions reached by the Bergier Report. On the basis of considerable research, such "traditionalists" demonstrate how Switzerland was in fact spared a German attack because of the deterrent effect of the Swiss army's clear willingness to defend the country and because of the creation of a Swiss fortress Réduit in the Alps. They object to the revisionists' preconceived and prejudicial critiques of Switzerland's economic and financial links with Nazi Germany, and especially to their downplaying of the role played by the Swiss military. [28] They are convinced that the Swiss army did indeed have a deterrent effect and that the moral tone of defense was in fact maintained at a high level by none other than General Guisan. They are also convinced that foreign observers were impressed by the army's readiness to defend the country. [29]

Among this group of historians are well-known scholars such as Walther Hofer and – in spite of critical statements in his final report – Jean-François Bergier, who reject as arbitrary the accusation in the preface of the Eizenstat Report [30] that Switzerland prolonged the war. They also assess Jean Ziegler's theory – that Switzerland was responsible for a prolongation of the war by several years and thus should have millions of dead on its conscience – as wildly excessive. [31] In fact, the Independent Expert Committee on Switzerland in World War II – after extensive studies – *unanimously* rejected this accusation of Switzerland prolonging the war. [32]

Nonetheless, there are certain notable Swiss historians, including Hans Ulrich Jost, who have labeled Eizenstat's theory that the gold stolen by the Nazis in Europe – in part traded by Swiss banks – played an important role in financing and thus prolonging the war, as a "fact not seriously disputed by anybody

---

[28] Hans Senn, "Die Schweizer Armee stand bereit," in: Kenneth Angst, (ed.), Der Zweite Weltkrieg und die Schweiz. (Zurich, 1997), pp. 87-98; Hans Senn, Der Schweizerische Generalstab, vii: Anfänge einer Dissuasionsstrategie während des Zweiten Weltkrieges. (Basle, 1995); Walther Hofer, "Warum die Schweiz verschont blieb" in: Schweizer Illustrierte (September 18, 1989), pp. 133-138; H. R. Kurz, Operationsplanung Schweiz. Die Rolle der Schweizer Armee in zwei Weltkriegen. (Thun, 1974); Werner Roesch, Bedrohte Schweiz. Die Operationsplanungen gegen die Schweiz im Sommer/Herbst 1940 und die Abwehrbereitschaft der Armee im Oktober 1940. (Frauenfeld, 1986) and Alfred Ernst, "Die Bereitschaft und Abwehrkraft Norwegens, Dänemarks und der Schweiz in deutscher Sicht," in: Neutrale Kleinstaaten im Zweiten Weltkrieg. (Münsingen, 1973), pp. 59-60.

[29] For example in the context of the general willingness to defend Switzerland, the US Military Intelligence Division of the War Department General Staff received a memo dated April 3, 1941 from its military attaché at the Berne embassy, Lt. Colonel B.R. Legge, which contains the following final summary: "...in case of a threat of invasion, the Army and the people will follow General Guisan and the Swiss Army can be depended upon to fight. It is always ready and can be mobilized to full strength in 48 hours." National Archives of Records Administration (NARA), RG 165, MID 2043-72/32

[30] Eizenstat (1997), p. iii.

[31] Jean Ziegler, Die Schweiz, das Gold und die Toten. (Munich, 1997); Walther Hofer, "Wer hat wann den Zweiten Weltkrieg verlängert? Kritisches zur merkwürdigen These einer Kriegsverlängerung durch die Schweiz," in: Kenneth Angst (ed.), Der Zweite Weltkrieg und die Schweiz. (Zurich, 1997), p. 111.

[32] Bergier Report, pp. 543-544.

today." [33] When he made this statement in 1997, Jost put his reputation on the line as an internationally renowned historian to stand behind a theory which seriously incriminated Switzerland and gave Eizenstat's claim an aura of truth.

In the final Bergier Report's chapter on the *Armament Industry and War Material Exports*, the Commission was unable to make a precise statement on the actual effect of Swiss exports of war materials. Instead the Commission peculiarly concluded: "Whether the contribution of Swiss exports to the German arms capacity is estimated to be slightly higher or slightly lower would not make any difference to the central findings of our research. Swiss contributions *before 1933* were of much more importance when Switzerland – along with other European states – was the location of clandestine German armament production." [34] Before 1933, however, the German Reich was *not* Nazi Germany! Here again one can discern how revisionist historians, in their eagerness to solidify an image of Switzerland as making an important contribution to the Nazis' armaments efforts, use evidence that leads to a different conclusion.

According to British historian Neville Wylie, there is no proof that an attack on Switzerland was ever an important element of German strategy. [35] Yet one cannot conclude with certainty that such a danger was not present after the summer of 1940. As Hans Senn detailed in his history of the Swiss general staff, the German "Tannenbaum Plan" for attacking Switzerland remained on the table until November 1940. The deployment of the 12th German army on Switzerland's western border cannot be trivialized as merely "training exercises for younger officers." [36] The danger of a German attack on Switzerland passed by only when Hitler turned his attention to the Soviet Union and Operations Barbarossa ordering on December 18, 1940, that the German army prepare for an attack on the Soviet Union, which occurred on June 20, 1941. The Damocles' Sword hanging over Switzerland then moved to the east, even though it was by no means certain that it might not return in a more dangerous form. Just two years later the south of Italy was occupied by the Allied powers and the north by the Germans. Again Switzerland found itself directly in the center of a war zone, and no one could predict how the future would turn out.

There is no question that a number of military plans were drawn up for invading Switzerland. To date absolutely no definitive proof has emerged as to why such plans were never implemented, and so the question of why Germany did not attack Switzerland must remain finally unanswered (unless new materials emerge).

In fact the shape and implementation of Swiss neutrality was influenced by a range of critical factors which all deserve close appraisal. Nevertheless, many Swiss who have actively experienced the war years find the revisionists' judg-

---

[33] Hans Ulrich Jost, "Die Schweiz im Zielkonflikt zwischen Neutralität, Solidarität und 'legitimem Egoismus," in: Tages-Anzeiger of May 15, 1997.

[34] Bergier Report, p. 223.

[35] Neville Wylie, "Switzerland: a neutral of distinction?," in: Neville Wylie, European Neutrals and Non-Belligerents During the Second World War. (Cambridge, 2002) pp. 346-347.

[36] Ibid. VCf... Klaus Urner, Die Schweiz muss noch geschluckt werden! Hitlers Aktionspläne gegen die Schweiz. (Zurich, 1991).

ments biased. They not only resent the shutting out of other relevant studies, they also see the real efforts they made to defend their country belittled. [37]

In any comprehensive analysis of the behavior of states during World War II, there are many reasons to criticize a good number for their conduct. But one cannot avoid the impression that, when it comes to Switzerland, some Swiss and non-Swiss historians choose to pay insufficient attention to the complexities of a war – and how what emerges from those complexities can influence the decisions of a nation's leadership and a people's emotional state of mind.

In this regard, they by and large pass over the fundamental geo-economical location of Switzerland which, even before the outbreak of World War II, was shaped by an overwhelming dependency on trade with other states. Swiss behavior can be better understood by the fact that before the war 60% of Switzerland's imports and about 55% of its exports were with only five countries – Germany, France, Italy, Great Britain and the USA – *all of which became warring parties*. [38] Each of these countries was an important supplier of essential goods to Switzerland; Germany in particular had become the most important trading partner in the pre-war years, being both the biggest customer and the most significant supplier. The Swiss government was not really in a position to oppose even one of these countries. It could merely try to keep its trade links free in all directions, by means of strenuous, tough and long negotiations, to help its population survive through the war years.

It is astonishing to which lengths some revisionists have gone in enumerating every single mistake, contradiction and confusion of Swiss policies during the war years. However, one should not forget that *any* country's government is obliged to use all of its resources for the benefit of its population. Even in peace time, extremist groups exist and excesses and problematic behavior can be found at all levels in all countries of the world. By definition periods of war, including in this case the years after 1935, were states of emergency when survival became the highest priority. The Swiss government was faced with just such an emergency and still continued to base its actions on the principle of neutrality. It was successful in obtaining essential supplies from all warring parties and thereby safeguarding the survival of both its own citizens and the many war refugees who flooded into the country.

Switzerland might, of course, have interpreted neutrality to mean refusing to supply either Allies or Axis powers with military goods. It might not have granted loans to any of the warring parties. It might have censured all controversial political opinions and blocked all forms of political expression and action. If Switzerland had *not* done all the things it is accused of today – how long might the country have survived? Is it self-righteous or even hypocritical to expect that the Swiss government should have thrown away all possible considerations to remain unoccupied and sought moral purity at the cost of losing everything? The Swiss government chose to act according to a principle repeatedly annunciated by the head of the Swiss Economic Ministry, Councilor Dr. Walther Stampfli: "Life first,

---

[37] Peter Stadler, Epochen der Schweizergeschichte. (Zurich, 2003), p. 335.
[38] Schweizerische Handelsstatistik, Jahresbericht 1945, Eidgenössische Oberzolldirektion (ed.) Part 2 (Berne, 1946), p. 4.

philosophy later." Stampfli was also quoted as saying: "I am not interested at all in the opinion of future generations. Rather I am interested in the opinion of today's generation if they were to get no coal and nothing to eat." [39] As the Swedish minister of justice, Karl Gustav Westman, pragmatically told his Swiss government colleague, neutrality should not be upheld as an abstract idea, but as a practical policy for keeping the country out of war. [40] But even if this is your goal, you need both the will and the ability to defend yourself and have an intact economy.

In early 1930, the financial, social and economic repercussions of the 1929 crash of the New York Stock Exchange became noticeable. In 1931, the world economic crisis spilled over to Britain and Europe as the so-called Great Slump. Yet certain critical works overlook this critical period of time in Swiss history which otherwise would require greater consideration for the international political and economic challenges that Switzerland faced. Had such authors perhaps given more due consideration to the impact of the Great Depression on Switzerland, then their premise about the global political and economic influence on Switzerland would have led to giving more praise to the Swiss government in walking a tightrope through five critical years of uncertainty. Encircled by the overwhelming military might of the Axis and subject to extreme demands from *both* the Axis and the Allies, the Swiss government had really no alternative but to engage in tough and very difficult economic negotiations with *both sides*. Only then was it possible for Switzerland to manage and maintain its military options for defense, its will to resist as well as (albeit restricted) independence – even its very survival as a democratic state.

There was indeed massive German pressure on Swiss authorities and on Swiss media. The government had to deal with efforts by considerable numbers of fellow-travelers of the National Socialists to undermine Swiss neutrality. On this topic, Swiss historian Jean Rudolf von Salis said shortly after the war: "One cannot ignore that, apart from the chess moves of diplomacy, the suggestive power of Fascism and National Socialism spread far beyond the borders of the German Reich. Which people could claim that it had no Quislings and no Pétains among its citizens – even if the Germans were not present in their country? Which truthful person could deny that anti-Bolshevist and even the anti-Semitic slogans had great attraction and that because of them innumerable Europeans and Americans forgave the Hitler regime many excesses, at least in the beginning?" [41]

With the country subjected to these manifest dangers, the survival of the economy and the survival of Switzerland as an independent state were understandably given absolute priority. Therefore it was inevitable that compromises had to be made between the good and the bad. But wherever possible, Switzerland offered

---

[39] Georg Hafner, Bundesrat Walther Stampfli (1884-1965). (Olten, 1986), p. 261 – He was the head of the war economy during World War II and the "father" of the AHV (Department of Social Security) in the Council.

[40] Sten Carlsson, "Die schwedische Neutralität – Eine historische Übersicht," in: Rudolf L. Bindschedler et al. (ed.), Schwedische und schweizerische Neutralität im Zweiten Weltkrieg. (Basle, 1985), p. 28.

[41] J.R. von Salis, "Kriegsende in Europa," in: Neue Schweizer Rundschau, 13 1945/1946, p. 67-88. Cf. also Hans Ulrich Jost, Politik und Wirtschaft im Krieg: Die Schweiz 1938-1948. (Zurich, 1998), p. 148.

resistance. The Allied blockade and Axis counter-blockade negotiations in the early phase of World War II are a good example of Swiss persistence. Although the Hague Convention of 1907 expressly grants neutral states *the right to trade with all warring parties,* in spring of 1940 the Allies imposed a blockade against Switzerland and other neutral countries. [42] Between September 1, 1939 and May 10, 1940, the Swiss delegation had to fight both the French and the British for virtually every import and export permission for essential products. [43]

If Hans Ulrich Jost writes that the Swiss used their neutrality to slip out of Allied demands, his assessment is simply wrong. [44] It is true that after the outbreak of the war Switzerland tried to play its "neutrality card" to oppose French and British demands for arms deliveries and British demands for loans. But the Swiss soon found that this supposed trump card didn't have the expected effect on the Allied side. Instead, the French threatened to cut off supplies of food to Switzerland. Food dependence was one of the main reasons for the Swiss decision to renege on their neutrality ruling of April 14, 1939. This law had included a ban on exporting arms, ammunition, explosives and other war materials and components to warring parties. [45] Thereafter, French arms orders could be fulfilled legally in return for the release of essential food stuffs and other products from that country.

Swiss neutrality, though changing in its focus and emphasis, remained consistent. Even though Switzerland indeed made (sometimes secret) deliveries to the Allied powers, at the same time contacts with the Axis were also maintained. Those who criticize the latter should also recall that Switzerland acted as a representative for protecting the interests of a number of states which had broken off formal diplomatic contacts. During World War I, 25 states entrusted Switzerland with this task. In World War II this number increased to 43. [46] The services rendered by Switzerland in this regard were a major benefit to the Allied powers and many other countries as well. How could Switzerland have fulfilled these obligations without maintaining good relations with all warring powers?

Swiss refugee policy has also come under attack and has been criticized though often without justification or even complete knowledge of what actually happened. The gap between perception and reality is well illustrated in Swiss Counselor Eduard von Steiger's often quoted "the boat is full" speech. Von Steiger said: "Whoever has to command an already very full life boat with limited capacity and equally limited supplies while thousands of victims of a shipping disaster are crying for help must seem hard if he cannot take everybody on board. But still he remains humane if he warns people in time not to harbor false hopes and if he at least tries to save those already taken in." [47]

---

[42] Robert U. Vogler, Die Wirtschaftsverhandlungen der Schweiz zwischen der Schweiz und Deutschland 1940 und 1941. Basle / Frankfurt am Main, 1997), pp. 26-31.

[43] Walther Hofer and Herbert R. Reginbogin, Hitler, der Westen und die Schweiz. (Zürich, 2001).

[44] Hans Ulrich Jost, Politik und Wirtschaft im Krieg: Die Schweiz 1938-1948. (Zürich, 1998), p. 226.

[45] Amtliche Sammlung eidgenössischer Gesetzeserlasse, "Verordnung über die Handhabung der Neutralität vom 14. April 1939", p. 810.

[46] Hans Ulrich Jost, "Bedrohung und Enge (1914-1945)," in: Geschichte der Schweiz und der Schweizer. (Basle, 1986), p. 738.

[47] Carl Ludwig, Die Flüchtlingspolitik der Schweiz seit 1933 zur Gegenwart. (Bern, 1957), p. 394

Critics often don't consider the 320,000 refugees and internees taken aboard by Switzerland during a very difficult food situation. In a landlocked, mainly mountainous region and an encircled country, Switzerland's supplies of food 1940-1944 were largely controlled by the Axis powers which could cut off deliveries at will. In this light, Switzerland did more for refugees than most other states, certainly much more than the USA which has been so vociferous in its criticism of the Swiss.

There is no denying that influential people and groups of various stripes opposed a more open refugee policy in general and the admission of Jewish refugees in particular. The aversion to refugees was an international problem, and the treatment of refugees remains one of the darkest chapters of the war, both in Swiss and European, indeed in world history. Consider the persecution of Jews in unoccupied Vichy France and the handing over of Jewish children to the Nazis. [48] Likewise one can criticize the inhumanity of Cuban and American authorities who denied the ship St. Louis permission to dock – a ship loaded with Jewish refugees, men, women and children. In spite of urgent appeals to Congress and President Roosevelt, the St. Louis was ordered to return to Germany in 1939. During the vessel's return journey, Britain, France, Holland and Belgium declared their willingness to take in a certain number of its Jewish passengers, and finally the ship was given permission to dock in Antwerp. However, only the refugees taken in by Britain managed to survive the war more or less unharmed. After the German invasion of the other three countries, the passengers of the St. Louis became victims to the Nazi dictatorship after all. [49]

With today's knowledge of the horrific dimensions of the Holocaust and of the use of forced laborers and concentration camp inmates in German industry, and with the accusation and counter-accusations concerning the so-called collaboration of Switzerland with Nazi Germany, there would seem to be a pressing necessity to take a much closer look at the international framework – in trade, finance and politics – in which this small alpine country had to move, and to compare its actions with those of other nations.

The present book analyses the international context of political, economic, military and historical events before and during World War II which had a significant influence on Switzerland, in order to give a better understanding of the geopolitical situation and the resulting narrow scope of action for Switzerland during the time of National Socialism and Fascism. At the same time, it seeks to lay out the spirit of those times, the situation of Switzerland in the world, and to

---

Recent studies increased the number of refugees taken in by a further 30,000 people, so that we would need to talk about 320,000 refugees. Cf. Joerg Krummenacher-Schoell, Flüchtiges Glück: Die Flüchtlinge im Grenzkanton St. Gallen zur Zeit des Nationalsozialismus. (Zurich, 2005); Urs Rauber, "Rettungshafen St. Gallen. Der Ostschweizer Kanton nahm mehr Nazi-Flüchtlinge auf als bisher angenommen," in: Neue Zürcher Zeitung (NZZ Sunday paper) of September 18, 2005, p. 81.

[48] Bergier Report, p. 171; Jean Matteoli, Summary of the Work by the Study Mission on the Spoliation of Jews in France, cf. www.ladocfrancaise.gouv.fr April 17, 2000.

[49] J. E. Georg and Mautner Markhof, Das St. Louis-Drama: Hintergrund und Rätsel einer mysteriösen Aktion des Dritten Reiches. (Graz and Stuttgart, 2001).

compare – systematically and as far as possible objectively – the positions and actions of Switzerland with those of other neutral countries.

It is the goal of the present work not only to reassert facts which have been ignored and to point out historical distortions, but to shed light on the complex obligations faced by the decision-makers of those days. Our understanding of policies and laws of those years can be complete and balanced only when the whole story is known. In addition, the international comparisons laid out in the pages which follow show how other countries – both neutral and belligerently warring states – acted throughout the war period and what role the principle of neutrality played in meeting the challenges and dangers they faced.

CHAPTER I

SWITZERLAND BEFORE AND DURING WWII

NEUTRALITY – SWISS IDENTITY

After decades-long Napoleonic Wars, Europe's smaller states were granted an important role in keeping the peace, as part of the so-called "Balance of Power" policy. Switzerland was one of those states which had adopted neutrality as its foreign policy. Indeed, the leading European powers issued a guarantee for the practice of neutrality in 1815. This guarantee articulated both respect for the borders of neutral countries and for their political integrity. The declaration of March 20, 1815, acknowledged the permanent status of Switzerland's neutrality and guaranteed the integrity and inviolability of its territories. [50]

Over a hundred years later during World War II Switzerland's international relations was based on this deep-seated belief in neutrality, its historical evolution and political culture, a belief which was long inculcated in the Swiss people. Subsequently, neutrality not only set the tone for the Swiss attitude towards other countries, but its own domestic security policies. Moreover, during World War II the upholding of the principles of neutrality meant survival, not only to cope with the demands of the Axis Powers but the Allies alike. Domestically, the common belief in neutrality strengthened the national feeling of solidarity and counteracted the danger of ethnic fragmentation always present in any multi-cultural society. Neutrality was a powerful unifying factor for French-, German-, Romanic- and Italian-speaking Swiss, and as a nation, neutrality helped in reducing the temptation on the part of their citizens to look across the border and identify themselves with their linguistic and cultural "roots" or other dominant national identities beyond Switzerland.

Historically, the United States of America was the most influential and powerful state ever to take up the principle of neutrality. In the 19th century the USA pursued a policy of neutrality, if not isolationism. In the 20th century, too, or rather before the American entry in World War I, the interests of Switzerland and the USA, as far as neutrality and freedom of trade were concerned, definitely coincided. Moreover, American foreign policy was more oriented towards being

---

[50]   See http://hypo.ge-dip.etat-ge.ch/www/cliotexte/html/suisse.histoire.1815.2.html – "Les puissances signataires de la déclaration de Vienne du 20 mars font, par le présent acte, une reconnaissance formelle et authentique de la neutralité perpétuelle de la Suisse, et elles lui garantissent l'intégrité et l'inviolabilité de son territoire … " the signatories of the Vienna Declaration of 20 March have in this present act recognized in a formal way the eternal neutrality of Switzerland, and they guarantee the integrity and the inviolability of its territory… See also Edgar Bonjour, Geschichte der Schweizerischen Neutralität. Vier Jahrhunderte eidgenössischer Aussenpolitik. Vol I (Basle, 1965), p. 215.

neutral in the event of a war in Europe and therefore was very active to codify neutrality law, especially as regards guarantees for free trade for neutrals in times of war

The policy of free trade was to Switzerland already since the 19th century an essential part of its economic development causing industrial and banking expansion to occur. In a step to meet the challenges of an industrialized state at the beginning of the 20th century, the Swiss banking system was in need of modernization. A central bank was founded in 1907 which together with an up surging economy based on the principles of free trade would later contribute to making Switzerland into a center of international finance.

By the early 20th century, the concept of "neutrality" was well respected. Over the centuries the practices of neutrality were never systematically recorded until they were codified in 1907 at the Hague Conference. Neutral countries, among them the United States, welcomed the adoption of legislation specifying the rights of neutrality. But other non-neutrals, such as Great Britain, considered the establishment of legal neutrality a detriment. Britain had continually opposed the idea of neutrality and as such at the outbreak of World War I in 1914 adopted a strict blockade policy causing serious trade problems for neutral countries. Invariably, the foreign policies pursued by Switzerland and the United States illustrate several similarities, with the USA expressing a strong interest in the development of the rights of maritime neutrality in respect to the "freedom of the seas", while a land-locked country like Switzerland was primarily concerned with rights of passage of goods along land routes to serve its internal market needs. [51]

The beginning of World War I in 1914 put the USA in a certain dilemma. On the one hand, the country considered itself a neutral power. On the other, the USA rapidly became the most important supplier of war materials and foodstuffs to the Entente (Great Britain, France, Italy etc.) and financiers through the purchase of bonds of Allied governments. Although legally permitted under the Hague Convention, this one sided neutral trade led to domestic and international tension. American trade vessels shipped millions of tons of goods to England until the Germans gave up the attempt to keep the United States out of the war. Germany reopened unrestricted submarine warfare on February 1, 1917 thus ending maritime neutrality adding America to its enemies on April 6, 1917 following the sinking of several American ships in February and March. [52] America's approach to neutrality in World War I – a zigzag course under a neutral flag – was symptomatic for that country's very flexible interpretations of neutrality laws of the 1930s before entering the Second World War in December 1941.

With the United States entry into the First World War President Wilson fundamentally changed course and moved away from a policy pursuing peace between nations guaranteed by the so-called "Balance of Power" to a peace guaranteed by [international] law. [53] The *Realpolitik, a "politics of reality,"* long pursued in

---

[51] Jürg Martin Gabriel, The American Conception of Neutrality After 1941. (Basingstoke, 1988), pp. 14-41.

[52] John W. Coogan, The End of Neutrality. The United States, Britain, and Maritime Rights 1899-1915 (Ithaca, 1981).

[53] Erich Angermann, Die Vereinigten von Amerika. Vol. 7 (Munich, 1975), p. 25.

Europe was to give way to the "collective security" of the League of Nations. Wilson's hard fought battle for a new world political order did not include the kind of absolute neutrality practiced by the Swiss in terms of participating in military operations as part of the collective security arrangement. The League of Nations – initiated by the American president, but ironically never joined by the USA – did, however, ultimately allow "military neutrality" and exempted Switzerland, a League member, from taking part in military operations. In return, Switzerland agreed to participate fully in economic sanctions. This mutual agreement was embodied in the "London Protocol" of 1920 allowing Switzerland to practice its own brand of "differentiated neutrality". [54]

Both neutrality concepts were integral parts of classic international law, which viewed war as the sovereign prerogative of all nations. Seen from this perspective, wars were legal, rational, and even normal. War was legal, insofar as its declaration, conduct and termination were at least partly regulated by international law. War was also seen as rational, if it could be justified by a cost-benefit calculation. Though far removed from today's way of thinking, wars were seen as normal occurrences, and all nations prepared for them. War was the "continuation of politics by other means" (Clausewitz). Therefore war was neither just nor unjust. [55]

As part of this classical law of the sovereign prerogative of all nations, neutrality was also perceived as legal, rational and normal without any value judgements. Neutrality was justified so long as the gain derived from abstaining from war was higher than the costs incurred in fighting, i.e. in effect a simple profit versus loss calculation. If not particularly noble, neutrality was not held to be ethically reprehensible. It was neither less nor more than another foreign policy instrument available to states. In hindsight, the American decision to enter into war in 1917 proved to have far-reaching consequences for international relations, since it was America's turnabout which led to the end of classical 19th century neutrality. [56]

THE RISE OF FASCISM – DECLINE OF THE LEAGUE OF NATIONS

The years between 1931 and 1937 witnessed a chain of economic and political crisis which caused the people of Europe to realize that the horrifying lessons experienced from the First World War had been quickly forgotten. Power-hungry and revengeful leaders of different countries once again subscribed to a new wave of imperialism demonstrating unmistakably that legal declarations of international law, moral condemnations, or even world public opinion had little or no relevancy. In 1932 Japan brazenly snatched Manchuria from ailing China, and the League of Nations' hesitant reaction made plain the indecisiveness and impotence of this alliance of nations. When the League of Nations finally voiced disapproval of the Japanese attack, the Empire of the Rising Sun simply withdrew from the League in March 1933. Just six months later, in autumn 1933, Hitler Germany did the

---

[54] Dietrich Schindler, "Dauernde Neutralität", in A. Riklin/H. Haug/H.C.Binswanger (ed...), Handbuch der schweizerischen Aussenpolitik., (Berne, 1975), pp. 159-180.

[55] Jürg Martin Gabriel, Sackgasse Neutralität. (Zurich, 1997), pp. 19-27.

[56] Nils Orvik, The Decline of Neutrality, 1914-1941. (London, 1971).

same, not seeing any necessity to burden itself any further with the rules imposed upon it by the League. Thus, two highly aggressive powers placed themselves beyond the jurisdiction of the community of nations.

The League of Nations did succeed in pushing through sanctions against Italy following its Abyssinian campaign. Switzerland participated in these sanctions. On October 22, 1935, the Swiss Federal Council ordered the freezing of all Italian assets in Swiss financial institutions, both at home and abroad. However, the League's sanctions were partial and ineffectual due to the fact that they conflicted with other boycott legislation by different countries. For instance, according to U.S. interpretations of neutrality, supplying crude oil and other resources to warring countries was not banned. In fact, American crude oil exports to Italy increased threefold in the last quarter of 1935 compared to the earlier quarter, thus providing Mussolini with valuable resources to complete his military campaign. [57]

The League of Nations' inability, in 1935/36, to impose effective economic sanctions on Italy, and its acceptance of the occupation of the Rhineland by Hitler in 1936, only deepened Swiss uncertainty concerning the League of Nations' ability to safeguard international security. As a result, a major turning point took place in Swiss foreign policy. Switzerland began to back away from cooperating with international organizations as a means of guaranteeing its own safety and survival, and gradually distanced itself from the community of nations.

International relations became even bleaker in 1938. National political differences hampered economic growth and international trade. The Spanish Civil War (July 1936–March 1939) provoked increasing confrontation between major European powers. Britain and France were not drawn into that war, but Russia, which had joined the League of Nations in 1934, supported the mainly Communist-dominated Spanish government. Germany and Italy sided with General Franco. Both sides welcomed the opportunity to use the Spanish war theatre as a testing ground for their modern weaponry and sent in "volunteers", fighter planes and tanks. In March 1939, fascist-oriented Generalissimo Franco triumphed in Spain, and shortly thereafter, on May 8, 1939, pulled out of the League of Nations.

Meanwhile, France was plagued by domestic unrest. During the 1930s, attempts by France's left-leaning "Front Populaire" to introduce social and economic reforms were bitterly fought by bourgeois-military groups. In England, the appeasement policy pursued by the British Prime Minister, Neville Chamberlain, in his dealings with European dictators between 1937 and the outbreak of World War II did not contribute in reducing the general climate of insecurity, revealing once again Britain's political weakness. Therefore, without any difficulties Austria was annexed by the German Reich through the "Anschluss" in March 1938 as the German National Socialists seized power. [58]

On September 28, 1938 a meeting of the British and French prime ministers with the German Chancellor, Adolf Hitler and Italy's prime minister Mussolini, in Munich seemed to affirm the impotence of France and Britain against the demands of the "Führer". The "Sudetenland" was incorporated in the German Reich, de facto, rendering impossible any defense of Czechoslovakia, since the Czech bor-

---

[57] Ibid., p. 576.
[58] Ibid., p. 231.

der defenses were located in the annexed area. Two of the world's most powerful democracies without the agreement of or even consultation with the party concerned -Czechoslovakia – handed over parts of a country which were not theirs to give. A disastrous unholy alliance ensued between compromises to buy peace and a truly 'boundless' arrogance of power.

With that capitulation, a continuous threat of war hovered over Europe. To Switzerland's north and east, the new German Reich sought hegemony, while to the south Italy increasingly allied itself with Germany. Independent and neutral Switzerland seemed caught in a political vise, a closing ring.

A centuries-old tradition obliged the leaders of Switzerland to remain neutral and against taking sides with foreign powers. The growing strength of National Socialism and Fascism, the impotence of the League of Nations, and the decline of the two leading western democracies, France and Britain, could not but influence Switzerland's outlook on world affairs.The obvious break down in upholding a collective security policy strengthened Swiss public opinion that their national security could only be safeguarded by returning to strict neutrality.

In March 1938, Switzerland made the decision to return to "integral neutrality" which the country had practiced prior to its joining the League of Nations. This step was largely a reaction to the failure of the policy of collective security (e.g. German breaches of international law, such as the occupation of the de-militarized Rhineland in 1936, without any countermeasures being taken), the worsening political and economic conditions in Europe, as well as Germany's (1933) and Italy's (1937) withdrawal from the League of Nations. "This obvious shift within the European power-political order in itself was bad enough. The fact that the then world organization of states which had taken up the cause of collective security had suffered unforeseeable damage, not only concerned those states which were immediately involved in the Rhineland crisis, but all members of the League of Nations, in particular the smaller and weaker ones among them, such as Switzerland." [59]

In addition, the "funeral oration" for the policy of collective security given by the British Prime Minister in February 1938, may have played a significant part in Switzerland's decision. [60] In this speech, Neville Chamberlain openly stated that it would be tantamount to misleading the small states if they were allowed to go on believing that the League of Nations was still in a position to protect them against attacks. On May 14, 1938, Switzerland's decision to revert to "integral neutrality" took effect. This step was acknowledged by the League of Nations and by Germany and Italy. [61] So Switzerland was released from the obligation of participating in the League of Nations' economic sanctions and, in addition, demonstrated its determination to keep its economic independence. [62] But, unlike Japan and Ger-

---

[59] Walther Hofer and Herbert R. Reginbogin, Hitler, der Westen und die Schweiz. (Zurich, 2001), p. 56.

[60] Walther Hofer, Neutraler Kleinstaat im europäischen Konfliktfeld: Die Schweiz, in Helmut Altrichter and Josef Becker (ed.), Kriegsausbruch 1939: Beteiligte, Betroffene, Neutrale. (Munich, 1989), p. 221.

[61] Op. cit., p. 231.

[62] Klaus Urner, "Neutralität und Wirtschaftskrieg: Zur schweizerischen Aussenhandelspolitik 1939-1945," in: Rudolf L. Bindschedler et al. (ed.), Schwedische und schweizerische Neutralität

many, Switzerland did *not* leave the League of Nations. Subsequently, the accusation that it joined the fascist block of states opposed to the League of Nations is completely unfounded. [63]

Some historians contend that the return to "integral neutrality" meant distancing themselves from the League of Nations, thus indicating their desire to adapt to or even approach the Axis Powers. This step was not an attempt to find favour among Fascist dictatorships. Rather, it was a reaction to the changed security architecture, particularly around the Swiss borders. [64] The one – the return to neutrality – is not equivalent to the other – an approach to the Nazi dictatorship. To equate the two could suggest a subliminal ideological bias, and certainly displays an astounding ignorance of both the essence of Swiss neutrality and how it is deeply rooted in the Swiss peoples' culture and tradition.

The Swiss Confederation's national security policy had traditionally been based on the principles of neutrality and by pursuing this policy it proved over and over again to have benefited the country the most. What's more, strict "integral neutrality" had not only played a decisive role against the challenges of national aggrandizement in Europe in the late 19th century, it had also ensured the country's survival in World War I. [65]

At the beginning of World War II, the danger to Switzerland was abundantly clear. Surrounded by Axis Power, it watched as other small states were invaded and gobbled up while making every effort to convince its neighbours, Germany and Italy, to preserve its integral neutrality. [66] Between April and August of 1940 alone, eight smaller states became a victim of Hitler's war machine. These were states which were declared neutrals. Denmark, Norway, the Netherlands, Belgium and Luxemburg, as well as the three Baltic States, Lithuania, Latvia and Estonia were invaded. The latter had been annexed by the Soviet Union on the basis of the Hitler-Stalin Pact. The Soviet Union, incidentally, was no better or worse than Nazi-Germany's in its disregard for the rights of smaller states. On May 16, 1940 – in parallel to the German Reich's Pan-German ambitions – the Soviet Union announced that there was little hope for small countries to continue to exist which had not enough resources to sustain themselves. It is worth pointing out that many facts are not mentioned in the Final Bergier Report surrounding Russia's policies at the beginning of World War II. Looking closely at the chronology of events in the report a distinct tendency to overlook certain events can be observed. [67] A more un-biased report might have greatly benefited from mentioning the following facts:

– The German-Soviet Non-Aggression Pact of August 23, 1939, including the division of Poland

im Zweiten Weltkrieg. (Basle, 1985), p. 266.

[63] Ibid.

[64] Ibid., p. 230.

[65] D. Schindler, "Dauernde Neutralität", in: A. Riklin, H. Haug and H.C.Binswanger (ed.) Handbuch der schweizerischen Aussenpolitik. (Berne, 1975), pp. 159-180.

[66] Walther Hofer, "Neutralität im totalen Krieg," in: Mächte und Kräfte im 20. Jahrhundert. (Zurich, 1985), pp. 98.

[67] Bergier Report, pp. 91-95.

- The pincer movement by these two countries in 1939 – Germany's attack on Poland on the 1st of September, and that of the Soviet Union on the 17th of September
- The Soviet attack on Finland in 1939 which had a major psychological effect on Switzerland; and
- The annexation of the Baltic states by the Soviet Union in 1940, followed by elimination or deportation of different groups of the population.

The full story is larger still. Before the war, Austria (very voluntarily) and Czechoslovakia (very involuntarily) had gone under.[68] Further countries were to follow. Yugoslavia was completely shattered in the wake of the Balkan War. In fact Switzerland was on the list of countries under consideration. There were specific plans in dividing up Switzerland between National Socialist Germany and Fascist Italy. However, in contrast to these developments, a few new small countries emerged, such as Croatia and Slovakia, which were not really independent states and soon vanished from the map after the collapse of the Third Reich.[69] (After the break up of the Soviet Union, Slovakia again became independent on January 1, 1993, and in 1998, Croatia, formerly part of Yugoslavia, retained its territorial integrity.)

But there were other historical "lessons" to be remembered by the Swiss. In World War I, Switzerland had been unprepared for such a long military conflict, and even less prepared for the concurrent economic war. This time, Swiss leaders had read the writing on the wall, and had made major efforts to promote agricultural production and increase food stocks well before the beginning of World War II.[70] Nevertheless, because of its shortage of natural resources, Switzerland had to rely on imports of raw materials and semi-finished products in order to produce both goods for domestic needs and world-wide export – vital to a significantly industrialized country such as Switzerland with a very small domestic market. For this reason, and because of its own longstanding free market economy, it was impossible for Switzerland to retreat to some sort of autarchy.

However, once the war broke out, the Swiss had no option but to comply with Britain and France's wish to sign a War Trade Agreement on April 25, 1940 after several months of negotiations. Under the terms of this agreement, Swiss banks granted Britain a loan of 100 million Swiss francs which was to enable the British to continue purchasing weaponry from the Swiss. Yet on May 15, 1940,

---

[68] Republik Österreich Historikerkommission (Vienna, 2003) The historians' commission reached the conclusion that the image of Austria as the first victim of Hitler's policy of aggression is not accurate. Rather, the "Anschluss" was implemented with considerable enthusiasm.

[69] Walther Hofer, "Gestaltung der diplomatischen Beziehungen der Schweiz zu neuen oder untergegangenen Staaten sowie zu Staaten mit grundlegenden Systemänderungen," in: Rudolf L. Bindschedler et al. (ed.), Schwedische und schweizerische Neutralität im Zweiten Weltkrieg. (Basle, 1985), pp. 176.

[70] H. Keller and F. T. Wahlen, "Sektion für landwirtschaftliche Produktion und Hauswirtschaft," in: Die Schweizerische Kriegswirtschaft 1939/1948. Bericht des Eidgenössischen Volkswirtschaftsdepartementes. Die Eidgenössische Zentralstelle für Kriegswirtschaft (ed.), (Berne, 1950), pp. 257-298.

Switzerland unilaterally cancelled this agreement, due to the deteriorating military and political situation in Europe. [71]

Based on this development, the Swiss army high command, entered into a secret agreement with France (which was eventually discovered and became known as the La Charité Affair). This secret agreement allowed French troops to cross the Swiss border in defence of Switzerland in the event that the German army bypass the Maginot Line in the south with the purpose of marching into Switzerland to attack France. [72]

As armies mobilized, Swiss diplomats were busy calming the waters in soothing German irritation allegedly caused by the publication of "non-neutral" articles in the Swiss press. They attempted to defend the Swiss economy against the stranglehold of an Allied blockade and stop the Allied powers from abusing the League of Nations to further their war aims. At that point, the Swiss government wished to limit the activities of the League of Nations on its territory. As early as summer 1938, fearing the Nazis' wrath, Switzerland refused to hold a conference on Swiss territory which was to deal with the issue of Jews fleeing from Germany and Austria. The conference was therefore held in France, in the town of Evian, 50 kilometers from Geneva. It proved rather unsuccessful since very few of the 32 participating states could make up their mind to even take in a limited number of Jewish refugees. So Switzerland remained on its own faced with streams of refugees pouring in from all different neighboring countries.

WORLD ECONOMIC CRISIS

In addition to turbulent political events, the 1930s were also marked by profound economic disruptions. As a consequence of the crash of the New York Stock Exchange in September 1929, the steady flow of American loans to Europe dried up. This resulted in a recession which in turn triggered a world economic crisis. The following years, 1931-1937, were characterized by major economic and political problems around the world.

Banking and currency crises were the order of the day. Like falling dominoes there were chain reactions in other countries. The London Stock Exchange, Wall Street, Paris, Zurich, Berlin, to name but the most important ones were all interlinked. Panic selling at one stock exchange spread like a shock wave, leading to a collective fall in the share index in other stock exchanges, with London suffering more severe losses than New York. Between August 30 and December 27, 1929, British share prices fell by 45.4%. On Wall Street, continuous liquidations of foreign shares until 1930 led to the American stock market falling through the floor. [73]

---

[71] Walther Hofer and Herbert Reginbogin, Hitler, der Westen und die Schweiz. (Zurich, 2002), pp. 537-542.

[72] Georg Kreis, Auf den Spuren von La Charité. Die schweizerische Armeeführung im Spannungsfeld des deutsch-französischen Gegensatzes 1936-1941. (Basle, 1976) The Maginot Line extended from Basle to the north for about 300 kilometers to Sedan.

[73] Irving Fisher, The Stock Market Crash and After. (New York, 1930). Fisher argues that the London Stock Exchange Panic, also known as Harty Panic, triggered the American stock market crash of 1929.

Government attempts to stem the crisis worsened it. The introduction of the protectionist Smoot-Hawley Customs Tariff almost completely disrupted American trade worldwide, and led numerous stock markets to experience significant decreases on June 13 and again on June 20, 1930. The financial markets became even more nervous when Adolf Hitler in Leipzig on September 25, predicted that the National Socialist Party would be strengthened by the coming elections and would then proceed to renounce and cancel all post-war reparation agreements which had been imposed on Germany.

Between July 3 and December 18, 1931, the US industrial index plummeted 45.9%. In the same period, the French stock market experienced a 50.75% decrease in share prices, while the British industrial index fell by 31.8%. The insolvency of the Austrian Credit-Anstalt (Austrian Credit Institute) triggered a financial crisis in Germany and Britain decided to give up the gold standard, with many countries following suit. [74]

Debtor countries defaulted because of this collapse of international trade prices and low production figures. They were forced to reduce the repayments on their loans and finally cease payments altogether. The USA, France and Italy were among the first countries to be affected by the repercussions of the banking crisis.

Switzerland is Not Spared Either

While major financial centers went from one financial crisis to the next, in 1931 the shock waves finally reached Switzerland, which until that point had coped reasonably well. Because of the stability of Swiss currency, large amounts of foreign capital had been transferred to Switzerland since the mid-1920s. In 1929/30 particularly, much of that foreign capital was flight capital from Germany. Although Swiss banks were well aware of the high risk of that capital being called back into Germany due to political changes, they still invested it abroad at extremely attractive interest rates, which meant that a significant part of the foreign capital then flowed back both to Germany and to other states as investment [75]

But soon Swiss financial centers with their large, internationally renowned banks could no longer escape the same economic turmoil that was rocking the banks in other countries. The German banking crisis of 1931 had a major impact on Swiss financial institutions which were actively dealing abroad. Well over 1 billion Swiss francs – Swiss banking capital – were frozen as a result of the German Bank Moratorium [Standstill Agreement]. From that point, transferring Reichsmark to Switzerland became increasingly difficult, and finally completely impossible due to German foreign currency restrictions. The only way to avoid losses was for Swiss banks to reinvest this "captive" capital in Germany again.

In July 1931, some estimated 16% of German short-term debts were owed to Switzerland, and by year end, loans granted to Germany by major Swiss banks amounted to roughly half their total loan portfolios. [76] This risky commitment to

---

[74] Charles Kindleberger, The World in Depression, 1929-1939. (Berkeley, 1973).

[75] Joseph Jung, Von der Schweizerischen Kreditanstalt zur Credit Suisse Group – Eine Bankgeschichte. (Zurich, 2000), p. 51.

[76] Bergier Bericht, p. 268.

loans outside Switzerland and loss of liquidity caused by foreign currency controls ultimately proved fatal to a number of Swiss banks.

Geneva was the first victim. The Banque de Genève had already been weakened through losses related to its portfolio of foreign loans. On top of the banking crisis, the deteriorating political confidence in managing the crisis led to massive withdrawals of bank deposits. Unable to cope with the outflow of funds, in June 1931 Banque de Genève was forced to close its doors. The collapse of such a renowned Swiss bank increased the general climate of insecurity and undermined public confidence in Swiss banks as a whole, which had until then remained relatively unharmed. The next victim was to be the Schweizerische Diskontbank (Swiss Discount Bank, formerly Comptoir d'Escompte de Genève). Despite emergency support by the Swiss government, Diskontbank had to suspend operations at the end of 1934. Several reasons are put forward for the survival of the Schweizerische Volksbank (SVB) which in the late 1920s was still Switzerland's leading bank. According to the final report of the Bergier Commission, SVB managed to escape bankruptcy only through a at the time gigantic infusion of 100 Million Swiss francs from the state. Banking historian Joseph Jung, however, considers the new Swiss banking law to be the decisive factor. [77] In April 1931, the Basler Handelsbank Bank (Basel Commercial Bank – BHB) started reducing its open loans in Central Europe. The Eidgenössische Bank (EIBA), whose books showed 46% of its financial commitments to be in Germany, started cancelling its German loans in June 1931. Both banks, in conjunction with the Bank Leu & Co. – which also had to struggle with enormous losses – tried to prop up prices by buying up their own shares. But the effort was in vain. [78] As more and more banks struggled and collapsed, the Swiss Federal Council passed a new Swiss Banking Law on November 8, 1934, aimed at protecting banks and their customers by stipulating a guideline of careful business practices. [79]

Not all banks were equally affected by the world-wide economic crisis. The Schweizerische Bankverein (Swiss Bank Corporation) and the Kreditanstalt (Credit Suisse) were the only banks to survive the economic crisis without government support or a reduction in capital stock. Both institutions were able to offset loan losses and withdrawals by tapping into their reserves. [80] Shareholders of The Schweizerische Bankgesellschaft, (Union Bank of Switzerland – UBS) however, saw shareholder value sharply decline due to the bank selling shares of company stock.

---

[77] Cf... Marc Perrenoud, "Aspects de la politique financière et du mouvement ouvrier en Suisse dans les années 1930," in: Gerald Arletaz (ed.), Die Finanzen des Bundes im 20. Jahrhundert. (Berne, 2000), p. 99; Bergier Bericht, p. 266; Also cf. Joseph Jung, Von der Schweizerischen Kreditanstalt zur Credit Suisse Group – Eine Bankgeschichte. (Zurich, 2000), p. 36.

[78] Bergier Bericht., p. 266; cf. Marc Perrenoud, Rodrigo López, Florian Adank, Jan Baumann, Alain Cortat and Suzanne Peters, La place financière et les banques suisses à l'époque du national-socialisme: Les relations des grandes banques avec l'Allemagne (1931–1946). (Zurich, 2002).

[79] Joseph Jung, Von der Schweizerischen Kreditanstalt zur Credit Suisse Group – Eine Bankgeschichte. (Zurich, 2000), p. 52.

[80] Ibid., p. 32.

1934 was highlighted by widespread renewal and shifting of jeopardized loans while German, French and US authorities increased their inquiries about Swiss involvement in capital flight.

Swiss financial centers did manage overall to survive the crisis of the 1930s, in part through support given by the Swiss government. Some banks managed to cope with losses on their own, or benefited from the new banking law. But the years between 1930 and 1939 fundamentally changed the banking landscape in Switzerland. Within that nine-year period, some 60 banking institutions had to be taken over or liquidated altogether. [81]

No End to the Crisis in sight . . .

Belgium and the Scandinavian countries of Denmark, Finland, Norway and Sweden likewise did not manage to escape the economic debacle. The customs union between Germany and Austria led to considerable withdrawals of German capital from Sweden. Shortly afterwards, on May 11, 1931, the Creditanstalt-Bankverein, reputed at that time to have assets equal to the assets of the Austrian state, had to suspend payments. The second-largest German bank, Darmstädter and National-bank (Danat Bank), failed as well on June 13, 1931. During June and July 1931, German banks hemorrhaged reserves, as accountholders withdrew their deposits from banking institutions and converted them to non-German currencies and gold specie. The British pound, convertible to specie, was especially desirable and bid up, but the combination of pound acquisitions and conversions put the currency under pressure. British banks had to deal with major capital withdrawals in mid-July.

On September 18, 1931, the Berlin Stock Exchange had its worst week ever, with share prices falling 14%. This was partly in reaction to political events in Berlin, unrest in Austria, Hungary and other parts of Europe. Insolvencies amongst smaller German private banks, fears about the consequences of the [bank] moratorium [82] and concerns about the financial crisis in Romania, all contributed to increased feelings of financial insecurity.

The withdrawal of Pound Sterling deposits from British banks by foreign creditors in Britain, which had started in July 1931 because of the events in Germany, continued through the following months. By early September such withdrawals had reached 200 million pounds. The British government reacted by suspending specie payments (free conversion of pounds to gold) by the Bank of England on September 20, 1931, which basically amounted to a suspension of the gold standard. [83] The British government justified this step as a consequence of the con-

---

[81] Robert U. Vogler, "The Genesis of Swiss Banking Secrecy: Political and Economic Environment," in: Financial History Review. Vol. 8 Part 1 (Cambridge, 2001), p.75. and Robert U. Vogler "Swiss Banking Secrecy: Origins, Significance, Myth", Association for Financial History (Switzerland and Principality of Liechtenstein), Contributions to Financial History, Volume 7, Zurich, 2006.

[82] The moratorium was a temporary emergency measure intended to protect financial institutions which had come close to bankruptcy because of loans they had granted to Germany. cf. Neil Forbes, "London Banks, the German Standstill Agreement, and 'Economic Appeasement' in the 1930s", in: Economic History Review, 2nd Series, Vol. XL, no. 4 (London, 1987), p. 585.

[83] Joseph Jung (ed.), Zwischen Bundeshaus und Paradeplatz. Die Banken der Credit Suisse Group im Zweiten Weltkrieg. (Zurich, 2001), p. 52.

tinued pressure on the pound sterling caused by foreign investors "who had little confidence in the stability of their own countries."[84] This statement, made with typically snide British humour, was ironic since Britain itself had gone abroad to take out loans from both the United States in June and from France in August 1931.

Within a few days, the value of the British pound decreased by 30% finally releasing a long term build-up of forces against "economic internationalism" – the ideal of monetary cooperation between nations – broke loose. In a series of rapid measures, Britain embraced the principle of "imperial preference", signalling the end of an era.[85] The liberal world economic order established in the previous century was over.[86]

In the Netherlands the combination of a budget deficit and the events described above brought the Amsterdam Stock Exchange to the verge of a forced shutdown. But when the Dutch thought "it couldn't get worse," widespread rumors began to circulate of yet undisclosed banking problems, which further damaged the stock exchanges. In late September 1931, Sweden abandoned the gold standard. Denmark turned away from sterling currency and announced that its currency would henceforward be tied to the Dollar. Yet the fact that Britain had abandoned the gold standard also undermined the confidence that the American Dollar would remain convertible. The panic of the financial world now spilled over from Britain to America. Due to the withdrawals (for gold) of both domestic and international deposits, the number of American bank closures rose steeply, and the Federal Reserve Bank saw a drain in its gold reserves. The Fed's unwise and ill-informed decision to increase the prime rate in October 1931 – a move intended to protect the dollar – actually worsened the situation.[87]

In spite of repeated declarations by American authorities that they intended to keep the gold standard, in early October 1931, news began circulating that American gold reserves were exhausted. The consequences were major withdrawals from foreign accounts and further plunges in share prices on stock exchanges. "Bank runs" forced credit institutions in the USA to suspend withdrawals. News of banking problems in Germany added to global financial tension, and had an especially negative effect in countries which had made major loans to Germany, such as the USA, France and Switzerland. Between 1931 and 1932, within just one year, 2400 US banks were forced to close their doors. Bank closures resulted in a downward spiral with ever increasing withdrawals of foreign deposits.[88]

Hitler's September 25th 1931 speech in Leipzig also resulted in massive withdrawals of French investments from Germany which eventually mounted to several hundred million francs. 70 million French francs were withdrawn from a sin-

---

[84] Peter Temin, "Transmission of the Great Depression." In: Journal of Economic Perspectives No. 7 (1993), pp. 87- 102.

[85] Robert W.D. Boyce, British Capitalism at the Crossroads 1919-1932: A Study in Political, Economic and International Relations. (Cambridge, 1987), p. 2.

[86] Joseph Jung (ed.), Zwischen Bundeshaus und Paradeplatz. Die Banken der Credit Suisse Group im Zweiten Weltkrieg. (Zurich, 2001), p. 53.

[87] Peter Temin, "Transmission of the Great Depression." In: Journal of Economic Perspectives No. 7 (1993), pp. 87-102.

[88] Op. cit.

gle Cologne branch of the Reichsbank. On October 9, 1931, due to a major selling spree, share prices at German stock exchanges fell by an average 25% from July 11 levels. One week later, news about German-British financial difficulties resulted in a dramatic drop in share prices on eight international stock exchanges. On November 20, 1931, news was leaked that Germany was unable to make outstanding interest payments, which led to a sharp decline in share prices on various markets.

There was no end insight to bad tidings. One week later, there was more negative news on Germany's financial situation which was mainly due to reparation payments and the bank moratorium, as well as to France's refusal to revise German reparation payments. The speech delivered by Prime Minister Pierre Laval to the French Parliament, when he refused to review German reparation payments and referred to France's "holy right" to reparations, caused great concern in Germany and led to sharp drops in share prices in several countries, with the worst decline on the UK stock exchange following Britain's abandoning the gold-exchange-standard. During this week, the British industrial share index fell by over 10%.

On December 4, 1931, further unfavourable news concerning Germany and a depressed New York stock market resulted in worsening share developments, especially in Switzerland and in the Netherlands.

December 18, 1931, witnessed major share sell-offs a consequence of unpleasant financial developments, in the most important European capital markets. Britain and the Scandinavian countries were unable to stabilize their currencies.

In March, 1932, following the suicide of Ivar Kreuger, co-proprietor of the Swedish multinational company, consisting of Kreuger and Toll as well as Swedish Match, news spread like wildfire that Kreuger had forged promissory notes after a European government refused to grant him a major loan secured by his monopoly in the match industry. Ivar Kreuger's death had such wide repercussions in the financial world that the Swedish stock exchange was obliged to close for a week. When it reopened on March 25, the Swedish stock market plummeted 14%. Later in April, the existence of falsified accounts was confirmed, revealing that the Kreuger group indeed had major problems. This news did enormous damage to the already shattered confidence of investors, and in connection with other disaster reports on economic crisis in Central and Eastern Europe led to immense liquidations on most European and American stock exchanges. [89]

In the first week of June 1932 the German cabinet headed by Chancellor Brüning resigned. The shift to the right in German government politics caused a drop in share prices on four international stock markets. In mid-July, the news made the rounds that Austria could not fulfill its repayment obligations on a loan granted by the League of Nations in 1923, and in Switzerland, Italy and Austria share prices went through the floor.

---

[89] H. Lindgren, Bank, Investmentbolag, Bankfirma. Stockholms Enskilda Bank 1924-1945. (Stockholm, 1988), p.439-441; Peter Hedberg and Mats Larsson, "Banks, Financial Markets and the Swedish State During the Second World War," in: Joseph Jung, Herbert R. Reginbogin and Robert U. Vogler (ed.), Financial Markets of Neutral Countries during the Second World War. (in preparation by the Association of Financial History and the Principality of Liechtenstein), foot notes 7-10.

By the spring of 1933, the currencies of 34 countries had been devalued, and 26 states had decided to introduce foreign currency controls. [90] The world-wide financial debacle was the backdrop for the emergence of National Socialism which had been already lurking in the wings, and for what followed world wide.

GOLD STANDARD AND SOCIAL AWAKENING

In the inter-war years, the gold standard did not in fact function as well as it had before World War I. The essential reason was that after 1913 the political and social landscape in many countries changed dramatically. This had repercussions on the credibility of the international order demanded by the gold standard.

Under the gold standard, participating countries had an obligation to fix the price of their currencies against a specified amount of gold. Nations maintained these fixed prices by buying and selling gold at a predetermined price. [91] The period of this so-called "classic gold standard" lasted from 1821 to 1914, and the heyday of the gold standard, between 1880 and 1914, was a remarkable period for the world economy. These years were characterized by rapid economic growth, free exchange of labor and capital across borders in spite of political differences, practically free trade and – by and large – world peace.

By the beginning of the 20th century – and in some countries not until after the First World War – a large part of the so-called working class did not have the right to vote, and thus were excluded by taking a direct part in the country's political decision-making processes and thereby reaping potential financial benefits. After the war, many exclusions and inequalities in the area of voting rights were abolished and replaced by (mostly) male suffrage. Although the working classes were slow to challenge their "betters," extended suffrage slowly gave socially and economically weaker segments of the population a voice in their government. State activities increasingly came under scrutiny and monetary problems could no longer be tolerated by accepting monetary measures, which cut back on social programs and increased the burdens of the poor.

The petit-bourgeois population became more and more self-confident. After World War I, all across Europe, political organizations representing the working class sprang up like mushrooms. In Austria, Sweden, Denmark, France and Norway, social-democratic parties recruited steadily increasing numbers. The membership of the British Labor Party also continued to grow. [92] In Germany, the Social Democrats were already an important party in the 1890s. But it was only in the years 1919-1920 and then again in 1928 that the party became a serious participant in the German government. Between 1924 and 1928 France, for the first time, experienced the control of a moderate left-wing government. The leftists took over the government again from 1932 to 1933, and a more radical coalition of Socialists and Communists acceded to power between 1936 and 1938.

---

[90] Joseph Jung (ed.), Zwischen Bundeshaus und Paradeplatz. Die Banken der Credit Suisse Group im Zweiten Weltkrieg. (Zurich, 2001), p.53.

[91] Ibid., p. 150.

[92] Stefano Bartolini, "The Membership of Mass Parties: The Social Democratic Experience, 1889-1978," in: Hans Daalder and Peter Mair (ed.), Western European Party Systems. (London, 1983), p. 177-220 .

In Norway, the workers' party held some seats in parliament, and election victories in 1935 allowed the party to form a government. The Social Democratic Party of Belgium showed a similar pattern. Although all these social democratic movements had many different programs, it can be said that workers gained unprecedented influence in continental governments after World War I.

Apart from this rise of social democratic political parties, the trade union movement also became increasingly influential around the turn of the century, and made substantial gains during World War I. After the war, in the 1920s, widespread strikes broke out across Europe, causing severe disruptions in the economy. Organized labor demanded more political access and jobs, sufficient pay, and sought to establish minimal social safety nets. All these demands would ultimately conflict with government commitments to maintain the gold-exchange standard.

In the field of foreign trade, the 19th century gold standard put great emphasis on maintaining an even balance of payments between countries. However, this monetary "balance" often could only be achieved at the cost of severe domestic economic restraints and putting pressure on the social fabric of society. With large segments of the population having limited voice in government, it was relatively easy to convince those who did vote that additional financial burdens were necessary to maintain international trade and a healthy investment climate. [93] However, when suffrage was expanded in the course of social reform there was far less chance in making the case for the balance of trade and currency stability. For the very first time, most governments were now faced with competing for important political goals. In Britain, France, the Netherlands, Belgium, Sweden, and Norway, the struggle between capital and labor over income levels led to major imbalances and, in some national economies, generated inflationary pressure. [94]

Since the 1880s, Switzerland had gradually developed into a federal state which intervened in many areas of life. Moreover, leading officers in Switzerland's militia army often held high positions in industry, so that a rather authoritarian mentality arose in Switzerland. This was particularly obvious during World War I, but also continued during the 1930s. When the winner-takes-all electoral system was abandoned in favor of proportional representation in 1918, the aim was to extend democracy. The Social Democratic Party was among the parties benefiting most from the new electoral system. But while the Social Democrats got bogged down in their endless "class struggles" in fact fomented by the bourgeois classes, the other election winner, the Farmers', Craftsmen's and Bourgeois' Party, successfully positioned itself as a bastion against Socialism. The bourgeois coalition tried to build a new national community opposed to urbanization and industrialization and took a defensive posture against both the left-wing party and the liberal intelligentsia.

In the years since 1919 there had been no major change in the balance of power among the political parties. On average, the three largest parties each gained between 20% and 30% of the vote. After World War I, the Freisinnige Partei (Lib-

[93]   Theodor Emanuel Gregory, The Gold Standard and Its Future. (London, 1932).
[94]   Colin Crouch, "Inflation and the Political Organization of Economic Interests," in: Fred Hirsch and John H. Goldthorpe, The Political Economy of Inflation. (Cambridge, 1978), pp. 217-239.

eral Democratic Party) could claim leadership with 32%. In the 1930s, the Social Democrats then managed to snatch this position away from them, becoming the strongest party for a short time. But obviously, the Socialists' fighting days were over. The threat posed by National Socialism caused even those Social Democrats who were ideologically most active to seek a closer cooperation with political bourgeois party circles. But it was only in 1943 that the Social Democrats finally gained a seat on the Federal Council for the first time. [95]

In 1937 Trade unions and employers' associations in the machine and metal industry, one of the most important sectors of Swiss industry, signed a *Peace Agreement* which stipulated that there would be no more mutual reprisals – strikes and lock-outs – in future conflicts. This achievement was extremely unusual, then and since. It was reached on a voluntary basis because of the then high unemployment rate. But the state exerted quite a lot of influence on the process, because the employees' salary demands were threatening to undercut the export expansion brought about by the devaluation of the Swiss Franc in 1936. [96] This Peace Agreement concluded between trade unions and employers was one of the decisive reasons why Switzerland, as compared with other European states, experienced so little social tension.

The after effects of World War I including the dramatic changes in Russia through the Bolshevik Revolution had serious repercussions for the region in Central and Eastern Europe. In Germany, Austria and Bulgaria, pre-war governments fell. While the first two countries moved towards becoming unstable democracies, Bulgaria adopted an uncompromising stance towards property and capital that its economic policy paralyzed the economy for years to come. Hungary got a first taste of Communist leadership as it started out in 1918 as a republic, and a year later its leader, Bela Kun, attempted to found a Hungarian Soviet Republic which in 1919 brought back counter-revolutionaries in support of a Hapsburg monarchy. The country emerged in 1920 as a monarchy under a dictatorship called Admiral Miklos Horthy. Poland became involved in a war with the Soviet Union to restore its boundaries before the immense partitions of the 18th century, which thereafter became an autocratic and reactionary government.

The whole range of problems arising in the inter-war years – the emergence of new political forces and demands for a more extended democracy – was an unprecedented challenge for most countries. Some gave up the struggle and abandoned democratic forms altogether. Others remained faithful to their understanding of democracy and, step by step, worked towards a domestic political consensus which included the new demands made by left-wing groups. Still others went through prolonged periods of instability, changing governments at an alarming rate, as they sought to address competing social demands.

Although countries took different paths as they attempted to reconcile competing demands, it was unavoidable that decisions would come into conflict with

---

[95] Hans-Ulrich Jost, "Bedrohung und Enge (1914-1945)," in: Geschichte der Schweiz und der Schweizer. (Basle, 1986), p. 738.

[96] Wolf Linder, "Entwicklung, Strukturen und Funktionen des Wirtschafts- und Sozialstaats in der Schweiz," in: Alois Riklin (ed.), Handbuch Politisches System der Schweiz. Vol. I. (Berne, 1983), pp. 255-382.

commitments to the gold standard. The time was over when practically all European governments based international economic policy on obligations to the gold standard, defending their currencies against inflation and devaluation while disregarding whatever social hardships ensued domestically.

Dwindling Willingness for Co-operation of Central Banks

Barry Eichengreen wrote that between 1870 and 1913, the central banks of most countries sought to counteract pressures on their currencies – pressures caused by an uneven balance of payments – by manipulating minimum lending rates or interest rates. But higher interest rates made short-term financing more difficult, slowed new investment, dampened domestic economic activity, and brought about a decrease in prices. This lessened the deficit and reduced the pressure to sell [a declining] currency. However, the price of keeping a sound foreign trade balance with other countries could only be achieved at the expense of shrinking expenditures related to the domestic economy. [97]

Comparing the pre-war and post-war years, it is obvious that a fundamental change in the maintenance of the gold standard had taken place. Before World War I, there was a certain trust among the member countries of the so-called "Gold Standard Club" that individual governments would make sure their macroeconomic policies respected the balance in foreign trade and fixed currency exchange rates. If one of the member states experienced a financial run on its reserves, it could rely on international co-operation and support granted by the central banks of other countries.

This 19th century "golden age" of mutual willingness to co-operate was in marked contrast to the way nations regarded their gold standard obligations in the inter-war years. World War I and the Versailles "Peace" Treaty sowed seeds of conflict which grew to wreak havoc on international monetary relations. Allied war debts and German reparations poisoned the relations between France, Britain and Germany, and in 1924, thwarted the plan to stabilize the German Reichsmark. Any feeling of alliance between Britain and the United States had long evaporated, and there was a quarrel brewing concerning the advantages and disadvantages of the gold standard. [98]

The necessities of financing World War I basically brought about the collapse of the gold standard. It was restructured after the war and between 1925 to 1931 known as the "Gold Exchange Standard". This new standard allowed all countries to stock their reserves with either gold or in dollars or pound sterling. Only the reserves of the United States and the United Kingdom were to consist exclusively of gold. However, when the Bank of England suspended free conversion of paper pounds into gold specie on September 20, 1931, due to massive gold and capital movements, this Gold Exchange Standard collapsed as well. [99]

---

[97] Barry Eichengreen, (ed.), The Gold Standard in Theory and History. (New York, 1985), pp. 6-9.

[98] S.V.O. Clarke, Central Bank Cooperation, 1924-1931. (New York, 1967)

[99] Ibid., p. 159 – In 1931, it became obvious how much customs had changed. When the British had difficulties in maintaining the parity of the pound sterling, foreign central banks were not – as previously – prepared to assist the Bank of England, but instead asked the Labour Party to implement larger cuts to unemployment benefit than they had been prepared to make.

The diminished international willingness to co-operate on maintaining an exchange based on gold was based in part on the fact that the sources for emergency capital, i.e. the central banks, ministries of finance and private investors, no longer trusted the political will of governments to hold down domestic expenditures and stay within their budgets. Reliable and immediate international cooperation, on which the stability of the gold standard in the inter-war years depended, was only seen sporadically. [100]

Against this increasingly bleak background, Switzerland managed to keep its macro-economic policies consistent with its international obligations regarding the gold exchange standard. Other countries, one after the other, were unable to cope with the destabilization of their capital markets as potential investors lost trust in different governments' willingness to pursue a deflationary policy and make socially painful cutbacks in support of a favorable foreign trade balances. Most governments felt that the social and political costs were too high a price to pay for maintaining the gold standard. As a result, the stability of the international monetary system fell by the wayside in the inter-war years. In the 1930s, only a few countries, Switzerland being one, were willing and able to keep their foreign trade balances in line with the demands of the gold standard.

WORLD TRADE

Resort to Clearing Agreements and State Interventionism

Between the New York Stock Exchange crash of 1929 and the so-called Great Slump of 1931, many countries tried in vain to find quick fixes which might counteract the collapse and restart their economies. Around the world governments introduced "political" trade measures, clearing and payment agreements, as well as outright currency controls.

France and Switzerland undertook clearing initiatives; Germany's Weimar Republic sought self-sufficiency; the USA introduced the work-creation programs of the "New Deal." All these programs embodied a certain degree of intervention by the state. In Argentina, state-devised "import substitution" incentives sought to promote domestic production of goods which had previously been imported. Industries which introduced such goods into their product lines not only enjoyed high profitability, but benefited from government measures which protected their products against foreign imports with tariffs and strict import rules.

Switzerland, too, felt that politics could influence industry and considered government intervention a viable solution to its problems. Government intervention protected the domestic Swiss economy against foreign competitors with an array of import limits, and the Swiss government became a shareholder in various companies. [101] Not only did this combined-ownership approach give Swiss industrial associations more leverage to influence economic policy, the enlarged

---

[100] Beth A. Simmons, Who Adjusts: Domestic Sources of Foreign Economic Policy During the Interwar Years. (Princeton, 1994).

[101] Wolf Linder, "Entwicklung, Strukturen und Funktionen des Wirtschafts- und Sozialstaats in der Schweiz," in: Alois Riklin (ed.), Handbuch Politisches System der Schweiz. Vol. I. (Berne, 1983), p. 282.

co-operation between industry and the state also made it possible after 1936 to organize a wartime-economy underground organization. [102] Additionally, Switzerland signed temporary bi-lateral payment agreements with Britain, and a trade balance clearing agreement with Germany.

British banks, traditionally liberal in trade policy, did not go this route. They put up determined opposition against import quotas and clearing agreements. In other words, they opposed the interventionist measures chosen by Germany. Instead, Britain raised its customs duties and abandoned the gold standard, hoping thereby to repair the damage caused by the financial collapse. Additional government interventions were rejected as being an infringement on Britain's long-established tradition of economic liberalism. Moreover, London banks viewed government intervention as the expansion of the state's authority to control business to be damaging to their long-term interests. So, those speaking for London's financial interests, i.e. the "City", were opposed to those who favored action by the government to mitigate the effects of the crisis. However, Britain's economy was heavily dependent on Germany, its primary market for exports, and as a result British policymakers were forced to show some willingness to compromise in regards to German desires to create trade clearing agreements while supporting the financial service industry at home. Moreover, within the framework of its trade relations, the government provided foreign currency to London banks, insurance companies and financial service companies within the scope of certain trade agreements with other countries – Payment Agreement with Germany 1938 – so that such foreign currency would be used to purchase British goods and Britain's position as a private financial clearing center was not undermined by separate, bilateral clearing agreements between states.

German Financial Crisis

In the months after the Reichstag elections of September 20, 1930, on account of dwindling trust in the political stability of the Weimar Republic and the rapid economic decline German banks were inundated with mass recalls of foreign short-term loans to Germany. Reich Chancellor, Heinrich Brüning thereupon demanded an end to the reparation payments which had been imposed on Germany by the victorious powers in the Versailles Treaty.

Eventually, on the initiative of US president Hoover (Hoover Moratorium), the allied creditors, i.e. the signatories of the Versailles Treaty, agreed on a one-year moratorium on German reparations payments. This moratorium became effective as of July 1, 1931. In the meantime, a run on German financial institutions worsened the situation in Germany so much that banks had to be closed for three weeks. On July 15, 1931, the Weimar Republic again decided to introduce foreign currency controls. [103] This included the Reichsbank's monopoly on foreign currency trading and the setting, by fiat, of an "official" value of the Reichsmark.

---

[102] Wilhelm Bickel, Die Volkswirtschaft der Schweiz. Entwicklung und Struktur. (Aarau, 1973). p. 69.

[103] Gerald D. Feldman, "Die Deutsche Bank vom Ersten Weltkrieg bis zur Weltwirtschaftskrise 1914-1933," in: Lothar Gall et al., Die Deutsche Bank 1870-1995. (München, 1995), pp. 138-314; Die Devisenverordnung von 1925 hat das Gesetz von 1915 aufgehoben, um freien Devisenverkehr zu ermöglichen.

The risks of German reparations and loan defaults were central. The Bank for International Settlements in Basel (*Bank für Internationalen Zahlungsausgleich or BIZ*) – also known as the "reparations bank" – was instructed to establish a committee to work out the overall amount of all German commercial foreign debts whose payment period needed to be extended. The committee determined that the German debt with foreign banks amounted to about six billion Reichsmarks, and recommended a moratorium on repayment of German short-term debts to foreign banks. [104] In fact, the committee succeeded in persuading the foreign creditor banks to sign a "standstill agreement" and a renewal of a central bank loan to Germany of 100 million dollars. This way, a Germany credit collapse could be avoided, and the willingness of foreign banks to co-operate was maintained: they agreed not to recall their loans, at least for the present. The Standstill Agreement, valid for six months, was signed on September 19, 1931. It was a temporary emergency measure for protecting financial institutions which were on the brink of disaster because of the loans they had granted to Germany. This Agreement was also intended to calm widespread fears of a total collapse of the capitalist system, a general panic which would deny that recovery was even possible.

The payment moratorium did not, however, rebuild trust in the German economy. Bank loan cancellations from abroad kept flooding in. After the expiry of the Hoover Moratorium in June 1932, countries were still in the throes of their own economic crises. A resumption of reparation payments by Germany was simply out of the question. The creditor countries had no other choice but to declare, during the Lausanne Conference, that German reparation payments would be officially suspended as of July 9, 1932,

For those British and American banks whose loans within Germany were based on trade transactions, the largest part of outstanding loans (72.4%) consisted of short-term credits against commodity shipments (documentary acceptance credits). In Britain, banks such as Kleinwort, J. Henry Schroder or Lazard Brothers, which had close relations with Germany, were most severely affected. Lazard Brothers was on the brink of ruin, and was only saved by support from the Bank of England. [105]

By contrast, German commodity credits only involved about one third (32.5%) of the capital of Swiss financial institutions. Their largest outstanding debts consisted of loans (42.2%), mainly granted to German companies. Naturally, the Swiss banks were interested in the fastest possible restoration of German solvency, and considered the restructuring of German outstanding debts a promising possibility. A recommendation by the Swiss banking committee that short-term loans should be commuted into long-term investment was in fact incorporated as Article 10 in the 1932 Standstill Agreement which replaced the six-month agreement of September 1931. On the basis of this article, Swiss creditor banks commuted loans worth 23.3 million Reichsmarks by 1933 (amounting

---

[104] Gian Trepp, Die Bank für Internationalen Zahlungsausgleich im Zweiten Weltkrieg: Bankgeschäfte mit dem Feind. Von Hitlers Europabank zum Instrument des Marschallplans. (Zurich, 1993), p. 20.

[105] Robert W.D. Boyce, British Capitalism at the Crossroads 1919-1932: A Study in Political, Economic and International Relations. (Cambridge, 1987) p. 344.

to about 3/4 of all transactions of this kind) and thereby were able to achieve a long-term reduction of assets heretofore blocked in Germany. However, in 1934 German debts still amounted to the considerable sum of 900 million francs. By the beginning of World War II, this amount had shrunk to 250 million, and at the end of the war, only 153 million francs were owed. [106]

Like the creditors who had granted short-term loans, bondholders also were forced to coordinate their actions at the international level. They founded the "Committee of British Long-Term and Medium Term Creditors of Germany". This association was set to grant bondholders the same periods of repayment and conditions as the Standstill Agreement. However, when the Committee tried to organize a united front – preferably led by the "City" – of all creditor countries, Hjalmar Schacht, the president of the German Reichsbank, was able to thwart the agreement. He played a game of "divide and conquer" by emphasizing the differences in various types of loans, and succeeded in breaking up the united front of the creditors and convincing the British banks to follow his lead.

Schacht had still other ideas to escape creditors. He was successful in luring additional creditors away from a British-led front by giving the impression that he had offered Switzerland special conditions in the form of "additional exports" and that this suggestion had been accepted by Switzerland in signing the 1934 Trade Agreement.

On January 30, 1933, Adolf Hitler came to power – the Weimar Republic had come to an end. In Britain, the government, business and the financial circles hoped that the storms raging in the global economy and financial world eventually would subside. Further there was hope that the fundamental structures of the capitalist system in Europe and the world would remain intact. Many British politicians, bankers and industrialists really believed that National Socialism would have a revitalizing effect on the German economy and lead to an economic and financial turn-around. [107] This assessment by British foreign policy experts reveals an unbelievable misjudgement of the true character of Hitler and his goals.

The economies of both Britain and Germany had considerable excess production capacity at that time. Moreover, both countries were experiencing a major demand for natural resources which could not be met by domestic sources alone. But Germany, obsessed with self-sufficiency, refused to actively promote interna-

---

[106] Bergier Report, p. 270; See Neil Forbes, "Doing Business with the Nazis: Britain and Germany in the 1930s," in: Society for European History Fourth Annual Workshop: The Management of Political Risk in Dictatorial Environments: European Foreign Investment: 1918-1980. (Paris, 21/22 March 2002), p. 6. Not all creditors were so successful. In contrast to the Standstill Agreement, the long-term and medium-term debts amounting to over 60 million British pounds were considerably higher than the short-term "stand-still" debts of 34 million on the London market There were two categories of long-term loans: the Reich bonds, such as e.g. Dawes and Young, and bonds which had been circulated by German cities and energy suppliers. Investors and institutions around the world had subscribed to both types of loans.

The debts had one fundamental difference, though: it was only the Reich bonds which were guaranteed by the participating states, while non-Reich bonds did not enjoy this kind of protection. So the international community of creditors of Germany was confronted with the choice either to liquidate its assets and incur great losses, or to work within the restrictions of foreign currency controls.

[107] R.J. Overy, War and Economy in the Third Reich. (Oxford, 1994), p.37.

tional trade of natural resources with Britain. The German government instead increased controls on foreign currency movements. The British, nevertheless, were reluctant to give up their hope of a reviving German economy.

Bank Espionage in Switzerland

It was completely in keeping with the National Socialist conception of legality that on December 1, 1936, a law was adopted stipulating the death penalty for any violation of German foreign currency regulations. This law had already been preceded by the anti-Jewish Nuremberg Racial Laws of 1935, and it was followed by further legislation – laws which banned Jews from the civil service and other professions, promoted economic boycotts, the preparation for the confiscation of all Jewish property, right through to the removal of all civil rights for Jewish citizens as stipulated by the Reich Citizenship Law of November 25, 1941. This law stipulated that Jewish property fell to the Reich in cases where people, because of their residence abroad, lost their German nationality. [108] However, foreign currency trading was still permitted, so long as it consisted of clearing trade, i.e. if before or after a transaction, a clear equivalent could be negotiated with the clearing partner countries, as for example in the "Payment Agreements" concluded with Britain in 1934 and 1938.

Like Germany, France had also introduced foreign currency controls which threatened punishment for any violations. However, no disobedient Frenchman had to fear that he would be transported to the hereafter for this type of misdemeanour. But governments need money (nothing new, really) and such intrusive regulations gave them a welcome opportunity to control their citizens' private assets. Naturally, faithful subjects immediately tried to move their money out of government clutches, and since Switzerland (as well as the USA) had not introduced foreign currency controls, the country became a welcome safe haven for such "illegal" capital flows. Then it was again up to governments, especially those of Germany and France, to find all those hidden nest eggs by sending eager employees of their tax authorities to Switzerland to uncover possible violations of foreign currency regulations. In the context of the New Deal, the USA was also interested in finding out about its citizens' foreign treasures, although the government went about it in a much more moderate way. It did not look for foreign currency, but for gold which had been taken abroad. As a consequence of these collective "scouting" activities, Switzerland experienced a spectacular increase in spying activities by overzealous French and particularly German tax authorities. In some cases the agents even succeeded in obtaining customers' names and data from bank employees, although Swiss banks, even before the adoption of the banking law, had always been careful to protect their customers' privacy. There was already the draft of the banking law, dated February 24, 1933, containing a regulation against bank espionage – this was *before* the Germans had started their attempts at systematically tracking down the assets of Jewish fellow citizens. Because of increasing amounts of French capital flowing into Switzerland, and

---

[108] Andre Botur, "Privatversicherung im Dritten Reich. Zur Schadensabwicklung nach der Reichskristallnacht unter dem Einfluss nationalsozialistischer Rassen- und Versicherungspolitik," in: Berliner juristische Universitätenschriften, Reihe Zivilrecht, Vol. 6 (Berlin, 1995).

because of the Third Reich's attempts at bank espionage, the Federal Council and the Parliament felt obliged to introduce more protective measures. So, in article 47 of the bank law, in force since March 1, 1935, they introduced further protection of the customer's right to privacy which until then had only been guaranteed under civil law. [109] In the case of violation, considerable fines and prison sentences were stipulated. [110] Later, it was alleged that these laws had been adopted to protect the assets of Jewish customers from access by the Nazi regime. However, the Bergier Commission in its final report comes to the conclusion that this allegation is incorrect and completely unfounded, and that the same applies to a diametrically opposite accusation, found in some literature, that this legislation was adopted in order to get access to the assets of persecuted Jewish customers, i.e. that it was motivated by pure greed. [111]

SWITZERLAND AND THE USA – FINANCIAL HAVENS

On March 6, 1933, President Roosevelt proclaimed that the USA could issue bank notes not backed by gold, and the export of gold was prohibited. [112] Until 1934, it was generally allowed to exchange US bank notes for gold, and the Treasury Department was obliged by law always to hold a minimum gold reserve. The world economic crisis put an end to this freedom, and resulted in the adoption of the Gold Reserve Act of January 30, 1934. This act prohibited private trading in gold and authorized the Treasury Department not only to control all future gold transactions, but also to issue new regulations for acquiring, holding, transporting, melting, trading, importing and exporting gold. Furthermore, the Treasury was authorized to "purchase gold in any amounts, at home or abroad, at such rates and upon such terms and conditions as he [the Secretary of the Treasury] may deem most advantageous to the public interest". [113]

Immediately after the Gold Reserve Act had been adopted, President Roosevelt, always the "public interest" in mind, raised the gold price considerably, from $20.67/oz. to $35.00/oz. The consequences of this manoeuvre were imme-

---

[109] Joseph Jung, Von der Schweizerischen Kreditanstalt zur Credit Suisse Group – Eine Bankgeschichte. (Zurich, 2000), p. 49.

[110] Cf. Bergier Report, p. 267 article 47 section 1, lit. (b) "Wer vorsätzlich als Organ, Beamter, Angestellter einer Bank...die Schweigepflicht oder das Berufsgeheimnis verletzt,...wird mit Busse bis zu Fr. 20'000 – oder mit Gefängnis bis zu sechs Monaten bestraft,...[oder beides]; handelt der Täter fahrlässig, so ist die Strafe bis zu Fr. 10'000.-." [Any wilful breaches of professional confidentiality or professional secrecy ...by institutions, officials, employees of a bank ...will be punished with a fine of up to 20,000 Swiss francs – or with prison of up to six months [or both]; if the offender was grossly negligent, the fine may be up to 10,000 Swiss francs.]

[111] Ibid.

[112] Joseph Jung (ed.), Zwischen Bundeshaus und Paradeplatz. Die Banken der Credit Suisse Group im Zweiten Weltkrieg. (Zurich, 2001), p. 53.

[113] 48 Stat. 337, Sect. 8; the earlier wording comes from Sect. 2. See U.S. Statutes at Large, 73rd Congress, 2nd Session, – Jan. 30, 1934, 337, 341. On 24 March, 1937, the Federal Bank of New York was issued a Treasury license for this type of gold transactions. U.S. Treas. Dept., Spec. Form TGL-18, License No. NY-18-1, "License to Transport, Import, Melt and Treat, Export, Earmark and Hold in Custody for Foreign or Domestic Account," Mar. 24, 1937, Princeton University., Seely Mudd Manuscript Library. Harry Dexter White Collection, Box 3, File 82 [223773-774].

diately obvious. Enormous amounts of capital were literally pulled out of Europe and transferred to America. Some explained this draining of funds as "autonomous private transfers of hot money from Europe in part due to the new price", while others saw "the growing threat of Nazism in Hitler Germany" as the real reason. [114]

Between February 1 and March 14, 1934, i.e. within a period of only six weeks, gold worth over half a billion dollars was imported into the United States. [115] These phenomenal flows of riches into the USA was, however, not a matter of days or weeks, but continued to flow, month after month, for the next *eight* years, from February 1934 until October 1942. This gold run brought the USA an annual average increase in gold reserves worth 1.5 billion dollars. Ultimately, gold worth 15 billion dollars was transferred to the United States. [116]

With the adoption of the new Banking Act, Switzerland had a wide spectrum of financial services to offer. After the major drain of deposits between 1931 and 1935, these new bank services triggered considerable capital flow to Switzerland, mainly from Germany and France, but the reasons varied widely. While some Germans transferred their assets to Switzerland in order to circumvent strict German currency and registration laws, which demanded almost complete disclosure of financial assets, many French citizens shifted assets to Switzerland, as well as to London and New York, because they feared that the election of the "Front Populaire" (Popular Front) in 1936 would result in tax increases and a devaluation of the French currency. A devaluation was indeed announced on September 25, 1936. A day later, on September 26, the Swiss Bundesrat devalued the Swiss franc as well for, it maintained, primarily economic considerations. The "lighter" Swiss franc was intended to stimulate exports and, through an increase in domestic productivity, to reduce unemployment in Switzerland which had risen from 8,131 in 1929 to 93,009 by 1936. [117] The 30% devaluation achieved its aims. The export industry recovered, and foreign capital increasingly flowed into Switzerland. [118] The number of job-seekers decreased noticeably after 1937, although there was nothing approaching full employment in sight. [119] But devaluing the currency was not the only measure taken by the Bundesrat. The Swiss government acted in the

---

[114] Greg Bradsher, head archivist of the National Archives and Record Administration (NARA) until the 1990s, held the opinion that banking secrecy had been introduced to profit from the emergency Jews were experiencing in Germany.

[115] Griffeth Johnson, The Treasury and Monetary Policy 1933 – 1938. (Cambridge, 1939), p.54

[116] Plunder and Restitution: Findings and Recommendation of the Presidential Advisory Commission on Holocaust Assets in the United States and Staff Report (Washington, D.C., 2001). Senator Knowland was a member of the Senate Appropriations Committee, and on April 14, 1952, asked the Treasury about the annual gold flow to and from the USA. The Treasury answered in early May. United States Treasury Department, "Material in Reply to Questions from Senator Knowland," NARA, RG 56, Entry 69A7584, Box 4. However, no statistical records from the years themselves are quoted about the annual gold inflow in the years 1934–1940. Records were not used to reconstruct annual gold inflow to the United States until years later.

[117] Statistisches Jahrbuch der Schweiz 1945, Eidgenössisches Statistisches Amt (Berne, 1946), p. 380.

[118] Joseph Jung (ed.), Zwischen Bundeshaus und Paradeplatz. Die Banken der Credit Suisse Group im Zweiten Weltkrieg. (Zurich, 2001), p. 54.

[119] Op. cit.

belief that no country can assert its political will on its economic strength alone, but needs to rely, in part, on a credible military defence as well. Later on, the combination of military, political, diplomatic, economic, and also intellectual defence of the country became integral components of the Swiss mentality. [120] So it was not only the devaluation of the currency, but also an economy turned towards the production of armaments which contributed to Switzerland's economic upswing.

In the 1930s, Germany's restrictive foreign currency laws and strict official controls caused more and more German companies to begin using services offered by Swiss banks. In addition, the discrimination against German Jews and the territorial expansion of Nazi-Germany resulted in additional capital flight to Switzerland. Since neutral Switzerland was located in the geographical center of Europe and had successfully maintained its neutrality throughout World War I, many European investors sought to open Swiss bank accounts. They did so on the assumption that Switzerland would keep its neutral status even if another war should break out and thus their deposited capital would remain safe. But by no means did all of this incoming capital remain in Switzerland. Many Europeans used Switzerland as a financial transit point, later moving their assets on to still "safer" financial havens such as the United States. [121]

Movements of capital to the United States were periodically disrupted. When, in July 1937, the dollar's exchange rate decreased, large sums of European capital were again withdrawn from the USA and moved, mainly to Great Britain although some found its way back to Switzerland. [122] The capital drain from the United States caused by the weak dollar was accelerated by a sharp fall in prices at the New York Stock Exchange in 1937 and by the worsening American economic situation. [123] Assets were mainly transferred to London, but also to Amsterdam, Paris, and Zurich. Capital movements in those years may be likened to great waves flowing back and forth, not moved by any natural tide, but by world-wide economic insecurity and the constant search for the safest haven.

In September 1938, the threat of war became obvious to everyone and European investors once more began transferring assets to the United States. Even though the Munich Conference succeeded in averting war (for the time being), capital transfers continued unabated, and part of this transfer of assets, which became known as the "Golden Avalanche", included funds transferred from Switzerland to the United States. Correspondingly, relations between Switzerland and the United States intensified, either via London or directly, and close working relations with American financial institutions were established. [124] Finally, consider-

---

[120] Walther Hofer, Neutraler Kleinstaat im europäischen Konfliktfeld: Die Schweiz, in Helmut Altrichter und Josef Becker (ed.), Kriegsausbruch 1939: Beteiligte, Betroffene, Neutrale. (Munich, 1989), pp. 206-207.

[121] Mira Wilkins, "Swiss Investments in the United States 1914-1945," in: Switzerland and the Great Powers. (Geneva, 1999), pp. 119-122.

[122] The French, especially, took rather swift action, because they feared that the American and French governments might make an agreement for the purpose of stimulating capital flow to Paris. Cf. Joseph Jung (ed.), Zwischen Bundeshaus und Paradeplatz. Die Banken der Credit Suisse Group im Zweiten Weltkrieg. (Zurich, 2001), p. 65.

[123] Op. cit., p. 55.

[124] Ibid., p. 122.

able assets invested in Switzerland were repatriated to the USA where they were held out of investment markets as cash. [125] Standing back, it is clear that the massive flight of gold from Europe to the United States began well before the war.

The USA was not Interested in the Origin of Gold

The Federal Reserve Bank monitored the volume of inflowing capital, and the Treasury Department considered various methods to put a stop to the incoming flow of gold. However, this flight gold was of major importance for the recovery of the American economy after the recession of 1937. [126]

Harry Dexter White, head of the Division of Monetary Research in the United States Treasury Department considered gold as "... the best medium of international exchange yet devised ... [constituting] one of the effective cushions for insulating the domestic economy from adverse repercussions of economic changes abroad." [127]

In his opinion "the fact that every country in the world will sell goods for gold and no country will refuse gold in settlement of debt or in payment for services rendered" [128] was much more important than the more technical considerations of the Treasury. It seemed that all Europe – individuals, companies, institutions and even central banks and governments – were moving assets out of Europe to the USA for safekeeping. Still, American's own assets invested abroad in late 1939 amounted to the staggering sum (for the time) of 11.4 billion dollars. [129] While huge sums of risk capital continued fleeing to the American safe haven, investments continued around the world.

After the German invasion of the Netherlands, Belgium and France in May 1940, quite suddenly the issue of determining the origin of the gold imported into the USA became of major concern to Britain. It was not out of moral principles that such gold might have been unjustly seized by the Nazis. Instead the British government worried that Dutch and Belgian gold in private hands might fall into German hands and be used to finance the German war effort. The new issue of the provenance of imported gold becomes clear in a section quoted from the final report of the "Presidential Advisory Commission on Holocaust Assets in the United States": the Financial Counselor of the British Embassy, Pinsent, sent a note to the US Treasurer Morgenthau, asking "whether he would be prepared to

---

[125] Paul Erdman, Swiss-American Economic Relations: Their Evolution in an Era of Crisis. (Tübingen, 1959), p. 26

[126] Op. cit., Memo by White to Secretary Morgenthau, "Gold Imports in the United States", May 9, 1939, NARA, RG 56, Entry 67A1804, Box 50, Divisional Memo #2; An earlier unsigned draft memo of 17 March 1938, titled "Merits of a Proposal to Place an Embargo on Gold Imports" states that the disadvantages of such an embargo by far outweighed its advantages. If desired, gold inflow might be regulated by other means. NARA, RG 56, Entry 67A1804, Box 50, Division Memoranda No.1

[127] H. D. White, "The Future of Gold", corrected copy, Dec. 20, 1940, Princeton University, Seely Mudd Manuscript Library, Harry Dexter White Collection, Box 3, section III, p. 4.

[128] Ibid., p. 6.

[129] Department of Commerce (Hal Lary and Associates), "The United States in World Economy" (Washington, D.C., 1943), p. 123.

48

scrutinize the gold imports with a view to rejecting those suspected of German origin?" [130]

In his reply memorandum dated June 4, 1940, Harry Dexter White stated that the US Treasury had always taken the position in Congress that it was not in a position to make effective distinctions between the different origins of the gold, because, due to sales in other countries, gold lost its identity and further that there was no system of international co-operation in place which would stop such gold movements. [131] Dexter White's memorandums clearly show that he considered the unconditional acceptance of gold to be the correct procedure, regardless of its origin. [132] White also added that the most efficient contribution to be made by monetary agencies in the USA and elsewhere would be "to leave inviolate the unquestioned acceptability of gold as a means of international payment". [133]

So, while the Stuart Eizenstat Report of May 1997 implies that the United States made an effort to limit trade, especially trade involving stolen gold and foreign currency, the Treasury's correspondence paints a completely different picture. Treasury officials of this Department, including Harry Dexter White, were perfectly clear in stating that the origin of gold was of secondary importance to the USA when commercial transactions were concerned. Such commercial transactions were of prime importance for maintaining a stable world economy and thus were to be given absolute priority.

Based on these facts, it would certainly have been appropriate for the Jewish World Congress, US Senator d'Amato, Under-Secretary of State Eizenstat, Federal Judge Korman and the Volcker Commission to have focused their inquiries into the gold trade and dormant accounts of Holocaust victims not *only* on Switzerland, but also on the banks and financial service providers in the USA who have been spared investigations of this kind. As will be shown in the following chapter, in addition to the USA, other neutral countries also avoided awkward investigations into the origin of gold they bought or accepted in payment. [134]

The American government's unconditional acceptance of dubious gold was also applied to Russia after the Russian attack on Poland in the second half of September 1939. During the subsequent Russian attack on Finland, the so-called "Winter War" beginning in November 1939, trade activity between Russia and Germany had been stepped up. In early 1940, the Soviet State Bank sent gold from its depository with the German Reichsbank to the Schweizerische Bankverein (Swiss Bank Corporation), which recast it in its gold foundry in Le Locle. So, during the first four months of 1940, Russian gold weighing 23.7 tons and worth

---

[130] Note handed by Mr. Pinsent, Financial Counselor at the British Embassy, to Mr. Cochran of the Treasury on 27 May, 1940. NARA, RG 56, Entry 67A1804, Box 49

[131] Memo by White to D.W. Bell, Cochran and Foley, 4 June, 1940, NARA, RG 56, Entry 67A1804, Box 49 Among nations trading in gold, the ingots were usually melted down, re-shaped and then marked with the national stamp, so that it was no longer possible to trace their original provenance.

[132] H. D. White, "The Future of Gold", March 1, 1940 Princeton University, Seely Mudd Manuscript Library, Harry Dexter White Collection, Box 4, Section III, and corrected notes in Box 3 with last corrected version of 20 December, 1940.

[133] Ibid., corrected memo December 20, 1940, p. 7.

[134] Eizenstat (1997), p. xxi.

US\$ 26.6 million (SFr 115.2 million) obtained new Swiss "parentage". [135] This activity helped to disguise the Russian origin of the gold so that it could be used in payment for oil and other goods imported from the USA to the Soviet Union. It was important to eliminate the Russian die stamp. Otherwise there was the risk that the gold would be confiscated and used to pay off older, outstanding financial claims against Czarist Russia which the Soviets had repudiated. [136]

However, the American Embassy maintained statistics on Swiss gold imports and exports, and these records led the Swiss National Bank, the Americans and the French to discover the Soviet ruse. The US government was immediately informed that very likely large amounts of this Russian gold would shortly arrive in the United States. US authorities voiced "serious disapproval" of transactions of this kind. Still, the United States government undertook no specific measures to identify, block or seize the recast Soviet gold – even though the Soviet Union was still classified by the US as an enemy power. [137]

Switzerland has been accused of being the most important channel for gold coming out of occupied or Nazi-controlled countries before and during World War II. This is the conclusion of the Bergier Report. However, it may be that the American government and media, in their broad and unqualified accusations against Switzerland, were really attempting to pre-empt whatever accusations could be made against the USA for actions which were exactly the same – the "crime" of channelling unchecked gold out of Europe. The Presidential Counsel on Holocaust Assets, established in 2001 especially to investigate gold flows, dug out a list drawn up for the 1941 hearings of the American Stabilization Fund. This listing supposedly proved that, during the gold run into the USA between 1934 and 1940, the value of gold coming into the USA from Germany amounted to just \$94 million, with gold worth \$60.5 million originating from Italy and \$692.5 million from Japan. The overall value of gold imported to the USA from Germany, Italy and Japan thus was said to amount to just \$753 million, a sum equal to less than 5% of the increase in US gold reserves. The US government commission then expressed satisfaction that most of the gold which came to the United States did not originate in Axis countries.

But in fact, three quarters of all gold imported to the USA came from just three countries: Canada (55%), Britain (14%) and France (5%). [138] So, despite the "complete" listing of Axis gold, the true origins of a much greater part of American gold are by no means clear. The US Treasury Department had more than once stated its inability to check the origin of gold imported to the United States. Thus, the possibility cannot be ruled out – particularly in view of the vast capital

---

[135] Goldbericht Bergier-Kommission, p. 55 Chapter 1; About 1 ton of gold went to the Schweizerische Bankgesellschaft (today UBS); cf. also Bergier Report, pp. 243-244.

[136] Bergier Report, p. 244.

[137] Unabhängige Expertenkommission Schweiz – Zweiter Weltkrieg (ed.), Die Schweiz und die Goldtransaktionen im Zweiten Weltkrieg. Vol. 16 (Zurich, 2002), pp. 241-243.

[138] Treasury Dept., Div. of Monetary Research, "Net Movement of Gold to the United States by Countries, 1940," NARA, RG 56, Cf.: Plunder and Restitution: Findings and Recommendation of the Presidential Advisory Commission on Holocaust Assets in the United States and Staff Report (Washington, D.C., 2001). Entry 67A1804, Box 50, Div. Memo #4 [202562] and [202561]

flows across international financial markets during this period – that additional European gold had been stored intermediately in countries such as France, Canada or Britain – or Switzerland for that matter – by Germany, Japan and Italy, for smooth and "undetected" transfer to the United States at some later point.

The ready acceptance of this superficial and unchecked listing might arouse suspicion that both the 1941 hearings and the 2001 Presidential Commission simply avoided, for domestic political reasons, investigating a rather obvious question: Did the USA in fact support the Nazis by its unconditional acceptance of any and all gold, however dubious its origin and allow such precious dollars to be used in trade by the Nazis for war materials – gold which may well have been seized from Jews?

The Independent Commission of Experts Switzerland – Second World War (also known as the Bergier Commission) has loudly condemned Switzerland for being a center of trade in illicit German gold. The Commission's approach might have been more balanced – and fair – had it at least raised the question of the way other neutral countries assessed and addressed the problem of stolen gold.

At least Eizenstat, in his second report of June 1998, tried to tone down his perhaps injudicious remarks in his first report of May 1997 by describing the trade between other neutral countries and Germany during World War II. His second report indeed criticized activities of the US government and of the military after the war. Unfortunately, the reports do not deal with the role of the United States in the years leading up to its entry into World War II. [139]

THE BEGINNING OF WORLD WAR II

Switzerland is Surrounded

On May 10, 1940, the Germans attacked the Netherlands, Belgium, Luxemburg and France. German tanks rolled towards the English Channel and forced the French army and British Expeditionary Force to draw back to an enclave at Dunkirk. The Belgian army was not able to stop the German advance, and nor were the densely forested Ardenne mountains the obstacle to German tanks that France had thought they would be. Within four days, German troops crossed the Meuse near Sedan and fanned out across open country. The expected advance on Paris, however, was temporarily held back. Instead, the lead attack units of the German army advanced westward, destroyed the French Ninth Army, cutting off the French First Army and the British Expeditionary Force as well as the Belgian army in Flanders from the main French force in the south.

On May 19, 1940, German units reached Abbeville. The French Prime Minister, Reynaud, discharged the Commander of the French forces, Gamelin, replacing him with General Maxime Weygand who wanted to cut through the narrow and extended German attack corridor and re-unite with the allied armies trapped in

---

[139] William Slaney, U.S. and Allied Wartime and Postwar Relations and Negotiations with Argentina, Portugal, Spain, Sweden, and Turkey on Looted Gold and German External Assets and U.S. Concerns About the Fate of the Wartime Ustasha Treasury. (June 2, 1998), http://www.state.gov/www/regions/eur/rpt_9806_ng_links.html (Referring to the Eizenstat Report of 1998).

the north and west of France. That, at least, was the plan but it was not successful. On May 25, Lord Gort ordered the evacuation of the British Expeditionary Forces from Dunkirk. That evacuation was carried out under fire between May 27 and June 4. The bulk of British forces as well as a substantial part of the French northern army managed to escape by sea. The evacuation was complicated by the collapse of the Belgian army. On June 5 German troops broke through the hastily improvised defense front along the Somme and Aisne which Weygand had considered to be his last line of defense. Mussolini felt that he was on safe ground and brought Italy into the war as a German ally June 10, 1940. The French government was in panic and about to collapse. On June 10, it abandoned Paris for Tours, and moved on to Bordeaux in the south a few days later. That same day, Paris fell into German hands. Germany occupied half of France, while General de Gaulle, in London, swore to continue the struggle in the French colonies with the help of the Free French Forces. On the evening of June 16, Prime Minister Reynaud resigned. His successor was Marshal Pétain, who immediately tried to negotiate conditions with Germany to end the fighting. On June 22, 1940, a German-French armistice was signed. [140]

This totally unexpected French defeat left Switzerland completely surrounded by countries which were either allies to Germany or under German occupation. The only connection between Switzerland and other democratic countries was a narrow corridor between Geneva and the unoccupied south of France. Within the course of a single month, neutral Helvetia found itself surrounded by dictatorial governments. At that critical point, the then Federal President, Pilet-Golaz, in a speech delivered on June 25, 1940, maintained that Switzerland must adapt to the "New Order" in Europe. [141] Assessing Pilet-Golaz's intentions, the British envoy in Berne reported back that he was "the leading advocate in the Federal Council for the maximum of collaboration with the Axis which the Swiss public could be induced to stand" [142]

The vast majority of the Swiss population, however, showed an increased willingness to defend Switzerland at all costs, including war. That attitude had been expressed back in November 1938 when the Swiss people agreed to increase the country's armaments. The call to defense was also a main theme of General Guisan's "Rütli-Rapport" of July 25, 1940: "As long as millions of armed troops are standing in Europe, and as long as considerable forces may proceed to attack us any moment, the army must stand guard." [143] In this speech, General Guisan portrayed Switzerland as a country which was able and willing to defend itself against all intruders and to fight for its democracy and political freedom, despite finding itself in the middle of a continent turned totalitarian.

---

[140] L.F. Ellis, The War in France and Flanders, 1939-1940. (London, 1953); Brian Bond, France and Belgium, 1939-1940. (London, 1965); Guy Chapman, Why France Collapsed. (London, 1968); A. Horne, To Lose a Battle (New York, 1969); and William Shirer, The Collapse of the Third Republic: An Enquiry into the Fall of France in 1940. (New York, 1969)

[141] Werner Rings, Schweiz im Krieg 1933-1945. (Zurich, 1997), p. 176.

[142] Luzi Stamm et al. (ed.), Dignity and Coolness. (Lenzburg, 2004), doc. 126, p. 188 – British envoy, David Victor Kelly, to Foreign Minister Anthony Eden, (written Berne, 4 June 1941, received 20 June 1941).

[143] Hans Rudolf Kurz, Dokumente des Aktivdienstes. (Frauenfeld, 1965), pp. 90-91.

The subsequent shift of large parts of the Swiss army to the Réduit fortress area in the Alps was aimed at threatening Adolf Hitler and Benito Mussolini with consequences which both the Germans and the Italians wanted to avoid at all costs, namely the destruction of the two critical railway lines through the Simplon and Gotthard passes and interdicting any easy passage through the Alps. By deploying its army in this fashion, Switzerland could indeed exert political pressure on Germany and Italy, and not only in negotiations concerning economic issues. As early as 1939, huge amounts of goods moved over these vulnerable supply routes between Germany and Italy. [144] So the army deployed to block those supply movements [by destroying the tunnels] was a clear and present danger to Germany's plans for additional conquests. Alternative transport was possible but extremely difficult, and would have certainly resulted in major problems for the German-Italian war machines. The enormous importance of the traverse across the Alps for Germany was confirmed in 1940 by a remark made by the head of the German trade delegation, Hemmens, that the end of transit [through the Alps] would also spell the end of Switzerland. [145]

One fact should be given special emphasis here, though: at no time did the Swiss government permit German soldiers to put as much as the tips of their toes on Swiss soil. This is a marked difference with Sweden where the government consented to German units crossing Swedish territory. [146]

Like the USA, Switzerland referred to international agreements to justify certain activities. In the Gotthard Treaty concluded with Germany and Italy on October 13, 1909, Switzerland had undertaken to permit regular transport of goods through its territories, *with the exception of war materials*. When the Allied powers demanded, as they regularly did, that Switzerland reduce the volume of goods transported across its territory it consistently referred to this still valid agreement to justify their resistance to reductions. [147]

Through all this, Swiss domestic supplies, foodstuffs and industrial materials suffered substantial difficulties. Following the German invasion of Denmark and Norway in April 1940, guaranteeing supply of foodstuffs and raw materials was immediately given top priority while rationing foodstuffs and textiles. The export of high quality precision goods and the large currency reserves of the Swiss National Bank helped sustain the economy. However, tourism came to a standstill, and the Swiss hotel industry collapsed. Trade and presumably existential problems were emerging. On July 6, 1940, the Swiss Federal Council issued regulations for foreign currency trading with countries occupied by the German Reich, and Switzerland, as a major financial center, was closely tied to events affecting greater Europe. With the start of the German attack on its neighbouring coun-

---

[144] Urs Schwarz, Vom Sturm umbrandet. Wie die Schweiz den Zweiten Weltkrieg überlebte. (Frauenfeld, 1981), pp. 112-113.

[145] Edgar Bonjour, Geschichte der Schweizerischen Neutralität. Vier Jahrhunderte Eidgenössischer Aussenpolitik. Vol. VI (Basle, 1970), p. 213.

[146] Detlev F. Vagts, "Switzerland, International Law and World War II," in: American Journal of International Law vol. 91 No. 3, July 1997, p. 467; Urs Schwarz, The Eye of the Hurricane: Switzerland in World War II. (Boulder, 1980), p. 65

[147] Op. cit., p. 271.

tries, the ensuing financial chaos brought trading at Swiss Stock Exchange to a complete halt between May 10th and July 8th 1940.

Support by the Banks

Swiss banks played an important role during the war. They granted loans for obtaining critical industrial and food resources, such as oil products, coal, animal feeds, coffee, textiles etc. At the same time, by granting lines of credit, they made it possible for both Swiss and non-Swiss companies within Switzerland to fulfil orders placed by foreign governments.

During 1940 a wide range of clients availed themselves of credit from the major Swiss banks (SBG, SKA, SBV, SVB). It was these four banking "giants" who in March 1940 declared their willingness to grant the British government a loan of 100 million Swiss francs. [148] At the same time, the Eidgenössische Bank and the Basler Handelsbank provided credit to primarily Germany-based borrowers.

Loans of various types were granted to customers, both at home and abroad. Borrowers included the Spanish Treasury Department, the IG Farbenindustrie, Berlin, Standard Oil of New Jersey, General Motors (Suisse), Brown Boveri & Co. (Baden), Bulova Watch Co. Inc., New York, Lonza AG, Ciba AG, J.R. Geigy AG, Basel, etc. The numerous transactions included a great variety of financing arrangements. Some involved transactions based on ingots of gold and silver. Others were merely letters of credit. In the case of arms transactions, the banks mainly offered letters of credit (basically advances against products to be delivered) for arms supplies, e.g. by Waffenfabrik Solothurn to the Swedish army, by Zurich Werkzeugmaschinenfabrik Örlikon-Bührle & Co. to the Russian state, by Tavaro SA in Geneva for the supply of ignition devices for the artillery to the British War Office, for gold transactions with the Russian State Bank. Swiss banks even financed the supply of 20 mm guns for planes and anti-aircraft artillery to France, shortly before the French capitulation. This diverse portfolio demonstrates that the banks were exclusively interested in transactions which earned a profit, without ideological preference for or against the allied powers, the Soviet Union or Nazi Germany. [149]

The "New Order" in Europe also meant that the Swiss had to deal with the "Executive Order" issued by President Roosevelt on April 10, 1940. This order gave the United States legal justification for freezing assets, not only assets of the governments of countries occupied by Germany, but also assets of companies and private citizens of those countries. The Danes and Norwegians whose countries had been occupied by the Germans on April 9 were the first to be hit by Roosevelt's rigorous executive order. With Hitler's additional conquests in spring 1940, the number of "victims" continued to multiply due to this American blanket approach to freezing all assets of Nazi-occupied territories.

With the war continuing in and on the seas around Europe, the Swiss economy had to adjust to various new demands: German rule within the "New European Order", a British naval blockade, assorted "black lists" of forbidden trades,

---

[148] Walther Hofer and Herbert Reginbogin, Hitler, der Westen und die Schweiz. (Zurich, 2001), pp. 532-538.
[149] Bergier Report, p. 244.

Roosevelt's "Executive Order" in the context of foreign assets in the USA. A continuing barrage of new demands and conditions forced both Swiss business and government to deliberate how to balance competing and often contradictory requirements by warring parties which might conflict with rules of Swiss law and Swiss neutrality.

Swiss banks differed in the approaches they used to assist their customers in protecting assets from being frozen in the United States, as well as in the ways they dealt with transactions on the Swiss securities markets involving shares belonging to residents of countries occupied by Germany. If the USA should enter the war, confiscation of American subsidiaries of German companies was to be expected. Swiss banks tried to assist their German customers in escaping this fate by adjusting share ownership. With chemical and pharmaceutical companies, transactions were devised which had the effect of concealing ultimate ownership. So, for example, in the case of the German Schering Corporation, shares linked to its American subsidiary were transferred to a Swiss company called Chemical and Pharmaceutical Enterprises Ltd. (CHEPHA), and the Swiss Bank Corporation held majority ownership of that company. Management know-how continued to come from Germany, while the company was Swiss-owned for official purposes. [150]

But for residents of German-occupied regions, the situation was completely different: at the beginning of the war, the warring countries prohibited the payment of interest and dividends to inhabitants of enemy states. Bonds due for repayment could not be redeemed if they were owned by people from enemy countries. Repatriation of securities was not illegal on principle, so long as detailed affidavits on origin and the length of ownership were produced. [151] The 'Swiss Ownership Declaration' was a form created for such requirements. In using this form, intended as it was to circumvent foreign regulations; some banks did permanent damage to the national and international reputations of Swiss banks in allowing their employees the use of forged affidavits, and with that discrediting the Swiss affidavit system. Sometimes, Swiss authorities – in particular the Federal Department of Economic Affairs – turned a blind eye to clearly fraudulent certificates. However, other banks, among them Credit Suisse, were not inclined to take affidavit risks and refused to participate in such transactions. [152]

But if banks in Switzerland were sometimes careless in filling in declarations on share ownership, [153] American banks were guilty of the same oversights, and disclosures were often accepted even though they were known to be incomplete or inaccurate. "The companies could enter in the forms whatever they thought suitable." [154] There was no clear explanation of what information was needed and

---

[150] Mira Wilkins, "Swiss Investments in the United States 1914-1945," in: Switzerland and the Great Powers. (Geneva, 1999), pp. 122-123.

[151] Gerard Aalders and Cees Wiebes, Die Kunst der Tarnung., (Frankfurt, 1994), p. 160.

[152] Bergier Report, p. 276; cf. also Hanspeter Lussy, Barbara Bonhage and Christian Horn, Schweizerische Wertpapiergeschäfte mit dem "Dritten Reich". Unabhängige Expertenkommission Schweiz – Zweiter Weltkrieg UEK (ed.), Vol. 14 (Zurich, 2001), pp. 189-236

[153] Ibid., p. 198

[154] National Archives of Records Administration (NARA), RG 56, Entry 45080211, Box 47. "General Information on the Administration, Structure and Functions of Foreign Funds Control,

important to retain permits for business enterprises. What's more, this vague state of affairs remained unchanged for many months, while control of capital transfers was extended to include foreign assets from practically all countries of the world. It was only in spring of 1941 that form FRBE-1 was introduced which specifically required any company doing business in the US to comply with the regulations of the "Freezing Control", namely to provide information on ownership, type of business, names of directors, officials, subsidiaries etc. [155] Nevertheless business licenses were not thoroughly checked until a year later after President Roosevelt introduced Order 8389 in April 1940. In the meantime, some American banks continued to comply routinely with German finance regulations.

Switching to War Economy

As early as in the mid-1930s, as the threat of another war spread across Europe, Switzerland recognized the danger. [156] At the outbreak of World War I Switzerland had been totally unprepared and had suffered as a result many bitter social problems. Now, with another dark shadow lurking over Europe the country wanted to be better prepared should war come again. [157] As early as 1936, the Swiss parliament empowered the Federal Council to begin a transition from a peacetime to a wartime economy. [158] On September 29, 1936, the Council's power to take economic emergency measures took effect. It was authorized to take precautionary actions which were not otherwise specified or limited by existing legislation. In spite of these preventative measures people hoped that "the good Lord would spare them", but as the decade wore on, it was widely recognized war was indeed imminent. On March 8, 1938, the Federal Council set out a series of preparatory measures for organizing and coordinating the economy on a war footing. The measures entrusted the Federal Department of Economic Affairs with the ultimate management of the war economy. A few major sectors, however, remained exempt from its control – including military procurement, railways and shipping as well as finance. [159] So, a year before the actual outbreak of World War II, Switzerland had prepared an organization empowered to take over command of a large sector of the Swiss economy in wartime. [160]

Of course, armaments are both extremely expensive and crowd out domestic consumption, so financial policy needs to be integrated into the fiscal 1938 plan-

---

1940–1948," chpt 3, p. 36 (on history of FFC) The Executive Order 8389 of April 10, 1940 was unclear about what information was required to attain a permit to keep a company from being frozen by FFC.

[155] Ibid., p. 37

[156] Hans Schaffner, "Eidgenössische Zentralstelle für Kriegswirtschaft," in: Eidgenössische Zentralstelle für Kriegswirtschaft (ed.), Die Schweizerische Kriegswirtschaft 1939/1948. (Bern, 1950), p. 2

[157] Ibid.

[158] Edgar Bonjour, Geschichte der Schweizerischen Neutralität. Vier Jahrhunderte Eidgenössischer Aussenpolitik. Bd. III (Basel, 1967), p. 404

[159] Hans Schaffner, "Eidgenössische Zentralstelle für Kriegswirtschaft," in: Eidgenössische Zentralstelle für Kriegswirtschaft (ed.), Die Schweizerische Kriegswirtschaft 1939/1948. (Berne, 1950), p. 2.

[160] Edgar Bonjour, Geschichte der Schweizerischen Neutralität. Vier Jahrhunderte Eidgenössischer Aussenpolitik. Vol. III (Basle, 1967), p. 404 .

ning. [161] Just two years earlier, in 1936, nearly half the Swiss state expenditures were allocated towards defence. This was accomplished by issuing government bonds amounting to 235 million Swiss francs. In the following years, the share of military spending rose continually, from the "loan of 90 million (1935) to a little over 200 million (1938) to 1.3 billion francs in the years 1940-1944, which corresponded to four fifths of the entire Swiss federal budget." [162] These extraordinary expenditures met with the approval of Swiss citizens. Follow-up legislation, entitled "Reinforcing National Defence and Fighting Unemployment" submitted for approval by the Federal Council, was adopted by a large majority of the electorate on November 27, 1938. The bill set out a government loan totalling 415 million francs, 213 million of which were earmarked for military purposes, and the rest for creating more jobs. [163] The military share was used for building a complex net of fortifications, as well as for the procurement of airplanes.

When the Austrian people, by an overwhelming majority, voted to join the Third Reich in 1938, it was clear that more trouble was coming. The Swiss government realized that building up the military was not enough. Careful attention had to be paid to social and economic aspects as well, if the calamities which occurred during World War I were to be avoided. The government also sought to achieve the closest possible unity of all Swiss for the defence. The government thus pursued a two-track policy to maintain maximum social stability while building up the armed forces. On April 6, 1939, a credit of 327 million Swiss francs was applied across the "two fronts" of reducing unemployment and strengthening national defences. [164]

Handling the Export of War Materials

Regulations of the Hague Convention V of 1907 prohibited the neutral states (although not their citizens) from supplying war materials to parties in conflict. [165] This rule remained in effect even after Switzerland joined the League of Nations. In accordance with this regulation, on March 31, 1934, the Federal Council issued a ban on export of war materials to both Bolivia and Paraguay, at that time engaged in what was called the Chaco War. When the League of Nations called for sanctions on Italy because of its Abyssinian War, the Swiss government banned the export of war materials to both Italy and Abyssinia. Switzerland also honoured The Hague Convention regulation during the Spanish Civil War by issuing an export ban which extended to Spanish possessions and the Spanish zone in Morocco. [166] In October 1938, however, the Schweizerische Bankverein (Swiss

---

[161] Hans Ulrich Jost, Politik und Wirtschaft im Krieg: Die Schweiz 1938-1948. (Zurich, 1998), p. 17.

[162] Ibid., pp. 9 and 15.

[163] Ibid., p. 17.

[164] Christian Kubitschek, Die wirtschaftliche Situation der Schweiz im Zweiten Weltkrieg, (Wei-, den, 1994), p. 26

[165] Convention Respecting the Rights and Duties of Neutral Powers and Persons in Case of War on Land., The Hague V. October 18, 1907, 36 Stat. 2310, 1 Bevans 654

[166] Klaus Urner, "Neutralität und Wirtschaftskrieg: Zur schweizerischen Aussenhandelspolitik 1939-1945", in: Rudolf L. Bindschedler et al. (ed.), Schwedische und schweizerische Neutralität im Zweiten Weltkrieg. (Basle, 1985), p. 265

Bank Corporation) granted a "private" loan to Franco's anti-Communist Spanish insurgents. [167]

The arms race of the 1930s underlined the League of Nations' inability to act to control international trade in armaments. Swiss citizens, too, had recognized the dangers of an uncontrolled armament industry and tried to control it with domestic initiatives. A petition for an arms-control referendum was, however, turned down on February 20, 1938. But a counterproposal made by the Swiss Federal Assembly was adopted, and was added as article 41 of the Swiss Constitution. It set up measures to monitor the private defense industry. Henceforth, both manufacture and export of war material required government permits. As early as April 14, 1939, i.e. at roughly the same time as the USA returned to "proper" neutrality (May 1, 1939), the Federal Council approved a draft concerning Swiss neutrality, and Article 3 of that draft disallowed the "export of weapons, ammunition, explosives, other war materials and their components to warring states, as well as any accumulation of such objects in the border areas or for transportation across the borders." [168]

Due to a range of economic and financial reasons as well as out of fear of unemployment and social unrest, the government was soon forced to give up this self-imposed ban on the export of war materials to warring countries, so readily set out in 1939. Switzerland became concerned that other countries would respond with trade reprisals if the export ban was strictly enforced. Also the powerful Swiss armament industry lobbied against the measure. [169] The reversal by the Federal Council also acknowledged that war materials were important leverage in negotiations and in exerting pressure for safeguarding foreign trade. On September 8, 1939, the decision was made to drop the absolute export ban, and on September 22, 1939, replacing it with specified conditions under which future export of war materials would be allowed:

- The needs of Switzerland's own army were given absolute priority, with the exception of certain counter trade transactions furthering the interest of the military defense of the country.
- The raw materials for any orders received from abroad were to be supplied by the customer.
- The armament companies were subject to permissions and monitoring. Export permits were only granted if the orders were supplied to foreign governments. All deliveries had to be made on cash terms only or in exchange for essential supplies. [170]

So the Council of Ministers reinstated the rules of The Hague Convention V of 1907.

---

[167] Hans Ulrich Jost, Politik und Wirtschaft im Krieg: Die Schweiz 1938-1948. (Zurich, 1998), p. 35.

[168] Amtliche Sammlung eidgenössischer Gesetzeserlasse, "Verordnung über die Handhabung der Neutralität vom 14. April 1939", p. 810

[169] ., Klaus Urner, "Neutralität und Wirtschaftskrieg: Zur schweizerischen Aussenhandelspolitik 1939-1945", in: Rudolf L. Bindschedler et al. (ed.), Schwedische und schweizerische Neutralität im Zweiten Weltkrieg. (Basle, 1985), p. 266

[170] Ibid., p. 268.

America's Neutrality and the Supply of War Materials

Officially the United States, as a neutral state, abided to the principle of banning exports of war materials to conflicting parties as codified in "Third Neutrality Act" of May 1, 1937. This act reiterated the ban on both arms exports and financial support to warring states. It was, however, supplemented with an important additional clause. This so-called "Cash-and-Carry Clause", limited at first to two years, permitted warring parties to purchase American *products and raw materials* (not arms) on a cash only basis and transport them on their own vessels. Thanks to this inventive clause, lucrative US sales of much needed war materials such as crude oil, cotton, copper, steel, trucks etc. could continue. [171]

When, in the same year, a new conflict between Japan and China loomed on the horizon, the contradictions inherent in American legislation on neutrality and the Cash-and-Carry Clause became obvious. The exceptions allowed in the clause in reality only applicable to powerful states which could both pay cash and maintain naval forces strong enough to protect the cash-and carry purchases. So this regulation was not even handed and did not serve peace, but granted assistance to financially strong, even aggressive, states. Further weaknesses in the American neutrality position became obvious when Roosevelt decided not to impose an embargo – an embargo aimed at protecting American interests – on China and Japan who were fighting but not yet officially "at war." Such an embargo would have had to include *both* China and Japan. However Roosevelt wanted to keep the option open to supply China with arms and also to station American warships in China. Japan might have easily put a stop to shipment of American arms and other goods to China by officially declaring war on China. This would automatically have triggered American neutrality legislation and the application of the Cash-and-Carry clause. China was no naval power and would lack the muscle to buy and transport much of anything from the USA. The snag was, though, that after officially declaring war on China, Japan would also have lost the opportunity of buying *finished arms*, because the Cash-and-Carry clause permitted only the purchase of raw materials and semi-finished products but no weapons and ammunition. Since Japan refrained from officially declaring war on China, the buying of considerable amounts of war materials from America could continue. [172] This obvious contradiction in American neutrality policy was never revised.

The historian Akira writes: "...the American people were confronted with a neutrality crisis and compelled to recognize that in a world so sharply divided between forces of democracy and totalitarianism, the policy of neutrality was not something to be innocently indulged in but would have serious implications for the struggle between these forces". [173]

The historian Foster Rhea Dulles remarks that later on Roosevelt considered the neutrality legislation "an error". [174] In August of the election 1936, an election

[171] Ibid., pp. 209-210.

[172] Max Silberschmidt, Der Aufstieg der Vereinigten Staaten von Amerika zur Weltmacht. (Aarau, 1941), p. 433.

[173] Akira Iriye, The Cambridge History of American Foreign Relations – The Globalizing of America, 1913-1945. Vol. III. (New York, 1993),pp. 155-156.

[174] Foster Rhea Dulles, Amerikas Weg zur Weltmacht 1898-1956. (Stuttgart, 1957), p. 180.

year, the American President said: "We shun political commitments which might entangle us in foreign wars... We are not isolationists except in so far as we seek to isolate ourselves completely from war." [175]

The restrictions of American neutrality policies limited Roosevelt to give effective support to the arming of the Western powers. It was impossible for him to achieve a repeal of the neutrality legislation. In the spring of 1939, he therefore tried at least to find a Congressional majority for prolonging the Cash-and-Carry clause which was to expire on May 1. Congress refused to go along. A week later, during a dramatic session, the American president was defeated by a combination of neutralists led by William Borah, who maintained that fears of war breaking out in that year were unfounded.

After the German invasion of Poland, America *explicitly* declared its neutrality on September 5, 1939. At that time, the majority of Americans were only moved by one thought, the desire to keep out of the war at any cost. However, when Britain and France both came to the defense of Poland and declared war on Germany, public opinion had changed. Three weeks after the invasion of Poland, Congress met in a special session and
– extended the Cash-and-Carry clause,
– repealed the president's authorization for imposing armament embargos, and
– decided on a return to "neutrality under international law." [176]

Although the United States insisted of being recognized as a neutral power – at least as long as it did not enter the war – however, the country did slowly, but consistently move away from the principles of neutrality, when such principles conflicted with economic or political self-interests. These activities differed considerably from the legally accepted types of actions by a neutral state, as for example, in the case of the American Lend-Lease Act.

SWISS FOREIGN TRADE

As a small country with neither seacoast nor established access to the sea, Switzerland had recognized early on that its economic security and the full employment of its population depended on the maintenance of wide-ranging trade. Moreover, Switzerland has very few natural resources, and must import raw materials and semi-finished goods for the manufacture of products both for domestic consumption and for export. In order to compete in world markets – then as now – Switzerland needed highly specialized processing and finishing industries. It met this challenge in a masterly way. In 1938 – one year before the outbreak of World War II – the country had the third-largest per capita export turnover world-wide. [177]

But dependence on foreign trade creates problems, too. During World War I, Switzerland's fate had depended on the dominant warring countries – Germany, France, Britain, Italy and the USA, both for imports (about 55%) and for exports

---

[175] William L. Langer and S. Everett Gleason, The Challenge to Isolation 1937-1940. (London, 1952), p. 16.

[176] Samuel Eliot Morrison and Henry Steele Commager, The Growth of the American Republic. (New York, 1962), p. 538

[177] Max Heuberger, Die Strukturwandlungen des schweizerischen Aussenhandels in den Jahren 1938 bis 1949. (Basle, 1955), p. 8.

(about 60%). [178] At the beginning of World War II, Switzerland was in a similar situation.

The following brief summary of Swiss import and export relations with the Axis and Allied Powers in 1938 gives an overview of this dependence:

USA:	Important supplier of food products to Switzerland, along with Canada and Australia. In addition, the United States supplied considerable amounts of copper and cotton. Swiss exports to the USA consisted mainly of watches and clocks, chemical products and cheese. In 1938, the USA's share of Swiss foreign trade was 8% for imports and 7% for exports.
Great Britain:	Supplier of coal, sugar, and wool. Britain was much more important for Switzerland as an export market for machines, aluminum, watches and clocks, chemical products and silk. In 1938, the British share of Swiss foreign trade was 6% for imports and 11% for exports.
Italy:	Important supplier of food products, such as citrus and exotic fruits, fruit and wine. Switzerland exported watches and clocks, machines, instruments and large amounts of cheese. In 1938, the Italian share of Swiss foreign trade was 7%, both for imports and exports.
France:	Close behind Germany, Switzerland's most important trading partner, supplies vegetables, potatoes, coal, iron and chemical products. Switzerland also exported chemical products to France, as well as hardware, machines, instruments, watches and clocks. In 1938, the French share of Swiss foreign trade was 14% for imports, 9% for exports.
Germany:	Germany was both Switzerland's most important customer and its most important supplier, providing the lion's share of key imports such as machines, hardware, chemicals, fertilizer, but also coal and iron. Switzerland exported watches and clocks, machines and chemical products to Germany. In 1938, the German share of Swiss foreign trade was 23% for imports, and 16% for exports.

This summary shows that while Swiss exports in 1938 were not overly concentrated on any one market, Swiss imports were much more problematic: the goods supplied by Germany and France – likely opponents in a future war –

---

[178] Schweizerische Handelsstatistik, Jahresbericht 1945, Eidgenössische Oberzolldirektion (ed.) part 2 (Berne, 1946), p. 4.

amounted to nearly 40% of all Swiss imports. And these were strategically important materials which would be hard to replace. [179]

Thus each of these countries had economic leverage over Switzerland and could threaten – or easily carry out – trade reprisals on Switzerland's vulnerable sectors. Moreover, the loss of one or both of these trading partners would have a major negative impact on the Swiss economy, both in terms of domestic consumption and on the country's ability to manufacture for export. So, from the Swiss point of view, a major storm was brewing and Switzerland's economic livelihood was under threat. In hard economic terms, Switzerland had few alternatives. The country had to adopt a strategy of attempting to reconcile conflicting interests, and surviving through difficult political and trade negotiations.

The Beginning of Economic Warfare

When Germany suddenly attacked Poland in the fall of 1939, Britain and France did not immediately launch a military action against Germany – as they were obliged to do by the terms of their Agreement on Mutual Assistance. Rather they declared an economic boycott of Germany, and tried diplomatic means to win the support of the neutral countries of Europe and, especially, of the then still neutral United States.

On September 3, 1939, Britain and France commenced an economic blockade of Germany which immediately affected neutral states. The blockade sought to interdict export of German goods transited through third countries. It focused to cut off German imports, both direct shipments and, again, shipments routed through neutral territory. In effect, a blockade on Germany meant controlling both imports and exports from neutral states. Ironically, Britain and France accused the Swiss government of violating the obligations of its neutral status. But it was Britain and France who ruthlessly disregarded the neutrality and sovereignty of smaller states when it was in their interest to do so.

Try as they would, it was nearly impossible for the Allies to cut off German trade completely. They moved on to requesting that neutral countries of Europe contribute to the economic war against Hitler-Germany by reducing their German trade and, in certain sectors, shutting it down completely. The Allied Powers lent weight to their "requests" by imposing blockade measures which gave no consideration to the economic needs of neutral states, and rode roughshod over their sovereignty. Threatened with the outright confiscation of trade goods and the reality of nearly strangled trade, neutral countries had no alternative but to enter into blockade negotiations with the Allied Powers. In those negotiations, they tried to use broader Allied interests to keep at least some trade alive and work out conditions which would allow their economies to survive. Britain used the blockade, with its extensive regulation of trade, to undermine its international competitors.

Belgium, the Netherlands and Sweden quickly yielded to this pressure. As early as December 7, 1939, they signed the War Trade Agreement laid down by the Allied Powers. Switzerland held out much longer, and continued to resist intrusive

---

[179] Wilhelm Bickel, Die Volkswirtschaft der Schweiz. Entwicklung und Struktur. (Aarau, 1973), p. 69.

and harassing Allied requests. However on April 25, 1940, after protracted and often bitter negotiations, Switzerland signed the agreement sought by the Allies.

The procedure used by the Allies was the so-called "navicert" system already used during World War I. By submitting to a naval search at the port of origin, neutral importers and exporters were issued navigation passes (navicerts) by the blockade authorities. A navicert gave some security that certified cargoes would not be intercepted or seized on route to their destination ports. At the outset, navicerts covered all neutral maritime traffic from overseas to Norway, Sweden, Denmark, Italy, Belgium and the Netherlands. In 1940 the coverage was extended to include all other European nations as well. [180] In the case of Switzerland, the navicert system meant the country could only import products which had been approved – at some point in transit – by the Allied Powers. As the war expanded, the navicert program became less and less effective, since Germany itself came to control all of continental Europe.

In its continuing economic negotiations with both the Allied Powers and Germany, Switzerland was consistently led by the principles of neutrality. After the war, Switzerland was repeatedly accused of having been biased in its supply policy. But the facts speak for themselves. During the war years, Switzerland imported much more from the Axis powers than she exported to them both in value and volume. From Germany alone, Switzerland imported goods worth roughly half a billion francs, much more than she exported to that country.

Switzerland was actively trading with Allied and other overseas countries as well. The Swiss succeeded in exporting goods worth about 1.7 billion francs despite the double [Allied/Axis] blockade. Imports from Allied and non-aligned countries amounted to about 2 billion francs, roughly a third of the trade with the Axis Powers. Yet it should be remembered that Sweden, as just one example, supplied Nazi Germany with over a quarter of its iron supplies over the course of World War II, an economic and political tradeoff which was much more important to the Third Reich's war economy. [181]

The War Trade Agreement [182] of April 25, 1940, between Switzerland and Britain and France – as similar agreements between the Allied Powers and other neutral countries – was an attempt at restructuring the production output of the Swiss economy in favor of the Allied Powers' war interests. With the defeat of France, this agreement was soon overtaken by events, as were the agreements which had previously been negotiated with other neutral countries. Nevertheless, this agreement is interesting for two reasons:

First – The War Trade Agreement remained formally valid until the end of the war, and so constituted a counterbalance to German-Swiss economic negotiations during World War II. In these negotiations, the Swiss government made every effort to resist the pressure exerted by Nazi Germany, even risking the com-

---

[180] Adolph Vaudaux, Blockade und Gegenblockade. Handelspolitische Sicherung der schweizerischen Ein- und Ausfuhr im Zweiten Weltkrieg. (Basle, 1948), p. 36.

[181] Klaus Urner, "Neutralität und Wirtschaftskrieg: Zur schweizerischen Aussenhandelspolitik 1939-1945," in: Rudolf L. Bindschedler et al. (ed.), Schwedische und schweizerische Neutralität im Zweiten Weltkrieg. (Basle, 1985), p. 252.

[182] Walther Hofer and Herbert R. Reginbogin, Hitler, der Westen und die Schweiz. (Zurich, 2001), pp. 517-543.

plete break-down of economic relations. Britain was well aware of these efforts and appreciated them, so much so that in a tacit agreement with the Swiss government, Britain kept intact the Anglo-Swiss Trade Agreement of April 1940, and in practice permitted modifications to accommodate new conditions after the French defeat in June 1940. On closer examination, this concession should not be seen as overly generous, since Britain, in signing the War Trade Agreement, had already acknowledged that it was impossible for Switzerland to break off all trade relations with Germany.

By late 1940, the British understood that Switzerland was determined to defend its independence, and as a result the British government was more liberal in allowing imports essential to the Swiss. Switzerland was not permitted to reship such imported goods to Germany, but this exception on imports at least made it possible for the Swiss economy to keep functioning. In practice, the British allowed Switzerland to accumulate a two-month stock of essential supplies. Nevertheless, Swiss authorities considered it in the interest of their country to leave the Swiss public in ignorance of these stockpiles. They knew the inevitable rationing (of imports) would lead to unrest in the population, and the government could not – for security reasons – disclose the actual amount of reserves available. Also the authorities, having secret reserves, were in a better position to resist German demands. [183]

The issuance of navicerts for more important goods was also slightly simplified: after 1940, navicert applications could be coordinated through the Swiss government. Italy also showed an unexpected sympathy for the Swiss, and allotted cargo space on Italian ships, solving one of Switzerland's main transport problems. Moreover, eventual concessions by Switzerland's other neighbor states were of enormous importance to this landlocked and surrounded country, because permits were needed not only for loading and unloading Swiss cargos in foreign ports, but also for further transport across foreign territories. [184]

Second – The War Trade Agreement was the first important agreement Switzerland had to conclude during World War II under pressure from the Allied Powers. Already, neutral Switzerland's policy of selective optimization had become apparent, a policy which allowed the country to negotiate a tight-rope through demanding economic negotiations both with the Axis Powers and the Allied Powers. This may be illustrated by two examples:

At the beginning of the war, Britain, in order to conserve and protect necessary wartime resources, had imposed an embargo on imports considered non-essential. This led to an abrupt downturn in Anglo-Swiss trade. As a result, in subsequent talks with Britain, Switzerland was obliged to refuse certain proposals Britain advanced to pay for Swiss goods, proposals which would have favored British wartime interests at the expense of the Swiss. Switzerland did, however, declare

---

[183] Luzi Stamm et al. (ed.), Dignity and Coolness. (Lenzburg, 2004), doc. 124 p. 188 – British envoy, David Victor Kelly, to Foreign Minister Anthony Eden, (written Berne, June 4, 1941, and received June 20, 1941).

[184] Klaus Urner, "Neutralität und Wirtschaftskrieg: Zur schweizerischen Aussenhandelspolitik 1939-1945," in: Rudolf L. Bindschedler et al. (ed.), Schwedische und schweizerische Neutralität im Zweiten Weltkrieg. (Basle, 1985), p. 252.

its willingness to loan the British 100 million francs, linking this offer to Britain's agreement to allow an increase in Swiss exports to Britain. This government-to-government loan was to be disguised as an agreement between British and Swiss banks so that one principle of neutrality, namely that of parity between Swiss treatment of combatants, would not be infringed. However, because of the abrupt change in the military and political situation in Europe following the invasion of France, the Swiss banks withdrew their loan offer on May 15, 1940. [185]

All the same, Switzerland had succeeded, against Allied interests, in maintaining the country's right to supply goods to other countries, although in reduced amounts. In spite of the withdrawn loan offer, the Swiss, with stubborn negotiating tactics, had also managed to get British permission to continue trading with Germany – a trade which was absolutely necessary to Swiss survival as a nation – albeit with fixed quotas. Switzerland continued, throughout the war, to pursue its neutral and necessary strategy of balancing the competing interests of both the Allies and the Axis.

It is easy to criticize specific decisions in retrospect. But such historical criticism does not always take into account the grim realities of the national and the international environment of the times. The following section, using several negotiations as examples, will attempt to show what the Swiss delegation experienced during its tough, nerve-racking and bitter tug-of-war on products, supply quotas, and export markets. Readers should note that, for Switzerland this struggle on blockade issues was about the very survival of the country. It was also part of the country's war to maintain political and economic independence. They should also be aware that Swiss delegations were dealing with global powers that – not least because of their colonial pasts – were not used to tolerating principled opposition from smaller countries.

BLOCKADE NEGOTIATIONS

The blockade negotiations with Allied and Axis Powers resulted in a whole series of trade agreements containing detailed regulations governing export quotas and payment transactions. Moreover, in the first three to four years after the war's outbreak, Swiss political and military leaders also faced the possibility of an outright German invasion. Hence trade and quota negotiations were influenced by real and potential military confrontations which triggered ever new constraints, difficulties and bottlenecks. There was no clear solution to Switzerland's predicament, since any resolution depended on the outcome of the wider war.

The so-called 'Phony War' of 1939/1940 (the Sitzkrieg after the invasion of Poland but before the German Blitzkrieg into France) saw an inexorable transition from peacetime to wartime economies. Both sides sought to weaken each other's economic base. Switzerland was caught in the middle of these maneuvers – badgered both by the Allied and Axis Powers. Like a swimmer in high waves, Switzerland tried to fight for its economic survival, seizing on any available opportunity to stay afloat.

---

[185] Walther Hofer and Herbert R. Reginbogin, Hitler, der Westen und die Schweiz. (Zurich, 2001), p. 542.

Switzerland's economic ties to Britain – not to mention England's naval superiority on the high seas – gave that country enormous leverage over the Swiss. By manipulating the concessions game, i.e. allowing increased imports of raw materials into Switzerland, Britain could maintain considerable control over war materials ordered from Switzerland, including the financing of such orders. The French, in contrast, had less strategic leverage and adopted more direct measures to exert pressure, such slamming physical restrictions on border transit. However, the overarching concern of both Britain and France in blockade negotiations was insuring that Switzerland continued to supply them with war materials. [186] German restrictions were, initially at least, less onerous. Just like the neutral countries, Germany depended on imports from overseas and benefited from any type of trade.

Naturally, Switzerland was interested in keeping the discussions focused on blockade issues. But a Swiss proposal to hold combined British-French-Swiss negotiations in London was not well received. The British wanted to be the final arbiter in the trade wars, and made it perfectly clear that they would only sign a War Trade Agreement with Switzerland after such an agreement had been concluded between Switzerland and France. [187] They would not commit to anything approaching final conditions of their own until they had pinned down the French position. In the meantime Swiss-British negotiations focused mainly on general trade issues.

Beginning of Talks

Swiss/British negotiations on trade relations were in fact opened in London on November 7, 1939, and another negotiation on Allied economic boycott measures began on November 14 in Paris.

The Allied Powers wanted a blockade agreement which would destroy the German economy, but they also sought to manipulate economic changes imposed on neutral states – the consequences of the blockade – to favor Allied needs. In the case of Switzerland, they wanted to use any production capacity which was freed up because of the new export restrictions to be turned to fulfilling war material orders placed by the Allied Powers.

Switzerland, in other words, could only avoid its own economic strangulation resulting from the blockade by working out a trade agreement with the French. [188] This was easier said than done. First, it proved virtually impossible to separate the more limited blockade issues from much broader trade relations between Switzerland and France. Second, not only the French Trade Ministry, but other affected

---

[186] Schweizerisches Bundesarchiv, Troutbeck and Fraser. London, March 7, 1940 FO 371/23174 Economically Switzerland was heavily dependent on Britain, but Britain, too, had considerable interest in concessions the Swiss might grant them. This particularly applied to the supply of war materials and to the granting of a loan by the Swiss. The British need for wood (classified as war material) was so great that Britain was even prepared to accept wood from Germany via Switzerland. In Switzerland, this [German] wood was mainly used for constructing huts which were supplied to Britain, in addition to wooden parts. Schweizerisches Bundesarchiv, Bericht über den Stand des schweizerischen Holzverkaufs. Berne, February 26, 1940 7110 EVD 1973/134 Vol. 14 and meeting Setchell-Glesinger of March 11, 1940 7110 EVD 1973/134 Vol. 14.

[187] Schweizerisches Bundesarchiv, E 1004-1 Bundesratsprotokoll, February 24, 1940.

[188] PRO: FO 371/24532 Alphand an Le Ministère du Blocus. Berne, October, 31, 1939.

French ministries soon took an exceedingly lively interest in the course of the negotiations. The ensuing complexity – not to mention the Byzantine French bureaucracy – meant it was only a matter of time before the blockade talks ground to a halt. Conflicting government interests pervaded discussions in England as well, and despite London's desire to work things out, Swiss initiatives were engulfed in a government labyrinth. For Switzerland, a resolution was a matter of economic life or death and, in the face of bureaucracy and delay in both London and Paris, the Swiss resorted to unusual measures. They suggested that the negotiations should be hurried along by talks between special missions and moved permanently from Bern to Paris and London, respectively. [189] In London, the talks were to be held by Swiss Minister H. Sulzer, an industrialist, [190] and Professor P. Keller, delegate for trade agreements, and in Paris by the Swiss envoy, Minister Walter Stucki.

When the Allied Powers met the Swiss delegation, the Allies expressed their dissatisfaction with a trade agreement concluded on October 24, 1939, between Switzerland and Germany. For their part, the Swiss complained of the economic pressures forced onto their country by the Allied blockade. [191]

In their opening statements, Swiss negotiators described the existing state of German-Swiss economic relations. They also explained that after the beginning of the war, Allied purchases of Swiss products had decreased sharply, and as a result they had been forced to continue trading with Germany in order to pay for the raw materials needed to keep Swiss manufacturing afloat. They detailed how 50% of the final value of German exports to Switzerland consisted of expenses tied to goods, commissions and agency fees. The remaining 50% of value due from Switzerland could be used by Germany for purchasing Swiss goods. Only under this arrangement could Switzerland acquire German coal, iron and steel necessary for its factories, while supplying Germany with manufactured goods as counter trade. The Swiss delegation emphasized that this was essentially a barter arrangement. In other words Germany did not receive convertible Swiss currency in exchange for raw materials supplied to Switzerland, but was reimbursed only with processed raw materials. Moreover, they maintained that the total value of German raw material coming into Switzerland amounted to twice the value of processed goods exported back to Germany. They referred to a law adopted in 1935 which forbade non-Swiss finished goods being used in clearing trade with Germany. Switzerland could support its trade with Germany only by processing of imported raw materials. [192] They emphasized that Switzerland had few raw materials of its own, and thus had no alternative but to import them. With this detailed description the Swiss tried to dispel Allied suspicions that raw or semi-processed materials allowed into Switzerland by England and France might be passed on to Germany to support the German war effort.

---

[189] Schweizerisches Bundesarchiv, E 1004-1 Bundesratsprotokoll October 30, 1939.

[190] Hans Sulzer was a very well-known Swiss industrialist, Director of Gebrüder Sulzer, President of the Vorort industrial association.

[191] PRO: FO 371/24532 Stanley Irving, the English observer at French-Swiss negotiations, to Troutbeck. Paris, November 14, 1939.

[192] Ibid.

The French were reluctant to accept the Swiss explanation, and bristled at the mention of German raw materials flowing into Switzerland. [193] They threatened and sporadically imposed summary confiscation of Swiss goods in transit, saying that an accumulation of supplies within Switzerland might be yet another reason for a German attack of that country. At the time – October/November 1939 – there was in fact intelligence concerning German troop concentrations in Southern Germany and the Black Forest, reported by H.L. Setchell, Trade Secretary at the British Embassy in Bern. In the event of an attack, France and Britain said they would be prepared to release confiscated Swiss goods back to Switzerland. But it remained unclear how such a transfer would be carried out and who might ultimately profit from it. If there was no German attack on Switzerland, impounded Swiss goods would continue to be set aside and protected in France, an arrangement worked out previously for Belgian manufactures. [194]

The Swiss delegation resisted. On the following day, November 15, 1939, they again protested the allegation that Switzerland was a trade center for Germany, pointing out that Switzerland could not survive without maintaining the manufacture and delivery of products to its main suppliers of essential raw materials, of which Germany was one. The Swiss reiterated that all goods originating from France, Britain or elsewhere overseas – goods that came under contraband control regulations – would not be exported to any countries except back to their country of origin or to other neutral states. They gave assurances that the only goods excepted from this regulation were those which were subject to basic processing in Switzerland. But this time, too, negotiations faltered. The Swiss did not succeed in persuading the French of the benign nature of such processing. [195] They were requested to provide a list of goods to be considered for quotas and controls for the next meeting, and to come up with additional proposals for a blockade agreement. [196]

These proposals were presented by the Swiss on November 16 and, in a subsequent meeting, were in a large part refused by the French. However, the French Trade Minister H. Alphand set out to draw up a new draft of a blockade agreement which would include at least parts of the Swiss goods listing.

Breaking off Negotiations

By November 1939, Switzerland saw its economic situation decline precipitously due to Allied blockade politics. Sensing an emergency and even before formally responding to the new French draft, Swiss negotiators presented the French with a provisional measure to release Swiss goods confiscated due to blockade measures. [197] This occurred on November 21, 1939.

France refused to accept this measure, even on a provisional basis, maintaining that final resolution of the matter was imminent. [198] This French hauteur infuriated

---

[193] Ibid.
[194] Ibid.
[195] Ibid., Paris, November, 21, 1939.
[196] Ibid.,
[197] PRO: FO 371/24532 Irving to M.E.W. Paris, November, 21, 1939.
[198] Ibid.

the Swiss. On November, 23, the Swiss came out and openly insisted on their right to trade with all neutral states at their own discretion and without interference by others – blockade or no blockade. [199] By doing so they undercut French efforts to limit export trade to certain neutral countries to current account transactions. The French curtly requested the Swiss delegation to clarify the contentious points with the Swiss government in Bern, and the entire Swiss delegation abruptly left Paris. [200]

In the meantime, Minister Stucki in Bern tried to smooth the waters. By December, 5, 1939, all participants had calmed down enough to resume talks. [201]

The "Accords Spéciaux"

On December 5, 1939, the Swiss delegation suggested that private supply agreements (*accords spéciaux*) should be concluded solely between affected French and Swiss companies without official participation of the Swiss government. France flatly refused this suggestion and insisted that the Swiss government should issue guarantees for any such agreements. [202] The French believed that the existence of a government guarantee behind an order between a French and a Swiss company would ensure that the company in question would deliver the goods on schedule.

The question of timely deliveries seems to have been one of the issues addressed already in the agreement on arms supplies to France concluded secretly and without official approval by the Swiss government on September 22, 1939. In that agreement, parties in Switzerland had guaranteed to deliver Swiss-made weapons to France, but with the proviso that production for Switzerland's own national defense would take priority. Only when the government approved delivery of any given shipment of arms could a specific delivery date be set. However, the Swiss government was not permitted to make blanket promises on delivery dates, because this would have violated a Swiss national decree of July, 8, 1938. This decree stipulated that the government had to grant permission for each and every arms order, and it had been issued with an eye to unexpected circumstances, including urgent and unforeseen needs of the Swiss army. Granting broad export permissions would also have been ruled out by a later decision taken by the Federal Council on February, 16, 1940. This decision made it clear that the Swiss Military Department could label its own orders as urgent and that, in such a case, the manufacturer had to postpone fulfilling any other orders until the Swiss orders had been completed. [203] Finally the Swiss had to recognize that all their arguments for achieving compromise were getting nowhere, and they agreed to comply with French demands. [204]

---

[199] Ibid., Paris, November, 24, 1939.

[200] Ibid.

[201] PRO: FO 371/24532 Irving to M.E.W. Paris, December, 5, 1939.

[202] Ibid.

[203] Schweizerisches Bundesarchiv 7110 EVD 1967/32 G.B. 821 Fierz to Trade Department of EVD. Berne, April, 22, 1940.

[204] Op. cit.

In continuing negotiations, French Trade Minister Alphand suggested that the Swiss should review the blockade agreement between France and Belgium signed the previous day to find formulations which might be useful to Swiss interests. [205]

But the Swiss delegation remained angry and frustrated at being ordered to comply with the unilateral demands of the Allied Powers. While they agreed to study the Belgian agreement, Swiss negotiators wanted to demonstrate that they were not completely powerless. They abruptly introduced restrictions on the import of certain French goods and, more importantly, on Swiss armaments exports to France. Armaments were the Achilles heel of the French and the Swiss blocking such exports was unacceptable to them. The French delegation immediately broke off all negotiations. [206] Some days later, both sides had calmed down, and the negotiators entered the next round of talks. In a conversation between Hotz and Alphand on December 8, 1939, the French promised Switzerland relief for exported silk, embroidery, clocks and watches, in return for the Swiss lifting trade restrictions. [207]

On December 10, negotiations on the blockade agreement resumed, lasting until December 21. [208] According to the well-established pattern, modifications suggested by the Swiss found little favor with their French neighbors. After two days, Minister Alphand suggested that a commission consisting of Juge, Stechell and a Swiss expert should work out lists in four categories affecting Swiss products, modeled on the Belgian agreement: [209]

1. Goods subject to a total export ban
2. Goods subject to export limits, compared to previous years
3. Goods subject to special quota agreements
4. Goods subject to no export control

The Swiss agreed to these conditions.

NEGOTIATIONS WITH BRITAIN

Since the beginning of hostilities in 1939, relations between France and Britain had improved somewhat, at least to the point where the two powers were able to coordinate on blockade negotiations with Switzerland. Parallel to the blockade negotiations held in Paris, talks on economic issues had started in London on November, 7, 1939. Since the British position was that Britain would only take up blockade issues once a French-Swiss agreement was concluded, the talks held in London initially focused on broader issues of trade. However, Britain and France were still wide apart on the timing of any ultimatum issued to Germany, the strategy towards the Balkans and the Baltic States, possible bombing of the Ruhr industrial region (which the French opposed), and the question of sending troops into German-occupied neutral Belgium. Forced into cooperation during the

---

[205] Ibid.
[206] PRO: FO 371/24532 Irving to Troutbeck. Paris, December, 8, 1939.
[207] Ibid. and Schweizerisches Bundesarchiv E 1004-1 Bundesratsprotokoll, December 27, 1939.
[208] Ibid., Irving to Troutbeck. Paris, December, 10, 1939.
[209] Ibid., Paris, December 21, 1939.

first months of the war, ancient enmities between Britain and France continued to flare up. The French complained that the British military contribution was ludicrously small in view of a million unemployed in England. Britain had in fact provided only two divisions compared with France's eighty five. France suspected, not completely without justification, that Britain was using the war to increase its own exports instead of concentrating all available resources on mobilization. [210]

The Swiss were by now quite proficient fighters in bureaucratic hand to hand combat and seized every opportunity to take advantage of the British failure to understand how important Swiss exports to Germany were. [211] Overall, however, the London talks were less acrimonious than those in Paris. On December 1, 1939, the London negotiation reached a fundamental point – the negotiation of a crucial payment agreement proposed by the British Treasury Department. [212] The proposal covered acceptable methods of payment on trade contracts backed by the British and Swiss governments. On the Swiss side, the draft was discussed by P. Keller and A.C. Nussbaumer (one of the presidents of the Swiss Bank Corporation and member of the delegation). On the British side, the negotiators were S.D. Waley (Under-Secretary of State at the Treasury), Carr of the Board of Trade, Jones and another Bank of England expert. The Swiss delegation received the opening proposal from the British. [213]

Essentially, the agreement provided that British payments for goods supplied by Switzerland were to be made in pounds – the amount calculated at the official exchange rate between the pound sterling and Swiss francs – into a special Swiss account maintained at the Bank of England. Against this pound credit balance, the Swiss National Bank would then make corresponding payments in Swiss francs to the appropriate Swiss exporters. But the Swiss National Bank could use the *pounds* in its special Bank of England account freely for payments within the British Commonwealth. The domain of such pound sterling payments included Egypt, Iraq and Sudan, but not Canada, Newfoundland or Hong Kong. The pounds sterling in this special account were to be guaranteed by a gold security, and the total balance in favor of Switzerland should never exceed 5 million pounds (100 million Swiss francs). If Swiss credits were to go above this ceiling, Switzerland could request payment in another free foreign currency. Initially, the draft covered payments to be made by the British state to Switzerland for government contracts, but it was evident that private sector contracts would likewise be included in this regulation. British companies would make payments for goods received from Switzerland to the special Swiss account at the Bank of England. [214]

---

[210] D. Johnson, "Britain and France 1940," in: Trans. Royal Historical Society. Vol. xxii (1972), p. 142-146; J.C. Cairns, "Great Britain and the Fall of France: A Study in Allied Disunity," in: Journal of Modern History. Vol. xxvii No. 4 (1955); and G. Wright, "Ambassador Bullitt and the Fall of France," in: World Politics. Vol. x No. 1 (1957), p. 76.

[211] Schweizerisches Bundesarchiv E 1004-1 Bundesratsprotokoll, February 24, 1940.

[212] Schweizerisches Bundesarchiv 7110 EVD 1973/134 Vol. 15 Exposé Professor Keller. 28. December, 1939.

[213] Ibid., Schweizerische Wirtschaftsverhandlungen mit Grossbritannien. London, December 1, 1939.

[214] Schweizerisches Bundesarchiv 7110 EVD 1973/134 Vol. 15 Exposé Professor Keller of December 28, 1939.

In further discussions, Under Secretary of State Waley pointed out that Switzerland had made arrangements with Germany in a trade agreement of October 24, 1939, whereby the Reich's delinquent payments owed to Switzerland would be paid down. The Swiss delegation maintained that such advances were not, in fact, loans to Germany and pointed out that – in compliance with its neutrality policy – Switzerland would not grant government loans. But Swiss private banks, with permission of the Swiss National Bank, were allowed to grant foreign loans. Now that loans had entered the discussion, Waley said that while the British government was not requesting any such loans, private loans might indeed be welcomed to facilitate transactions by the British private sector. The Swiss responded that the issuance of Swiss bank credits to Britain could only be of interest to Switzerland if such credits served to increase the whole range of Swiss exports to Britain. They were definitely not interested in granting credits solely for the purpose of financing Britain's purchase of Swiss armaments. Waley replied that any loans granted by Switzerland could certainly have a beneficial effect on British decisions concerning the import of goods from Switzerland. The Swiss delegation again promised to study the matter. [215]

The overarching strategy of the Bank of England was to protect the British pound from inflation and possible devaluation. So long as British imports could be paid for with a counter trade of British goods or through limited bilateral agreements, then the supply of British pounds on the free market could be held to a minimum. There was, however, no legislation restricting foreign exchange on the part of Britain. The British preferred bilateral agreements, as opposed to across-the-board currency restrictions, since such agreements were more flexible and could be customized to the special conditions of any partner country. In the payment agreement between Britain and France, for example, there was no provision at all for cash transfers. The terms of the payment agreement between Britain and Sweden stipulated that all trade payments were to be processed through a special, limited account. [216]

The Swiss were in a dilemma. In spite of Waley's blandishments, it was obvious that Britain in fact did desire an agreement that would allow loans for British purchases of war materials from Switzerland. [217] But accepting such a proposal would have led to a whole list of negative repercussions on the Swiss:

– Swiss neutrality legislation demanded parity treatment of warring parties, and in granting loan rights to England, Switzerland would have been forced to accord equal rights to Germany, which would certainly result in Allied countermeasures against Switzerland. It should be noted here that at the time of these blockade negotiations with the Allies, Switzerland was not yet completely surrounded by Axis Powers and Germany had not yet demanded Swiss loans to finance purchases of war materials.
– Apart from immensely complicating Switzerland's relations with Germany – reason enough to refuse – a loan agreement with Britain would penalize

---

[215] Ibid.
[216] Schweizerisches Bundesarchiv 7110 EVD 1973/134 Vol. 16 Waley to Keller London, December 16, 1939.
[217] Op.cit.

Switzerland with foreign exchange losses due to Britain's control of the official exchange rate. [218]
- Switzerland's status as a neutral would be severely compromised by an agreement which would be so clearly a ruse to allow financing British contracts for war materials.
- The Swiss population remembered World War I and harbored a strong aversion to some Swiss companies supplying war materials and profiteering from war. [219]

However, the Swiss did not reject the British suggestions out of hand but looked for ways to accommodate British interests, for example by permitting Swiss exporters to grant the British extended terms of payment in normal goods trade, but not trade of war materials. They also sought to verify that the measures to be taken would assist Swiss export industry rather than British currency policies. [220] The Swiss moved away from strict parity considerations, noting that economic relations with Britain on the one side and Germany on the other were by nature too different in structure to be given analogue treatment. [221] Nevertheless, the Swiss Political Department, on December 7, did recommend to the Federal Council "... to strive for a formal parallel (between Britain and Germany), as far as possible." [222] On the delicate issue of government advances to prop up the accounts receivable of Swiss exporters, the delegation was instructed to follow the German-Swiss trade agreement of October 24, 1939.

After lengthy discussions in Bern with experts from the Political, Finance and Customs Departments, as well as representatives from the National Bank, on December 11, 1939, the Swiss government unanimously decided that it could not accept the British draft payment agreement because it would have resulted in the Swiss economy becoming a service provider for British currency policy and the British war economy. In addition the government was concerned that, by accepting this British proposal, the door would be opened to British demands for a much more restrictive clearing agreement which would cut even more deeply into Switzerland's trade and finance. [223] The Swiss were reluctant to accept the restrictions in foreign exchange embodied in the agreement. An imbalance of trade could arise. Swiss exporters were free to make their own trade decisions. They could not be forced to sell their goods to Britain if they could not get the desired price or for any other reason. But according to the agreement, the Swiss Nationalbank was required to buy British pounds at an officially fixed exchange rate for payment of the goods bought from Britain. The Swiss felt this would lead to an unacceptable risk for the national bank. The ensuing trade deficit would not be balanced by the sale of Swiss goods but by the forced purchase of pounds. Finally, the government decided that an agreement which set out financing for war

---

[218] Schweizerisches Bundesarchiv 7110 EVD 1967/32 G.B. 821 EPD to EVD. Berne, December 7, 1939.
[219] Schweizerisches Bundesarchiv 7110 EVD 1973/134 Vol. 15 Meeting at the Bank of England of December 18, 1939. London, December 19, 1939.
[220] Op.cit.
[221] Ibid.
[222] Ibid.
[223] Schweizerisches Bundesarchiv E 1004-1 Bundesratsprotokoll, 11. Dezember 1939.

materials ordered by Britain in Switzerland violated Swiss neutrality policy. [224] At this point, Switzerland could still afford to reject the proposal on the basis of its neutrality alone. Later on, when the country was completely surrounded by Axis Powers, Switzerland could not have accepted an agreement – an agreement seen to favor the British – without incurring immediate and severe economic reprisals from Germany and Italy.

The Swiss government did agree to soften its rejection of the British payment proposal by offering the British a loan of 100 million francs. Through this loan, they hoped to smooth the way for easing the normal exchange of goods, based on earlier pre-war agreements. Although a government loan, this credit was to be structured as an agreement between private British and Swiss banks to avoid openly compromising Swiss neutrality and the principle of parity. [225] The Swiss delegation informed the British of this decision on December 12, 1939. [226] In his written answer of December 16, S.D. Waley of the Treasury acknowledged the Swiss offer, but rejected the loan because it did not meet with English intentions. [227]

On December 20, 1939, the Swiss delegation received a second draft of a payment agreement from the British. It was an extension of the first draft of December 1, and showed British intended to regulate payment transactions between Switzerland and Britain through a payment agreement. [228] The Swiss delegation returned home for the Christmas holidays and discussions with the government on the new proposal. [229]

Again, the Swiss summoned their experts to study the proposal, and on January 9, 1940, the Swiss Federal Council decided to accept the British clearing proposal in principle, seeing such an acceptance as the only option remaining since Britain had rejected the Swiss loan offer. However, there were still questions which needed to be clarified and the Swiss hoped to negotiate these to their advantage. The Council did not want to comment formally on the British proposal until these points were cleared up. So the Swiss negotiators set off for London again. They had been authorized by the Federal Council to begin talks on the clearing proposal, as soon as certain preconditions had been settled:

– A guarantee of active measures by the British on the import of Swiss goods to Britain, to include (currently) prohibited goods such as silk material, silk ribbons, shoes etc. which had traditionally been part of British-Swiss trade.
– The British government was to liberalize supply quotas and facilitate a general increase in the purchase of Swiss goods. Switzerland would consider granting Britain a sum of up to 5 million pounds to be used to extend the terms of payment and avoid balance difficulties, despite the fact that the Swiss balance of

---

[224] Ibid.

[225] PRO: FO 371/24532 Memorandum. London. December 11, 1939.

[226] Ibid., J.G. Owen (M.E.W.) an S.D. Waley (Under Secretary of State in the Treasury). London, December 12, 1939.

[227] Schweizerisches Bundesarchiv 7110 EVD 1973/134 Vol. 16 Waley to Keller. London, December 16, 1939.

[228] Schweizerisches Bundesarchiv E 1004-1 Bundesratsprotokoll, December 11, 1939.

[229] PRO: FO 371/24532 Waley to Fraser (Board of Trade). London, December 21, 1939.

trade was already strained due to the losses expected to be incurred on trade with Germany.

The willingness of the British to acquiesce to these Swiss concerns would be put to the test in the negotiations which followed. [230]

The Swiss delegation arrived back in London on January 16, 1940, and a meeting with British counterparts from the Treasury, the Bank of England and the Ministry of Economic Warfare (M.E.W) was scheduled for the following day. To the considerable surprise of the Swiss, the representatives of the Treasury and the M.E.W. at once seemed to acknowledge the reasons for Swiss reservations, even though the representative of the Bank of England expressed objections. To the Swiss, it seemed that the Bank was pursuing different goals than the government. The Bank wished to restrict circulation of the pound out of currency and trade policy considerations. The Treasury, for its part, was seeking for ways to improve Britain's poor trade balance with Switzerland.

However, on January 26, 1940, the Board of Trade accepted the Swiss loan proposal. [231] By doing so, the British authorities seemed to abandon the policy of seeking payment agreements with countries where Britain's trade balance was negative. Britain had signed such an agreement with Sweden, for example, at the beginning of the year which limited Sweden's free payment transactions. The Netherlands was about to receive a demand for the same. In the case of Switzerland, however, the British departed from their usual practice, apparently because of Switzerland's ability to provide financial assistance to Britain. It seemed that the Treasury and M.E.W. had succeeded in convincing the Board of Trade that Swiss financial considerations for Britain were of more importance than the currency concerns of the Bank of England. [232]

The Swiss immediately made use of this change. They submitted new requests to the Board of Trade concerning the terms of the loan, demanding that old contracts be reinstated and that imports of non-military goods from Switzerland be increased. In addition, the Swiss asked for a relaxation of Britain's blockade policy against Switzerland and requested general permission from the Ministry of Economic Warfare to export goods to Germany.

The most important reasons for offering a 100 million Swiss francs loan to Britain were the following:
- avoid the imposition of a restrictive clearing agreement with Britain;
- finance the import of Swiss goods, which the Bank of England had calculated to show a surplus of about 200 million Swiss francs in the current year;
- secure a favorable British response on the blockade issue and permission for increased Swiss imports, particularly for products manufactured by Switzerland's weaker industries, such as textiles, aluminum foils and weaved hats.

As mentioned earlier, this loan was granted only to be cancelled later by the Swiss. But the British loan is a good example of how Switzerland put its financial power and the power of the freely-traded Swiss franc to good use in negotiations

---

[230] Op. cit., January 9, 1940.
[231] Schweizerisches Bundesarchiv E 7110 1973/134 Vol. 15 Memorandum. London, January 30, 1940.
[232] Ibid.

on vital trade issues. Manoeuvres to protect the trade necessary to Swiss survival were behind the granting of clearing loans to the Axis Powers. After 1939, currency restrictions became general across Europe, and only the US dollar and the Swiss franc continued to be traded freely. [233] After the USA entered the war in December, 1941, the Swiss franc was the only currency which continued to be accepted world-wide. [234]

FRENCH/BRITISH REQUESTS FOR WAR MATERIALS

In early 1940, the French and British came to the conclusion – after extensive discussions – that they needed to present a united front and should develop a basis for permanent co-operation after the war. In a declaration signed on March 28, 1940, both parties agreed not to conclude a separate armistice or peace treaty without consulting the other. They wanted to demonstrate to Germany how determined they were to proceed in a unified and coordinated manner.

By March 19, 1940, there was agreement in principle on a blockade agreement, with only a few issues remaining unresolved. The same day, the French tried to use the occasion to press the Swiss delegation for a firm date for the delivery of orders for war materials. The Swiss assured them that their orders would receive the same attention as Swiss orders. They repeated – as several times before – that setting a firm delivery date would violate Swiss legislation giving absolute priority to Swiss defense interests, explaining that Switzerland would only use its right to prioritize production for national defense orders in absolute emergencies. Switzerland would try, if at all possible, to ensure timely processing of Allied contracts for war materials. [235] This declaration of goodwill did not meet with the response the Swiss had hoped for. On the contrary, the French reaction was unexpectedly harsh: Paris insisted on written guarantees of delivery dates without any priority being given to Swiss needs. [236] The French insistence on these terms was no accident. On February 28, members from various government departments had met with the British negotiators: J.M. Graham of the British Board of Trade, Irving, Setchell, and their French counterpart, Alphand. Together, they backed the French plan to use the blockade negotiations as a means to exert pressure on Switzerland to deliver the arms exactly as ordered. [237]

On their own, the British had pressed the Swiss on war material deliveries as well. The British envoy to Bern, David Kelly, had managed to get delivery guarantees for the British war materials order, by skillfully putting pressure on Messrs. Fierz (director of the Military Technical Services) and Minger (head of the Swiss Military Department). But these efforts seemed in danger again when Switzerland

[233] Markus Heiniger, Dreizehn Gründe. Warum die Schweiz im Zweiten Weltkrieg nicht erobert wurde. (Zurich, 1989), pp. 131-132.

[234] Gian Trepp, Die Bank für Internationalen Zahlungsausgleich im Zweiten Weltkrieg: Bankgeschäfte mit dem Feind. Von Hitlers Europabank zum Instrument des Marshallplans. (Zurich, 1993), p.10.

[235] PRO: FO 371/23174 Irving to M.E.W., March 19, 1940.

[236] Ibid.

[237] Ibid. Report on Blockade Negotiations February 28 – March 5, 1940 from Graham, London, March 8, 1940.

tightened its legislation on arms supply on February 16, 1940. All contracts for arms deliveries henceforward had to be submitted to the Swiss Military Department for approval which gave the state a new right to control priority on deliveries. Kelly therefore proposed to the Foreign Office that contracts which had already been accepted and the guarantees issued should be tied to an economic agreement between Britain and Switzerland. [238] To this end the British devised a text to present to the Swiss delegation in the context of the London talks on a broad trade agreement between Switzerland and Britain. [239] The wording of the text specified that whenever the Swiss government accepted British orders for war materials, it should guarantee that these orders would not be delayed because priority had to be given to Swiss orders. The British likewise recommended that the French should base their demands on this British formula – as a condition for the conclusion of the blockade agreement – that Switzerland grant them delivery guarantees for the war materials ordered by France. [240]

Clearly, Britain was cooperating with the French on tactics to ensure guaranteed scheduling of deliveries of Swiss arms (Swiss confirmation of on-time deliveries of arms to France was still pending). The British were due to sign the blockade agreement on March 19, 1940, but signature was postponed on the excuse there had been insufficient time to study the agreement. [241]

A week later, on March 27, 1940, the British announced that they wanted additional changes to the agreement, particularly with reference to an export of arms from Switzerland to Russia with a value of some 2 million pounds and such shipments to pass through Germany. The British feared that the Germans would confiscate the arms (a fear which did not prove well-founded). Britain also objected to the fact that Germany would be paid in foreign currency for the transfer of weapons materials, since Britain wanted, with a few exceptions, to restrict German access to convertible currencies. The British also demanded additional controls over goods traffic between Switzerland and other neutral countries, as well as input into how neutrals should be classified. "Bad" neutrals, such as Russia and Finland, were to be put on a "Black List" which would also designate individuals or companies which, in the Allies' opinion, belonged to or supported the enemy. The lists were constantly updated and being on the Allied black list could have extremely unpleasant repercussions:

– Property owned by blacklisted persons or companies in the Allied sphere of influence was subject to confiscation;
– Blacklisted persons or companies could not transport goods over routes controlled by the Allies; and
– Trade between Allied nations and blacklisted persons or companies was forbidden. [242]

---

[238] Edgar Bonjour, Die Schweiz und Europa. Vol. III (Basle, 1973), p. 132-133.
[239] Ibid.
[240] PRO: FO 371/23174 Setchell to Cross. Paris, Paris, March 5, 1940.
[241] Ibid., M.E.W. an Irving und Setchell. London, March 20, 1940.
[242] Catherine Schiemann, Neutralität in Krieg und Frieden. Die Aussenpolitik der Vereinigten Staaten gegenüber der Schweiz 1941-1949. (Zurich, 1991), pp. 27-28.

Given the way the war was developing, the signature of the blockade agreements between Britain and Switzerland in Bern, and between France and Switzerland in Paris, on April 25, 1940, was an important milestone. Issues which were not yet resolved by that date:

– Swiss credits granted to Britain
– British coal deliveries to Switzerland
– Import of Swiss luxury goods to Britain
– Arms for Britain.

were to be worked out in the course of the negotiations on the trade agreement between Switzerland and Britain after the blockade agreement had been signed. However, the German invasion of Belgium and the Netherlands on May 10, 1940 pushed these negotiations into the background. [243]

SWITZERLAND IN THE GERMAN SPHERE OF INFLUENCE

Switzerland at the beginning of the war did not have the same strategic value it would have later on. The Germans mainly focused on its acquisition and manufacture. Few Swiss goods were considered vital to the war effort. The Swiss potential for manufacturing war materials and other industrial products had not yet been fully recognized. Germany's attention was concentrated mainly on south-Eastern Europe, Scandinavia and occupied Western Europe, whose industrial and agricultural resources were of much greater interest to the Nazi Reich. However Switzerland was still considered by Germany to belong to the German sphere of influence and to be a state which it controlled – at least economically.

Even before the French capitulation and before the German tank corps of General Guderian reached the Swiss border near Pontarlier on June 17, 1940, the Nazi regime – whose behavior towards Switzerland had been friendly during the so-called "Phony War" or "Sitzkrieg" after the invasion of Poland – abruptly changed its tone. The Germans informed the Swiss of their demands, and, by way of direct intimidation, imposed a coal embargo in the same month. The Nazis demanded that Switzerland break off all economic relations with the Allied powers and re-channel all arms deliveries to Germany. Like Wagner's pompous dramas, the demands of the Reich were made against rumblings in the background by the German ambassador, Ritter: that Switzerland was "nothing but a huge armament workshop, almost exclusively working for England and France." [244] In so far as it went, this statement was accurate, since until March 1940, the German share of Swiss war materials contracts amounted to but a fraction of the Allied share. [245]

Before the outbreak of war, Germany was Switzerland's main source of coal, supplying up to 53% of the total Swiss coal imports of 3.34 million tons. [246] The abrupt embargo on coal in the second half of June, 1940 gave Switzerland a taste

[243] Schweizerisches Bundesarchiv E 1004-1 Bundesratsprotokoll, May 21, 1940.

[244] Akten zur Deutschen Auswärtigen Politik 1918-1945 (ADAP), D, Vol. IX No. 377 Memo Ritter, Berlin, May 27, 1940.

[245] Robert U. Vogler, Die Wirtschaftsverhandlungen der Schweiz zwischen der Schweiz und Deutschland 1940 und 1941. Basle / Frankfurt am Main, 1997), p. 59.

[246] Georges-André Chevallaz, The Challenge of Neutrality. Diplomacy and the Defense of Switzerland. (Oxford, 2001), p. 165.

of the methods the Germans were prepared to use to push through their demands. Switzerland found itself in an extremely difficult situation. The country depended on German coal, as the Allied powers could not and would not supply it. A prolonged coal embargo would result in unemployment for at least 300,000 people. [247]

The absolute will on the part of Sweden to maintain peace at any price was clearly discernible as was Switzerland's absolute will to fight the specter of unemployment and factory shutdowns, which was like a red thread interwoven through all of the economic negotiations with Germany during the Second World War. The Swiss imperturbable desire to preserve employment can be seen early on in the "speech of rapprochement" delivered by Pilet-Golaz: "Work! The Federal Council will supply the Swiss people with work at all costs, at any price." [248]

The Swiss therefore decided to comply with German wishes, integrating German contracts into the production program at short notice, re-routing aluminum deliveries intended for Britain to Germany, and stopping deliveries of war material to the Allied powers including those 'ready for transport' to France and Britain. [249]

How much longer would the Axis powers, who controlled all of west and central Europe, allow isolated Switzerland to remain unoccupied? One of the Alpine republic's strongest defenses against invasion must have been its ability and clearly expressed readiness to destroy the Gotthard and Simplon railway tunnels, as well as all other routes across the Alps which were the main arteries for the transport of German war supplies to Italy. Nevertheless, a permanent threat of German invasion remained, even after Switzerland had demobilized some of its troops and partially adapted its export policies to German wishes. At the same time, Switzerland took whatever measures it could to assure that its foreign trade relations were to be honored whenever possible. It also recognized the principles laid down in the War Trade Agreement by upholding trade relations with Britain and other member states of the British Empire.

There were two reasons for the demobilization of Swiss troops on June 6, 1940: on the one hand, troops were withdrawn in order to avoid antagonizing the German colossus, since Germany had followed the arming of Swiss troops closely and with great suspicion. [250] On the other, the re-orientation of industry and the introduction of a war economy had created a considerable demand for workers, which could only be met by demobilizing. A core of 150,000 soldiers was kept for defense tasks – and for dealing with the Gotthard and Simplon tunnels, if necessary. However, plans remained in place whereby the Swiss army could be fully mobilized again within two days.

Under the prevailing conditions – Switzerland cut off from Allied trade routes, practically surrounded by Axis powers, and an armistice concluded between Germany and France – Switzerland was forced to grant a clearing loan of 150 million

---

[247] Adam Jost, Die Haltung der Schweiz gegenüber dem nationalsozialistischen Deutschland im Jahre 1940. Diss. (Berlin, 1972), p. 241.

[248] Edgar Bonjour, Geschichte der Schweizerischen Neutralität. Vier Jahrhunderte Eidgenössischer Aussenpolitik. Vol... VIII (Basle, 1975), p. 162.

[249] Juerg Fink, Die Schweiz aus der Sicht des Dritten Reiches 1933-1945. (Zurich, 1985), p. 145-146 notes made by Hemmen, July 9, 1940 in: Akten zur Deutschen Auswärtigen Politik 1918-1945 (ADAP), Series D, Vol. X, (Bonn, 1963), pp. 144-146.

[250] Op. cit., p. 45.

Swiss francs to Germany in a trade agreement of August 9, 1940. The agreement also stipulated that Switzerland was supposed to curtail all exports to Britain. In return, Germany guaranteed to supply Switzerland with coal, iron, seeds etc. [251]

Neither the Allied nor the Axis powers showed any understanding for Switzerland's difficult situation. Swiss actions provoked the question: How serious should Swiss neutrality be taken? It was interpreted as a purely political concession to Germany.

All agreements with Germany were closely linked to loans, but it soon became clear that the increase in Swiss credit to Germany were resulting in an increase in arms supply to the Axis powers. Besides additional exports of weapons and ammunition valued at 100 million Swiss francs, the Swiss hoped that the first clearing loan would also lead to aluminum exports worth some 20 million Swiss francs, and extra exports of machines and agricultural produce worth about 40 million Swiss francs. [252] In addition, Switzerland agreed to pay 11.8 million of its clearing obligations in Swiss francs. [253]

The clearing agreements which are so viciously criticized today were an instrument used skilfully by the Swiss to acquire raw materials and prevent unemployment if not outright economic disaster:

– Clearing agreements permitted Switzerland to cope with German requests for Swiss deliveries without incurring major negative repercussions on its own economy. [254]
– By granting loans, Switzerland gave Axis Powers the impression that it continued to be interested in co-operation. [255]
– Since clearing loans were closely linked to economic agreements, the import of vital raw materials could be secured.
– Last but not least, these loans resulted in an increase in contracts and brought work to many export companies, some of whose traditional trading partners no longer existed.

Not only the clearing agreements but also the readiness of Swiss banks to exchange German gold – including gold of unknown origin – against valuable foreign currency provoked international criticism after the war. The convertible Swiss franc gradually made Switzerland a centre of currency exchange, not exclusively, but to a large extent for the Third Reich. Swiss banks had until then been bankers for the world, but because of these gold transactions they had to endure the contemptuous label of being 'Hitler's bankers'.

---

[251] Schweizerisches Bundesarchiv E 1004-1 Bundesratsprotokoll, 1/Vol 400 of August 12, 1940 – Final Report of the EVD on economic negotiations with Germany.

[252] Klaus Urner, "Neutralität und Wirtschaftskrieg: Zur schweizerischen Aussenhandelspolitik 1939-1945," in: Rudolf L. Bindschedler et al. (ed.), Schwedische und schweizerische Neutralität im Zweiten Weltkrieg. (Basle, 1985), p. 279.

[253] Unabhängige Expertenkommission Schweiz – Zweiter Weltkrieg, (ed.), Die Schweiz und die Goldtransaktionen im Zweiten Weltkrieg. Vol. 16, (Zurich 2002), p. 108.

[254] Edgar Bonjour, Geschichte der Schweizerischen Neutralität. Vier Jahrhunderte Eidgenössischer Aussenpolitik. Vol. VIII (Basle, 1975), pp. 166-168.

[255] Ibid., p. 67-68.

Switzerland was encircled by the Axis powers, almost as if they were being strangulated. The Swiss had no choice but to yield to German demands on many points. Nevertheless, they continued to resist German demands for a total ban on exports to Allied countries. Their negotiators succeeded in convincing the Nazis that any ban on exports would lead to an end of Allied supplies reaching Switzerland, which in turn might affect Switzerland's ability to supply goods to Germany. They argued that the risks of such a ban would be higher than the anticipated benefits. Switzerland succeeded again in fending off new German protectionist endeavors.

Because of its stubbornness on these issues, as early as September 1940 Switzerland was granted permission by Germany to continue economic relations with Britain, albeit at a reduced level and only supplying products which had of no strategic value. [256]

What the Nazis did not know was that, in spite of the German stranglehold, Switzerland had surreptitiously continued exporting Swiss goods to Britain. Under extremely difficult circumstances war material was exported between August 1, 1940 and May 26, 1941 amounting to 6.1 million Swiss francs. Very likely, the Germans were also not informed that Switzerland was regularly supplying British intelligence with detailed information about its ongoing economic negotiations with Germany. [257]

As might be expected, the Allies responded negatively to German-Swiss economic cooperation by tightening the blockade, refusing navicerts for industrial raw materials and limiting food stuffs and consumer goods. [258] These measures dealt a heavy blow to Swiss foreign trade. On June 14, 1941, the American governmentblocked all Swiss accounts in the USA, then worth about 5 billion US dollars overall. [259] Generally restrictions became a lot tighter between summer 1940 and late 1941.

Switzerland found itself being pressured from all sides. While the Allied powers were primarily interested in controlling Swiss imports, so that no goods would fall into the hands of the enemy or would be used to produce things which were important for the Axis war effort, the Axis powers kept a close watch on Swiss exports to keep the amount of goods leaving the country to a minimum. [260]

---

[256] Bergier Report, p. 186.

[257] Jürg Stüssi-Lauterburg, "Die Schweiz zwischen dem 5. Mai und dem 5. August 1941," in: Schweizerzeit of March 12, 2004.

[258] Catherine Schiemann, Neutralität in Krieg und Frieden. Die Aussenpolitik der Vereinigten Staaten gegenüber der Schweiz 1941-1949. (Zurich, 1991), p. 35.

[259] Herbert R. Reginbogin, "The Financial Market of America During World War II," in: Joseph Jung, Herbert R. Reginbogin and Robert U. Vogler (ed.), Financial Markets of Neutral Countries during the Second World War. (in preparation by the Association of Financial History and the Principality of Liechtenstein); Gian Trepp, Die Bank für Internationalen Zahlungsausgleich im Zweiten Weltkrieg: Bankgeschäfte mit dem Feind. Von Hitlers Europabank zum Instrument des Marschallplans. (Zurich, 1993), p. 64.

[260] Max Steiner, "Die Verschiebungen der schweizerischen Aussenhandelsstruktur während des Zweiten Weltkrieges. Diss. (Zurich, 1950), p. 15.

The Compensation Deal

The Allied powers – not interested in dealing with Switzerland's economic situation and the resulting constraints – never concealed their irritation about the conclusion of the German-Swiss economic agreement and successively increased economic pressure on Switzerland. Over the course of 1942, supplies of raw materials flowing into Switzerland greatly decreased.

To break this closing circle, Switzerland attempted to negotiate a compensation deal with the Allied powers, including several talks in both London and Berlin. The meetings were not easy. The Swiss needed to get London to agree to trades, while Berlin had to issue the necessary transport approvals. In London, the Swiss quickly realized that the Allies had very limited enthusiasm for their plan, since the American armaments industry had come rapidly up to speed and Swiss armaments deliveries were hardly needed any more. [261] But because they still attached value to relations with the last democratic state in central Europe, the British agreed to a so-called "Compensation Deal". [262] Thereupon the Swiss managed to obtain the necessary transport approvals from Berlin. In convincing the Germans, the Swiss once more argued that without Allied raw materials, Swiss deliveries to Germany would be endangered. [263]

The arrangement was officially signed on December 14, 1942. It granted Switzerland import of raw materials including copper, nickel, rubber etc. In return, the Allied powers were to receive machine tools, clocks, watches and precision tools. Nevertheless, the overall result accounted for little, since the Allies only agreed to a one-time delivery worth 2.5 million Swiss francs. [264] A further unpleasant outcome for Switzerland was the realization that caught between blockade and counter-blockade, it had virtually no leverage to influence Allied decisions in its favor.

Italian Needs

In parallel with its negotiations with the Nazi regime, Switzerland also held talks with Italy which had entered the war on Hitler's side on June 10, 1940. In addition to import and export increases, the representatives of the Italian government sought to explore the possibility of foreign currency loans from Swiss banks and – after Switzerland had granted Germany concessions to that effect – a clearing loan. The Swiss finance sector and the export sector of Swiss industry had long supplied services important to Italian industry and Italian political leaders – granting loans, gold purchases, concealed assets transfers, and movements of flight capital, to name just a few. At the core of Swiss-Italian relations, however, was a highly sought foreign currency loan of 75 million Swiss francs granted by a consortium of Swiss banks led by the Schweizerische Bankverein (Swiss Bank Corporation), in August 1940, to "ISTCAMBI" (the foreign currency department

---

[261] Catherine Schiemann, Neutralität in Krieg und Frieden. Die Aussenpolitik der Vereinigten Staaten gegenüber der Schweiz 1941-1949. (Zurich, 1991), p. 70.

[262] Ibid., p. 74.

[263] Heinrich Homberger, Schweizerische Handelspolitik im Zweiten Weltkrieg. Ein Überblick auf Grund persönlicher Erlebnisse. (Erlenbach, 1970), p. 83.

[264] Ibid., p. 84.

of the Italian central bank). In addition, the Federation confirmed an advance of 125 million Swiss francs from a consortium of banks. In December 1940, Italy knocked on the Swiss door again, requesting a further loan, this time of 140 million Swiss francs, which was granted in March 1941. It was perfectly obvious that these loans were primarily used for purchasing war materials from the company Oerlikon-Bührle, as well as for aluminum and machine tools. Switzerland always placed a series of conditions on the granting of the loans, and was granted transit permits and raw material supplies. Switzerland justified these loans by its need to maintain economic viability and as leverage against the Axis powers. [265]

Further Agreements with Germany

The concessions Switzerland had to make to the Axis powers in August 1940 continued to have a formative influence for the entire war period, confirming the economic aspect of the military reality across Europe. In return for Switzerland's accommodation, Germany issued a guarantee to supply Switzerland with vital goods. Switzerland now depended on trade with Germany for the survival of its economy and its work force.

The agreement of August 9, 1940 was not yet signed and sealed when German officials responsible for military equipment began looking covetously at Swiss production, especially of weapons and weapon accessories. In October 1940, the German navy, air force and army made their requests for war materials known. It was obvious that the political and military leaders of Nazi Germany intended to seek supplies. In talks held in February 1941, the German chief negotiator, Gottfried Seyboth, said that Switzerland had now become a supplier "of important weapons in considerable amounts." [266] In a provisional protocol of February 7, 1941, Switzerland granted Germany a new clearing loan of 156 million Swiss francs, and in return was assured that monthly coal deliveries would remain unchanged at 150,000 tons. But that was not the end of it. On January 28, 1941, Göring's air force had let the German Foreign Office know that it needed further materials which would by far exceed the agreed clearing loan of 165 million francs. When they needed something – they took it. In the following weeks, the Germans requested an extension of the credit to 850 million Swiss francs. A corresponding agreement was signed on July 18, 1941, with a contract until the end of 1942. Switzerland hoped to get longer-term security of supplies of coal, iron, petrol and lubricating oil promised by the Germans, in return for the extension of the contract period. But by late 1942, German coal and iron deliveries fell far short of the agreed amounts. The Nazis were not in the habit of limiting themselves by either contracts or treaties. Moreover, at this time Nazi arrogance was at its height and so – although Germany had not kept its commitment to supply materials – the Germans demanded that the Swiss credit be extended to an unlimited amount.

The original agreement on the 850 million Swiss franc credit was due to expire in December 1942, and by then the shortfall in supplies promised but not delivered

---

[265] Klaus Urner, "Neutralität und Wirtschaftskrieg: Zur schweizerischen Aussenhandelspolitik 1939-1945," in: Rudolf L. Bindschedler et al. (ed ...), Schwedische und schweizerische Neutralität im Zweiten Weltkrieg. (Basle, 1985), p. 280.

[266] Ibid., p. 279.

by Germany had reached 960,000 tons of coal, 130,000 tons of iron, and 78,000 tons of fuel. [267] After fruitless negotiations during which the Swiss began to show less willingness to supply goods – in part due to increasing Allied pressure – Switzerland refused to budge and took the risk that negotiations might fail. As of January 15, 1943, trade relations between Germany and Switzerland ceased to be constrained by any signed contract.

The Carrot-and-Stick Approach

On March 18/19, 1943, when the Germans were expecting the Allied landing in Italy, Bern was informed by its intelligence service that Germany was planning to invade Switzerland. There was news from Munich that mountain troops had been assembled. This information was considered credible, particularly since hostile articles had appeared in the German press. [268] Walter Schellenberg, head of the SS foreign intelligence service, subsequently confirmed the threat to Roger Masson, head of the Swiss intelligence service, which by that time was part of a more comprehensive secret service network. This led to the so-called 'March Alarm' in Switzerland. [269] By now, Germany had declared what it called a "total war" with new and serious repercussions for the populations of occupied and annexed countries and territories. Hitler was unpredictable and everything seemed to wait on one of his whims or strategic inspirations. The German army was believed to be poised to execute a well-planned lightening strike into Switzerland.

About one (agonizing) week after this alarming information, the news arrived that the danger was now over – and had never really existed. After the war, no definitive operative Wehrmacht or Army plans for an attack on Switzerland during this period of time could be found. Most probably, the attack story had been fabricated by the Nazis to keep Switzerland under pressure so that it would agree to more economic concessions in the current negotiations. [270]

News of alleged German plans 'to deal with Switzerland' regularly reached the Swiss, either openly or via the Swiss intelligence service. A source from Himmler's entourage stated that the Germans were determined to take military action in May 1941, if no agreement could be reached in that summer's German-Swiss negotiations. [271] Swiss fears of German military action – for one reason or another – were not completely unfounded.

The Nazi regime made good use of the Swiss population's fear of German occupation by adopting a carrot-and-stick approach. In March 1941, Göbbels made the reassuring remark that Germany had no intention of occupying Switzerland. Sighs of relief in Switzerland! But just when Swiss heart-rates had almost returned to normal, Göbbels came out with a vitriolic tirade in May 1941, threaten-

---

[267] Op. cit., p. 280.

[268] Alfred Ernst, Die Konzeption der schweizerischen Landesverteidigung 1815 bis 1966. (Frauenfeld and Stuttgart, 1971), pp. 32 and 69.

[269] Pierre-Th Braunschweig, Geheimer Draht nach Berlin: Die Nachrichtenlinie Masson-Schellenberg und der schweizerische Nachrichtendienst im Zweiten Weltkrieg. (Zurich, 1990), p. 259-294.

[270] Hans Rudolf Kurz, "Waibels fünfte Kolonne," in Die Woche of September 18, 1981, p. 13.

[271] Edgar Bonjour, Geschichte der Schweizerischen Neutralität. Vier Jahrhunderte Eidgenössischer Aussenpolitik. Bd. V (Basle, 1971), pp. 246-247.

ing Switzerland with "Germany's answer", if the country's press should continue to insult National Socialism in reports and commentaries. [272] Unpredictability was one of the constants of German foreign policy.

Turning Point 1943

Three months after negotiations broke off, Switzerland discovered that the 850 million Swiss francs line of credit agreed to in July 1941 had been exceedingly overdrawn. The Nazis had gone over the line of credit through the issuance of foreign currency certificates amounting to up to 1350 million Swiss francs. By the time the Trade Department became aware of this maneuver, it was too late. It remains unclear, however, whether this overdrawing of the credit limit went really undetected or if Switzerland was in fact tacitly agreeing to a credit extension. [273] The latter assumption is supported by the facts that payment arrangements in the clearing agreement called for all payments to be accounted for by the Schweizerische Nationalbank (Swiss National Bank) and the Deutsche Reichsbank, thus giving Switzerland the ability to manage and control the foreign trade arrangements with Germany as laid out in the clearing agreement of July 1941. However, these German 'help yourself' activities came finally to an end when in 1943 the war had reached a turning point in favor of the Allies. As the Allies were becoming stronger with every passing day so was the pressure mounting against the neutral powers, providing them with moral support against Berlin. Henceforth, the Swiss government and its negotiators were able to demonstrate a bit more self confidence in their negotiations with the Reich with the result that the relations with Germany began to worsen.

After a tense prolonged period in which there was no official trade agreement, a provisional German-Swiss accord was concluded on June 23, 1943, followed by a new agreement on October 1, 1943. Both the provisional and final agreement aimed at reducing Swiss war material supplies to Germany step by step and easing the German counter-blockade. Although the balance seemed ever so slightly to tilt in favor of Switzerland, the Germans forced the Swiss to accept some unpleasant contractual terms in form of a 'coal loan' which required that Switzerland pay Germany 50 Swiss francs in advance for each ton of coal delivered to Switzerland and repayable by Germany *after* the war. [274] For these concessions, Switzerland agreed to the German negotiator's demand for yet another extension of the credit line.

However, the October 1, 1943 agreement had a very short life span. New negotiations were needed as early as spring 1944. This time it appeared as if a comprehensive economic agreement was no longer of primary concern to the German negotiators. The question about deliveries of goods and electricity from Switzerland was significant, but now it was superseded by the so-called transit issue. Since Italy had entered the war in June 1940, Alpine transit had grown to become a cru-

---

[272] Ibid.

[273] Markus Heiniger, Dreizehn Gründe. Warum die Schweiz im Zweiten Weltkrieg nicht erobert wurde. (Zurich, 1989), p. 109.

[274] Werner Rings, Raubgold aus Deutschland. Die "Golddrehscheibe" Schweiz im Zweiten Weltkrieg. (Zurich, 1985), p.138.

cial part of German-Swiss relations. After Mussolini's fall in July 1943, large parts of Italy were occupied by German troops, and so traffic across the Alps played an even more decisive role. [275]

A short-term agreement concluded in March 1944, assured Germany of important Swiss services and the continuation of trans-Alpine traffic. Between February and May 1944, an average 400,000 tons of goods were transported from north to south and about 50,000 tons from Italy to Germany each month. [276]

After October 1939, when the clearing agreement between Germany and Switzerland was first signed, supplementary protocols were attached to the agreement which took into consideration the new developments on the ground by fulfilling the increasing German demand for armaments and related war materials. Accordingly, the estimated importance of Switzerland as a supplier of high quality machines, instruments and weapons to the German economy had increased while the role Switzerland played in counter trade transactions became ever more important.

In addition, the transit routes to Italy were considered very important by the Germans. [277] As earlier portrayed, in early 1943, the Swiss were prepared to risk a break down in negotiations before allowing Germany a greater use of their country's production capacity. Henceforth, Switzerland successively decreased its deliveries to Germany – yielding to increasing Allied demands in spite of Nazi reprimands. As "flexible" as the German side was known to be, they increasingly focused their attention on the Swiss financial service industry where they could obtain freely convertible Swiss francs for gold, i.e. foreign currency to pay their other trading partners for raw materials and products necessary for the war effort. Every month, about 5 tons of gold were exchanged for foreign currency. [278] The precondition for these transactions was a German-Swiss trade agreement with the longest contractual period possible. The agreement formally acclaimed that transit traffic to Italy will be maintained and guaranteed without any stipulations as to the content of the transit traffic or about Switzerland supplying Germany with only small amounts of goods. [279]

On June 29, 1944, the March Agreement was replaced by a new agreement. Under Allied pressure, the Swiss negotiators were able to reduce substantially Swiss supplies to Germany compared with 1942. According to Edgar Bonjour, exports to the Third Reich – primarily weapons and war materials – were reduced from about 55 million to about 23 million Swiss francs. [280]

---

[275] Christian Leitz, Nazi Germany and Neutral Europe During the Second World War. (Manchester, 2000), p. 39.

[276] Ibid.

[277] Willi A. Boelcke (ed.), Deutschlands Rüstung im Zweiten Weltkrieg. Hitlers Konferenzen mit Albert Speer 1942-1945. (Frankfurt am Main, 1969), p. 137.

[278] Militärisches Bundesarchiv Freiburg BA / MA RW19/440 war diary 8 appendix for the period April 1 June 30, 1944.

[279] Stefan Frech, Die deutsche Kriegswirtschaft und die Schweiz 1943-1945. Bedeutung der Schweiz als Handelspartnerin und Warenlieferantin. (Bern, 1998), p. 106.

[280] Edgar Bonjour, Geschichte der Schweizerischen Neutralität. Vier Jahrhunderte Eidgenössischer Aussenpolitik. Vol. VI (Basle, 1970) p. 266.

While trade between the two countries continued, a clear downward trend was noticeable. Switzerland restricted deliveries to Germany as a consequence of Germany's failure to fulfill its contractual obligations. However, despite an export ban introduced by the Swiss on ball bearings, weapons and weapon accessories as of October 1, 1944, and the blocking of German assets in Switzerland on February 16, 1945, economic relations with the Third Reich were never completely broken off. On February 28, 1945, the two countries signed another economic protocol which dealt with the remaining German-Swiss trade relations.

ALLIED PRESSURE

After entering the war, the United States of America, which recently had classified itself a neutral and demanded that the rest of the world respect their neutrality, almost immediately abandoned that principle. The USA displayed no sign of respect for contracts concluded by a neutral country like Switzerland – especially if they happened to be contracts concluded with the Axis. The Americans considered even the transport of merely civilian goods to be of strategic value, and this became a bone of contention. America's position was that the transport of civilian goods by third parties freed up enormous railway capacities for the transport of oil and steel along railway lines in German hands, which could be hardly denied to have no strategic value.

In June 1943, the British and American governments demanded that Switzerland desist from transporting oil between Germany and Italy. Switzerland responded by pointing out that the Allied powers had blockaded Swiss oil supplies, and the country, therefore, depended on oil deliveries from Romania, which would only be allowed to pass through Germany as long as Switzerland permitted the passage of oil across the Alps to Italy. The Allied powers simply ignored the Swiss predicament and repeated their demand in August 1944, extending it to the transport of all goods, even though Switzerland had in March 1944 unilaterally reduced the amount of goods transported to pre-war quantities of goods. [281] On October 1, 1944, Switzerland issued a ban on all weapon-deliveries to Germany. Arms trade was permitted to continue with other countries but at a reduced level.

The Americans refused to acknowledge any difference between military and civilian goods. They were unable – or unwilling – to recognize the strategic problems Switzerland faced. To the Americans, the issue was black-and-white – 'who's not for us, is against us'. Any country claiming neutrality supported the enemy according to the Americans, and they weren't interested in the fact that Switzerland was a small neutral country fighting for survival, a country which had to use every means to win small concessions from their enemy located along its borders. Neither did the USA acknowledge how few concessions Switzerland

---

[281] Urs Schwarz, The Eye of the Hurricane: Switzerland in World War II. (Boulder, 1980), p. 65; cf. Richard Ochsner "Transit von Truppen, Einzelpersonen, Kriegsmaterial und zivilen Gebrauchsgütern zugunsten einer Kriegspartei durch das neutrale Land," in: Rudolf L. Bindschedler et al. (ed.), Schwedische und schweizerische Neutralität im Zweiten Weltkrieg. (Basle, 1985), p. 222. According to Ochsner, Switzerland did not rate mineral oil as war material, but then – after an Allied note of June 10, 1943 and in spite of German protests – struck it off the list of goods permitted for transfer. This concerned only relatively minor amounts.

itself had made to the Axis powers during the four years when it was completely surrounded. [282] For Washington, the fighting against Nazi Germany was an ideological, total war.

The U.S. position on neutrality was ironic because, when the United States itself was still neutral, it *insisted* on its "natural right" to trade with warring Nazi Germany. But once America entered the war, it sought to ban all other neutral nations from enjoying that same right.

The British were somewhat more restrained, not least because they were already thinking about post-war developments and how they would re-establish the financial and trade relationships prior to the outbreak of the war. [283] Nevertheless, the strategic Sankt Gotthard pass not only separated Switzerland from Italy, it also was a fulcrum for Allied attitudes concerning the moral and legal rights of neutral countries, and as the war moved towards conclusion, conflict on those moral and legal rights was unavoidable heading on a collision course. [284] The Third Reich was on the brink of losing the war, and when American forces reached Switzerland from Grenoble, they declared the counter-blockade – German restrictions on exports to the Allies – and all until then agreed to conditions to be invalid as of September 7, 1944. [285]

The next phase of the war saw ever increasing Allied pressure on Switzerland to break off all relations with the Third Reich. [286] Yet even in 1944 Switzerland was still for the most part surrounded by Germany, with its economy largely dependent on shipments of German raw materials. Switzerland could not just terminate relations. Nevertheless it continued to reduce its exports to Germany. [287] At the same time, exports to the Allied powers started to increase again. This was the result of Switzerland's desire rather than demand by the Allies by re-routing its deliveries and trying to counteract unemployment caused by reductions in exports to Germany.

There were also new developments in conjunction with the Alpine crossing, which had been a long standing issue throughout the war. The Allied powers repeatedly demanded that Switzerland should reduce transit traffic across the Alps. Only now, in 1944, was Switzerland prepared to make concessions. It issued both transit restrictions and bans on transit. In October 1944 Switzerland closed the Simplon Tunnel completely for German goods in transit. [288] But Switzerland still

---

[282] Dean Acheson, Present at the Creation: My Years in the State Department. (New York, 1969), p. 58.

[283] Cf. Walther Hofer and Herbert R. Reginbogin, Hitler, der Westen und die Schweiz. (Zurich, 2001).

[284] Op. cit., p. 66.

[285] Klaus Urner, "Neutralität und Wirtschaftskrieg: Zur schweizerischen Aussenhandelspolitik 1939-1945," in: Rudolf L. Bindschedler et al. (ed.), Schwedische und schweizerische Neutralität im Zweiten Weltkrieg. (Basle, 1985), p. 280.

[286] Catherine Schiemann, Neutralität in Krieg und Frieden. Die Aussenpolitik der Vereinigten Staaten gegenüber der Schweiz 1941-1949. (Zurich, 1991), p. 103.

[287] Heinrich Homberger, "Die Schweiz in der internationalen Wirtschaft," in: Aussenwirtschaft (AS). (Berne, 1949), pp. 109-111.

[288] Details on Allied demands, the conflict of interests and the step-by-step adoption of restrictions on the transit of goods, weights and finally bans on transport by Switzerland may be found in: Richard Ochsner "Transit von Truppen, Einzelpersonen, Kriegsmaterial und zivilen Ge-

irritated the Allied powers by stubbornly refusing to halt transit altogether, referring to The Hague Convention V of October 18, 1907 and the Gotthard Treaty of October 13, 1909. [289] But as the Allies pushed the Nazis back and broke through the counter-trade blockade in the fall of 1944, it blocked all access routes into Switzerland issuing an ultimatum that all transit should stop. At once, the situation was critical for Switzerland. A "Legal Rescue" came from Italy in February 1945, when the Italian government withdrew from the Gotthard Treaty, allowing Switzerland to impose an almost complete ban on transit. But at that point deliveries from Germany had fallen dramatically. In trade negotiations with Germany in late 1944/early 1945, Switzerland made the north-south transport of goods, particularly coal and iron, contingent upon Switzerland importing the same amount. But since it became obvious that such a trade agreement would never materialize, on February 9, 1945, the Swiss Federal Council decreed that coal transit was to stop, and on March 9, 1945, that iron transit was all but to cease. [290]

In early 1945, Federal President von Steiger, Head of the Swiss Department of Justice and Police (EJPD), had replied very politely, but in a form that the Americans had not expected, to a letter from President Roosevelt requesting that Switzerland should support the Allies in their fight against the Nazis. He wrote that it was totally out of the question, due to reasons of principle that the Swiss government could break off trade relations with Germany. He maintained that this Allied request went against neutral trade and financial policy. As long as Germany met its contract obligations, Switzerland was obliged to maintain the mutual traffic of goods. [291] He added that there was also a problem of supplies. The Allies had cut off Switzerland from all supplies of industrial raw materials over the last four years, and precisely because of this reason Switzerland was now dependent on the supply of such raw materials from Germany. The Allied powers did not share this view, maintaining that Switzerland had sufficient reserves to last until the end of the war. [292] They were not completely wrong in this assumption, for in May 1945, Switzerland still possessed 1 million tons of coal. [293]

---

brauchgütern zugunsten einer Kriegspartei durch das neutrale Land," in: Rudolf L. Bindschedler et al. (ed.), Schwedische und schweizerische Neutralität im Zweiten Weltkrieg. (Basle, 1985), p. 224; Gilles Forster, Transit ferroviaire à travers la Suisse (1939-1945). (Zurich, 2001); Christine Uhlig, Petra Barthelmess, Mario Koenig and Peter Pfaffenroth, Tarnung,Transfer, Transit. Die Schweiz als Drehscheibe verdeckter deutscher Operationen (1939-1952), in: Unabhängige Expertenkommission Schweiz-Zweiter Weltkrieg (ed.), Vol. 9. (Zurich, 2001); Eugen Kreidler, Die Eisenbahnen im Machtbereich der Achsenmächte während des Zweiten Weltkrieges. Einsatz und Leistung für die Wehrmacht und Kriegswirtschaft. (Frankfurt/Zurich, 1975), p. 107.

[289] Felix Bosshard, Der Gotthardvertrag von 1909, Ein Beitrag zur schweizerischen Innen- und Aussenpolitik vor Ausbruch des Ersten Weltkrieges. Diss. (Zurich, 1973).

[290] Richard Ochsner "Transit von Truppen, Einzelpersonen, Kriegsmaterial und zivilen Gebrauchgütern zugunsten einer Kriegspartei durch das neutrale Land," in: Rudolf L. Bindschedler et al. (ed.), Schwedische und schweizerische Neutralität im Zweiten Weltkrieg. (Basle, 1985), p. 228.

[291] Edgar Bonjour, Geschichte der Schweizerischen Neutralität. Vier Jahrhunderte Eidgenössischer Aussenpolitik. Vol. VII (Basle, 1974), pp. 363-364 Roosevelt to von Steiger and pp. 376-378 von Steiger to Roosevelt.

[292] Catherine Schiemann, Neutralität in Krieg und Frieden. Die Aussenpolitik der Vereinigten Staaten gegenüber der Schweiz 1941-1949. (Zurich, 1991), p. 135.

[293] Georg Hafner, Bundesrat Walther Stampfli 1884-1965. (Olten, 1986), p. 266.

With the exception of stock-piled coal, however, Swiss supply problems had indeed increased with the southern and western Allied advance in winter 1944/1945, placing more pressure on the Swiss population. Allied commanders blocked the shipment of overseas supplies whose delivery had been the subject of long negotiations, and tightened blacklist restrictions, resulting in more difficulties for Swiss exports than at the time of the counter-blockade.

The Swiss had compelling reasons to maintain contact with Germany, even in the last year of the war. Notwithstanding the openly expressed irritation of the British and American governments, Switzerland insisted that its neutral status prevented it from breaking off relations with just one of the warring parties. While Swiss deliveries to Germany declined to virtually nothing during the last months of the war, Switzerland stubbornly followed the principle of neutrality and maintained economic and diplomatic relations with Germany right up to the end of the war.

The Swiss did not change their attitude until in February 1945 a US-British-French delegation led by the American Laughlin Currie initiated the post-war negotiations. The 'Currie negotiations' lasted for two months, and during them, the Alliance succeeded in persuading the Swiss to freeze all German assets and to draw up an inventory. This was in accordance with the so-called 'Safehaven Policy' issued by the US Treasury, a policy designed to block all German financial transactions in neutral countries.

During the very hectic end phase of the war, the Swiss managed to shift public policy more towards meeting expectations of the Allied powers without ending trade relations with Germany. Swiss business and financial circles assumed that trade with Germany would continue even after Germany's defeat, and tried at least to keep some type of business contacts with German companies. In this regard, they were not unlike the British companies which throughout the war anticipated that business would continue as usual.

But Switzerland was asked by the Allies to pay a price. France obtained a loan of 250 million Swiss francs which was supposed to ease the transition period for those countries liberated by the Allies, Belgium and the Netherlands as well as France. In return, the Allied powers agreed to open transport routes through France and allow limited exports of various Swiss products. [294]

In spite of the Swiss loan, however, Switzerland got little out of the transaction. The Allies did not supply coal, and Germany for all practical purposes was no longer a supplier. Moreover, the Allies did not release Swiss assets seized in their countries. Restrictive blacklisting was also continued. [295] These bans were of particular importance to Switzerland since, in 1944, 10% of the 150,000 names on the "Black Lists" were Swiss companies. [296]

---

[294] Op. cit., p. 151.

[295] Ibid., p. 152.

[296] Klaus Urner, "Neutralität und Wirtschaftskrieg: Zur schweizerischen Aussenhandelspolitik 1939-1945," in: Rudolf L. Bindschedler et al. (ed.), Schwedische und schweizerische Neutralität im Zweiten Weltkrieg. (Basle, 1985), p. 274.

"Black Lists"

Starting as early as 1943, Switzerland became a target of British and American combined war efforts to curtail countries from trading with the enemy. An especially hard blow to the Swiss business community had been the blacklisting of a leading Swiss manufacturer, Gebrüder Sulzer AG in Winterthur, in the fall of the same year because Sulzer would not sign an 'undertaking' obliging him to accept Allied demands to cease deliveries to the Axis powers voluntarily. Sulzer continued to trade with the Germans holding out until 1944.

Allied blacklisting continued long after the war had come to an end causing strong public indignation outcry suspecting that the lists were aimed at eliminating Switzerland as a world competitor in a post-war era. The so-called 'Brugg Speech' by Federal Minister of State, Dr. Walther Stampfli, on September 9, 1945, gave full vent to these suspicions: "... Our economy is being dismantled from the outside. And worse: Swiss companies no longer follow the orders of Swiss authorities, but the threats of foreign authorities. It is clear that such interference cannot be reconciled with our sovereignty, nor with the solemn declarations made by the great democracies when going to war against the violation of small nations by the tyranny of National Socialist imperialism. Economic war must end, too." [297] In a subsequent speech delivered to the Swiss National Council on September 18, 1945, Stampfli caused even more of a stir: "Sometimes you cannot fail to form the impression that they just want to finish off competitors they don't want to meet on the world market any more, or that this is all about resentment towards companies which, in their opinion, showed bias during the war. ... It is an outrage if it is no longer our own national authorities who decide which domestic companies may supply other Swiss companies, but when this depends on the permission of foreign authorities." [298]

The Washington Agreement

The Allied powers resented the fact that the Swiss – in spite of finally freezing German assets on February 16, 1945 – had still refused to yield control of those assets to the Allies under the Safehaven Program. [299] In an economic war strategy of tit for tat, the Allies refused to unblock Swiss assets frozen in Allied countries, and continued to apply pressure on Switzerland, putting the very existence of companies concerned on the line, until Switzerland conceded to its demands.

Negotiations which began in March 1946 in Washington called upon Switzerland to hand over German assets to the Allied powers and to return the greater part of purchased gold bought from Germany. Gold worth 560 million Swiss francs ($130 million) was supposed to be returned. [300]

Once again Switzerland refused these demands of handing over the German assets to the Allies by arguing that such an action would contradict international

---

[297] Sigmund Widmer, Geschichte der Schweiz. (Zurich, 1973), p. 398.
[298] Hans Schaffner, Die Schweizerische Kriegswirtschaft 1939/1948. (Berne, 1950), p. 2.
[299] Eizenstat (1997), p. 1-89.
[300] Ibid., S. 72; cf. Edgar Bonjour, Die Schweiz und Europa. Vol. V (Basle, 1977), p. 179.

law. [301] However, the Swiss delegation succeeded in reducing the value of German assets in question from around 1 billion Swiss francs to about half that amount [302] by excluding the assets of Germans who had been Swiss residents before 1939. Stolen property found in Switzerland and returned to its rightful owners was also excluded. A further reduction of German assets was achieved by recasting Swiss property ownership rules. [303]

In April 1946, the Washington negotiations were declared a failure. But one month later, on May 25, 1946, a compromise was nonetheless achieved. German assets in Switzerland were liquidated – with one half of the proceeds going to the Allied powers, the other half remaining in Switzerland to satisfy Swiss claims against Germany. As for German gold, Switzerland paid 250 million Swiss francs for gold that had been bought by the government's central bank – Schweizerische Nationalbank (Swiss National Bank) – without prejudice. [304]

It was not until this Washington Agreement signed in May that the last restrictions on foreign trade were removed and blacklisting of Swiss companies was discontinued. So the trade war against Switzerland lasted a year longer than the military conflicts of World War II.

REFUGEES

Whenever social challenges conflict with national priorities, the former are as a rule sacrificed to the latter. So when it came to handling the Jewish refugee problem before the war, the moral social conscience among European democracies yielded to a policy of "Appeasement" towards Nazi Germany.

Neither the Jewish associations nor the 32 represented governments, including those of the USA, Britain and France, which took part in the Evian Conference in France on Jewish Refugees on July 1, 1938, were prepared to pursue a solution to the refugee issue by trying to force Germany to change its anti-Semitic attitude through economic sanctions – a method commonly used today – or through direct confrontation. [305] It must be said, though, that in 1938, European governments and the leaders of the USA could not foretell what would follow. At the time of the Evian Conference, not only governments but also many Jews and non-Jews living in Germany and elsewhere believed that somehow it would be possible to reach a type of accommodation with Hitler on Jewish refugees. They trusted in the power of diplomacy and their blindness permitted Hitler and his countless willing henchmen to establish concentration camps where all "unwanted elements"

---

[301] Schweizerisches Bundesarchiv Bern, Expert report by Dietrich Schindler of January 25, 1946. E 2801 1968/84, 30.

[302] Linus von Castelmur, Schweizerisch-Alliierte Finanzbeziehungen im Übergang vom Zweiten Weltkrieg zum Kalten Krieg. Die deutschen Guthaben in der Schweiz zwischen Zwangsliquidierung und Freigabe 1945-1952. (Zurich, 1992), p. 98.

[303] Schweizerisches Bundesarchiv Bern, Sitzung des Schweizerischen Bundesrates, Bern, 8. März 1946 E 2801 1968/84, p. 30.

[304] Op.cit., p. 83-84.

[305] Alfred Cattani, Hitlers Schatten über Europa: Brennpunkte der Zeitgeschichte 1933-1945. (Zurich, 1995), p. 40; S. Adler-Rudell, "The Evian Conference on the Refugee Problem," in: Year Book, Leo Baeck Institute, (ed.), Vol. XIII (London/Jerusalem/New York, 1968), p. 238.

– Jews, Roma and Sinti, other victims of German racial mania, Catholic priests and Protestant ministers, as well as political opponents – were imprisoned and murdered, and also to carry out the countless horrors in ghettos, transit and work camps. [306]

From today's perspective, the behavior of the major democratic powers, France, Britain, the USA and other states, may seem inhumane, cowardly and selfish. But it should be remembered that at the time the concept of human rights – certainly in terms of law – was nowhere near what it is today. International law didn't acknowledge basic human rights we so often take for granted today and such safeguards which did exist were based either on voluntary compassion or on rulings of inviolate sovereign states. There were no international legal norms on the status of refugees. Individuals without country were literally at sea, with no court or tribunal to hear their case or to protect them. [307]

In pre-war Switzerland, the definition of 'refugee' was still shaped by 19th century attitudes and was much narrower than it is today. The Swiss had a long tradition of granting political asylum but that right could only be sought by people persecuted for prohibited political activity in their country of origin. Only such individuals had a legal right to asylum and protection against repatriation. People, who were persecuted for other reasons, such as race, religion etc., received no particular protection under Swiss asylum law. Strictly speaking, there was no legal obligation for states to take in Jewish refugees. Even the practice in some countries of interning refugees did not contravene any national and international law. [308] This difference in time and outlook should not be forgotten, even though criticism is justified.

After Austria's 'Anschluss' to Germany, which began on March 12, 1938, states bordering Germany, such as Switzerland, but also more distant countries, such as Sweden, held bilateral talks with Germany in April and May to try to find ways of coping with the wave of Jewish refugees. When no international agreement on taking in refugees was in sight following the Evian Conference, it became more difficult for those who had sought temporary refuge in Switzerland to leave for other countries. No other country would accept them. [309]

The Swiss police division responsible for non-Swiss residents imposed the cost of the stay of Jewish refugees in Switzerland, and for their departure, on the Swiss Association of Jewish Congregations and the Swiss Association of Jewish Institutions for Poor Relief. [310]

---

[306] United States Holocaust Memorial Museum (ed.), The Holocaust. (Washington, 1994).

[307] Bergier Report p. 411-414; Max Frenkel, "Die Flüchtlingspolitik in rechtlicher Sicht: Juristisches Lehrstück für historische Arbeit," in: Neue Zürcher Zeitung (NZZ), December 11/12, 1999, No. 289, p. 91.

[308] Ibid.

[309] Diplomatische Dokumente der Schweiz 1934-1949 (DDS)., Vol. 12. Document No. 363 (Berne, 1994), pp. 833-835.

[310] Ibid. See Unabhängige Expertenkommission Schweiz – Zweiter Weltkrieg, Die Schweiz und die Flüchtlinge zur Zeit des Nationalsozialismus. Vol. 17. (Zurich, 2001), p. 282 hereafter called "Refugee Report" (Flüchtlingsbericht). Concerning the controversy in the UEK Refugee Report, that the SIG pronounced in favor of barring Jewish refugees from entering Switzerland cf. Urs Rauber "Von Kooperation zum Widerstand: Der Schweizerische Israelitische Gemeindebund und die Flüchtlingspolitik von 1938 bis 1942" in Neue Zürcher Zeitung of March 15, 2000,

The Jewish organizations reacted by increasing their efforts to ease the public burden by raising relief funds both nationally and internationally. [311] In spite of these efforts, the Swiss government wanted to introduce compulsory entry visas for all German citizens, which after the 'Anschluss' also included Austrians. [312] Such a requirement would render legal entry into Switzerland for Jewish refugees practically impossible after October 1938. [313] Given the failure of the Evian Conference to come up with broader resettlement options, the Swiss had to assume that Jewish refugees entering Switzerland would be unable to travel on to any other country. And since very high numbers of refugees had to be expected, Swiss authorities maintained they did not have the resources to allow unrestricted immigration of Jewish refugees. So Switzerland and Sweden asked Germany to aid in controlling the flow of immigrants by taking measures to distinguish Jewish refugees. Germany, however, was not prepared to accept obligatory visas for all German citizens, and so its envoy apparently suggested that passports of German citizens of the Jewish faith should be marked with a letter 'J'. [314] New research

---

No. 63, p. 16. According to the minutes of the Federal Council session of August 18, 1938, Saly Mayer, president of the SIG (Schweizerischer Israelitischer Gemeindebund) and Silvain Guggenheim, head of the Jewish Institutions for Poor Relief, expressed fears that they would be unable to continue to raise sufficient funds to host Jewish refugees. At a meeting with Heinrich Rothmund, head of the Police Department of the Swiss Department of Justice and Police (EPJD) he (Silvain Guggenheim) is reported to have said: "... but if the crowds coming in during the past few days continued, [he] could see no other possibility than a ban on entry to Switzerland." However, the SIG Central-Comité minutes of this meeting recast his statement. According to those minutes, Silvain Guggenheim said that first all possible ways of raising money from the Jewish congregations should be exhausted. Otherwise the authorities would take their own measures and would decline any responsibility for the consequences. When the SIG representatives finally had to declare to the authorities that the relief organizations' funds were nearly exhausted, the authorities interpreted this as the SIG's agreement to border closure.

[311] Ibid.

[312] Diplomatische Dokumente der Schweiz 1934-1949 (DDS)., Vol. 12. Document. No. 414 (Berne, 1994), pp. 933-939.

[313] Op.cit., Refugee Report, p. 283.

[314] Max Keller, "Eine unglaubliche Verwechslung-Die Schuldzuweisung an Heinrich Rothmund für den J-Stempel beruht auf einem fatalen Irrtum" in: Schweizerzeit Issue 19 of September 14, 1998. Corrects the widespread belief that the idea of the "J" stamp came from Switzerland. In 1998, the former civil servant, Max Keller, had an extensive correspondence with the then editor-in-chief of the "Beobachter", Peter Rippmann, concerning the controversy on the 'J' stamp. But Dr. Peter Rippmann has admitted that "actually a mistake had been made: the roles of the German envoy, Köcher, and (the Swiss) Rothmund were reversed by the "Beobchter" in a fateful error." In plain English: editor-in-chief Rippmann himself, in 1954, had confused the two persons (a "fatal" error indeed) and erroneously attributed Köcher's words to Rothmund. So the myth of the alleged Swiss "suggestion" was born. Cf.: http://www.luzi-stamm.ch/ziele/weltkrieg/08.pdf. "In view of the importance of the correspondence between Dr. Peter Rippmann and me and of his admission for future historic research and for the shaping of political ideas, I have submitted photocopies of this correspondence to the Federal Archive. I have also informed the Bergier Commission of the essential points of Dr. Rippmann's admission. Furthermore, I have informed the Schweizerische Israelitische Gemeindebund (SIG), whose comments and attitude about a year ago led me to look into the issue of the 'J' stamp more closely. While Dr. Peter Rippmann displayed the insight and humanity to admit his error, the SIG is not interested in this new state of affairs, and considers my documentation – which in the meantime has been recognized by Dr. Rippmann as essentially correct – as merely the 'expression of an opinion'." Cf. Max Keller, Das Ende der J-Stempel-

has shown that the Swiss Heinrich Rothmund was not the individual who came up with the idea of the 'J' stamp. Nonetheless, Swiss politicians and historians maintain that, even if the Swiss did not invent the "J" stamp, Swiss refugee policy was inhumane.

In spite of the introduction of the 'J' stamp, many refugees were still admitted to Switzerland. The director of the Council for German Jewry (London) estimated the number of Jewish refugees during the summer of 1939 alone as 12,000 in Belgium, 5,000 in the Scandinavian countries, and 10,000 in Switzerland (after the annexation of Austria in 1938 between 5,000 and 6,500 people fled to Switzerland). [315]

In spring 1942, the Germans began deporting Jews to the east, starting first in Belgium and the Netherlands, and then in France, too. The Vichy government, which had been quick to work out its own anti-Jewish laws, handed over Jews who had fled to French territory to the Nazis. More and more refugees started appearing at Swiss border stations and a second wave of refugees flooded into Switzerland – just as happened four years previously after the annexation of Austria. This time, most refugees came via the western border. On August 13, Heinrich Rothmund issued an order to Swiss border authorities to deport any person who had come across the border illegally. Escaped prisoners of war, deserters and political refugees were exempt from this order. Refugees, who were persecuted for racial or religious reasons, however, were not to be granted the status of political refugees. Apprehended illegal immigrants were allowed to leave Switzerland freely (without being reported to opposite border authorities), but some border guards cautioned them that if they attempted re-entry, they would be handed over directly to foreign border police.

The order to close the Swiss border to further refugees as of August 13, 1942 was certainly morally questionable. But in dealing with Swiss behavior on the refugee problem, the "Refugee Report" published by the Bergier Commission in 2001 *Die Schweiz und die Flüchtlinge zur Zeit des Nationalsozialismus* (*Switzerland and Refugees during National Socialism*) goes much father and paints a picture of Switzerland as an inhumane country. [316] In its final report, the Bergier Commission even claims that Swiss refugee policy helped National Socialism achieve its goals. [317] The commission maintains that the Swiss government remained stubbornly unmoved by the most horrific human suffering, and favored a border policy accommodating to Nazi Germany. But the commission report failed to mention that Swiss authorities faced the very real problem of dealing with a flood of refugees which threatened to overwhelm the country's ability to house, feed and employ them – at a time when other states were refusing to do so. Moreover, the official policy was widely circumvented and in practice the borders were

Saga, Schriftenreihe Pro Libertate No. 11 (Berne, 1999) and F.F. Müller, Stockholm und der J-Stempel, Neue Zürcher Zeitung (NZZ), January 3, 2000). The Bergier Commission did not deal with the hypothesis presented by Max Keller.

[315] op. cit., footnote No. 38, p. 59 and p. 11.

[316] Refugee Report, p. 73, 126, 290, 350.

[317] Bergier Bericht, p. 172.

not closed to refugees. In the months following the official border closure, more Jewish refugees were taken in than ever before. [318]

Many Swiss objected to the government's decision to close Swiss borders to additional refugees. Protests ensued all over the country and individuals and organizations conveyed their dissatisfaction with the ruling of the Federal Council: Christian, Jewish and women's organizations, refugee relief organizations, socialist organizations, the press, and even politicians. National Council member Paul Billieux, mayor of Pruntrut, weighed in against the border decision stating that unless it was overturned "barbarism will go even further, and all values which allow us to call ourselves civilized will be treated with utmost contempt." [319] The historian, Marc Vuilleumier, reports that the theologian Karl Barth, the historian Edgar Bonjour, and other Swiss citizens, such as Gertrud Kurz from Bern, Zurich minister Paul Vogt, and Social Democrat Regina Kaegi-Fuchsmann, the director of the Swiss Workers' Relief Organization in Zurich, voiced their protests. [320] Because of the severe domestic criticism, Federal Councillor, Eduard von Steiger, after an "in parts very turbulent meeting" with the central association of Swiss Jewish refugee relief organizations on August 24, ordered that the decree on border closure should be handled with more flexibility. Cases should henceforward be examined on an individual basis, with the exception of "people who for serious reasons should be considered as unwanted persons". [321]

Discontent with Official Measures

On September 22 and 23, 1942, the National Council held a major debate on refugees. Federal Councillor von Steiger emphasized the necessity to control the inflow of refugees. "If we don't take any action, the inflow will increase so much the problem will simply get out of control." [322] In addition to the issue of food supplies, there were those who felt uneasy about "undesirable elements", including Jews. Those concerns had led the National Council to adopt the government's refugee policy with a large majority in the first place. On September 23, the Federal Council's refugee policy came under a strong attack from minority members of Parliament, including socialists, radicals, liberals and independents. [323] But the decree to turn away refugees officially remained in force. [324] Nevertheless, between September and the end of 1942 alone, 7,372 refugees legally entered Switzerland. [325] Obviously, not all border stations obeyed the orders issued by Bern. What is also surprising is that the inflow of Polish-Jewish refugees to

---

[318] Jean-Christian Lambelet, Le Mobbing d'un petit pays: Onze thèses sur la Suisse pendant la Deuxième Guerre Mondiale. (Lausanne, 1999), p. 41-52.

[319] op. cit., S. 125.

[320] Marc Vuilleumier, Flüchtlinge und Immigranten in der Schweiz. Ein historischer Überblick. (Zurich, 1987), p. 91.

[321] Carl Ludwig, Die Flüchtlingspolitik der Schweiz seit 1933 zur Gegenwart. (Berne, 1957), p. 210.

[322] BAR, E 1301(-) 1950/51, Vol. 352 – Refugee debate of the Swiss National Council of September 22/23, 1942.

[323] Marc Vuilleumier, Flüchtlinge und Immigranten in der Schweiz. Ein historischer Überblick. (Zurich, 1987), p. 91.

[324] Op. cit.

[325] Refugee Report, p. 35.

Switzerland had its most marked increase just at this time, in the late summer/early fall of 1942, when the Swiss authorities had just decreed that the borders should be closed. [326] According to the Bergier Refugee Report, an additional decree was issued on December 29, 1942, repeating the regulations concerning repatriation of refugees and confirming that "refugees facing repatriation should be prevented from getting in touch, directly or indirectly, with relatives, lawyers, relief organizations or foreign diplomats. However, in 'cases of hardship', those responsible should refrain from turning refugees away." [327] The numbers seem to indicate that not many cases of hardship were turned away.

But it is a fact that, in the first ten days after the issue of the decree in mid-August 1942, the regulations concerning the closure of borders were rigidly adhered to. Many Jewish refugees were turned away, some to face a tragic fate. Interesting research conducted by the historian, Paul Stauffer, has shown, however, that after September 1942, thousands of Polish-Jewish refugees were admitted to Switzerland, in spite of the seemingly restrictive refugee policy. [328] From this, one must conclude that, as far as the directive was concerned, the exception was more often applied than the rule.

In 2000, a detailed study by J.-Ch. Lambelet showed how the border stations of the Canton of Geneva implemented the orders issued by Bern – or rather didn't implement them. He also provided evidence that those who were initially turned back usually made several further attempts at entering the country via other border stations, until they were finally admitted to the country. Research in archives in Geneva found that about 86% of all those seeking asylum and over 90% of refugees of Jewish origin were admitted. [329] A further study commissioned by the Canton of St. Gallen from Joerg Krummenacher also corrected the findings of the Bergier Commission on Swiss refugee policy during World War II, and increased by about 30,000 – to 320,000 – the estimated total number of refugees admitted to Switzerland. [330] Nevertheless, to this day, there are no countrywide studies of the way Swiss border stations implemented the orders received from Bern.

Refugee Camps

The regulations on the admission of refugees were frequently criticized, and people questioned why other solutions were not considered. As early as 1940, the Fed-

---

[326] Paul Stauffer, Polen, Juden, Schweizer. (Zurich, 2004), p. 140.

[327] Refugee Report, p. 131.

[328] Op. cit., pp. 140-143.

[329] Jean-Christian Lambelet, Evaluation critique du rapport Bergier sur "La Suisse et les réfugies à l'époque du national-socialisme" et nouvelle analyse de la question. (Lausanne, 2000); Jean-Christian Lambelet, "Kritische Würdigung des Bergier-Berichts 'Die Schweiz und die Flüchtlinge zur Zeit des Nationalsozialismus'," in: Schweizer Monatshefte, No. 3 (2000); Pierre Flückiger, Les réfugiés civils et la frontière genevoise durant la Deuxième Guerre mondiale sous la direction de Catherine Santschi. (Geneva, 2000). Cf. Arbeitskreis Gelebte Geschichte, 'Wir ziehen Bilanz' (Stäfa 2005): Jean Christian Lambelet, 2. Refoulements et refoulés, pp. 117-124.

[330] Joerg Krummenacher-Schoell, Flüchtiges Glück: Die Flüchtlinge im Grenzkanton St. Gallen zur Zeit des Nationalsozialismus. (Zurich, 2005); Urs Rauber, "Rettungshafen St. Gallen. Der Ostschweizer Kanton nahm mehr Nazi-Flüchtlinge auf als bisher angenommen," in: Neue Zürcher Zeitung (NZZ am Sonntag) of September 18, 2005, p. 81; Carl Ludwig, Die Flüchtlingspolitik der Schweiz seit 1933 zur Gegenwart. (Berne, 1957), p. 394.

eral Council had decided to establish work camps for refugees, which increased in number with the mounting number of refugees, and which were often located in empty hotels. Refugee labor was not supposed to compete with the private sector, and this is why refugees were not allowed to pursue gainful employment. The camp inmates, whether they were craftsmen, poets, scientists or musicians, had to work for the state, doing forestry work, road building etc., under the strict supervision of the military, who demanded discipline. Very often, married couples were separated, with women assigned to washing or sewing tasks, again with no consideration for any other skills they might possess. [331]

Relief Organizations

While the Nazis waged their merciless campaign against people of Jewish origin everywhere, including the occupied countries, there were many Swiss who protested against this persecution and offered help. In doing so, they followed their own consciences rather than obeying rules that refugees should be turned away and that Swiss citizens should not help foreigners who had not been granted "political refugee" status. They usually worked in small groups supported by larger organizations located in Switzerland or abroad. Those who helped included both simple citizens and some prominent figures, which did everything in their power to ensure that humanitarian considerations were given more weight than the so-called "reasons of state" which were influenced by fear of Nazi Germany.

A remarkable number of aid organizations in Switzerland were very energetic and raised considerable funds to save and support refugees. [332] Some were organizations partly supported by foreign embassies in Bern. The standard works of Holocaust research contain numerous references to the importance of the Polish link between Bern and New York or London, respectively. Although the borders of Europe and the USA were almost completely closed, people such as Nathan Schwalb, "Onkel Schwälbchen" (Uncle Little Swallow) succeeded in saving the lives of 250,000 people. He directed Zionist rescue activities in Switzerland from a center in the *Rue des Philosophes* in Geneva, with additional bases all over Europe. [333]

Although the acquisition of source material remains difficult, Paul Stauffer in his book *Polen, Juden, Schweizer* (*Polish, Jews, Swiss*) reports that the enormous amount of assistance provided by orthodox American Jews to their persecuted brothers in faith in Europe would not have been possible, if it had not been for the life line of the Polish diplomatic channel to and from neutral Bern. [334] It is said that without neutral Switzerland, some 100,000 people would not have survived. In this context, the statement by JWC Secretary General Israel Singer made in January 2005 in Berlin calling Swiss neutrality during World War II a *crime* is nothing else than polemic. Until Pearl Harbor, the United States was also a neutral country. Neutrality was accepted and renowned American jurists such as Philip Jessup,

---

[331] Marc Vuilleumier, Flüchtlinge und Immigranten in der Schweiz. Ein historischer Überblick. (Zurich, 1987), p. 93.

[332] Refugee Report, p. 80.

[333] Andrea Koehler, Neue Zürcher Zeitung (NZZ), "Der 'Aufbau' am Ende? Of April 15, 2004.

[334] Paul Stauffer, Polen, Juden, Schweizer, (Zurich 2004), pp. 142-143.

Charles Hyde, and Edwin Borchard made articulate defenses of strict neutrality. Was it a *crime* that the USA claimed strict neutrality and acted accordingly?

There is no doubt that anti-Semitism existed in America, in Switzerland, in Sweden and in many other countries of the world. Even representatives of aid organizations, such as diplomat Carl Jakob Burckhardt, the League of Nations High Commissioner in the City of Danzig between 1937 and 1939 and an influential person in the International Committee of the Red Cross, were not without anti-Semitic bias. Burckhardt was by no means an ideological Nazi anti-Semite, but his remarks, maintains historian Urs Bitterli, show a slight unease with the social advancement of Jewish intellectual circles, Bitterli suggests that Burckhardt's emotional aloofness towards Jews could well have been a barrier in terms of a more active commitment on his part to help persecuted Jews. [335] But Burckhardt did not join others in official silence. Rather in the fall of 1942, he had his intermediaries passed on intelligence concerning planned mass killings at the camps to the Consul General of the USA in Switzerland, with the assertion that Hitler had given orders to make Germany "free of Jews" by the end of 1942. [336] Such orders were never issued in written form (although there were many speeches demanding the elimination of all European Jews.)

When Rabbi Wise led a delegation of representatives of the most important Jewish organizations in the USA into a meeting with President Roosevelt on December 8, 1942 to urge the president to do everything in his power to stop the genocide, Roosevelt told him that he had already been informed of these events by American diplomats in neutral countries. [337] Roosevelt failed to mention, of course, that he did not consider the admission of German Jews to the USA a priority, an attitude mirrored in U.S. State Department's policies. Not without reason, FDR had made his old friend, Breckenridge Long, an anti-Semite and determined opponent of refugees, director of refugee policies. [338] Is this perhaps why, in 1944, the USA failed to bomb the rail link to Auschwitz? While a bombing might not have stopped the genocide, it might have sent a moral message, and possibly even more saved lives by interrupting, or at least delaying, the process of mass murder. The American explanation that "these targets were not of vital importance for the course of the war" sounds odd, given that efforts were made to save the famous Lipizzaner from falling into Russian hands and food parcels were dropped by parachute on Warsaw although it was known that they might fall into German hands. The Roosevelt administration automatically rejected all requests to bomb the railways or roads to concentration camps because the fate of Jewish refugees was not a priority for the American president. In principle there was, however, no contradiction between the Allied victory and the rescuing of Jews. In 1944, Roosevelt, yielding to strong pressure exerted by the Congress, Jewish activists and

---

[335] Urs Bitterli, "Humanitärer Auftrag und politische Ambition: Paul Stauffers neues Buch über Carl J. Burckhardt," in: Neue Zürcher Zeitung of September 1, 1998, p. 13.

[336] Paul Stauffer, Sechs furchtbare Jahre… "Auf den Spuren Carl J. Burckhardts durch den Zweiten Weltkrieg. (Zurich, 1998), p. 229.

[337] David Wyman, Das unerwünschte Volk, Amerika und die Vernichtung der europäischen Juden. (Munich, 1986), p. 86.

[338] Lawrence Davidson, "The State Department & Zionism 1917-1945: A Reevaluation," in: Middle East Policy Vol. VII No. October 1, 1999, p. 12.

Treasury Secretary, Henry Morgenthau Jr., took a step towards rescue by establishing the War Refugee Board. Although this commission had very little money or other support from the White House, it still played an important role in the rescue of over 200,000 refugees. Moreover, the commission's activities were not detrimental to the war effort. If it had been established earlier, many lives might have been saved. [339]

It was only on December 17, 1942, that the USA, at the urgent request of Britain, issued a common declaration with the other Allied governments condemning "in the strongest possible terms this bestial policy of cold-blooded extermination" and expressing a "solemn resolution to ensure that those responsible for these crimes shall not escape retribution." [340]

From today's perspective, it appears there were unambiguous references to the policy of the extermination of European Jews in numerous contemporary papers. But at the time there were many rumors and dubious reports as well. After all, the Germans had been the victims of cynical atrocity propaganda by the British during World War I. Given the scale of the mass murder reported, could it not be imagined that readers would view such information as mere propaganda? Could it be that – in spite of the knowledge that the final solution was being implemented right then – there was a collective refusal to believe such a horrific truth? Is it for this reason that President Roosevelt and all states which possessed information about the mass killings did not initiate emergency measures to help those affected? As late as 1944, even Jews did not believe eye witness reports about the murder of Jews in Auschwitz, or denied that people from the country of Bach, Beethoven, Schiller and Goethe were capable of this type of atrocity and barbarism. Why should a Swiss Federal Councillor of state, Eduard von Steiger, who today is accused by the Refugee Report of the Bergier Commission to have ordered the closure of Swiss borders, supposedly in full knowledge of the killing of Jews, not also have had reason to doubt the truth of what was happening? [341] Or was the reason rather that the fate of the Jews of Europe was not of sufficient importance to political leaders such as Roosevelt and others all over the world and that therefore nobody did anything to oppose Hitler's obvious intention to eliminate the Jewish people?

Critics accuse the International Red Cross of giving priority to the interests of prisoners of war in Germany and failing to protest the maltreatment of civilians, particularly in the context of Holocaust. [342] Would such protests have impressed

---

[339] The David Wyman Institute for Holocaust Studies, "History Channel Distorted FDR's Response to the Holocaust." www.wymaninstitute.org .

[340] Op. cit., cf. Dokumente zur Deutschlandspolitik. Vol. 3 (Frankfurt am Main, 1988/1989), p. 1162.

[341] Rudolf Vrba, "Die missachtete Warnung. Betrachtungen über den Auschwitz-Bericht 1944," in: Dietrich Bracher et al (ed.), Vierteljahrshefte für Zeitgeschichte. Issue 1 (Munich, 1996), p. 1-24; Yehuda Bauer, "Anmerkungen zum 'Auschwitz Bericht' von Rudolf Vrba," in: Dietrich Bracher et al (ed.), Vierteljahrshefte für Zeitgeschichte. Issue 2 (Munich, 1997), p. 297-307 This deals with the fact that as late as 1944, eye witness reports on the murder of Jews in Auschwitz were not believed by Jews or even denied by them.

[342] Jean-Claude Favez, Une Mission Impossible? Le CICR, les déportations et les camps de concentration nazis. (Lausanne, 1998), p. 367-375; cf. Jean-Claude Favez, The Red Cross and the Holocaust. (Cambridge/New York, 1999).

the architects of the final solution? It is doubtful that Hitler would have refrained from implementing the final solution. Might protests about the treatment of Jews have led Germany to disregard the Geneva Convention concerning the treatment of prisoners of war? This possibility cannot be ruled out. In regard to the treatment of prisoners of war in Germany, British Foreign Secretary Anthony Eden wrote to U.S. Ambassador John Winant in late August 1944 that "there was a genuine fear that the Gestapo might run amok and commit wholesale murder of British and American prisoners of war, unless there was a Protective Power that would have an influence of restraint on the Nazis." [343]

If Switzerland had publicly condemned Germany for the mass killing of Jews, it would have spelled the end of diplomatic relations between Germany and Switzerland and would have prevented Switzerland's intervening diplomatically to help Allied prisoners of war. [344] As Paul Stauffer stated at the end of his book, "The question will remain unanswered – probably for ever – whether it might have been possible to find a middle course between publicly denouncing Nazi crimes and more or less silently accepting them, a middle course which might have made it possible to rescue human lives from mass extermination." [345]

Individual Fighters

In pursuing the mandate as a protecting power, there were Swiss that did play a role in mitigating the savagery of Nazi policies, including some notable figures such as Swiss Consul Carl Lutz, who was sent to Budapest in early 1942 and soon promoted to head of the Department of Foreign Interests at the Swiss embassy. [346] Through the Swiss consulate, Lutz represented the diplomatic and consular interests of the United States, Britain, Belgium, Yugoslavia, Egypt, Uruguay, Haiti, Venezuela, Honduras, El Salvador and Romania in Hungary.

Shortly after the German occupation of Hungary in March 1944 and after the start of the mass deportation of 450,000 Hungarian Jews, Lutz developed a brilliant strategy for saving tens of thousands of Jews from the gas chambers of Auschwitz.

Although it was not in his instructions and not Swiss policy, he approached Adolf Eichmann in Budapest and declared that, as diplomatic representative for British interests, he held 7,800 Palestinian certificates which would permit Jews to emigrate from Hungary to Palestine. Lutz emphasized that any person holding such a document was automatically under the protection of the Swiss embassy until it was possible to emigrate to Palestine. During the ensuing negotiations, which dragged on for months, Lutz insisted that these protective letters also included the holders' families. When Budapest was again occupied, this time by the Russians, Carl Lutz continued his Palestinian letter campaign. Through unwavering persistence, he succeeded in bringing some 50,000 persons under the protection of the

---

[343] Eizenstat (1997), p. 26.

[344] Detlev F. Vagts, "Neutrality Law in World War II," in: Cardozo Law Review. Vol. 20 No. 2 December 1998 p. 47.

[345] Paul Stauffer, Sechs furchtbare Jahre... "Auf den Spuren Carl J. Burckhardts durch den Zweiten Weltkrieg. (Zurich, 1998), p. 369.

[346] Meir Wagner, The Righteous of Switzerland: Heroes of the Holocaust. (New Jersey, 2001), p. 173.

Swiss embassy, saving their lives. [347] This number may even be a conservative estimate, for in a letter of thanks to Lutz of December 24, 1949, Michael Salomon, president of the Hungarian Zionist organization, confirmed that Lutz had saved the lives of 72,000 people. [348] Yad Vashem names Carl Lutz as a 'Righteous Among the Nations'. [349]

It should be mentioned, however, that the Swiss government in Bern did not show much appreciation for his extraordinary achievement. On the contrary, Lutz was reprimanded for exceeding his authority. [350] The Foreign Office thought little of the fact that he rescued people from certain death, because he had not acted in accordance with the letter of the law. A police commander, Louis Grüninger, who in 1938 backed the (illegal) admission of refugees in St. Gallen, as well as Louis Haefliger, who saved tens of thousands of human lives in Mauthausen concentration camp, and Peter Surava, a committed journalist writing for the magazine "Nation" was likewise reprimanded by the government. Their biographies were only written in 1990 when they were rehabilitated – 45 years after the end of the war. [351]

In its status as a neutral country, Switzerland represented the diplomatic interests of 43 nations during World War II, including the United States and Great Britain. Only by acting as neutral representatives with a protection mandate could Swiss diplomats such as Carl Lutz carry out their rescues actions and facilitate the humanitarian efforts of the International Committee of the Red Cross (ICRC), [352] which, technically, was entrusted to carry out the functions of a "protecting power" vis-à-vis of the prisoners of war – a role bestowed upon neutral Switzerland in 1929 under the Geneva Convention. [353]

In view of the criticism leveled at Swiss refugee policies, reference must be made to David Wyman's assessment that, with the exception of Palestine, Switzerland was the country, which, with 21,304 Jewish refugees [354] by the end of the war, had taken in more Jewish refugees for its size than any other country. [355] In addition, Joerg Krummenacher's most recent study points out that Switzerland took in about 30,000 more people than had previously been thought. This means that

---

[347] Ibid.

[348] Theo Tschuy, Carl Lutz und die Juden von Budapest. (Zurich, 1995), p. 335

[349] After World War II the wording "Righteous Among the Nations" (Hebrew:çñéã àåîâù äòâìí Chassid Umot ha-Olam) was adopted for non-Jewish persons who had dedicated their lives to saving Jews from the National Socialist Holocaust.

[350] Alexander Grossman, Nur das Gewissen. Carl Lutz und seine Budapester Aktion. (Wald, 1987); Theo Tschuy, Carl Lutz und die Juden von Budapest. (Zurich, 1995).

[351] Alphons Matt, Einer aus dem Dunkeln. Die Befreiung des Konzentrationslagers Mauthausen durch den Bankbeamten H... (Zurich, 1988); Peter Hirsch, Er nannte sich Peter Surava. (Stäfa 1991); Keller, Stefan, Grüningers Fall. Geschichten von Flucht und Hilfe. (Zurich, 1993).

[352] Meir Wagner, The Righteous of Switzerland: Heroes of the Holocaust. (New Jersey, 2001), p. xii.

[353] Detlev F. Vagts, "Neutrality Law in World War II," in: Cardozo Law Review. Vol. 20 No. 2 December 1998, p. 475.

[354] Refugee Report, p. 36.

[355] Carl Ludwig, La politique pratiquée par la Suisse à l'égard des réfugiés au cours des années 1939 à 1955. (Berne, 1957), p. 303 and David Wymann, The Abandonment of the Jews : America and the Holocaust 1941-1945 (New York, 1998).

the number of Jewish refugees could be considerably higher. [356] By comparison, the massive USA allowed just 21,000 Jewish refugees to stay on American soil between Pearl Harbor and the end of the war. While the mass murder of Jews was taking place in Europe, 90% of the 190,000 immigration visas available for the USA remained unused. [357]

No doubt, the life led by people who found refuge in Switzerland was not always easy. But they survived the persecution – thanks to the actions of Swiss citizens, aid organizations and above all Swiss Jews who made enormous financial sacrifices, but also thanks to a government which decided – if only in the summer of 1942 – to bear the cost of accommodating the refugees. [358] The Swiss government certainly could have done more to help save Jews. But this in no way justifies the claim that Swiss authorities, through their refugee policy, helped the National Socialists to achieve their goals. [359] Rather one should say that Switzerland used its neutrality to granting 27,000 Jewish refugees and a further 20,000 Jews of Swiss nationality or with a right of residence in Switzerland refuge and security for the duration of the war. [360] If you add on those Jewish people who were saved through Swiss embassies and the International Red Cross which was staffed by Swiss, as well as those who managed to reach other countries via Switzerland, when this was still possible, over 220,000 Jewish men, women and children were rescued from imprisonment and death with the help of this neutral country. [361]

FINAL REMARKS

Overall, Swiss efforts at maintaining close economic relations with Germany allowed Switzerland to survive. The Swiss economy, including its technology and financial bases, survived the war years more or less undamaged.

Switzerland was able to attain the central goals of its defense and economic policies. Without persistent and subtle use of the country's foreign trade relations, neither the government nor the country's enterprises would have been able to guarantee bread and work to the Swiss population [362], and Swiss military leaders would not have been able to obtain sufficient raw materials for weapons and fortifications. The continued existence of many banks, the foundation of the highly developed Swiss credit system, depended on the protection of foreign assets or at least on an orderly disposal of credits which did collapse.

---

[356] Joerg Krummenacher-Schoell, Flüchtiges Glück: Die Flüchtlinge im Grenzkanton St. Gallen zur Zeit des Nationalsozialismus. (Zurich, 2005).

[357] David Wyman, The Abandonment of the Jews. (New York, 1998), p. 136.

[358] Daniel Bourgeois, Das Geschäft mit Hitler Deutschland. Schweizer Wirtschaft und das Dritte Reich. (Zurich, 2000), pp. 228-229.

[359] Bergier Report, p. 172.

[360] Op. cit., p. 183.

[361] Carl Ludwig, Die Flüchtlingspolitik der Schweiz seit 1933 zur Gegenwart. (Berne, 1957), p. 318: "295'381 ausländische Flüchtlinge, Internierte, entwichene Kriegsgefangene sowie die zu gewissen Zeiten zahlreichen, bei der Polizei nicht gemeldeten Flüchtlinge; Andrea Koehler, Neue Zürcher Zeitung (NZZ), "Der 'Aufbau' am Ende?" of April 15, 2004".

[362] Jean Hotz, "Handelsabteilung und Handelspolitik in der Kriegszeit" in: Die schweizerische Kriegswirtschaft 1939-1948. (Berne, 1950), p. 85.

Switzerland ultimately succeeded as well in breaking out of the political and economic isolation imposed on it by the Allied powers. The decisive factor was the country's intact economy whose potential the victorious powers intended to use in rebuilding Europe and international trade. All in all, thanks to its financial resources and production capacity, Switzerland repeatedly managed to secure concessions despite the superior might of both the Axis and the Allied powers and to maintain a kind of flexibility in its position between the warring parties. By protecting its core economy, Switzerland was able to maintain political neutrality and secure its survival. In the tight-rope walk of negotiations with Allied and the Axis powers, terms which were minor for those powers were questions of national survival for the Swiss. The country's motto had to be 'Adaptation *and* Neutrality'.

Although Germany's military victories of summer 1940 persuaded Swiss leaders to place some restrictions on speech, free speech was never banned, or even curbed to the extent demanded by the Germans. Switzerland remained fundamentally faithful to democratic values, even though there was some press censorship of aggressive anti-German reports and editorials. The Neue Zürcher Zeitung only reported on the gas chambers of Treblinka, Poland, on June 20, 1943, [363] i.e. after the final solution had already been running for many months and millions of Jews murdered. Member of the National Council Feldmann, although a journalist himself and a harsh critic of state press control, stated that they [the Swiss press] had succeeded to a large extent in "... asserting and meeting the Swiss people's right to information on the major events of the war, as well as defending the Swiss point of view with great determination where this really concerned the protection of Swiss interests." [364] Critical voices were never silent in Switzerland.

---

[363] Tom Bower, Blood Money. The Swiss, the Nazis and the Looted Billions. (London, 1997), p. 66; Jacques Picard, Die Schweiz und die Juden, 1933-1945. Schweizerischer Antisemitismus, jüdische Abwehr und internationale Migrations- und Flüchtlingspolitik (Zurich, 1997), pp. 407-409 and Peter Kamber, Schüsse auf die Befreier. (Zurich, 1993) pp. 38-40 Neue Zürcher Zeitung, "Das Schicksal der Juden in Polen." June 20, 1943.

[364] Edgar Bonjour, Geschichte der Schweizerischen Neutralität. Vier Jahrhunderte Eidgenössischer Aussenpolitik. Vol. V (Basle, 1971), p. 196.

CHAPTER II

HOW NEUTRAL WERE THE NEUTRALS?

CONTROL OF NEUTRAL COUNTRIES

At the outbreak of World War II, Britain and France began to integrate the economies of all neutral European countries as part of their own overall war economy by pressuring them into submitting to an economic surveillance program. Once France was defeated in June 1940, the control of neutral country trade continued to be conducted by Britain on its own until the USA initiated a similar surveillance program after Japan's attack on Pearl Harbor (December 7, 1941), and Hitler's (December 10, 1941) subsequent declaration of war against America.

Initially Britain made major diplomatic efforts to win active support from Europe's neutrals and from the USA for its blockade against Germany. Gaining American goodwill was of vital importance since Britain could not control American business transactions outright. But negotiations on rationing, allocation rights, bans, etc., put Britain on a collision course with neutrals that in spite of major diplomatic efforts, were reluctant to submit to trade monitoring. The British ignored protests, however, and moved boldly ahead with closely tracking trade shipments by Portugal, Spain, Sweden, Switzerland and Turkey to ensure that their blockade was effective. They also devoted considerable efforts to following relations between neutral countries as well as those directly with Axis powers and so plotted critical check points within the flow of international trade. The British also quickly realized that not all neutral powers were equally neutral.

Sweden started to think about the definition of its rights and obligations as a neutral in 1938. [365] In the *United States* – neutral before it entered the war – Congress precisely defined the terms of American neutrality through legislation in the pre-war years of 1935, 1936, 1937 and 1939. *Switzerland* – in spite of joining the League of Nations in 1920 – was the only European country which had been officially neutral since 1815, and in fact displayed its neutrality on the nation's coat of arms since that date. Both in World War I and in the inter-war years, Switzerland had sought to remain scrupulously neutral. Even after the beginning of World War II, Switzerland – like the USA – insisted that its relations with the warring nations should be defined by its rights and obligations as a neutral country and that its neutrality should be respected. [366] This same contention was made by *Spain, Portugal* and *Turkey* when it declared neutrality at the outbreak of World War II.

---

[365] Neutrality has been a principle of Swedish policy since the 1854 Crimean War.

[366] Walther Hofer, Neutraler Kleinstaat im europäischen Konfliktfeld: Die Schweiz, in Helmut Altrichter and Josef Becker (ed.), Kriegsausbruch 1939: Beteiligte, Betroffene, Neutrale. (Munich, 1989), p. 205-227

But respect for neutrality did not rank high on the wartime agendas of the combatants. The Allied powers explicitly adopted total blockade as a means of cutting off German access to raw materials and goods from neutral countries. All neutral countries in Europe were expected to submit to Allied-dictated restrictions on their import and export activities.

In the case of *Switzerland*, such restrictions involved the export of weapons, ammunition, machines and locomotives, as well as gold transactions within the financial sector.

Sweden was a very significant trading partner for Nazi Germany and the importance of Swedish ball bearings for the German armaments industry can hardly be overestimated. Moreover Sweden supplied German industry with 40% of its iron ore requirements until other European suppliers could to some extent reduce German dependence on this neutral country. [367] *Spain* and particularly *Portugal* supplied Germany with tungsten. This metal was absolutely indispensable for armaments, used for hardening steel for products such as air plane engines and propellers, tanks and armored vehicles as well as for armor-piercing projectiles. Spanish exports to Nazi Germany also included iron ore, mercury and zinc.

Turkey supplied extremely rare and valuable chromium ore since chromium's properties resemble those of tungsten. Chromium ore was critical to the German armament industry and stocks were insufficient.

Finally *Vichy France*, the *unoccupied* part of France after the armistice, saw fit to assist Germany with its production capacity and supply of labor. As a result, Britain quickly classified defeated France as an enemy country subject to the blockade. Vichy France, on the whole, cooperated with Nazi Germany by keeping the French colonial empire in check and directing, in so far as possible, its services towards the war efforts of the Reich.

DIFFERENCES WITH THE USA

With the beginning of World War II and especially after the French defeat in June 1940, Britain imposed a system of wartime economic controls. These controls, targeting the flow of strategic goods from neutral and non-warring countries to occupied Europe, rapidly led to serious Anglo-American differences. [368]

---

[367] Eizenstat (1998), p. 91 – Academic assessment of Swedish trade with Germany during World War II, especially in respect of iron ore, led to the question whether Sweden might have stopped the war right at the beginning in 1939 by not exporting iron ore to Germany. Alan Milward and Joerg-Johannes Jaeger were roused by a provocative theory from Rolf Karlborb, who published an overview of Swedish iron exports to Germany between 1933 and 1944., and asked: "If Lapland's mines had stopped working, would this have shut down the furnaces in the Ruhr area?" Historians Gerhard Weinberg and Christian Leitz concluded that stopping Swedish deliveries would not have prevented the war, because the German economy had other iron ore sources. Cf. Gerhard Weinberg, A World At Arms: A Global History of World War II. (New York, 1994), pp. 73-74 and 77-78; Christian Leitz, Nazi Germany and the Neutral Europe During the Second World War. (Manchester, 2000), pp. 64-65

[368] Robert W. Matson, Neutrality and Navicerts. Britain, the United States, and the Economic Warfare, 1939-1940. (New York/London, 1994); W.M. Medlicott, The Economic Blockade, 2 vols (London, 1952 und 1959)

The restrictions were eased somewhat by the British after President Roosevelt confirmed neutrality legislation on November 4, 1939, prohibiting American vessels from calling at harbors in the so-called zone of conflict. America defined this zone as all harbors along the coasts of Norway, Sweden, the Baltic States and connected waters, as well as the coasts of Germany, Denmark, the Netherlands, Belgium, France and Spain. [369]

But as German troops took up positions within sight of Britain across the Channel, the British were determined to push through more extreme measures of economic warfare. These measures included forced quotas, search and seizure rights and a comprehensive blockade based on the navicert system involving permission certificates on virtually all naval cargo movements. Navicerts could only be issued by a British official at the loading port. In effect, Britain was claiming the sole right to control international trade. Vessels without proper papers could be stopped by the British Navy, escorted to the nearest harbor and any goods not permitted according to the British-dictated listing confiscated.

This strategy could not be fully implemented without the tacit cooperation of the United States. But when the British began putting American firms on its black list, summarily excluding them from trade with Britain, the Commonwealth and the Empire, American resistance rose. The US government suspected Britain was using navicerts to achieve trade advantages beyond purely military goals, and therefore set out to define very clearly what actions the British could take without provoking a hostile reaction from the USA. During a meeting between the Assistant Chief of the Division of European Affairs John Hickerson and senior staff of the British embassy in Washington D.C. on November 9, 1939, the British were handed a proposal, the so called 'Code of Practice', outlining what the Americans felt to be acceptable:

1. The navicert system was not to be used in any way which would compromise the normal volume of exports of obviously neutral character from the United States and any other neutral country.
2. The navicert system should not be used in any way which would discriminate against the United States and US export companies.
3. Granting or refusing navicerts should only depend on supply conditions in the importing country and should not be connected to any conditions imposed on American exporters or the United States itself.
4. If applications for navicerts were refused, the applicant should be given a short, precise explanation of the reasons for the refusal. [370]

Britain essentially rejected this American proposal, making it clear to the USA that Britain, as a country at war, felt obliged to prevent the delivery of forbidden goods to Germany and that the British navy would therefore continue to stop vessels and to check their cargo in the nearest harbor – including vessels from the United States.

---

[369] Foreign Relations of the United States Diplomatic Papers (FRUS), Vol. I. (Washington, D.C., 1956), p. 775 – Memo of Assistant Chief of the Division of European Affairs, John Hickerson, of November 9, 1939, concerning a meeting with leading members of the British Embassy in Washington. D.C.

[370] Ibid., p. 772

These expansive war rights claimed by the British were in conflict with the neutrality rights claimed by the USA, and led to increasing delays in the inspection harbors. The US State Department repeatedly and pointedly articulated that Britain must respect America's neutrality. In the words of US Undersecretary Adolf A. Berle Jr.: "... the neutral right to live transcends the belligerent right to make things unhappy for his enemy."[371]

But such American remonstrance went largely unheeded and the British still did not fully comply with the American conditions laid down on November 9, 1939. They continued their total economic war, stopping American vessels and confiscating all goods intended for the enemy.

However, after Hitler began the invasion of Denmark and Norway on April 9, 1940, the US became more supportive of the British position. On April 10 Roosevelt issued Executive Order 8389 which allowed the freezing of foreign assets. When the Germans rolled into Low Countries and France in May and June 1940, this decree was used to block all German attempts to access property held in America by the governments or inhabitants of these countries. [372] The freezing of foreign assets in the USA kept step with the conquests of the Third Reich. Paradoxically business links between America and Germany remained largely intact.

As the United States government attempted to represent and reconcile the interests of American companies trading on world markets, it extended its influence in other world regions besides Europe, including South America and the Orient. This process pushed American foreign policy step by step away from that of a pure neutral to the policies of a so-called non-belligerent country. [373] Until the French defeat in 1940, the USA became a *de facto* supporter of Britain and France and even before the Japanese attack on Pearl Harbor in early December 1941, tensions between America and Britain over blockade issues had subsided. But new trade issues between the two countries kept opening up, particularly in the early stages of the war. The treatment of Vichy France was problematic because, although technically independent and unoccupied, the Vichy state was effectively controlled by Germany.

While there were no diplomatic relations between Britain and Vichy France, the United States maintained official diplomatic relations with the Vichy regime. America did not seem bothered by the fact that this as yet unoccupied part of France was not only closely controlled by the Nazis, but also willingly supplied

[371] Robert W. Matson, Neutrality and Navicerts. Britain, the United States, and the Economic Warfare, 1939-1940. (New York/London, 1994), p. 29

[372] Herbert R. Reginbogin, "The Financial Market of America During World War II," in: Joseph Jung, Herbert R. Reginbogin and Robert U. Vogler (ed.), Financial Markets of Neutral Countries during the Second World War. (in preparation by the Association of Financial History and the Principality of Liechtenstein); Gian Trepp, Die Bank für Internationalen Zahlungsausgleich im Zweiten Weltkrieg: Bankgeschäfte mit dem Feind. Von Hitlers Europabank zum Instrument des Marschallplans. (Zurich, 1993), p.64, cf National Archives of Records Administration (NARA), RG 56, Entry 45080211, Box 47. "General Information on the Administration, Structure and Functions of Foreign Funds Control, 1940–1948" (FFC), ch 3, p. 28

[373] The term *'non-belligerent'* has no status in international law and seems to imply that a country is willing to do anything possible within the limits imposed by its neutrality to help one of the warring states to victory. Detlev F. Vagts, "Neutrality Law in World War II," in: Cardozo Law Review. Vol. 20 No. 2, December, 1998 p. 460

the German Reich with labor and other services. Moreover, the Americans took virtually no notice of Charles de Gaulle in London, who was calling himself the sole legitimate representative of France. The tense relations between the USA and Britain on the subject of France is illustrated by the diary entry of the American ambassador to Vichy France, Admiral William Leahy, who wrote that "the British blockade action which prevents the delivery of necessary foodstuffs to the inhabitants of unoccupied France is of the [same] order of stupidity as other British policies in the present war". [374] It must be emphasized, however, that whatever reservations the Americans regarding British blockade policy had changed abruptly when the USA was attacked and entered the war: from that point on, the United States was, if anything, even more rigorous than Britain in enforcing a wide-ranging trade blockade.

WHO WAS NEUTRAL?

So, who was neutral? In Europe, this definition certainly applied to Switzerland and Sweden, to a certain extent also to Turkey and Portugal, and to Spain with major reservations. In addition, there were the Vatican and Ireland. For a period, some Latin American countries claimed neutral status. Argentina and Turkey waited until shortly before the collapse of the Third Reich to declare war on Germany. The USA and the Soviet Union also belonged to the club of neutral countries before they entered the war themselves. All of these countries practiced neutrality in different ways, and neutrality itself came to be interpreted very differently by different states.

A status of neutrality – formally declared – naturally had repercussions on a country's foreign relations. But the Allied and the Axis powers attached different importance to neutral states according to wartime assessments of their importance to the war resulting in different standards of respect for the neutrality of different states.

This attitude was especially clear in the behavior of the British government. In September 1939, Britain had assured Switzerland and other neutrals that it would treat each neutral according to its own standards and not be influenced by the actions of the Axis powers. This 1939 assurance certainly sounded like a serious promise, but it soon fell by the wayside. England, just like its enemy Germany, was already violating Swiss air space. London was more concerned with the practical implementation of its war plans than in the legal application of neutrality. [375]

Apart from Switzerland, how did the other neutral countries – Spain, Portugal, Sweden and Turkey – handle their neutrality during the five and a half years of war in the areas of economy, trade, finance, procurement of raw materials and acceptance of refugees? They all to some extent were faced with the Allied blockade policy. What motivated them to support the Nazi regime and how important were the contributions made to the German war effort by the respective neutral states?

---

[374] James J. Dougherty, The Politics of Wartime Aid: American Economic Assistance to France and French North Africa 1940-1946. (Westport, 1978), p. 24

[375] Neville Wylie, Britain, Switzerland, and the Second World War. (Oxford, 2003), p. 12 – Alexander Cadogan of the Foreign Office to Charles Paravicini, Swiss envoy in London before the outbreak of War on September 9, 1939, BA E2001(D) 3/303

Spain

While countries such as Turkey and Portugal had relatively autocratic, repressive systems of government, other countries such as Sweden and Switzerland boasted liberal democratic traditions with established political parties and free speech, both for their citizens and for the press. With the exception of Spain, none of these neutral countries was ruled by a Fascist government.[376] In contrast with Switzerland and the other European neutral powers considered here, Spain – although unoccupied – had the closest sympathies to the Axis powers. There was a significant risk that Spain would enter World War II on Hitler's side.

The Spanish Civil War

To a large part, the domestic and foreign policy adopted by Franco during World War II may be explained by the circumstances of the Spanish Civil War.

In February 1936, the Popular Front, a colorful collection of left-wing Republicans, Socialists, Communists and various radical working class groups, won the Spanish national elections.[377] In the spring of that year, uprisings broke out in various parts of the country, and the new government proved unable to maintain order. Riots and demonstrations were fanned by working class representatives from the coalition, resulting in illegal land occupations, wide-spread strikes and incidents of violence triggered by left-wing and then right-wing radicals. In July, amidst growing chaos, the leader of the conservative forces, José Calvo Sotelo, was murdered by members of the security forces. Five days later, conservative units of the army took up arms against the legally elected government. Their action was countered by militants loyal to that government – and the Spanish Civil War began.

The republican Popular Front government never succeeded in achieving a high degree of unity among its disparate mix of supporters. At the beginning of the Civil War, because of its Marxist and pro-Russian attitude, the new Spanish republic had practically no support from the western democracies. Britain, France and the United States followed policies of non-intervention. The republican forces depended heavily on Russian assistance in their fight against nationalists led by General Franco. Those forces, in turn received military and financial assistance from Hitler and Mussolini.[378] It was a struggle of political extremes.

To pay for the war effort, both the popular front and the nationalists confiscated property and valuables from banks and civilians.[379] But such seizures were insufficient. Franco's nationalists made widespread use of foreign loans not only from Germany and Italy, but also from banks and companies in other countries.

---

[376] Paul Preston, Franco: A Biography. (London, 1995)

[377] Mercedes Cabrera and Fernando del Rey, "Spanish Entrepreneurs in the Era of Fascism. From the Primo de Rivera Dictatorship to the Franco Dictatorship (1923-1945)," Paper read at the conference held on November 26/27, 2002, by The Society for European Business History e.V. – SEBH on Enterprises in the Period of Fascism in Europe., pp. 9-11; cf. Walther L. Bernecker, "Neutralität wider Willen, Spaniens verhinderter Kriegseintritt," in: Helmut Altrichter and Josef Becker (ed.) Kriegsausbruch 1939. Beteiligte, Betroffene, Neutrale. (Munich 1989), pp. 153-177

[378] Paul, Preston, A Concise History of the Spanish Civil War. (London, 1996)

[379] Ibid.

One of the Franco regime's more unusual loan arrangements was with the Texaco oil company, which agreed to supply Franco with unlimited quantities of oil on credit – an unprecedented undertaking. [380]

Through the bloody, three-year war which savaged and impoverished the Spanish people, the nationalist junta slowly moved towards victory, in the process canceling all the democratic reforms decreed in April of 1931. On March 28, 1939, nationalist troops marched into Madrid, and from that time on Spain was ruled by the iron fist of Francisco Franco Bahamonde.

Franco won his victory with the decisive assistance of Hitler's and Mussolini's Fascist regimes. The new Spanish government was a personal dictatorship, with Spain developing a leadership cult on the model of the Duce and Führer cults in Italy and Germany. Franco became the Caudillo, leader of the Falange (Falange España Tradicionalista), a political party founded in 1937 to unite right-wing political groups. Its structure and popular appeal were much inspired by Fascist and National Socialist parties. The Caudillo laid out a political platform of limiting trade unions, respecting private property and imposing state controls on much of the economy. [381] The new Spanish regime combined traditional conservative beliefs with the more modern totalitarian impulses of Fascism. It was based on a single united party supported by a loyal and victorious army and a Catholic church reasserting itself after being oppressed by the popular front government.

Spain emerged from its civil war in 1939 overwhelmed with war debt. Both sides had taken loans from the Banco de España which, like so many Spanish institutions, had been divided during the war. [382] At the beginning of hostilities, a group of nationalist bank directors met in Burgos (the capital of Franco's Spain) and reorganized the bank as the Francoist Bank of Spain. However, the bank's headquarters remained in republican Madrid, as did the main deposits of precious metals. To prevent gold stocks from falling into nationalist hands, the republicans ordered that much of the reserves be sent to Russia. Ostensibly this gold was to serve as a guarantee for loans granted by the Soviet Union, the republicans' only ally. Republic Spain indeed faced a financial crisis, since the Allies' Non-Intervention Pact made it almost impossible for the popular front to purchase war materials in western countries. The Russian communists never returned the Spanish gold, arguing that the loans to the Spanish Republic for arms and supporting Russian military personnel far exceeded the value of the precious metal deposited

---

[380] Ibid.

[381] Herbert Feis, The Spanish Story. Franco and the Nations at War. (New York, 1966), p. 7

[382] The "Ley de Ordenación Bancaria" (banking law) for the first time regulated the relation between the Banco de España and private banks, with the aim of transforming this issuing bank into a proper central bank. Its capital was increased, it was granted the right to inspect private banks, a privileged interest rate was established, so other banks could obtain money from the central bank at favorable rates, and the Banco de España began regulating foreign currency policy.

in Russia. [383] (Franco repeatedly tried to retrieve this gold after the war, but to no avail).

Franco and the Axis Powers

Axis support helped Franco defeat the left-wing republicans, and relations between the Caudillo and the Axis powers were reaffirmed with Franco signing on March 31, 1939, a secret friendship and cooperation agreement with Germany which offered Spanish assistance as a transport link for goods from South America. [384] After his victory, he announced his accession to the Anti-Comintern Pact between Italy, Japan and Germany on April 7, 1939. A month later, on May 8, 1939, Spain withdrew from the League of Nations.

In spite of his obvious ideological affinity with the leaders of the Axis powers, Generalissimo Franco declared Spain to be neutral shortly after the outbreak of World War II in September 1939. But he continued to show his gratitude for the support the Axis powers had given him. The protracted civil war had exhausted Spain both economically and financially, so the country was in a desperate state when hostilities broke out across Europe just five months after the end of the civil war in Spain.

Contemporary press reports and documents paint a bleak picture of Spain's financial position. The government was isolated internationally and, compared with other neutral countries, was in an extremely desperate situation economically. It was not until after the end of World War II that France and Britain resumed diplomatic relations with Franco. Switzerland – economically stable, democratically ruled and with an impressive ability to maintain a functioning economic infrastructure – stood out sharply against devastated but neutral Spain before World War II.

Neutrality Tango

As the European war accelerated, Franco obviously favored a Fascist system, but he could never be totally sure that Spain itself might not someday fall victim to a German invasion. The Caudillo was therefore keen to prove his loyalty. The Spanish press was required to support only one side. In contrast to countries such as Switzerland and Sweden which were repeatedly criticized by the Nazis for news reporting biased against Germany, the pro Axis announcements in the Spanish newspapers were a real comfort for the Nazi-soul. [385] During the entire period of the so-called Phony War after the invasion of Poland, Franco again and again violated the legal obligations attached to claiming the status of a neutral.

These violations – according to historian Christian Leitz – included replenishing German destroyers and submarines with food and fuel in Spanish coastal

---

[383] Gabriel Tortella, "The Spanish Financial Sector During The Second World War" Herbert R. Reginbogin, "The Financial Market of America During World War II" in: Joseph Jung, Herbert R. Reginbogin and Robert U. Vogler (ed.), Financial Markets of Neutral Countries during the Second World War (in preparation by the Association of Financial History and the Principality of Liechtenstein).

[384] Eizenstat (1998), p. 63

[385] Stanley G. Payne, The Franco Regime, 1939-1975. (Madison, 1975), p. 299

waters and harbors. [386] Detlev Vagts, international law expert at Harvard University, wrote: "It is not clear which of Spain's activities on behalf of the German navy went beyond the bounds of neutrality. It was probably lawful to permit refueling stops, but not to allow German tankers to remain in Spanish ports for long stretches or to permit overland travel of replacement crews." [387]

Spain's foreign policy faced direct challenges both after Hitler's lightning conquest of France in 1940 and after the subsequent German occupation of southern France in November 1942. Effective German control of the French border had far-reaching repercussions on Spanish-German economic relations. With the fall of France, the French-Spanish border route now became more important than Mediterranean Sea lanes as the main corridor for the transport of goods into Germany. As a result, Spanish exports to the Axis powers increased from 970,000 tons in 1941 to 1.28 million tons in 1942. [388]

On June 13, 1940, encouraged by German successes, Franco proclaimed a Spanish foreign policy of non-belligerence. Essentially the new policy looked forward to an eventual Axis victory, and Franco declared that Spain would do everything in its power – within the limits of its neutrality – to support Germany and Italy on this path.

However, the Spanish Caudillo kept his options open and continued his efforts to speed up Spain's military preparations. His sympathies for the Axis powers were so obvious, however, that a Spanish declaration of war on the Allied powers could not be ruled out. The first step in this direction was taken on June 19, 1940, when Franco sent a letter to Berlin offering to enter the war on the Axis side. [389] At this time, a Third Reich victory seemed possible indeed, and Franco was hoping to acquire French North-West Africa for Spain.

Hitler was not particularly enthusiastic about the Spanish offer, irritated as he was by Mussolini's delay in entering the war. At that point, Hitler expected that a total defeat of the French was just a matter of time and that Britain must either accept German peace conditions or risk outright defeat. With victory so close, why – in the view of historian Christian Leitz – should he permit others to reap the fruits of his achievements? They had only made a small contribution and late in the game. [390]

However in the summer of 1940 Britain proved to be a tougher opponent than the Nazis had imagined in their first triumphant euphoria – their first error of judgment. It became clear that the massive operation to invade Britain might sink – true to its code name Sea Lion – into the English Channel, while the British Lion was beginning to roar. Plans of invading Britain were put aside and Operation

---

[386] Akten zur Deutschen Auswärtigen Politik 1918-1945 (ADAP), Series D (1937-1941), Vol. XII, No. 2, p. 657; cf. Christian Leitz, Nazi Germany and the Neutral Europe During the Second World War. (Manchester, 2000), p. 119; cf. Charles B. Burdick, "Moro": the Resupply of German Submarines in Spain 1939-1942," in: Central European History. No. 3 (1970), pp. 256-284

[387] Detlev F. Vagts, "Neutrality Law in World War II," in: Cardozo Law Review. Vol. 20 No. 2 December 1998, p. 468

[388] Eizenstat, (1998), p. 63

[389] Christian Leitz, Nazi Germany and the Neutral Europe During the Second World War. (Manchester, 2000), p. 122

[390] Ibid.

Felix – a plan aimed at occupying the Iberian Peninsula and cutting off the British from western access to the Mediterranean – was resurrected. [391] Suddenly Franco's offer to enter the war – unwelcomed in June but publicly repeated on July 18, 1940 – seemed a lot more attractive.

With Spain at its side, German military operations against Gibraltar, Britain's forlorn post at the southern end of the Iberian Peninsula would be feasible. Operation Felix called for two German troop contingents to cross Spain with Franco's permission. Once they were in position, the Nazis would attack Gibraltar both from land and sea with deadly efficiency. As soon as Gibraltar was in German hands, two divisions were to move across the strait to attack Morocco which remained under the control of the French army. [392]

Franco, of course, was well aware of Gibraltar's strategic importance. With the Pillars of Hercules – the mythical guardians of the entry into the Mediterranean – in German possession, the Reich would be able to control critical sea lanes. A British loss of Gibraltar would have immediate and disastrous repercussions for British bastions around the Mediterranean: direct links to Egypt and the Suez Canal would be almost completely destroyed, and oil tankers would take weeks longer on their voyage from the Middle East to Britain. British pressure on Italy, the weaker Axis partner, would inevitably decrease, and a German presence on Gibraltar would also intimidate Turkey, Britain's ally in the Mediterranean. Churchill wrote: "Spain held the key to all British enterprises in the Mediterranean." [393]

But in spite of his readiness to enter the war on the side of the Axis powers, voiced both publicly and in writing, Franco held out for his price: extending Spanish control into French Morocco and other colonies in Africa, perhaps even into Europe. In retrospect, it seems clear that Franco expected Operation Sea Lion to be a quick success, so he would not have to fear British retaliation against Spain from British forces in the Mediterranean.

However, Franco's demand for control of the French territories in West Africa would not have served Germany's security interests in the region, since Franco's troops in Africa were obviously in very bad shape. Moreover, on September 25, 1940, the French colonial army, which was loyal to the Vichy government, succeeded in beating back a British attack on Dakar, the capital of French West Africa. The British attack had been intended to prepare for a landing of de Gaulle's troops. [394] They wanted to prevent Dakar becoming a danger to Freetown, an important assembly point for convoys. It would also have been a welcome territorial base for British expeditions. Last but not least, banks in Dakar held gold from France, as well as Belgian gold reserves and Polish gold. For both the British and

---

[391] Gerhard Schreiber, "Die politische und militärische Entwicklung im Mittelmeerraum 1939/40," in: Das Deutsche Reich und der Zweite Weltkrieg. Vol. 3 Part 1 (Stuttgart, 1984), p. 213

[392] Op. cit., p. 140

[393] Winston S. Churchill, The Second World War: Their Finest Hour. Vol. II (Boston, 1949), p. 519

[394] A. G. Ploetz (Hrg.), Geschichte des Zweiten Weltkrieges. (Würzburg, 1960), p. 147

de Gaulle, these were good reasons for an attack. However, the strike was poorly planned and ended in failure. [395]

As another twist on neutrality, French authorities in Dakar had guaranteed their army's neutrality on condition that Germany respects the integrity of French Northwest Africa. Against this background, Hitler and Mussolini met on October 4, 1940, at the Brenner Pass to discuss Franco's demands. If Franco entered the war, Britain would immediately seize Spanish bases on the Canary Islands. Hitler also wanted to make sure, for his forthcoming meeting with Pétain, that Vichy would remain loyal to the Reich. Accepting Spanish colonial demands might possibly drive the Vichy leadership straight into the arms of de Gaulle and Britain. Hitler did not want to risk losing the many advantages of Vichy collaboration to gain the costly and dubious participation of a country which was hungry, defenseless and devastated. The Führer and the Duce therefore agreed that Hitler, in his next meeting with Franco scheduled for late October, would make no binding promises concerning Spanish entry into the war and certainly no territorial promises. They also ruled out explicit promises for German supplies of vital goods to Spain. [396]

Hitler met Franco in the town of Hendaye on the Spanish-French border on October 23, 1940, one day before his meeting with Marshall Pétain. As Hitler intended, no final agreement was reached on conditions for Spain to enter the war. But Franco, expecting a German victory, was eager to profit from post-war treasures and was prepared to sign a secret protocol in Hendaye making Spain a party to the Tripartite Pact. Spain committed itself to enter the war as soon as the Axis powers supplied Spain with the necessary equipment. The timing of this war entry was to be determined by mutual agreement of all three Axis powers. The secret agreement contained in principle an assurance that Spain would get Gibraltar and additional territories in Africa, but only to the extent that equivalent areas in Africa could be granted to the French as compensation. These assurances were not to impinge German-Italian claims on France. [397]

One week after the meeting, Hitler received a letter from Franco, confirming his intention to enter the war on the German side, but still insisting on his territorial demands. [398] But then Mussolini, eager to demonstrate his own independent power, attacked Greece from Albanian territory on October 28, 1940. Hitler expressed his dismay with this unilateral Italian action when he met Mussolini in Florence. He had good reason, since the Italians not only did not succeed in conquering Greece, the new front ended with the Greeks occupying more than a third of Albania. The Italian offensive also pulled the British into the conflict, since they had guaranteed Albania assistance against the Axis powers. British troops mined Greek waters, established air force and naval bases on Crete, and finally landed in Greece on

---

[395] R. T. Thomas, Britain and Vichy. The Dilemma of Anglo-French Relations 1940-1942. (London, 1979), pp. 62 and 65

[396] Elena Hernandez-Sandoica and Enrique Moradiellos, "Spain and the Second World War, 1939-1945," in: Neville Wylie (ed.), European Neutrals and Non-Belligerents During the Second World War. (Cambridge, 2002), pp. 256-257

[397] Ibid., p. 257

[398] Paul Preston, Franco, a Biography. (London, 1995), p. 403; Christian Leitz, Nazi Germany and the Neutral Europe During the Second World War. (Manchester, 2000), p. 125

March 7, 1941. In order to prevent an additional Allied front in the Balkans – similar to that of 1915 – Hitler was forced to stage a relief attack to protect the German south eastern flank. On April 6 he began the campaign against Yugoslavia and Greece. On April 12, 1941, the German 12th Army marched into Belgrade, and on April 24, 1941, Greece capitulated. [399] Mussolini's craving for glory of his own had far reaching consequences. Death and unspeakable suffering were the immediate bitter harvest. In addition twelve German divisions were mired down in Greece prompting Hitler to postpone the invasion of Russia. This and Hitler's outrage about Yugoslavia declaring its subservience to Germany as ended through a coup d'état on March 26, 1941 by the Serbs led Hitler to invade Yugoslavia with "unmerciful harshness" resulting in a postponement of four weeks for the beginning of Operation Barbarossa, which was probably the most catastrophic military decision of the entire war. [400]

Franco Refuses to Enter the War

Notwithstanding Franco's continuing territorial preconditions, in November 1940 Hitler became convinced that Spain would indeed enter the war on the Axis side, and he moved forward with plans and preparations for a coordinated attack on Gibraltar. The start of the attack was set for January 10, 1941. In preparation, Wehrmacht troops would move into Spain. Hitler sent Admiral Wilhelm Canaris, head of the German Abwehr (military intelligence), to Spain to make sure of Franco's support for Operation Felix. The meeting between Canaris and Franco took place on December 7, 1940. But instead of agreeing, as Canaris expected, Franco rejected an immediate Spanish entry into the war. Franco claimed it was not yet feasible for Spain to declare war, citing the growing discrepancy between Spain's economic and military needs and German offers. Hitler's attack plans were thrown into disarray. [401]

Franco was well aware of certain adverse events that may well have dampened his enthusiasm. First, the fierceness of the British in defending their home islands had made the expected invasion of Britain, planned for October 12, 1940, much less likely. Meanwhile the British navy's determination to maintain its dominance over Italy in the Mediterranean shattered Axis hopes to block the Suez Canal which was an absolute precondition for any attack on Gibraltar. The second reason for Franco's diminished enthusiasm was the opposition he was facing in his own camp. While younger officers of the Falangist party were in favor of Spain entering the war, Franco was faced with increasing resistance from top army commanders who had the support of the church and followers of the monarchy. Their resistance rested on Spain's military vulnerability and on the prospect of famine which appeared imminent in the winter of 1940. Moreover at that point Spain was ever more dependent on Anglo-American supplies of food and fuel. [402]

---

[399] Lothar Gauchmann, Der Zweite Weltkrieg. Kriegführung und Politik. (Munich, 1967), pp. 112-113

[400] John G. Stoessinger, Why Nations Go To War. (Belmont, 2005), pp. 35-36

[401] Elena Hernandez-Sandoica and Enrique Moradiellos, "Spain and the Second World War, 1939-1945," in: Neville Wylie (ed.), European Neutrals and Non-Belligerents During the Second World War. (Cambridge, 2002), p. 252

[402] Ibid., p. 258

Although Spain was not an inland country like Switzerland, the British sea blockade turned out to be extremely effective, and Spain became aware of how much the country's domestic stability depended on imports of food, fuel and raw materials. Remaining technically neutral helped Spain in two ways: on the one hand Spain's clearly Fascist proclivities reduced imminent danger of conflict with the Axis powers; and on the other, the country could maintain vital subsistence lifelines for the Spanish economy. Allied powers were still buying Spanish goods, not because they actually needed them, but in order to deprive the Axis of these products and materials. The Axis powers in their turn tried to get their hands on Spanish products by any means, foul or fair. But the Allied powers did not limit their efforts in Spain to purchases. In the early 1940s, both Britain and the USA sought to lure Spain away from the Axis by supplying the country with urgently required goods such as crude oil, food stuffs and textiles. The USA began shipping grain and petrol to Spain. However, Franco was not to be trusted. He gladly accepted American crude oil, took a small portion for Spanish needs, and transferred the remainder to the Third Reich. [403]

Franco's economy also continued to support the German war effort with a variety of products and services, including the shipment of clearly strategic goods such as leather, fur, iron ore, mercury and cork. Spanish deliveries of textiles were very welcomed indeed after summer-clad German troops spent their first winter on the Russian front. In response, the Allied powers ranked warm clothes immediately after tungsten ore in second place on the list of goods to be withheld from Nazi Germany. [404]

The private correspondence between Pedro Teotonio Pereira, Portuguese ambassador in Spain, and the Portuguese president, Antonio de Oliveira Salazar, offers interesting insights on Franco's behavior and the close political and economic coordination between British and Portuguese diplomats who sought to keep Franco from entering the war so that the entire Iberian Peninsula would remain officially neutral. [405] Skilful Portuguese diplomats succeeded in convincing Spain that it would be unwise to imitate Italy's folly.

With Spanish support problematic, Hitler backed off on Operation Felix and started preparations for Operation Barbarossa, the Wehrmacht's massive surprise attack on the Soviet Union. But Hitler never totally gave up on Spain, Felix and Gibraltar as strategic keys to a broad Mediterranean plan. In 1942, the plans for a German attack on Gibraltar were considered again (as is well known – to no avail).

But in the eyes of the British, a Spain – or rather continuing Spanish neutrality acquired major importance for Britain's security interests. Dominating the

[403] Dean Acheson, Present at the Creation: My Years in the State Department. (New York, 1969), pp. 86-90;

[404] Christian Leitz, Nazi Germany and the Neutral Europe During the Second World War. (Manchester, 2000), p. 132

[405] Fernando Rosas, "Portuguese Neutrality in the Second World War," in: Neville Wylie (ed.), European Neutrals and Non-Belligerents During the Second World War. (Cambridge, 2002), pp. 272-273; Elena Hernandez-Sandoica and Enrique Moradiellos, "Spain and the Second World War, 1939-1945," in: Neville Wylie (ed.), European Neutrals and Non-Belligerents During the Second World War. (Cambridge, 2002), p. 262

western Mediterranean, a hostile or simply pro-Axis Spain had the potential to seriously disrupt Britain's far-flung transport and supply system. Spain also constituted a latent political threat to other countries and especially Portugal. Historian Denis Smyth writes: "Spain's strategic location astride maritime, imperial and inter-continental lines of communication made its attitude toward the war crucial for the British fight to survive." [406]

All three parties, the Allies, Germany and Spain, now started a delicate and risky game:

– Germany wanted to get as many goods as possible from Spain, and at the same time keep it in reserve as a possible ally. The Nazis could not treat Franco too harshly or he might change sides and support the Allies.

– The Allied powers did not really need Spain – either economically or as a war partner. Their goals were to keep Franco from supporting the Germans too aggressively or even from joining forces with them. To achieve those goals they stepped up their economic warfare. They paid higher prices for key products sought by the Germans and exerted pressure on Spain by threatening to block the export of products on which the Spanish economy depended. But like Germany, the Allies had to tread carefully so as not to alienate the Spanish government and drive it into an even closer alliance with the enemy. It was British and American aid in the form of food and fuel that staved off what seemed to be imminent famine in Spain during the winter of 1940/1941. [407]

– Spain, the third party, was also walking on a tightrope. Franco had the advantage of being courted by both the Allied and Axis powers, but he was always in danger of being blocked or attacked, if either side or both sides at once felt he was being too devious and dishonest.

Franco continued to show his gratitude for Nazi Germany's assistance during the Spanish Civil War. On July 14, 1941 he started sending over 18,000 volunteers to assist the Germans in the war. That number increased to some 47,000 Spaniards serving in what was called the Blue Division after the Falangists' blue shirts. They fought on the Russian front as the 250th German Division between mid 1940 and February 1944. By supplying soldiers Franco definitely violated the rules of neutrality. His actions went far beyond the scope of a non-belligerent and doubtlessly contributed to the prolongation of the war in Russia. Besides troops for the Russian front, Franco also supplied Germany with 8,000 Spanish workers. [408]

---

[406] Denis Smyth, Diplomacy and Strategy of Survival: British Policy and Franco's Spain., 1940-1941. (Cambridge, 1986), p. 2; cf. Neville Wylie, Britain, Switzerland and the Second World War. (Oxford and New York, 2003)

[407] Fernando Rosas, "Portuguese Neutrality in the Second World War," in: Neville Wylie (ed.), European Neutrals and Non-Belligerents During the Second World War. (Cambridge, 2002), pp. 272-273.

[408] Klaus-Joerg Ruhl, Spanien im Zweiten Weltkrieg. Franco, die Falange und das 'Dritte Reich'. (Hamburg, 1975), p. 63-64; Gerald R. Kleinfeld and Lewis A. Tambs, Hitler's Spanish Legion. The Blue Division. (Carbondale, 1979); Stanley G. Payne, The Franco Regime, 1939-1975. (Madison, 1975), p. 272 – During a visit to Madrid by Reichsführer (SS) Himmler, it is assumed that they also discussed cooperation between the Gestapo and the Spanish police, as well as preparing security for the Hitler-Franco meeting in Hendaye. Fernando Rosas, "Portuguese Neutrality in the Second World War," in: Neville Wylie (ed.), European Neutrals and Non-Belligerents During the Second World War. (Cambridge, 2002), pp. 272 – 273.

Nonetheless, Spain did cooperate with the Allied powers on humanitarian issues, permitting shot-down Allied airmen to cross Spain safely and offering a safe haven to escaped Allied POWs, civilian prisoners and Jews with transit documents who managed to flee to Spain across the Pyrenees. [409]

Return to Neutrality

Although remaining ideologically close to Germany and Italy, the Spanish government's confidence in an Axis victory gradually declined. Moreover, it became increasingly clear that Spain could not rely on Germany for supplies of essential goods such as food and crude oil. The country was forced to look west – to the United States and Latin American countries – for delivery of such goods which required obtaining export licenses from the Allied powers. Faced with these realities, Franco slowly curtailed his tête-à-tête with the Axis leaders which had started with his obvious and early support for Hitler, followed by a phase as a non-belligerent ally of Germany, and later – at the climax – seriously considered entering the war on the Axis' side. But by October 1943, Franco's political attachments to the Axis, if not his ideological attachments, were radically diminished. As the war turned, Franco returned to Spanish-style neutrality. On the occasion of the annual reception for the diplomatic corps on October 2, 1943, he used the word "neutral" to define Spain's position for the first time. His rediscovery of neutralism led Franco to order the 25th Blue Division back from the Russian front at the end of October 1943. [410] However, their pullout was not complete until 1944. The Blue Division was replaced by a steadily diminishing legion of Spanish volunteers who fought alongside the Germans until the bitter end. [411]

By 1943 Allied victories in North Africa and the collapse of the German offensive in Russia allowed both the USA and Spain to put aside their concerns about a possible German invasion. Franco, accommodating to all sides, began to play down his links with the Axis powers even further, and to emphasize his relations with the Vatican. On May 9, 1943, in the guise of a worried neutral power, he preached peace between the Axis and the Anglo-Saxon countries, "to avoid Communism … Russian barbarism waiting for its prey." [412]

But months before he changed his tune and started putting on the sheep's clothing of a born-again neutral, Franco had met the American ambassador, Hayes, who urged him to declare Spain's unrestricted neutrality. On that occasion, Franco replied that he could not yet declare total neutrality but that he was making

[409] Arnold Toynbee and Veronica M. Toynbee (ed.), The War and the Neutrals, In: Survey of International Affairs 1939-1941. (London and New York, 1956), p. 264-266, 291-293; Comisión de Investigación de las Transacciones de Oro Procedentes del III Reich durante la II Guerra of April 8, 1998, cf. Chaim U. Lipschitz, Franco, the Jews, and the Holocaust (1984); Haim Avni, Spain, the Jews and Franco (1982) Both authors differ considerably in their reports. While Lipschitz states that 28,500 Jewish refugees were sheltered in Spain, Avni estimates that only 7,500 Jews succeeded in fleeing to Spain.

[410] FRUS, Vol. II (1943), pp. 620-621

[411] Detlev F. Vagts, "Neutrality Law in World War II," in: Cardozo Law Review. Vol. 20 No. 2 December 1998, p. 468

[412] Elena Hernandez-Sandoica and Enrique Moradiellos, "Spain and the Second World War, 1939-1945," in: Neville Wylie (ed.), European Neutrals and Non-Belligerents During the Second World War. (Cambridge, 2002), p. 264

efforts to move in this direction. [413] Franco seems to have moved very slowly indeed, for a 1947 US State Department memo states that during the first four years of the war, Franco had acted in a decidedly non-neutral manner by supplying Nazi Germany with considerable amounts of strategically important goods, as well as giving military and intelligence assistance. Spanish wartime intelligence passed on to the Germans was supplied by a network of spies operated out of the Spanish embassies in Washington and London. These spying operations seem to have started in 1942. The Spanish did not suspect, though, that their messages were being systematically intercepted and decoded, and that the content was known to the US administration. [414]

All along Franco was on the hook for Spanish debts to the Axis powers. Hitler and Mussolini took full advantage of these debts – run up between 1936 and 1939 during the Civil War – as a means of exerting pressure. Germany, the main creditor, was particularly insistent on an immediate reduction in the debt, to which end they would accept minerals, food stuffs and raw materials. [415] The Allies constantly complained about Spain's extensive trade with Germany, but Franco responded that he had to export because he owed the Axis powers $212 million for war materials and army equipment from the Civil War years.

Spain Isolated

After 1942 Axis victory was becoming increasingly unlikely. Spain was in a severe bind. Franco not only had the wrong friends who were on the brink of losing the war, they were no longer in a position to supply Spain with urgently needed goods such as food stuffs, oil, technical equipment and capital. So Franco had to rely on his ideological adversaries to meet his country's most basic requirements for oil, cotton and grain, and other imports which saved the country from famine in the winter of 1940 and later from total economic collapse.

In spite of their otherwise restrained approach to Franco, at two points the Allies decided to force Spain to change sides by stopping the supply of crude oil. In the winter of 1941, shortly after the United States had entered World War II, they interrupted shipments of crude oil until Franco reluctantly agreed to stop selling that crude to Germany and Italy. Franco also had to accept American supervision in the form of an Iberian Peninsula Operating Committee which oversaw the allocation and use of crude oil in Spain. Obviously, the Americans were well aware that their oil had been passed on to the Third Reich.

Again during the winter of 1943/44 the Allies withheld oil deliveries until the Spanish regime agreed to stop supplying tungsten to Germany. The kid glove treatment of Spain was over. Franco would now certainly not enter the war on Hitler's side, and the Allied powers were confident of their eventual victory in Europe. They put pressure on Spain to weaken German resistance and accelerate

---

[413] FRUS, Vol. II. (1943), p. 612 – Airgram – 368 U.S. Ambassador Hayes to Secretary of State Hull Memorandum of Conversation between Hayes and Franco.

[414] Eizenstat (1998), p. 62

[415] W. M. Medlicott, The War and the Neutrals. (London, 1956), p. 264-266 and 291-293; The April 8, 1998, report of the El presidente de la Comisión de Investigación de las Transacciones de Oro Procedentes del III Reich durante la II Guerra; Eizenstat, (1998), p. 59.

the end of the conflict. But the Spanish government resisted for more than four months before yielding to Allied demands. [416]

The Spanish Market

Apart from the considerable debt binding Franco to the Axis powers, Spain (as Portugal) had the advantage of owning extremely valuable minerals urgently needed by Germany. As early as 1936 the Sociedad Financiera Industrial (SOFINDUS) had been established in Spain for the purpose of controlling trade relations with Germany. This large commercial conglomerate soon became the hub of a large Spanish-German trade. In 1937 and 1939 SOFINDUS granted preferential economic treatment to German companies in special bilateral agreements and by the beginning of the war had established a trade empire. Under the secret protocol of a German-Spanish agreement signed on March 31, 1939, Spain agreed to become a communication channel in the smuggling of goods from South America to Germany. A veritable armada of 53 ships under Spanish flag was created for this purpose. [417] While the Allied blockade was very efficient at stopping bulky cargoes, smaller items such as industrial diamonds or platinum – used as a catalyst in the production of nitrates and sulfuric acid -formed the bulk of smuggled goods and often were not picked off by Allied control nets. [418]

In May 1940 Spain signed a 3-year treaty granting Mussolini's Italy supplies of important goods. In 1942 the bulk of Spanish-German trade, which until then had consisted of food stuffs, shifted to minerals needed for the war effort. 70% of the mineral trade between the two states consisted of pyrite, a high-grade iron ore of which Spain had rich deposits. Tungsten remained at the top of the German import list and for the most part was only available through purchases from Spain and Portugal. Other raw materials such as zinc, lead and mercury were also supplied to Germany.

The first attempt to woo Spain from German influence started in March 1940 when Britain signed a contract to supply Spain with materials such as crude oil and fertilizers for six months. Spain in turn would deliver iron ore, minerals and citrus fruit to the Allies. These agreements were renewed every six months for the duration of the war. The Allied powers were aware of Franco's dealings with the enemy but accepted these transactions without protest.

In May 1943, when increased amounts of materials destined for the Axis powers began to be smuggled from South America to Spain, the USA started a program for buying up such materials at the origin of supply. Moreover, as the balance of the war started shifting in favor of the Allies, they ratcheted up pressure on Spain to curb trade with Germany, particularly with regard to arms and other essential goods.

---

[416] Op. cit., cf. also Herbert Feis, The Spanish Story. Franco and the Nations at War. (New York, 1966) L. Caruana and H. Rockhoff, "A Wolfram in Sheep's Clothing: Economic Warfare in Spain, 1940-1944," in: The Journal of Economic History, No. 63 Part 1 (2003), pp. 100-126

[417] Eizenstat (1998), p. 62

[418] W. M. Medlicott, The Economic Blockade. Bd. II (London, 1959), pp. 289-290

The Fight for Tungsten

A critical focus in the Spanish trade was on tungsten. Unlike Portugal which had a quota system, Spain operated an open market for tungsten. This gave a small advantage to the Allied powers that had better access to hard currencies. Nevertheless, the amount of tungsten they managed to acquire was tiny compared to the amounts obtained by the Germans. The Third Reich was obviously in a much stronger position. Indeed, by 1941 the Germans had developed most Spanish tungsten mines, controlled the largest supplier, SOFINDUS, and had bought up almost the entire tungsten ore output. [419]

By way of contrast, Britain during that period had only succeeded in getting its hands on a meager 32 tons of this much coveted mineral. Something had to be done. So, in early 1942, Britain and the USA swept into Spain with bags of money with the intent of outbidding the Germans and buying up as much tungsten ore as possible. Spain profited immensely from its gold mine of tungsten. Production shot up to almost double the previous year's output, and the price went from a pre-war $75 per ton to over $16,000 per ton in June 1943. The Allies bought the market using the façade of a bogus company and in 1942 succeeded in snatching at least 1,000 tons of tungsten from the Germans, about half of the overall production. The Nazis were furious and negotiated a new trade agreement with Spain in December 1942 which set out more precise allocations. In this agreement Spain undertook to supply Germany with fixed quantities of strategically important products, including tungsten, in exchange for coal, arms, fertilizers, chemicals and finished products. In addition, Spain granted Germany loans of 552.5 million pesetas ($50.2 million) to help cover their purchases. This agreement was not to last long, and each side blamed the other for failed deliveries. Spain now thought it appropriate to rack up the price, increasing the minimum for tungsten to $20,500 per ton. In order not to interrupt the incoming stream of wealth, Spain granted the financially strong Allied powers special permission to exchange dollars and pounds sterling for pesetas, giving them the chance to snap up tungsten at a time when German peseta reserves were running low. But as early as February 1943, Germany and Spain signed yet another secret agreement.

In order to facilitate ore smuggling from Portugal and Spain, Germany started to buy smaller mines on both sides of the border. The bulk of illegal trade was from Portugal to Spain which bordered on Axis territory. The Allies estimated that Germany smuggled almost 50 tons of tungsten across the border in spring 1943, and tried to limit German access to this coveted ore by buying huge amounts of tungsten on the Spanish black market. [420] In the meantime, the Third Reich, in summer 1943, was reaching the end of its financial means. But Franco did not abandon Hitler. In November 1943, the Spanish government granted Germany a loan of 100 million Reichsmarks, with 57% of that sum to be used to pay for tungsten and the remainder for costs connected with the purchase. It was, of course, in Franco's interest that the profitable sales of tungsten continue. By subsidizing

---

[419] Christian Leitz, "Nazi Germany's Intervention in the Spanish Civil War and the Foundation of Hisma/Rowak," in: Paul Preston and Ann L. Mackenzie (ed.), The Republic Besieged; Civil War in Spain 1936-1939. (Edinburgh, 1996), pp. 53-86

[420] Eizenstat (1998), pp. 67-68

German tungsten purchases he could be sure that this trade would continue, as long as both warring parties were able to buy tungsten at the now grossly inflated price. [421] He knew that if Germany stopped buying tungsten, the Allied powers would not need to continue making expensive purchases. This finally happened in the second half of 1944. In the meantime, American ambassador Carlton Hayes had been informed of Franco's agreement with Germany and requested that the Spanish government refrain from further tungsten deliveries to Germany while the Allied powers and Spain were holding negotiations on a tungsten agreement. Reports from January 1944 show that Germany had received larger amounts of tungsten than before: 225 tons were purchased in that month alone. [422] The request made by the American ambassador fell on deaf ears, and the British ambassador, Sir Samuel Hoare, who also tried to stop Franco from delivering more tungsten to the Nazis did not fare any better. Allied irritation about the Spanish attitude resulted in an immediate oil embargo.

After February 2, 1944, German buyers were no longer granted Spanish tungsten licenses and some obstacles to export were established. Nevertheless in April 1944, the third month of the Allied oil embargo, Germany succeeded in importing 198 tons of tungsten from Spain. [423]

The US government was demanding a total embargo of Spanish tungsten deliveries but faced a stubborn Spanish administration. It finally agreed to a compromise suggested by its British ally. The British urged yielding to Spanish demands not because of good will or generosity but because Spanish banks had refused to grant Britain peseta credits and British peseta reserves were nearly spent.

On May 2, 1944, Spain signaled that it was prepared to restrict tungsten deliveries to Germany to 580 tons, 300 tons of which had already been delivered. So Germany only got about half the amount supplied in the previous year. But German inventiveness in acquiring needed raw materials was not short-circuited that easily. Deciphered telegrams between SOFINDUS and Berlin show Germany succeeded in receiving some 865 tons through smuggling, or 285 tons more than the May agreement had granted them for the entire year. Smuggling was accomplished through German companies which sold tungsten to Spanish companies in Spain who transported the ore to France and then sold it back to Germany. Illicit Spanish tungsten exports to Nazi Germany were only stopped in August 1944 with the closure of the French border. [424]

Operation Safehaven

In spring 1944, the Allies began Operation Safehaven. It was designed to capture all German assets – both public and private – in neutral states and use these for reparation payments. Germany was to be denied any possibility of having these assets at its disposal after the war. Samuel Klaus of the US Foreign Economic Administration (FEA) was the head of the Safehaven team. He reported that Spain

---

[421] Christian Leitz, Nazi Germany and the Neutral Europe During the Second World War. (Manchester, 2000), p. 135
[422] Ibid., p. 136
[423] Ibid.
[424] Op. cit., p. 70

was both the most discouraging and the most difficult of all neutral countries, and that even the American ambassador to Spain, Carlton Hayes, was not very co-operative. Klaus remarked that because of corruption within the Spanish government, it was a child's play for Germany to cover up business dealings there. He reported that Tangier was being used as a channel for smuggling assets from Spain and Portugal to Argentina. Incidentally, Klaus' statements seem to confirm the secret program – drawn up by Bormann, head of the National Socialist Party Head Office and Hitler's deputy – for moving capital out of Germany towards the end of the war. [425]

In the fall of 1944, the Allied powers issued the first *formal* request to Spain to cease all gold transactions in favor of their enemy. But it was only on May 5, 1945, that Spain was ready to issue a decree to freeze all Axis assets. On May 7, 1945, the day the German Wehrmacht capitulated in Reims, Spain finally agreed to allow a British-American property task force to set up a trust to assemble both the official and semi-official assets of the German state in Spain. For mysterious reasons, there were soon problems with this agreement, too. A year later, in July 1946, the property task force had only succeeded in getting control of $25.3 million of German assets in Spain as compared to an estimate of $95 million. [426]

A lot of clues point to Spanish gold transactions, including evidence provided by the Allied secret services, records captured from the German Reichsbank, official declarations by Swiss banks and confiscated records from the offices of the quasi-official companies SOFINDUS and Transportes Marion. The most accurate estimate was that Spain had received gold worth $138.2 million, either directly from Germany or indirectly via Switzerland. [427]

Years after the war, according to a report issued by a Spanish Investigation Commission on April 8, 1998, Spain purchased gold for $75.8 million during the war years. Additional published figures show that, in spite of its many financial problems, the Spanish government succeeded in increasing its gold reserves – which had only been worth around US $49 million in 1940 – to US $124.3 million by 1945. [428] To do this, Spain purportedly used its trade balance to buy gold from non-German banks. A considerable amount came from the Netherlands.

So Spain, impoverished and hungry after the Civil War, managed to amass considerable gold reserves – just as it did after World War I – thanks to its substantial trade surplus. The circumstances of the two wars, however, differed greatly. During World War I, Spain had used its neutral position to profit from its agricultural and industrial products. Trade expanded and there was some prosperity amongst sections of the population, although there was also considerable social friction. However, in the early 1940s, Spanish trade plummeted since the country had lost France almost completely as a primary trading partner. Germany replaced France in that role. Moreover, it would not be inaccurate to say that Spain was able

---

[425] Ibid., p. 71

[426] Ibid., p. 74

[427] Ibid., p. 75

[428] El presidente de la Comisión de Investigación de las Transacciones de Oro Procedentes del III Reich durante la II Guerra of April 8, 1998, Gold holdings increased from $49 million to $124.3 million between 1940 and 1945.

to build up its trade surplus during World War II because Germany and the Allies were trying to outbid each other for Spain's outputs of minerals and other raw materials.

However trade with Germany did not give Spain the opportunity to buy gold. Spain's trade surplus was used to pay its outstanding debts to Germany, and trade between the two countries was regulated by a clearing agreement which allowed no exchange of gold or foreign currency. It was Spanish exports of food stuffs and minerals which gave Spain convertible currency for buying gold. [429]

Spain bought gold, not exclusively, but primarily from central banks such as the Swiss National Bank, the Bank of Portugal, Bank of England and – to a lesser extent – from the Bank for International Settlements and a private German-Spanish bank, the Banco Alemán Transatlántico. [430] According to the Bergier final report, Spain was the second-largest purchaser of gold from the Swiss National Bank. [431] And it was not the Bank of Spain which bought the most of this gold but the Spanish Institute for Foreign Currency (IEME). With one exception, when it acted as a cover for the Deutsche Reichsbank in a transaction with the Banco Alemán Transatlántico, IEME never bought gold directly from the Deutsche Reichsbank. The Spanish government can certainly be credited with considerable cleverness in using IEME for gold purchases and thus avoiding any direct contact with the Reichsbank over gold.

After the end of World War II the victorious Allies established an Asset Control Council which was entrusted with the difficult task of finding the precious metals seized by Germany from central banks in conquered countries and the property stolen from private individuals – mainly, but not exclusively Jews – and restoring it to is original owners. This council also dealt with the origin of the gold in Spanish possession, but could not establish definite proof of whether this gold was indeed stolen gold. Only gold which had been purchased directly from Germany could be confiscated. Whenever the gold had come from other sources, it had to be assumed that the owner had purchased it in good faith. Such gold could not be confiscated unless there was proof – in the shape of a mark or stamp affixed by a bank – that it was stolen.

The negotiations between IEME and the Allied Control Council were long, difficult and complex. Out of sheer exhaustion and the outbreak of the Cold War, the Allied powers came to adopt a more lenient attitude towards Franco. Only eight gold ingots were confiscated from Spain in 1948 and returned to their rightful owner, De Nederlandsche Bank. However, in spite of its accumulation of gold, Spain recovered very slowly in the post-war years. This was partly due to Franco's political and economic mismanagement which made recovery difficult. The main reason, however, for the slow recovery was that Spain was considered a pariah and was treated accordingly in the post-war years. In the course of the Potsdam

---

[429] Gabriel Tortella, "The Spanish Financial Sector During The Second World War," in: Joseph Jung, Herbert R. Reginbogin and Robert U. Vogler (ed.), Financial Markets of Neutral Countries during the Second World War. (in preparation by the Association of Financial History and the Principality of Liechtenstein)

[430] Ibid., p. 35

[431] Bergier Report, p. 248 – Spain was the second-largest purchaser of gold from the Swiss National Bank.

Conference, the Allied powers decided to refuse Spain membership in the United Nations because of its Fascist behavior. In December 1945, American ambassador Norman Armour left Madrid and the post was only filled again in 1951. Other nations also withdrew their ambassadors. In May 1946, a UN sub-committee published a report containing proof of Spain's Axis-friendly attitude, pro-Nazi activities and post-war support for Germany, including sheltering Nazi criminals, and suppression of political opposition. [432]

PORTUGAL

Portugal's geographical situation and its political interests naturally brought the country into a close relationship with Spain. In Portugal, as in neighboring Spain, businessmen, civil servants and even policemen were involved in smuggling activities for both the Allies and the Nazis. The Portuguese government had a tolerant attitude towards these undertakings. [433]

During the war, Portugal practiced what Assistant Secretary of State Dean Acheson described as "classic legal neutrality". This implied that Portugal tried to balance its trade with both sides. [434] Economic historian Nuno Valério assessed Portuguese economic policy until the summer of 1940 and after the fall of 1943 as "biased neutrality" (leaning towards Britain) and in other years as "geometrical neutrality" (leaning opportunistically). [435]

The decision by Dr. Antonio de Oliveira Salazar, prime minister of Portugal, to proclaim Portuguese neutrality on September 1, 1939, was based on both ideological and economic considerations. Salazar's declaration implied greater autonomy from Britain but a continuing, if less intense, collaboration between the two countries and was of course continuously influenced by political and military developments. On the other hand, for Portugal neutrality opened the prospect of profitable business opportunities with both warring parties. [436] In early September 1939, Salazar was convinced that this war would have no winners and no losers. [437]

Britain and Germany were guaranteed open trading in Portugal's domestic market as well as in its valuable colonial resources. Neutrality indeed brought a rich harvest for Portugal: its economy boomed. Salazar had the satisfaction of a trade balance which had gone from a deficit of $90 million in 1939 to a surplus of $68 million by 1943. During the first four years, assets in private banks nearly doubled, and the holdings of the Bank of Portugal almost tripled. Like Spain,

---

[432] FRUS, (1946), Vol.V., p. 1065-1090.

[433] Douglas L. Wheeler, "The Price of Neutrality; Portugal, the Wolfram Question and World War II," in: Luso-Brazilian Review, Vol. XXIII, Part II (1986), p. 97

[434] Dean Acheson, Present at the Creation: My Years in the State Department. (New York, 1969), p. 87

[435] Nuno Valério, "The Portuguese Capital Market During World War II," in: Joseph Jung, Herbert R. Reginbogin and Robert U. Vogler (ed.), Financial Markets of Neutral Countries during the Second World War. (in preparation by the Association of Financial History and the Principality of Liechtenstein)

[436] Fernando Rosas, "Portuguese Neutrality in the Second World War," in: Neville Wylie (ed.), European Neutrals and Non-Belligerents During the Second World War. (Cambridge, 2002), p. 272

[437] Ibid., p. 276

Portugal reaped huge benefits from the trade war raging between Germany and the Allied powers, who tried to keep each other from getting their hands on coveted tungsten with threats and lucrative deals. In spite of huge profits, Portugal, like Spain, depended on American deliveries of crude oil, coal, ammonia sulfate and wheat. These were important reasons for Salazar to continue the relationship with the Allied powers. However, the country's newly proclaimed neutrality also had its risks. Portugal's weak economy, its strategic position on the southwestern edge of Europe, its valuable colonial properties in the Atlantic, Africa, and the Far East, as well as its output of strategic products made the country a desirable target and may have drawn threats to its sovereignty . . . [438]

For German naval forces Portugal occupied an important strategic position because its many harbors along its Atlantic coast were extremely hard to blockade effectively by the British. But Salazar also had to deal with the risk of a German invasion. He saw two potential scenarios: an invasion of Portugal by the Germans – after all the German Wehrmacht, following the occupation of France, was now less than 260 miles away from Portuguese borders – or an alliance between Hitler and Franco which would mean that German troops might well be stationed directly on the Portuguese border. [439]

British-Portuguese Relations

Until the summer of 1940 there were no good land links between Portugal and Germany. With some reservations, Portugal did not see itself as high on Germany's invasion list and continued to maintain its traditional relationships with Britain. While Portugal itself was rather at ease with this association, Britain had already taken into account a possible German attack on Portugal even before the defeat of France. In case of such an attack Britain had asked its Portuguese ally to reserve strategically important redoubts on the Cape Verde Islands and in the Azores for British occupation. [440]

The close political and emotional links between Portugal and Britain existed long before the outbreak of World War II, dating back to the Anglo-Portuguese Alliance of the 14th century. [441] During World War I, Portugal had joined Britain and sent 50,000 soldiers to the western front. In 1938, Britain was Portugal's most important trade partner. [442]

Portugal's links with Germany had no such deep roots. Relations dated only back to the time of the Spanish civil war, when Portugal's strong man, Dictator Antonio de Oliveira Salazar, openly sympathized with Franco and Hitler. Salazar had assisted Germany in smuggling arms to Franco's troops [443] and had also sup-

---

[438] Eizenstat (1998), p. 24

[439] Ibid., p. 23

[440] Glyn Stone, The Oldest Ally: Britain and the Portuguese Connection, 1936-1941. (Rochester, 1994), p. 157

[441] Fernando Rosas, "Portuguese Neutrality in the Second World War," in: Neville Wylie (ed.), European Neutrals and Non-Belligerents During the Second World War. (Cambridge, 2002), p. 268 The old alliance of 1386 was renewed by the Treaty of Windsor in 1899.

[442] Eizenstat (1998), p. 23

[443] Christian Leitz, Nazi Germany and the Neutral Europe During the Second World War. (Manchester, 2000), p. 145

plied volunteers to Franco. Salazar hoped that closer cooperation with the Axis powers would result in economic growth and lasting stability for his country. In late 1938 Portugal's trade with Germany was second only to its trade with Britain. However this did not prevent Salazar from protesting Hitler's invasion of Catholic Poland – and immediately thereafter declaring Portuguese neutrality. [444]

With the end of the Spanish civil war and the crushing of the Popular Front, National Socialist Germany and Fascist Italy had gained a foothold on the Iberian Peninsula. An expansion of the European conflict was becoming increasingly likely and Salazar wanted to make sure that Spain's support of the Axis powers would not have any negative consequences for Portugal. Quite rightly, Salazar feared that neutrality would not protect Portugal if Spain were to be drawn into the conflict. Salazar's top priority therefore was keeping Franco neutral.

In October 1940 cash-strapped Britain called upon long-standing links between the two countries to move Portugal to conclude a payments agreement. This gave Britain the option of buying Portuguese products with pounds sterling or getting credit for escudos and consequently a competitive edge in the struggle against Germany for Portuguese outputs. Britain's gold reserves were low and both Sweden and Switzerland, with whom no such financial good will relations existed, demanded gold for their products. [445] By the end of the war, this type of cash-on-the-barrelhead trade drove British debt to roughly $322 million. [446]

Portugal's Tungsten

Portugal's economic boom during the war years was also largely based on its rich tungsten resources. In addition to basic military applications, tungsten could also be used for the filaments of light bulbs. However in those days the metal was not attractive for its ability to shed light in the dark, but rather the opposite. Tungsten was essential for the production of ammunition. German industry almost exclusively used tungsten carbide to produce projectiles capable of piercing enemy armor. The Third Reich's armament production depended completely on the tungsten of two countries, Portugal and Spain, and on those countries' willingness to supply the ore.

In view of the amounts requested by Germany and its extraordinary efforts to secure supplies of ore, the Allies powers were bound to notice the German armament industry's Achilles heel in Portugal. While tungsten was equally important in Allied arms production, the Allies had other sources and did not have to rely exclusively on Spanish and Portuguese sources. But in order to withhold this valuable metal from the Nazis, the Allied powers bought any tungsten they could get – either legally or illegally – in Portugal and in Spain. As a consequence of intense competition between the warring parties for the coveted ore, the price for tungsten soared from a pre-war 2,800 Reichsmarks per ton to 60,000-65,000 Reichsmarks

[444] Op. cit.

[445] Neville Wylie, "The Swiss Franc and British Policy Towards Switzerland 1939-1945," in: Sebastian Guex (ed.), Switzerland and the Great Powers 1914-1945. (Geneva, 1999), pp. 461-480

[446] Op. cit., p. 25

per ton in the first two months of 1942. Production rose from 2,419 tons in 1938 to 6,500 tons in 1942. [447]

In order to balance out its neutrality, Portugal allocated quotas of tungsten in 1942. This system permitted all sides to export ore from their own mines as well as a fixed percentage from independent Portuguese mines. Britain owned the largest mine, France the second-largest, while Germany was the proprietor of two medium-sized combines and several smaller mines. Germany was awarded a favorable percentage of the output of independent mines because it agreed to supply Portugal with urgently needed products in return. In January 1942 the two countries concluded a secret trade agreement which included an export license for 2,800 tons of tungsten. In return, Portugal received coal, steel and fertilizer from Germany, products essential to Portugal which the Allies could not or would not supply. [448]

A year later the Allied powers tried to negotiate a new tungsten agreement. In return, Salazar demanded price reductions for various products, such as ammonium sulfate, oil derivatives and other goods. When the Allies declined, Portugal was angry and refused to increase Allied export licenses. Portugal moved immediately to conclude a new agreement with Germany.

Legal tungsten production eventually reached an annual average of 22,800 tons. The largest part, 14,000 tons, went to Britain, 1,600 tons were exported to the United States and 6,200 tons went to Germany. In addition, there were 300 tons for Italy and 500 tons for France. The remaining 200 tons were supplied to other countries. But these were just the legal allocations. [449]

As was to be expected, there was also illegal, unregulated ore production. The greater financial capacity of the Allied powers proved advantageous for transactions on the black market. But ultimately the quota system worked in favor of Germany and as a result Portugal became Germany's main supplier of tungsten by spring 1944. After this date the Allied ban on supply – although never completely enforced – and the later unavailability of usable land links between the two countries quickly curbed the supply of Portuguese tungsten to Germany. [450]

The value of all legal and illegal Portuguese goods going to Germany during the war is estimated to have been between 3,239 and 5,335 million escudos. Seen from a quantitative point of view, this amount provided a significant but not crucial contribution to the German war effort. [451] But qualitatively, tungsten was very different. It was perhaps the single most important product for the German war effort. So in the case of Portugal, it may be said that its tungsten deliveries to Nazi Germany definitely helped to prolong the war.

---

[447] Christian Leitz, Nazi Germany and the Neutral Europe During the Second World War. (Manchester, 2000), p. 158

[448] op.cit., p. 29

[449] Ibid., p. 8

[450] Ibid., p. 9

[451] Nuno Valério, "The Portuguese Capital Market During World War II," in: Joseph Jung, Herbert R. Reginbogin and Robert U. Vogler (ed.), Financial Markets of Neutral Countries during the Second World War. (in preparation by the Association of Financial History and the Principality of Liechtenstein)

Parallel to the tungsten negotiations, talks were held with the Allied powers concerning acquisition of military bases on the Azores. The sea war in the Atlantic was reaching a climax and the islands were to serve as important bases for Allied submarines. The Allies' original plan of taking over the Azores altogether had been given up so as not to provoke a German reprisals attack on Portugal. Instead the Allied powers implored long-standing Anglo-Portuguese relationships and Portugal finally agreed to sign a contract with Britain on August 17, 1943, permitting Britain to use these much coveted islands from October 1943. Towards the end of the year, use by the US Air Force was also included in this agreement. [452]

Portugal depended on the goodwill of the United States for its supplies of crude oil and other important products. In April 1944 the Allied powers exploited this fact by putting economic pressure on Salazar to force him to stop tungsten deliveries to Germany. On June 5, 1944, this blackmail proved successful, and Portugal officially stopped supplying Germany with tungsten. The Allied powers achieved their goal because Salazar could no longer withstand British pressure and because the threat of German reprisals was no longer to fear. [453]

Germany reacted to this decision by pretending its Portuguese tungsten mines were of no importance, selling them and buying other companies. By the end of June, the Allied powers estimated that the Nazis had salted away about 2 million dollars in hotels, cinemas, etc. At the same time, a German submarine stopped and seized a Portuguese vessel, an event which supposedly outraged the Portuguese, conveniently just in time for the end of the war. The USA took advantage of this shift in mood and started further negotiations with Portugal on establishing bases for the American Air Force on the Azores. The Portuguese insisted that any deal was dependant on reaching an agreement over necessary supplies and services. This happened on November 28, 1944, and the contract was signed. In return, the Americans generously permitted the Portuguese to take part in the fighting to liberate Portuguese Timor which was still occupied by Japan. [454]

Portugal's Gold

On May 6, 1945, under pressure from the Allies, Portugal confiscated all German government buildings on its territory. 5,000 gold sovereigns were found in the German embassy in Lisbon. On May 14, 1945, Portugal took a further step and adopted Law 34,600 which forced registration and freezing of all German assets in Portugal. In addition, a licensing system was created for releasing such confiscated assets. Trading in foreign currencies was strictly prohibited. On May 23, Portugal extended this legislation to all its colonies. [455]

On September 3, 1946, negotiations were started between Portugal and the Allied powers on taxing, liquidating and distributing German assets. However, no agreement could be reached on any of these issues during the Lisbon talks between 1946 and 1947. Portugal obstinately insisted that it was not obliged to return gold received during the war in return for supplying raw materials to the Nazis and

---

[452] op.cit., p. 34

[453] op. cit., pp. 35-36

[454] Ibid., p. 36

[455] Ibid., p. 38

even went so far as to claim that between 1938 and 1945 no gold at all had been transported from Germany to Portugal. Portugal maintained that its positive trade balance with Britain had led to British debts of about 81 million pounds and to the accumulation of a large sterling account with the Bank of Portugal.

Post-war investigations, however, showed that the Bank of Portugal received 49 tons of gold from the Deutsche Reichsbank. All German payments went via the Schweizerische Nationalbank (SNB) where Portugal kept three accounts. One account was used for the transfer of gold which served to pay for the SNB's purchase of escudos from the Banco de Portugal. The second account was used for gold with which the Bank of Portugal financed the purchase of Swiss francs. The third account essentially closed the circle, since it was used for the gold which Berlin had deposited in the Banco de Portugal's account with the SNB in Zurich.[456]

All in all, the following totals of gold arrived in the Bank of Portugal: 167 tons from the Federal Reserve Bank of New York, 104 tons from the Schweizerische Nationalbank and 28 tons from other countries. These deliveries occurred despite the absence of any positive trade balance with the senders. In the case of the Schweizerische Nationalbank and other sources, it must be assumed that Portuguese gold acquisitions were partly financed by Swiss francs coming from the Deutsche Reichsbank and partly by foreign currency brought into the country by refugees. In the case of the Federal Reserve Bank of New York, the Portuguese gold acquisitions implied the existence of a dollar account in the Bank of Portugal in spite of the negative trade balance with the United States during the period in question. This also supports the contention that significant so-called invisibles had been moved from the USA to Portugal during the war.[457]

At 14% of the total, German gold was only a small part of the gold amassed in the Bank of Portugal.[458] The Portuguese insisted that they had accepted the gold in good faith in payment for international transactions and therefore would not agree to return it.

In early August 1945, US financial attaché James Wood requested information concerning secret gold transactions with the Third Reich from the Secretary General and the Vice Governor of the Bank of Portugal as well as from the Portuguese Foreign Office. He received no answer. In May 1946 the bank's directorate still maintained that the bank never accepted gold from Germany.

In the meantime, Otto Fletcher of the State Department had prepared an estimate of Portugal's gold transactions during the war based on German wartime acquisitions of stolen gold, its sales to the Schweizerische Nationalbank, and statements by Swiss government officials and secret service data from the War Ministry concerning the transport of gold by truck from Switzerland to Portugal. Fletcher's modest estimate was that Portugal had received gold worth $139.3 million dur-

---

[456] Antonio Louca and Ansgar Schäfer, "Portugal and the Nazi Gold: The 'Lisbon Connection' in the Sales of Looted Gold by the Third Reich." cf.

http//www.yad.vashem.org.il/download/about_holocaust/studies/louca_full.pdf

[457] All figures on gold acquisition are based on the official reports presented by the Bank of Portugal and on the 1999 Report of the "Commission of Research on Gold Transactions between Portuguese and German Authorities during the Period between 1936 and 1945". They are in principle identical to the figures in the Eizenstat Report.

[458] Ibid.

ing the war. He was convinced that gold worth $22.6 million had been stolen from Belgium and at least 72% or $84 million of the remaining $116.7 million worth of gold which Portugal received from the Schweizerische Nationalbank was stolen German gold. [459]

The Allied powers suggested that Portugal should return $50.5 million. The amount was based on the argument that this was all gold that had been received after 1942 when it was generally known that the German gold reserves had increased by plunder all over Europe. Portugal responded that it had not been informed of these thefts and had accepted the gold in good faith. And that was that. The negotiations with Portugal dragged on until the 1950s, and finally the Allied demands for return of the gold failed miserably. The Portuguese were only prepared to return gold worth US $4.4 million. [460]

Documents show that the Portuguese authorities were not forthright in this matter. Victor Gautier, a high-ranking employee of the Schweizerische Nationalbank, sums up the content of a meeting with Albino Garble Peso, Secretary General of the Bank of Portugal, reporting that Peso told him the Bank of Portugal would not buy any Nazi gold directly, partly for political reasons and partly from legal caution. But if the gold went via the Swiss National Bank, these objections would disappear. Peso thought that someone ought to examine the matter. [461] This and other statements in the Gautier Report clearly demonstrate that the Portuguese were not only interested in Nazi gold, but also informed about its origin and that they wanted to keep a clean slate by choosing to purchase it via Switzerland.

At the beginning of the war, Portugal used the Bank for International Settlement (BIZ) and Yugoslav gold accounts with the Schweizerische Bankverein in Basel to transfer – and thereby conceal – purchases of Nazi gold. But the German invasion of Yugoslavia soon brought an end to this arrangement. In 1941 Portugal had to look for other routes. On January 8, 1942, the director of the BIZ, Thomas McKittrick, received a letter from Montagu C. Norman, director of the Bank of England, informing him: "As I hear, the BIZ organizes gold transports from Switzerland to Lisbon. I must warn you that our authorities look upon these gold transfers with an extremely suspicious eye." [462] This meant that Norman would no longer approve gold transfers from the BIZ to Portugal. Apart from the Bank of Portugal, the Portuguese Banco Espirito Santo also played a major role in financing business with Nazi Germany. An FEA report dated October 1945 accuses this bank of having been the financial agent for German tungsten transactions. After the Allied powers had forced the Banco Espirito Santo to sever its connections with Germany, the Germans transferred their accounts to the Banco Lisboa

---

[459] Eizenstat (1998), p. 42

[460] Ibid., p. 54

[461] Schweizerische Nationalbank, Zürich – Report by Victor Gautier "Voyage à Lisbonne et à Madrid du 12 au 26 Octobre 1941."

[462] Gian Trepp, Die Bank für Internationalen Zahlungsausgleich im Zweiten Weltkrieg: Bankgeschäfte mit dem Feind. Von Hitlers Europabank zum Instrument des Marschallplans. (Zurich, 1993), p. 63

e Açores. [463] The Banco Espirito Santo, however, also cooperated with American businessmen. [464]

In addition to official purchases, considerable amounts of gold were smuggled to Portugal. During interrogation after the war, the German commercial attaché in Madrid admitted that between 1943 and 1944 he transferred nearly a million dollars in English gold coins from Berlin to the German embassy in Lisbon by diplomatic courier. [465]

Another report points out that in June and July 1944 gold worth $360,000 was moved into Portugal and deposited with the Bank of Portugal under the name of the German ambassador. The bank's director admitted that various other high-ranking officials, including Franco's brother, then the Spanish ambassador in Portugal, as well as the Uruguayan ambassador and members of the German and the Vichy embassies in Portugal had smuggled in considerable amounts of gold, diamonds, bonds, banknotes and other valuables for deposit in private banks. [466]

As far as other German assets were concerned, the Allied powers and the Portuguese soon reached an impasse. As they had done with gold, the Portuguese now used the same arguments and refused to liquidate assets, even before the gold issue was resolved. These negotiations took place intermittently – sometimes formally, sometimes informally. They went on and on. By drawing out the talks, Portugal sought time to reduce – and perhaps conceal – the value of the confiscated German assets. They were masters in this field.

Incidentally, an OSS memo (the OSS or Office of Strategic Services was the precursor of the CIA) dated February 7, 1946, revealed that Portugal had received roughly 124 tons of Nazi gold worth $139.3 million and that American negotiators knew this. [467] Nevertheless they agreed to only $4.4 million worth of gold being returned. So, why this sudden modesty? As is so often the case, manifestly unfair decisions are reached at the price of resolving complex political interests. In the negotiations from the end of the war to 1953, the American stance on Portuguese gold may have been influenced by the fact that American negotiators were seeking permanent military bases on the Azores at the same time. [468]

Sought-After Azores

During the war, Portugal had granted the US Air Force permission to use British installations on the Azores but refused permission for a solely American base since "he (Salazar) is trying to remain neutral." [469] In July 1947, the State Department instructed its negotiating team to seek a compromise with Portugal on the

---

[463] Eizenstat (1998), p. 41

[464] NARA, RG 28, 370/13/33/02 Entry 98A File C-11-19711A Box 597 – Intelligence Report, June 30, 1943. According to an intercepted telegram of spring 1943 by Keith A. Wook in the context of the negotiations between the USA and Portugal concerning zinc, the "Banco Espirito Santo" was prepared to contribute $11 million for six months and without guarantee, for the purchase and financing of zinc transactions.

[465] op.cit.

[466] Ibid.

[467] Ibid., p.42

[468] Ibid., p. 54

[469] Ibid., p. 34

gold issue. The reason for this surprising change of position was the extraordinary importance the Azores had for the USA still after the end of the war. In 1945 the Joint Chiefs had put the islands on a list of the nine most important strategic bases for maintaining the security of the United States. So the gold issue was put on ice, at least until an agreement on Azores bases was signed and sealed.

How often are publicly proclaimed principles quietly moved aside when national security interests are at stake. In 1948, Treasury Secretary Robert Lovett wrote that "overriding political and strategic considerations of our foreign policy make it essential" to unfreeze Portuguese assets in the USA. [470] A week later, Portuguese accounts in the USA were unblocked by the Treasury Department and the USA permanently lost leverage to exert pressure on Portugal. [471]

On July 17, 1951, the State Department sent a telex to the American embassy in Lisbon with instructions to accept the Portuguese conditions. This decision was no doubt made because of what were considered pressing political and military concerns. [472] In 1949 Portugal had become a full member of NATO. Negotiating a long-term lease for an air force base on the Azores was high on the list of American priorities. The last agreement had resulted – in spite of the American restraint in the gold issue – in only a 5-year lease. Cold War priorities and consultations with the British led the State Department to recommend that the negotiators accept Portugal's returning only $4.4 million of gold, instead of the originally demanded $50.5 million – and with that at last have the troublesome gold problem off the table once and for all. However, the US Treasury was only prepared to agree to the State Department compromise upon receipt of a letter signed by an Assistant Secretary of State. Such a letter was necessary to confirm that political concerns justified the reduced settlement and that no agreement would contain clauses which might lead to claims later against the United States. This request was granted and the then Assistant Secretary for European Affairs James Bonbright signed an appropriate letter to Treasury Secretary Snyder along with a memorandum from US-Ambassador Lincoln MacVeagh noting his concurrence in the proposal. [473] On June 24, 1953, American gold negotiations with Portugal were ended. As they had done during the war, the Portuguese now made the conclusion of the agreement on American use of the Azores contingent a prior agreement with West Germany over gold claims. It was in June 1958 when Portugal finally signed such an agreement with the Federal Republic of Germany and only in 1959, fourteen years after the end of World War II, was Portugal prepared to return $4.4 million in gold.

---

[470] FRUS (1948), Vol. III, p. 1000-1001 Portuguese assets in the United States were frozen for a certain time in order to force the Portuguese government to negotiate. At the same time, the USA permitted Portugal to be one of the beneficiaries of the Marshall Plan. The crucial point in the negotiations was not the Nazi gold, it was the desire to get Portugal to accept permanent American military bases on the Azores.

[471] op. cit., p. 50

[472] Ibid., p. 53

[473] Ibid., p. 55

SWEDEN

When World War II broke out on September 1, 1939, both the United States and the Soviet Union declared their neutrality. They had little else in common and in the following years, their interests were directed at politically very different countries. The American administration under President Roosevelt started bending the laws of neutrality in favor of France and Britain. The Soviet government under Joseph Stalin was closer to Germany, aimed at keeping its credit agreement with that country of August 19, 1939, as well as implementing the Hitler-Stalin non-aggression Pact of August 23, 1939. The Soviet Union also supported the Third Reich by delivering raw materials of vital importance to the war effort, which Germany was not receiving because of the Allied blockade. In return, Hitler's Germany became the Soviet Union's most important supplier of armaments and weapons – armament technology in exchange for raw materials. [474]

On the western front all was still quiet. The French remained in their bunkers along the Maginot Line, the British – with very few troops deployed on the continent – did little but enforce their maritime rights, and the Germans held fast behind the Siegfried Line or rather the West wall. Instead, the demons of war had been unleashed in northeast Europe close to Sweden where the National Socialists and Communists were in the process of tearing up Poland. While Germany had rapidly subjugated the badly equipped Polish army and had occupied the western part of the country, the Soviets, acting on a secret clause in the Hitler-Stalin non-aggression Pact, marched into the eastern half of Poland two weeks after the German invasion.

For Hitler, the non-aggression Pact with the Soviet Union of August 23, 1939, was a precondition for his attack on Poland. This treaty gave him the assurance that he would not be involved in a war on two fronts. On the erroneous assumption that Britain and France – in continuation of their until now demonstrated submissiveness – would tolerate the German occupation of Poland and not intervene, Hitler believed himself to be safe.

The Hitler-Stalin non-aggression Pact in which those nations had undertaken to "refrain from any act of violence, any aggressive action and any attack on the other party, both individually and in conjunction with other powers" included a secret additional protocol. [475] In this protocol, the area between Germany and Russia was to be divided into spheres of interest. The states of Finland, Estonia, and Latvia were to go to the Soviet Union, while Lithuania would come under German rule. In addition, the further existence of a Polish state – although with a significantly reduced territory – was not excluded. But as early as September 20, 1939, the Russian foreign minister, Molotov, informed the German ambassador in Moscow that Joseph Stalin was not in favor of Poland surviving as an independent state at all and wished to negotiate a final German-Soviet border essentially eliminating Poland from the map. On September 28, 1939, German foreign minister Joachim Ribbentrop signed the German-Soviet Border and Friendship Agreement

---

[474] Hans-Jürgen Perrey, Der Russlandausschuss der deutschen Wirtschaft. (Munich, 1985), p. 293

[475] Horst Günther Linke (ed.), "Quellen zu den Deutsch-Sowjetischen Beziehungen 1917-1945". (Darmstadt, 1998), p. 202; Rolf-Dieter Müller, "Von der Wirtschaftsallianz zum kolonialen Ausbeutungskrieg" in: Das Deutsche Reich und der Zweite Weltkrieg. (Stuttgart, 1983), p. 165

defining the borders of the partitioned former Polish state as final. The division of territories in the secret August protocol was altered as well, so that now Lithuania would belong to the Soviet sphere of interest, and only a narrow strip of land in the southwest of the country was to come under German rule.[476] In January 1941, Germany sold its Lithuanian sphere of interest to the Soviet Union for the price of 7.5 million gold dollars or 31.5 million Reichsmarks.[477] By the time this deal was concluded, Plan Barbarossa – the German invasion on the USSR – had already been prepared.

So Poland was divided up for the fourth time in its history – one part for Germany, the other for the Soviet Union. There was a clear agreement that the two powers could do what they liked in the territories occupied by them. At the hands of these two totalitarian regimes, other states simply lost their independence, were annexed and exploited.[478]

The 'Winter War'

The Russians immediately started to build fortresses in the Baltic States of Estonia, Latvia and Lithuania, and also tried to do the same in Finland, which lay only about 25 kilometers away from Russia's second-largest city, Leningrad. However, Finland refused to let the Russians use Finnish territory or to concede them military rights inside its borders. When the Russians realized that negotiations would not allow even one Russian to put a foot on Finnish soil, Russia crossed the Finnish border invading Finland on November 30, 1939, which has come to be known as the 'Winter War'.

In response to this Russian act of aggression, the General Assembly of the League of Nations expelled the Soviet Union from the League, and requested that all other nations grant material assistance and humanitarian aid to Finland. Suddenly Sweden, which had been neutral since the beginning of hostilities, was put on the spot. Although Finland had not asked the Western powers for assistance, both France and Britain sought permission to use Swedish territory for transit privileges to support Finland with troops and materials. These Allied requests were not due to Christian brotherly-love, support for a democratic nation, or upholding international law. Instead Britain and France were seeking to establish a separate front in northern Sweden which would be problematical for Germany and in the process gain control of Sweden's valuable iron ore mines. Germany reacted quickly saying it would not tolerate Allied troops on Swedish soil and would respond with accordingly responsive measures – force.[479] Caught in the middle, Sweden refused transit to the Allied troops.

However in the meantime, weapons and ammunition were indeed supplied to Finland by the Western powers. But, according to an account by Prime Minister

---

[476] Lothar Gauchmann, Der Zweite Weltkrieg. Kriegführung und Politik. (Munich, 1967), p.32

[477] Akten zur Deutschen Auswärtigen Politik 1918-1945 (ADAP), Series D (1937-1941), Vol. XI, 2, p. 889

[478] Walther Hofer, Die Diktatur Hitlers bis zum Beginn des Zweiten Weltkrieges. (Constance, 1960), pp. 210-211

[479] Ulf Brandell, "Die Transitfrage in der schwedischen Aussenpolitik während des Zweiten Weltkrieges" in: Rudolf L. Bindschedler et al. (ed.), Schwedische und schweizerische Neutralität im Zweiten Weltkrieg. (Basle, 1985), p. 83

Chamberlain in the British House of Commons on March 19, 1940, the amounts were insignificant. [480] Why then should a special effort be made? After all Britain had not succeeded in its primary aim of stationing troops in Sweden and was in the midst of a hectic rearmament build-up leaving Finland more or less left to its own devices.

At the outset the American government vigorously condemned the Russian invasion of Finland and expelled Soviet technicians and engineers from the USA. [481] Nevertheless, the US administration wanted to avoid an open breach with Russia, and American assistance to Finland ultimately was, like that of the European Allied powers, minimal.

The Russo-Finnish war lasted only four months. The Finns put up a brave fight, but they could be no equal to the Soviet Union. In February 1940, the Russians used massive artillery to break through the Finnish Mannerheim Line and advanced north towards the town of Viipuri (Vyborg).

The Finns' failure to get weapons and supplies, if not from Britain or France, then at least from the United States, doomed the Finnish resistance. Without artillery or planes – which the United States would not supply – exhausted Finland could not hold out despite heroic efforts. So the Finnish foreign minister approached the Kremlin about an armistice. The Soviets, eager to end a campaign which had already lasted far too long and resulted in significant Russian losses, were prepared to negotiate. In the resulting Treaty of Moscow signed on March 12, 1940, Finland had to renounce parts of its territory and permit the establishment of a large Soviet naval base on the Hangö peninsula. However, Finland did manage to retain its sovereignty and its political system. [482]

The short duration of the war and the peace of March 1940 had spared Roosevelt considerable embarrassment as being portrayed as a liar before the entire world. There existed a stark contrast between the proclaimed great support for Finland and the silent inactivity of Roosevelt's administration to carry through. However, once the peace treaty was signed in March, the American export-import bank granted Finland a loan of $20 million, a sum which Secretary Morgenthau increased to $30 million – perhaps to assuage a guilty conscience – saying to his staff that the peace in Finland gave America an opportunity of doing "a constructive piece of work" there. [483] The Finnish government suddenly found itself with American dollars which it had urgently needed before the armistice to buy planes and artillery. During the short war, however, it was Sweden which had come to Finland's assistance and had tried to support its neighbor, who was ready to do battle with the Russians, with much needed weapons, food and some 7,000 to 10,000 volunteers. [484]

---

[480] Ibid., pp. 82-83

[481] Horst Günther Linke (ed.), Quellen zu den Deutsch-Sowjetischen Beziehungen 1917-1945. (Darmstadt, 1998), p. 410

[482] Max Jacobson, The Diplomacy of the Winter War. (Cambridge, 1961), pp. 261-266

[483] Henry Morgenthau, Morgenthau Diaries, March 14, 1940 pp. 247-249

[484] Neville Wylie (ed.), European Neutrals and Non-Belligerents During the Second World War. (Cambridge, 2002), p. 315; Christian Leitz, Nazi Germany and the Neutral Europe During the Second World War. (Manchester, 2000)

As early as September 1, 1939, after news of the German attack on Poland had spread, Sweden had declared its neutrality and reaffirmed that stance on September 3, 1939, in reaction to the French and British declaration of war with Germany. The country's chosen emphasis on *absolute* neutrality was manifestly intended to keep Sweden out of the war. Used this way – as an immediate, tactical maneuver – the concept of neutrality became less a matter of principle than something far more flexible, an option that could be chosen, and potentially reversed, based on the probable outcome of the war. [485] During the Winter War Sweden remained officially a non-belligerent, but favored Finland and gave that country, unlike all other nations, major support.

Neutrality had become a word which could take on many meanings. In Sweden itself the Winter War caused a political crisis over disagreements about what Swedish neutrality was supposed to mean, how it should be adapted to events abroad and what steps should be taken to keep Sweden out of any future war between Axis and Allied powers. It soon became clear that the two leading Social Democrats, prime minister Per Albin Hansson and his foreign minister Rickard Sandler, had completely different views about how Swedish neutrality was to be interpreted. Sandler insisted that democracy in Scandinavia would ultimately depend on the survival of democracies in other parts of Europe. He believed that absolute neutrality was morally impossible, particularly if Sweden were to make any contribution at all to the struggle for democracy and against fascism. [486] The prime minister, in contrast, was only interested in one goal: peace for Sweden. In a speech to the Swedish nation on September 1, 1939, he explained his reasoning: Swedes should "join together with calm determination around the great task of holding our nation out of war." [487] Hansson was to stand by his resolve to keep Sweden out of war throughout World War II – accepting peace-at-any-price in conflict with legal rules of neutrality.

In order to implement his plans for this 'Swedish' neutrality, Hansson formed in December 1939 a broad coalition with the bourgeois parties – excluding the Communists. Foreign Minister Sandler immediately resigned from office and was replaced by Christian Günther, a career diplomat without party affiliation. Sandler's replacement gave Hansson the freedom to reduce Swedish support for Finland since he had now an ally in Günther who strongly supported Hansson's goal of keeping Sweden out of the war at all costs. [488] In the following war years, Günther and Hansson were intent to defuse all dangerous points of contention with both the Third Reich and the Allied powers. [489]

---

[485] Martin Fritz, "Wirtschaftliche Neutralität während des Zweiten Weltkrieges," in: Rudolf L. Bindschedler et al. (ed.), Schwedische und schweizerische Neutralität im Zweiten Weltkrieg. (Basle, 1985), p. 48

[486] Paul Levine, Swedish Neutrality During the Second World War: Tactical Success or Moral Compromise?," in: Neville Wylie (ed.), European Neutrals and Non-Belligerents During the Second World War. (Cambridge, 2002), p. 311

[487] Ibid., p. 312

[488] Ibid., p. 320

[489] Ibid., pp. 315-316

But Swedish neutrality was immediately put to the test by the German invasion of Norway and Denmark on April 9, 1940. In reaction to the new situation the Swedish government declared that it would continue its neutral policy and that no foreign power was permitted to use Swedish territory. A Norwegian request to transport ammunition across Swedish territory was rejected and Norway was – as a precautionary measure – informed that earlier Swedish deliveries to Finland had been unique exception since the Finnish-Soviet conflict had been completely separate from the larger war between the Allies and Germany. [490]

While the German Wehrmacht had overcome resistance in Denmark quite quickly, the military campaign against Norway did not run so smoothly. More efforts and resources were needed than Hitler had planned. The battle for Narvik in particular was fierce, with the Allies supplying aid to the Norwegians. In the following weeks, the trio Ribbentrop, Göring and von Weizsäcker tried in vain to persuade the Swedish government to permit goods to be transported to German troops in Norway via Sweden. Their attempts were uniformly refused by the Swedish government. In late April, the Germans again approached Sweden with a request for the transit of clothing, food stuffs, bandages/surgical dressings and other articles for German soldiers. The Swedish government refused to allow the transit of articles for the 'equipment and maintenance of fighting troops', but permitted, in consideration of Narvik being a 'special case' – a single shipment of humanitarian aid in view of the crisis in and around Narvik. Hitler's personal intervention resulted in German personnel being allowed to escort the goods which Sweden thus far refused. The Germans used the one time pledge to allow over 30 railway carriages marked with red crosses through Swedish territory, including 40 so-called medical orderlies. [491]

During this early and successful phase of the war, the Germans were indeed arrogant. When Sweden remained reluctant to accept major violations of its neutrality, German diplomacy turned quickly into hostile intimidations. In a meeting with Swedish businessman Birger Dahlerus on May 6, 1940, Göring threatened to attack Sweden, if the Swedes continued to be uncooperative. [492]

On June 8, 1940, the British withdrew its last contingent of 24,500 troops from Norway. Two days later Norway capitulated. Since Sweden's shipping routes to the Baltic Sea and to the Atlantic were henceforth controlled by the German navy, the Swedish economy was now at the mercy of the Nazis. [493] The Swedish government, determined to keep the country out of the war, was now forced to make a whole series of concessions to the Third Reich which clearly conflicted with its neutrality.

On July 8, 1940, Sweden signed a transit agreement with Nazi Germany. This not only permitted transit of German goods of all kinds through Sweden, but also

[490] Ulf Brandell, "Die Transitfrage in der schwedischen Aussenpolitik während des Zweiten Weltkrieges," in: Rudolf L. Bindschedler et al. (ed.), Schwedische und schweizerische Neutralität im Zweiten Weltkrieg. (Basle, 1985), p. 84

[491] Ibid.

[492] Johann Wolfgang Brügel, "Dahlerus als Zwischenträger nach Kriegsausbruch," in: Historische Zeitschrift No. 228 (1979), pp. 70-97

[493] Christian Leitz, Nazi Germany and the Neutral Europe During the Second World War. (Manchester, 2000), p. 55

allowed the weekly transport of about 500 soldiers on leave in both directions like a kind of ant trail through Swedish territory between Oslo and Trelleborg on the southern Swedish coast. [494]

In granting such concessions, Sweden had certainly lost its unblemished image as a neutral, but did not escape from ever escalating German demands. In preparation for Operation Barbarossa the Wehrmacht sought to strengthen its military positions in Norway by harassing the Swedish government with more and more additional requests concerning the transit of troops and war materials through Swedish territories. The Swedes were forced to permit intermittent but increasing troop transports, which came to average 1,400 soldiers per day. According to later Swedish estimates, 670,000 German troops crossed Swedish territory during the war years. [495] Finally the Germans pushed through the transit of an entire, fully armed division – the 163rd infantry division led by General Engelbrecht – tasked to attack the fortress of Hangö in South Finland which, after the peace treaty of March 12, 1940, between Finland and the Soviet Union, was under Soviet rule. Such a massive movement of combat troops through Sweden made a mockery of official Swedish neutrality. For the sake of peace Sweden allowed itself to be used openly to further Nazi war aims.

Between June 22, 1941 – the date of the German attack on the Soviet Union – and the end of the year, Swedish trains transported 100,000 tons of goods for the Wehrmacht from Germany and Norway to Finnish borders, 60% of which were war materials. Over 15,500 injured German soldiers rode these same Swedish trains back to Oslo. [496]

Sweden's neutrality not only was rendered meaningless on land, but in the air and on the seas as well. Unarmed German military planes were permitted to fly over Swedish airspace in allocated corridors. German and Finnish vessels were given preferential treatment in being allowed to move through Swedish territorial waters. German vessels were even escorted by the Swedish navy when they did so. [497]

Economic Relations with Germany

Financial and economic relations between Sweden and Germany, which had always been extensive, were now expanded even further. At the beginning of World War II more than 130 companies or groups of companies in Sweden were German-owned. These companies gave the Germans a wide and useful spectrum of investments in Sweden. Bogus firms were set up to handle patent, brand and trust agreements as well as contracts. Moreover German companies had a way of becoming Swedish companies at very short notice so true ownership could be concealed to avoid Allied blockade and confiscation measures. [498]

---

[494] Ulf Brandell, "Die Transitfrage in der schwedischen Aussenpolitik während des Zweiten Weltkrieges," in: Rudolf L. Bindschedler et al. (ed.), Schwedische und schweizerische Neutralität im Zweiten Weltkrieg. (Basle, 1985), p. 83

[495] op. cit., p. 56

[496] Ibid., p. 79 footnote 56

[497] Ibid., p. 58

[498] Manfred Ertel, "Braunes Netzwerk im Norden " in: Spiegel Hitlers Krieg: Sechs Jahre, die die Welt erschüttern. No. 2/2005, p. 41

In certain critical sectors – machine tools, machine manufacture, timber, production of chemical raw materials, shipping, shipbuilding and steel production – German influence on Swedish industry was significant. Germany was particularly interested in iron ore and mining. Germany's armament industry depended on reliable supply of raw materials and Swedish iron ore played a particularly important role in German armament production. At certain points Sweden was supplying 40% of total German demand for iron ore which typically was low in phosphor. This allowed the German steel industry to keep its work force, blast furnace and coke needs lower than they would have been with less workable ore. It was estimated that savings in coal and coke alone amounted to 2 million tons per year. This meant the Germans could use fewer of their own workers in coal and iron ore mining, as well as in steel production. [499] Such high grade iron ore was of great importance for the production of high quality steel, and made up a significant part of the ore delivered to Germany. Correspondingly, Swedish deliveries to Germany kept increasing during the war. Stoppage of this supply would have had a major impact on Germany's armaments industry and would have dramatically increased stress on the German economy which was in any case mounting after 1941.

The cost of Swedish imports could not be entirely covered by the export of German products within the framework of existing German-Swedish clearing agreements so Germany was forced to resort to other methods of payment. So it happened that Sweden became one of the recipients of gold from Germany too in an amount which ultimately totaled some 28,300 kilograms. The Germans had looted this gold in Belgium and the Netherlands and recast it to avoid clues as to its origin. [500] Did the Swedish officials know – or should they have known – that the so-called German gold came from central banks in countries occupied by the Germans or might have been stolen from Jewish citizens and other opponents of the Nazi regime through use of terror and violence? [501]

The Allied powers made some attempt to stop Swedish supplies to Germany in part with military force similar to the Russians whose submarines attacked vessels transporting ore across the Baltic Sea. But more often than not the Allies relied on diplomatic and economic pressure. Until 1942 Sweden was in a rather fortunate position: Britain considered Swedish neutrality, as damaged as it was, still important to maintain and only exerted limited pressure on the Swedish government to reduce deliveries to Germany. The British also worried about driving Sweden even further into the German embrace. But when the United States entered the war against the Axis at the end of 1941, America saw no reason to adopt Britain's lenient policy towards Sweden. However, at the beginning of America's entrance into the war, it was too preoccupied with the military crisis in the Pacific than to draw up effective procedures against Sweden.

---

[499] Ibid., p. 72

[500] The Commission on Jewish Assets in Sweden at the Time of the Second World War., The Nazigold and the Swedish Riksbank – Interim Report – (Stockholm, 1998), p.28

[501] Cf. Walther Hofer and Herbert R. Reginbogin, Hitler, der Westen und die Schweiz. (Zurich, 2001), p. 605 Nothing as yet is known about the origin of the gold accepted – pre-war gold, looted gold or even victims' gold from conquered countries. However, it is hardly likely that the gold was pre-war gold.

Britain was well aware that Sweden had violated its neutrality by allowing the transit of German troops across its territory and by supplying Germany with strategically important products far in excess of the limits agreed in the War Trade Agreement Sweden had concluded with Britain on December 7, 1939. Nevertheless Britain, in a supplementary protocol of December 1941, allowed Sweden to import goods, in spite of the blockade, based on levels of Swedish imports reported in 1938 (*courant normal*). [502] These allowable imports were based on Sweden's normal consumption of food stuffs, semi-finished manufactured products, and industrial raw materials and, in the case of crude oil, on the amount required for the maintenance of Sweden's military. But even with those allocations, Sweden was not successful in importing the quantities allowed since during the war years items such as cotton, wool, furs and plant oils were difficult to procure in Europe. But imports were allowed to continue, and a major reduction in supplies would have had serious repercussions for all sectors of Swedish industry. On the other hand, Germany's counter blockade limited Swedish exports to Argentina and Chile for which German permissions were required. Despite the restrictions of the blockades, during the first half of 1942 Sweden managed to supply some strategic metals and half-finished machine parts to Britain which the British would have found difficult to obtain elsewhere. This illegal trade – illegal from the point of view of Germany – was accomplished through air links between Stockholm and Scotland. [503]

Although the blockade numbers create the impression that Sweden was able to import so much that in some cases it might have been in a position to make deliveries to Germany, Swedish imports were in fact limited in two ways. First, it was very difficult for the Swedes to acquire goods at all. Second, Göteborg traffic was restricted by both the Allied and Axis powers to five vessels per month in each direction and one tanker per quarter. Although the list of prohibited export goods had potentially weak points, it is likely that goods which did get into Sweden beyond the allowed quantity were not passed on to the Germany. Crude oil derivatives, for example, were used exclusively by the Swedish army. In spite of the War Trade Agreements, however, Swedish exports to Germany of Swedish goods such as iron ore and wool products increased compared with 1938.

But Sweden also supported the Allied powers by putting a substantial number of Swedish merchant vessels at their disposal. Swedish shipping capacity of some 400,000 tons outside the Baltic was either chartered outright by the Allied powers or served Allied interests. [504]

Throughout the war the British sought to avoid estrangement in their relations with Sweden. On October 25, 1942, Churchill wrote to Roosevelt: "I feel it most important that Sweden should be in with us all before the end, though the moment for bringing her in must be wisely chosen." [505] Britain feared Sweden might change

---

[502] Franklin D. Roosevelt Library, in the following called (FDR), Henry A. Wallace Collection, Box 61, Folder: President Roosevelt, Franklin D. July-December 1942, "Trade Policy Toward Sweden Revised Version," Board of Economic Warfare Analysis, November 3, 1942.

[503] Ibid.

[504] Ibid.

[505] Warren F. Kimball, Churchill and Roosevelt: The Complete Correspondence, Vol. I, p. 639 (London, 1985)

to the German side or that British pressure might lead to a shift in Swedish policies that would provoke a German invasion of that country. [506] Documents show that the USA had a completely different opinion about how Sweden should be treated. The debate got more heated when the US Board of Economic Warfare presented a report showing that Sweden had gone far beyond the laws of neutrality. [507]

Like the other neutral countries, Sweden had to continue a balancing act between Allied and German demands. This was a precarious undertaking for Sweden since Germany had achieved a monopoly over Swedish markets and Swedish industry was dependant on German production and on German willingness to deliver. Germany tried to take advantage of its dominant position and its trade policies became increasingly aggressive. Martin Fritz and Klaus Wittmann wrote that the Germans took advantage of their monopoly over Swedish markets to increase German prices for strategically important goods such as coal and coke. [508] Sweden, for its part, benefited from very strong German demand for raw materials. Supply and demand between the two countries drove export prices up with the main rise attributed to the German side. German domestic prices had increased continually in the space of about ten years while German export prices had remained nearly unchanged. Exports by Germany had been relatively unprofitable. Therefore, from the German point of view, pushing up their prices to Sweden was fully justified. At the same time the Germans also made sure they did not raise their prices so high as to curtail Swedish production and cause a problematic inflation in Sweden. Moreover, although the Germans were by and large in the driver's seat on trade, they could never get the Swedish government to make concessions which the Swedes considered disadvantageous for Swedish industry. While Turkey was widely held to be the so-called spoiled child of the Allied powers on trade, Sweden perhaps held a similar position in the Axis camp. Although Sweden was not exactly pampered by Germany, compared with how the Germans exploited the economies of other countries they remained relatively lenient with Sweden, at least as long as Sweden did the Nazis' bidding. [509]

As did Switzerland, the Swedes used clearing agreements to fend off German demands for deliveries. These bilateral agreements gave a certain amount of political and economic leverage to both Switzerland and Sweden and strengthened their negotiating positions. First, they hindered attempts by dominant Germany to obtain preferential rights in the interpretation of regulations. Second, Germany's demand for Swedish raw materials balanced the Swedish need for German fuel and finished products and so the two had a mutual interest in keeping the relationship intact. Third, functioning of the arrangement could only be maintained if there was constant communication. Questions and problems had to be dealt with swiftly, particularly since the clearing agreement was very sensitive to changes

---

[506] Ibid.

[507] Ibid.

[508] Martin Fritz, German Steel and Swedish Iron Ore 1939–1945. (Göteborg, 1974) and Klaus Wittman, Schwedens Wirtschaftsbeziehungen zum Dritten Reich 1933–1945. (Munich, 1978)

[509] Martin Fritz, "En fråga om praktisk politik. Ekonomisk neutralitet under det andra världskriget," in: Historisk tidskrift No. 3 (1982)

occurring on either side. [510] As in the case of Switzerland, sustained contact with Germany was also indispensable for Sweden in its function as a protecting power.

Compared with the pre-war years the volume of German-Swedish trade doubled between 1940-1944 as a result of mutual endeavors to maintain and improve the economic relationship. Although Germany was involved in a world war, its economic contacts, crucial to the war effort, were handled very efficiently. German demand and German supply were extremely reliable and so contributed to a steady growth in the Swedish economy. Overall, the war years dampened trade and even production, so that growth was slower than in the pre-war years, but there still was a continual upward trend. [511]

The Enskilda Bank

In addition to the SKF (Svenska Kullagerfabriken), the huge ball bearing operation which was part of the Wallenberg Empire, and ore mining enterprises, other parts of the Swedish economy also maintained excellent relations with the Germans. This included the Enskilda Bank, also owned by the Wallenberg family. With the aid of this bank, the Nazis were able to execute profitable business and financial transactions benefiting the Third Reich and even to conceal German assets in the USA.

The German Robert Bosch GmbH had a branch in the USA. As to avoid the risk of confiscation in the case of war, the Swedish Enskilda Bank bought in May 1940 the American Bosch Corporation (ABC) on the condition that it is returned to the Germans after the war. German chemicals giant I.G. Farben also profited from the assistance of the Stockholm Enskilda Bank. [512]

Safehaven documents prove that American authorities were aware of these activities for several years. Enskilda Bank was finally put on an American blacklist, investigations were opened, and the assets of American Bosch frozen. Treasury Secretary Morgenthau accused the Enskilda of widespread black market operations. The Swedish brothers Marcus and Jacob Wallenberg were put on a black list of barred foreign nationals in America while in Germany they were highly praised for their efforts. In 1941 Jacob Wallenberg was even awarded the 'German Order of the Eagle' by Hitler. – The long dispute between the Enskilda Bank and the US government concerning the bank's cooperation with Germany was ultimately settled out of court on September 20, 1950. [513]

The fact that the Wallenberg family had worked for both/sides led to a crisis in Sweden after the war in 1945. Chase Manhattan Bank in the USA had done

---

[510] Peter Hedberg and Mats Larsson, "Banks, Financial Markets and the Swedish State During the Second World War," in: Joseph Jung, Herbert R. Reginbogin and Robert U. Vogler (ed.), Financial Markets of Neutral Countries during the Second World War (In preparation by the Association of Financial History and the Principality of Liechtenstein).

[511] Ibid.

[512] Walther Hofer and Herbert R. Reginbogin, Hitler, der Westen und die Schweiz. (Zurich, 2001), pp. 609-610

[513] Ulf Olsson, "Stockholm's Enskilda Bank and the Bosch Group, 1939-1950," in: Banking & Enterprise. No I (Stockholm, 1998), p. 48; Gerard Aalders and Cees Wiebes, Die Kunst der Tarnung. Die geheime Kollaboration neutraler Staaten mit der deutschen Kriegsindustrie. Der Fall Schweden. (Frankfurt am Main, 1994)

some of the same things but no punishment was ever levied on Chase nor was there any crisis over its conduct. In the course of the Swedish crisis, Sweden's foreign minister Osten Unden pointed out that the Wallenbergs were no longer part of the inner circle enjoying special relations with the Swedish government. Raoul Wallenberg, a cousin, saved the lives of many thousand Jews in Hungary. When the Russian army seized Budapest from the Germans, he was arrested and carried off by the Soviet secret service on the charge of being an American spy and never returned. To this day no comprehensive research has been carried out on the fate of Raoul Wallenberg or on Count Folke Bernadotte, to whom many Jews also owed their lives. [514]

Pressure on Sweden

As the war evolved there was increasing Allied pressure on Sweden to impose sanctions on Germany for its violations. In January 1943, US Secretary of State Cordell Hull alarmed the Swedish government by abruptly demanding that Sweden fulfill its obligations as a neutral country lest the Swedish government face charges after the war. His actual words were: "The determining factor in American-Swedish relations during the war must be the extent of Sweden's resistance to Axis demands that were contrary to her rights as a neutral state and a democratic independent nation." [515]

This was essentially a demand for an end to Sweden's brisk and important trade with Germany. The signs were clear: Germany was fighting on all fronts and by 1943 it was becoming obvious that the Third Reich was losing the war. The victorious Allies would control the future international economy. This foreseeable change in conditions motivated the Swedish government to consider long-term re-alignment of both its economic and foreign policy. However while Sweden attempted to meet Allied demands, the fact remained that Sweden's economy still depended on Germany. Since, as was the case of Switzerland, there were no realistic alternatives to the German market, Sweden decided to continue German-Swedish trade, while at the same time struggling to fulfill the demands of the Allied powers where possible.

Finally on September 23, 1943, an agreement between the Allies and Sweden led to a substantial and progressive decrease in Swedish trade with Germany. [516] This occurred when the USA and Britain declared their willingness to increase Allied shipments to Sweden, including crude oil and rubber on the conditions that Sweden, on its part, agreed to prohibit transit of German war materials and troops, to reduce iron ore exports to Germany, to stop the Swedish navy from escorting German vessels in the Baltic Sea and to decrease its supply of ball bearings to Germany.

---

[514] Paul Levine, Swedish Neutrality During the Second World War: Tactical Success or Moral Compromise?," in: Neville Wylie (ed.), European Neutrals and Non-Belligerents During the Second World War. (Cambridge, 2002), p.325; In June 1996, the *US News and Reports* referred to declassified documents and reported that Raoul Wallenberg had acted as a spy for the OSS (Overseas Secret Service, precursor to the CIA).

[515] Cordell Hull, The Memoirs of Cordell Hull, Vol. II (London, 1948), p. 1345

[516] W. N. Medlicott, The Economic Blockade. Vol. II (London, 1959), pp. 471-472

Sweden now cautiously began a gradual winding down of Swedish-German trade. However, it tried to convince the Allies that it was cutting back on trade with Germany at a much faster pace than was actually the case. In the second half of 1943 and the early months of 1944, the United States concentrated its air raids on ball bearing factories in Germany in order to slow German weapons output. [517] Parallel to air force bombings, the Allies were offering to purchase Swedish ball bearings with the aim of cutting off Swedish ball bearing supplies to Germany. These efforts were not successful as German countermeasures and improvisation skills were able to avert serious repercussions. Dutch research has shown that Germany was able to continue to meet about 70% of its demand for the seven most important types of ball bearings used for aircraft construction with purchases from the Svenska Kugellagerfabriken. [518]

When concluding the agreement with Sweden in September 1943, Allied negotiators had only concentrated on a reduction of actual ball bearing deliveries, but had omitted to limit exports of the high quality steel used in the manufacture of ball bearings. So the Germans were able to use the steel to manufacture both ball bearings and more of the machines used to make them. [519] So long as Sweden was permitted to continue exporting steel to Germany, the shortfall in Swedish ball bearings could be made good in German factories. In this matter, the Third Reich retained the benefits of discreet Swedish cooperation.

As D–Day approached at the beginning of June 1944 the Allies were concerned the Swedish supply of ball bearings would facilitate the Wehrmacht's rearmament effort thus replacing the losses suffered at the new front in France. Again the Allies were determined to reduce the flow of Swedish ball bearings to Germany. Following a request from the Foreign Economic Agency, Stanton Griffiths, an influential American, was sent to Stockholm to push the Allied case. He finally convinced Svenska Kullagerfabriken (SKF) to yield to US demands, but only after making promises of Allied purchases, financial settlements and ultimately threatening blacklisting. SKF secretly agreed to delay 90% of its ball bearing deliveries during the critical invasion period and then to cut off supply altogether. For the remaining period of the war, SKF would stop supplying ball bearings to Germany although, in return, the Allies were committed to make substantial orders for ball bearings which would compensate the company for losses incurred from cutting off sales to Germany. [520]

In mid-July 1944, while Allied forces were advancing rapidly through France, US Secretary of State Cordell Hull, following conversations with Under Secretaries of State Stettenius, Patterson and other officials, concluded that more persuasion was needed to stop Swedish shipments to Germany. On July 12 he requested the American president give the go-ahead for new demands for an end to

[517] Eizenstat, (1998), p. 94

[518] Manfred Ertel, "Braunes Netzwerk im Norden," in: Der Spiegel, Hitlers Krieg: Sechs Jahre, die die Welt erschüttern. No. 2/2005, p. 40

[519] Martin Fritz, "Swedish Ball-Bearings and the German War Economy," in: Scandinavian Economic History Review Vol. XXIII (1975), p. 26

[520] FDR, Box 134 PSF: President's Secretary's File, Currie to FDR with attachments – Foreign Economic Administration (FEA,) memo Leo T. Crowley to Roosevelt May 25, 1944 with attached "Current Ball Bearing Negotiations with Sweden," undated

Swedish-German trade. [521] The next day, Roosevelt wrote to Churchill: "Swedish exports to the enemy are becoming a very pressing question here. All the circumstances of the war, particularly Soviet successes in the Baltic area, could now be favorably used by us to bring maximum pressure to bear on Sweden to eliminate exports to the enemy. I would appreciate your getting behind this matter personally as Winant [US-Ambassador to London] is now taking this question up with your people in the Foreign Office." [522]

British Foreign Secretary Anthony Eden agreed with Winant that Sweden should be pressured to cease all trade with Germany, but remarked that the Swedish government had already drastically reduced trade with the Nazis. Churchill made it even more obvious that he did not agree with the American position, telling Roosevelt that he did not want to endanger the advantages the Allied powers now enjoyed with Sweden. [523] In spite of this difference of opinion between their countries' leaders, the British and American Foreign Secretaries, Eden and Hull, presented a note to the Swedish government on August 24, 1944, supported by a separate, but identical demand from the Soviet Union, to the effect that the only response which would meet Allied demands would be an immediate end to all trade relations with the Axis powers and a radical change of Swedish policy. [524] These demands were backed up by serious threats should Sweden fail to comply.

On September 4, 1944, Swedish Foreign Minister Günther rejected the Allied demands, but Hull tried to appease Roosevelt by saying that the Swedes often rejected demands formally, only to move in the desired direction informally afterwards. He was to be proved right. While discussions were taking place in the Allied camp on whether to confiscate Swedish companies' assets and whether the government should be informed that after the victory over the Axis powers, Sweden's provisioning would depend on the country's policy towards Germany, US Ambassador in Stockholm Herschel V. Johnson reported that Sweden had decided to close all its harbors to German vessels. The Svenska Kullagerfabriken (SKF) agreed to stop all deliveries to Germany after October 12, 1944, and a month later said it was prepared to end all trading with Germany from January 1, 1945. [525]

This was not the end of all the problems, however. The Swedes meant trade would be stopped with Germany alone, while the USA understood a cessation to mean trade with all German-occupied territories, including Norway and Denmark with whom Sweden fully intended to continue trading. After several Swedish presentations and intercessions by the British, the USA permitted the Swedes to continue their trickle of exports to Denmark. [526]

[521] FDR, PSF Box 9, PSF: Confidential File: State Dept., Hull to Roosevelt July 12, 1944

[522] Warren F. Kimball, Churchill-Roosevelt Correspondence, Vol. III, p. 245, Roosevelt to Churchill July 13, 1944. (London, 1985)

[523] Ibid., p. 257, op. cit., Churchill to Roosevelt July 27, 1944.

[524] Cordell Hull, The Memoirs of Cordell Hull, Vol. II (London, 1948), pp. 1347-1348

[525] Ibid.

[526] Juerg Martin Gabriel, The American Conception of Neutrality After 1941. (Basingstoke, 1988), pp. 51-52

Sweden Insists on Its Rights

Why did the Swedish not react to growing Allied pressure earlier and with greater enthusiasm?

During the second half of the war, the Swedish government and the Swedish public, the majority of whom held pro-Allied attitudes, considered their trade with Germany a national right under international law. The British accepted this attitude while the Americans rejected it. [527]

Although the Swedish people and government were informed about Nazi atrocities, they insisted on trading with Germany – justifying this not by an existential emergency, but by reference to international law. In previous years, but particularly in 1944, when news of horrific Nazis crimes against Jews, minorities and prisoners of war was becoming widespread, this justification had a very hollow ring indeed. Concerning this vague justification for a neutral state to continue to trade with Germany, Holocaust historian Paul Levene suggests that Sweden's humanitarian efforts during the war were both an attempt to compensate for its feelings of guilt and a way of deflecting Allied economic demands.

Safe Haven Sweden

After the Austrian 'Anschluss', an enormous stream of refugees looking for a safe haven poured out of areas under Nazi control. For most of these unfortunates, the doors of European countries had been slammed shut and bolted. In view of the expected influx of refugees who were unlikely to be permitted to travel on to countries which would accept them as immigrants, Sweden – like Switzerland – contemplated introducing compulsory visas for all German citizens, now including Austrians. Both neutral countries, Sweden and Switzerland, accepted Berlin's suggestion of stamping passports of German Jews who wanted to emigrate with the letter 'J'.

Notwithstanding Sweden's humanitarian tradition, the historian Helene Lööw found that, as of January 1939, the hostility against Jews at Swedish universities was "supported by nearly all the country's student bodies." [528] In the three most important Swedish universities, students protested against the influx of Jews. Both Swedish authorities and the Swedish people reacted to Jewish distress with cold indifference rooted in what some have called a profound anti-Semitism. [529] Tobias Hübinette, a young man who researched the role of Sweden during World War II, discovered that a so-called brown network had apparently spread across the country. He found membership lists of Nazi-friendly Swedish organizations and bearers of the Iron Cross, including the names of many of the elite of Swedish society – jurists, doctors, teachers and journalists. Hübinette published the names of 28,000 Swedish Nazi sympathizers. His research showed that 400 to 500 Swedes voluntarily swore the oath of allegiance to Adolf Hitler out of principle and became SS

---

[527] Paul A. Levine, From Indifference to Activism: Swedish Diplomacy and the Holocaust 1938-1944. (Uppsala, 1996), p. 69

[528] Manfred Ertel, quoted from an article "Braunes Netzwerk im Norden " on the book by Helene Lööw. Nazismen i Sverige 1924-1979: pionjärerna, partierna, propagandan. (Ordfront, 2004) in: Hitlers Krieg: Sechs Jahre, die die Welt erschüttern". Der Spiegel No. 2/2005, p. 41

[529] Ibid., pp. 451-465

volunteers in so-called Viking and Nordland divisions. Some even served in Adolf Hitler's elite bodyguard regiment (Leibstandarte). Between 1933 and 1945 there was wide-spread xenophobia in Sweden. It was only when Hitler's genocide became obvious that Swedish efforts to rescue people persecuted by the Nazis came into play. [530]

While Sweden declared itself a neutral nation at the very beginning of the war, it maintained its restrictive immigration policy until late in 1942. To that point Sweden had taken in about 2,000 Jews, far less than most other European nations, including the smaller ones. [531] Sweden maintained this position until October of that year when the German final solution reached Norway. Then the switch from indifference to committed activism was primarily triggered by one man, Gösta Engzell, a career civil servant who during the war was the director of the Foreign Office's legal department. Led by Engzell, Swedish diplomats started to take advantage of their country's neutral status in becoming accepted negotiators for Jewish people – sometimes succeeding, sometimes failing. They succeeded in saving many lives, the majority of them not Swedish citizens. The final switch from indifference to active support of Jews kicked in when Sweden agreed to take in about 900 Norwegian Jews who were about to be deported to concentration camps. [532] Besides Jews, about 44,000 Norwegians managed to escape the harsh Nazi dictatorship by escaping to Sweden [533] This action was followed by the rescue of the Jewish population of Denmark, especially during October 1943, with over 7,000 Jews saved, and then again in Budapest where in 1944 between 15,000 and 25,000 Jewish lives were saved thanks to Swedish assistance. But not all Swedish efforts were successful. For example, in spite of violent protests, more than 1,200 Norwegian teachers and students were deported. [534]

In major European cities such as Paris, Berlin, and Amsterdam, Swedish diplomats again and again succeeded in bringing dozens of Jewish citizens under their wing of diplomatic protection. They included the amazing efforts of Swedish diplomat Raoul Wallenberg in Hungary, who rescued many ten thousands of people, and the famous white buses of Count Folke Bernadotte, who even in early 1945 succeeded in liberating from Himmler's concentration camps some 30,000 men, women and children, many of Jewish origin and made sure they were allowed to go to Sweden after May 1945. His rescue efforts remain an impressive monument to Swedish diplomacy. [535]

---

[530] Tobias Hübinette and Klaus Böhme, Den svenska nationalsocialismen: medlemmar och sympatisörer, 1931-1945. (Stockholm, 2002)

[531] op. cit.

[532] Bengt Åkerrén, "Schweden als Schutzmacht," in: Rudolf L. Bindschedler et al. (ed.), Schwedische und schweizerische Neutralität im Zweiten Weltkrieg. (Basle, 1985), pp. 115-116

[533] Werner Rings, Life with the Enemy: Collaboration and Resistance in Hitler's Europe, 1939-1945. (New York, 1982), p. 174

[534] Paul A. Levine, From Indifference to Activism: Swedish Diplomacy and the Holocaust 1938-1944. (Uppsala, 1996), p. 70-74 and 243-245; Steven Koblik, "Sweden's Attempt to Aid the Jews, 1939-1945" in: Scandinavian Studies, 56 (1984); Eizenstat (1998), p. 326

[535] Paul Levine, Swedish Neutrality During the Second World War: Tactical Success or Moral Compromise?," in: Neville Wylie (ed.), European Neutrals and Non-Belligerents During the Second World War. (Cambridge, 2002), p. 326

The Swedish neutrality was two–faced. In fact, the historian Paul Levine considers the rescue of Jewish lives as a violation of strict neutrality, though in the most positive sense and essentially an un-neutral action which could or should have been open to all other neutral countries. Levine argues that Sweden, at the very same time, was selling goods to Germany which was crucial for the continuation of the war and thus indirectly responsible for the enslavement of thousands of human beings as forced labor. Certainly there is sufficient guilt – and some praise – to go around. Sweden's humanitarian achievements were not only due to the heroic efforts of men like Raoul Wallenberg or Folke Bernadotte, but also to the stubbornness and commitment on the part of civil servants in the Foreign Office following the lead of Gösta Engzell who decided to counter inhumanity associated with bureaucratic resistance to change. [536]

Swedish diplomats made use of their recognized status as representatives of a neutral power by placing their 'good services' between suspected perpetrators and potential victims. They used the inefficiencies of bureaucracy to undermine the implementation of National Socialist racial policies against both individuals and, where possible, groups. Moreover being on the spot, diplomats were often in a position to intervene when deportation was most threatening. Most cases often turned into negotiations between a Swedish diplomat and his German counterpart to decide who was eligible for Swedish protection. Whenever the Swede could make the argument that this or that Jew was of political interest to the Swedish government, an application was filed confirming this state of affairs and demanding the continued well-being of the person concerned. [537] In spite of German protests, Swedish diplomats dodged through holes in German civil and diplomatic bureaucracies to help Jews who under normal circumstances would never have stood a chance of obtaining Swedish diplomatic protection. It is impressive that the Swedes managed to snatch people of Jewish faith from the Nazis' clutches even during the high points of deportations to the dreaded KZ camps. They were successful in holding actions few others tried or even contemplated during the war, not even the diplomats representing neutral countries, with the exception of the Swiss citizen Carl Lutz and some few representatives of the International Red Cross. But there were ambiguities in Nazi policies and ideology which they were able to exploit. Whenever German bureaucrats were confronted with a representative of a sovereign state who could submit a formal application in favor of a Jew, even the most subservient Nazis could claim they were deferring to a legitimate state power and grant the application with a clear conscience. Tangling the Germans in official paperwork did not work in every case, but it was an effective tactic after all. In one sense, these Swedish machinations could only pass through the German chain of command because Germany had a larger interest in maintaining normal diplomatic and economic relations with Sweden. As did so many of their colleagues in other countries, Swedish diplomats might also have pulled away from the conflict and closed their doors on the basis of their neutrality. They did not choose to take this easy option – and saved many innocent lives.

---

[536] Ibid.
[537] Ibid., p. 327

Besides Sweden other neutral European countries also protected Jews, their own citizens and immigrants alike. Switzerland, in particular, took in a higher percentage of Jewish refugees, in proportion to its population, than any other country.

Were Swedish humanitarian successes sufficient to compensate for the suffering caused by Swedish neutrality policies? Normally, governments strive to ensure their own people's survival and well-being. Under certain circumstances, governments may have to choose the lesser of two evils. Where issues of national survival are at stake, there may be little room for a broader-based morality in government policy. Perhaps the criteria for determining what is a justified or acceptable response to a threat posed by an enemy power depends on a nation's strength and its ability to defend the values it chooses. That may be why smaller nations and major powers assess these criteria so very differently.

Protective Power

Like Switzerland, Sweden took on the role of being the legal representative of foreign combatant states for the entire war. It represented the interests of one country with other countries, including that country's enemies. Looking after these interests did not include pushing political or national agendas. Rather, the primary task of a protecting power was managing the exchange of diplomatic and consular personnel as well as of civilians on the basis of agreements between warring parties. This included the administration of real estates – embassy or consular premises – belonging to the state represented, plus transport, storage and safeguarding of the state's property as well as protection of citizens living on enemy territory and their possessions. The search for individuals and the financial support for stranded persons, visits to various internee camps to check compliance with the Geneva Convention, advice on passport questions, as well as the issue of protective passports for people who could be considered under diplomatic protection were all part of the obligations of a protective power.

In September 1939, Poland was first to ask whether Sweden would be prepared to represent its interests in the event of war. Poland, of course, did not enjoy the benefits of the Swedish consent for long. By November 1939, Polish territory was completely occupied, and Sweden was informed by Germany that the Swedish mandate had ceased and was requested to hand over to the German authorities any Polish real estate administered by Sweden in Germany. However, this uncompromising attitude did not prevent the Germans on their part from requesting Sweden to represent German interests in France and Egypt. In turn, South Africa gave Sweden the mandate to look after its interests in the Third Reich. The request by the Finnish government to represent its interests in the Soviet Union failed because the Soviet Union no longer acknowledged the Finnish government. In spite of this handicap, Sweden acted as a mediator conveying political messages between the two states. 1940 brought a new series of mandates, including the request by Norway to represent its interests in Germany, Denmark, Italy and Vichy France, as well as Germany asking to be represented in Iceland, and Iceland requesting representation in Germany and Italy. The spread of war in 1941 resulted in a veritable avalanche of further mandates back and forth between Belgium, Bulgaria, China, Denmark, Finland, Germany, Hungary, Iran, Iceland, Japan, Mexico,

151

the Netherlands, Romania, Slovakia and the Soviet Union. In 1942, Sweden took on the mandates for Bolivia, Greece and Honduras, and in 1943 for Finland, Hungary and Japan. Even in 1945, requests for Swedish mediation continued, involving representations in 14 countries on Japan's behalf alone. [538]

Overall, Sweden had 114 official mandates to act as a protective power for 28 different countries, and represented foreign interests in 36 countries.

Safehaven Program

In 1944, according to the Eizenstat Report, Britain and the United States started to include Sweden in the Safehaven Program. The British, who were more lenient in this question wanted to restrict the program only to gold, while the USA wanted to include all German assets. The Americans interpreted trade agreements with the Reich as a form of collaboration. The Riksdag, or Swedish parliament, endorsed the Safehaven Program and in February, 1945 Sweden began to take stock of its gold and foreign currency to determine how much of it could be traced back to Nazi Germany.

That spring the British changed course and endorsed the American point of view, and drafted a proposal for Sweden which was also used as a basis for the Safehaven talks with Portugal and Spain. Until summer 1945, Sweden took measures to control German assets and extended its investigations to all German assets. In January 1946, under Allied pressure, Swedish laws were again extended to include all German subsidiaries as well.

In November 1945, Sweden presented a report on its gold transactions to the US Treasury Department. According to this report, Sweden had received gold of Belgian origin worth $22.7 million. In their own calculations, the Americans reduced this amount to $17 million. [539]

On February 11, 1946, the US embassy informed the Swedish government of details of the Allied Control Council Law No. 5 of October 30, 1943, which stipulated that German property in other countries, would revert to the victorious Allies. A Swedish delegation was invited to Washington to deal with this issue. Sweden expressed strong reservations about this Allied claim, but was prepared to join talks. [540] On April 5, 1946, Sweden let the American embassy know that the claim had to be brought before the Riksdag. They warned the Americans that parliament was likely to reject the proposal since Sweden maintained that the Allied claim had no foundation in international law and therefore constituted a violation of private property rights. In addition, Sweden demanded that its assets which had been frozen by the United States since June 14, 1941, must be released before talks could begin. Moreover, Sweden was to be allowed to inspect Swedish property in Germany. Both demands were refused. [541]

---

[538] Bengt Åkerrén, "Schweden als Schutzmacht," in: Rudolf L. Bindschedler et al. (ed.), Schwedische und schweizerische Neutralität im Zweiten Weltkrieg. (Basle, 1985), pp. 115-117

[539] Eizenstat (1998), p. 100

[540] Ibid.

[541] Ibid., p. 101; cf. Herbert R. Reginbogin, "The Financial Market of America During World War II," in: Joseph Jung, Herbert R. Reginbogin and Robert U. Vogler (ed.), Financial Markets of Neutral Countries during the Second World War (in preparation by the Association of Financial History and the Principality of Liechtenstein).

By late March, after talks with Britain and France, the United States believed it had assembled a picture of German assets in Sweden and pressed for negotiations to begin. Talks formally began in Washington on May 29, 1946. The US delegation was led by Seymour Rubin, Deputy Director of the State Department's Office of Economic Security Policy, with a British delegation led by Francis W. McCombe of the Foreign Office. France was represented by Christian Valensi, Financial Counselor of the French embassy in Washington. The head of the Swedish delegation was Judge Emil Sandstrom who at the beginning of the talks echoed Allied fears that Nazi assets might possibly be used for a revival of National Socialism, but also contended that the Allied claim to German assets abroad was not legally justified. [542]

The negotiations were harmonious, and were finalized by an agreement on July 18, 1946. Sweden assented to a division of the German assets on Swedish territory, estimated at 378 million Krona (about $90 million) as follows: 50 million Krona (about $12.5 million) for the Intergovernmental Committee on Refugees (later the International Refugee Organization), 75 million Krona (about $18 million) to the Inter-Allied Reparation Agency (IARA), excluding any amounts due to the United States, Britain and France. 150 million Krona (about $36 million) was to be used to fight disease and combat unrest in Germany.

On top of this, the agreement allowed liquidated property of Swedish or German persons to be remunerated in German currency, and allowed a Swedish delegation to travel to the American, British and French sectors of occupied Germany to inspect Swedish property there. The agreement supported the release of Swedish assets in the USA (amounting to about $200 million at the time), promised the elimination of all blacklists and approved the Allied claim to German property in Sweden. [543]

The agreement obliged Sweden to return 7,155 kilograms of refined gold (worth about $8 million). In return, the Swedes were released from all claims to return gold connected with transfers by the Swedish National Bank to third countries. [544] Finally, the agreement protected Sweden against all Allied claims to gold it had received from Germany before June 1, 1945, and transferred to third countries, as well as against additional claims after July 1, 1947. [545] In his report, US negotiator Seymour Rubin noted that the talks had been held in a calm atmosphere, lacking the bitterness dominating talks with Switzerland. [546]

Sweden ratified the agreement in November 1946. Shortly before July 1, 1947, the deadline for claims to gold, the Allied powers submitted an application for the return of 638 ingots ($10 million) of gold stolen in the Netherlands. Sweden contested parts of this claim, justifying their position by the fact that the gold had been bought before the adoption of the London Declaration of January 5, 1943. The Inter-Allied Declaration Against Acts of Dispossession Committed in Territories Under Enemy Occupation or Control, stipulated that transfer of property

---

[542] Ibid., p. 102
[543] Ibid., p. 104
[544] Ibid.
[545] Ibid., pp. 104-105
[546] Ibid., p. 106

from German-occupied countries was invalid, even if it appeared legal. [547] The Allied powers in return asserted that the agreement concluded covered the entire amount of gold bought. The debate on Dutch gold dragged on into the 1950s. In 1955, Sweden finally returned 6 tons of gold (about $6.8 million) to the Netherlands. [548]

After its final investigations, the Swedish Commission concluded in its report – Sweden and Nazi gold – that Sweden had received 59.7 tons of gold from Nazi Germany whose markings identified it as being of Dutch origin. In addition, a further 6 tons of gold of uncertain origin were discovered which were not included in the Safehaven operation. By this time, Sweden had returned 13.2 tons of gold to Belgium and the Netherlands. [549]. The investigation results were forwarded to the Swedish government. One of the investigators said that Sweden now had a moral duty, but not a legal duty, to return the gold. The Commission's report was finally published in 1997. [550]

TURKEY

The Republic of Turkey was founded in October 1923. Shortly after the outbreak of World War II its government decided to join various other countries in declaring neutrality. The Turkish president at that time was Ismet Inönü, successor of the founding father of the republic, Kemal Atatürk, who had built up the Turkish Republic after the collapse of the Ottoman Empire and had tried to make Turkey a secular state oriented towards Europe. Certainly Turkey, with its one party rule and complete lack of opposition, could not really be called a Western democracy. But the country began to move away from the rule of the sultans and Atatürk introduced policies to educate the nation about democracy over time. Moreover, his new secularization set out to do away with many traditional Islamic practices and introduce social and cultural reforms he considered necessary to turn Turkey into a modern Western society. [551]

While Turkey had been a German ally in World War I, Atatürk was wary of the Swastika façade. He voiced his misgivings about the increasingly aggressive nature of National Socialism and Fascism in the early 1930s, and his positions motivated his successor to be very skeptical about German offers to form an alliance, both before and during World War II. Although politics in Turkey rested on strong-man tactics which in some ways resembled those of the two fascist dictatorships, the country's ideology was far from that of Hitler or Mussolini. [552] In

---

[547] Ibid., p. 110

[548] Ibid., p. 111

[549] Sweden and the Nazi Gold. Stockholm: Commission on Jewish Assets in Sweden at the time of the Second World War, December 2-4, 1997. p. 19 (Conference paper presented at the 'London Conference on Nazi Gold', December 2-4, 1997)

[550] Sweden and the Nazi Gold. Stockholm: Commission on Jewish Assets in Sweden at the time of the Second World War, December 2-4,1997. p. 19 (Conference paper presented at the 'London Conference on Nazi Gold', December 2-4, 1997)

[551] Zehra Onder, Die türkische Aussenpolitik im Zweiten Weltkrieg. In: Mathias Bernath (ed.) Südosteuropäische Arbeiten Vol. 73 (Munich, 1977), p. 9

[552] Christian Leitz, Nazi Germany and Neutral Europe During the Second World War. (Manchester, 2000), p. 87

154

view of the imminent danger of war, the Turkish government was determined to continue Kemal Atatürk's policy and to keep well out of any conflict, as long as Turkey itself was not the victim of the attack.

The National Socialists' aggressive rhetoric and increasingly rabid ideology caused major misgivings in Turkey, which were further heightened by the manifestations of arrogance by Mussolini. His speeches of December 22, 1933, and March 19, 1934, described Africa and Asia as Italy's historic mission and demanded the occupation and remilitarization of the Dodecanese Islands in the Aegean off the southwest coast of Turkey. Those speeches moved Atatürk to strengthen both Turkey's relations with Britain for naval support and with the Soviet Union. Atatürk also took on a more active role in the League of Nations. The specific links with Britain and Russia dated back to bilateral agreements concluded in the early 1930s which had aided Turkey's industrialization, and they were now expanded by including additional security considerations. [553]

When in the mid-1930s the true territorial intentions of the German-Italian brotherhood started to emerge like rust through a painted surface, Turkey moved even farther away from Fascist and National Socialist ideologies. Turkey supported Ethiopia against Italy and the Republican side in the Spanish civil war. Turkey's strategic geopolitical location between the Balkans and the Middle East made it particularly attractive for powers who wanted to increase their political influence in this critical region. So they all tried to woo Turkey with economic and financial offers. Germany, for example, chose to overlook the Ottomans' reserves and granted the country a positive clearing balance with the Reichsbank in an effort to persuade Turkey to increase imports from Germany. Stable economic relations between the two countries had developed since the 1920s based to a large extent on German imports of Turkish agricultural products. The Germans, in spite of differences over foreign policy, were also very interested in Turkey's chrome ore and paid prices for Turkish agricultural products which were on average 30% above world market prices thus buying their way into increased trade for the valuable metal. [554]

From the mid-1930s the increasingly industrialized Turkish economy depended on the import of processed goods and raw materials, more than half of which were supplied by Germany – from 47.5% in 1938 to 50.7% in 1939. On the other hand, Germany absorbed over 44% of total Turkish exports. [555] Even during the great depression, in the years between 1932 and 1938, trade between the two countries quadrupled. While the Western powers were not prepared to grant interest-free loans, Germany granted major loans and accepted financial losses, thereby gaining economic and political influence in the south and southeast of

---

[553] Ibid.

[554] Brock Millman, " Credit and Supply in Turkish Foreign Policy and the Tripartite Alliance of October 1939: A Note," in: International History Review. Vol. XVI (1994)

[555] Willi A. Boelcke, Deutschland als Welthandelsmarkt, 1930-1945 (Stuttgart, 1994), p. 92-93

Europe. [556] The Turkish government observed this increasing trade dependency on Germany and, given developments in that country, was concerned. [557]

From the German point of view, the total volume of trade with Turkey was of relatively minor importance. But there was an irreplaceable pearl among Turkish exports. This was chrome ore, or rather chromic iron ore, which along with tungsten was high on the German armament industry's list of needs. Like tungsten supplied by Spain and Portugal, Turkish chrome ore had important characteristics for producing high temper steel, which was of major importance for the German armaments industry.

It was not only the Turkish government which was becoming increasingly concerned about the growing German influence on the Turkish economy. The British and French knew well the vital importance of that country's geopolitical situation and its chrome ore deposits. It secured the Balkan arena, served as a buffer against Russia, and could dominate trade routes in the eastern Mediterranean and into the Black Sea. It was obvious that their suspicious eyes also fell on Turkish chrome ore deposits. Countermeasures to block Germany were urgently called for and so on May 12, 1939, a British-Turkish, and on June 23, 1939, a French-Turkish, declaration were signed, in which Britain and France declared their intention to oppose any act of aggression in the Mediterranean. On October 19, 1939, a Treaty of Mutual Assistance, also called the Tripartite Alliance, was concluded between Britain, France and Turkey. These agreements aimed to foil any plans the Axis powers might have to move into the Balkans and Mediterranean, as long as Turkey was not involved in a war with Russia. [558]

As fate would have it, Ankara had received a loan of $55 million from Germany shortly before the outbreak of war. This loan was to finance purchases of machines and weapons from Germany. [559] In reaction to the Allied declarations Germany cancelled this loan. On January 8, 1940, Turkey signed a credit agreement for 43.5 million pounds sterling with Britain and France, with Britain as the main creditor providing 42 million. Of this sum, 15 million pounds sterling in gold was used to increase the reserves of the Turkish central bank. A second loan from Britain gave Turkey 25 million pounds sterling at an interest rate of 4% over 40 years. [560]

---

[556] Wilhelm Treue, "Das Dritte Reich und die Westmächte auf dem Balkan. Zur Struktur der Aussenhandelspolitik Deutschlands, Grossbritanniens und Frankreichs 1933-1939," in: Vierteljahreshefte für Zeitgeschichte, No. 1 (1953), p. 45-64

[557] Öner Günçavdı and Ertuğrul Tokdemir, "The Second World War And Capital Market Development In a Neutral Country: The Case of Turkey," in: Joseph Jung, Herbert R. Reginbogin and Robert U. Vogler (ed.), Financial Markets of Neutral Countries during the Second World War (in preparation by the Association of Financial History and the Principality of Liechtenstein).

[558] Eizenstat (1998), J.R.M. Butler, "The History of the Second World War", in: United Kingdom Military Series, Grand Strategy. Vol. II September 1939 – June 1941. (London, 1958), p. 301 and Sir Llewellyn Woodward, British Foreign Policy in the Second World War. (London, 1962), p. 13-14, 127 and 129

[559] Selim Deringil, "The Preservation of Turkey's Neutrality During the Second World War: 1940", in: Middle Eastern Studies, Vol. 18 (1982), p. 30–53

[560] Öner Günçavdı and Ertuğrul Tokdemir, "The Second World War And Capital Market Development In a Neutral Country: The Case of Turkey," in: Joseph Jung, Herbert R. Reginbogin and Robert U. Vogler (ed.), Financial Markets of Neutral Countries during the Second World War

This loan was the result of intensified Anglo-French diplomatic activities in Turkey and showed that the two countries, particularly Britain, were prepared to pay well for Turkish support. It was not the first loan or the last. The total amount given by the Allied powers to Turkey in loans or gifts between May 1938 and February 1940 totaled at least 58 million Turkish lira (about $250 million). 26 million Turkish Lira were given before the war and 32 million after the outbreak of the war. [561]

Relieved to have a way to avoid closer ties with the Axis, Turkey now came under pressure from the Allies. They sought to persuade the Turkish government to forsake neutrality and enter the war on the Allied side. For both camps, the Allied powers and the Germans, Turkey was a much coveted prize. The conclusion of the Montreux Convention of June 20, 1936, permitted Turkey to fortify the Turkish Straits and to close them to foreign warships in the event of war. [562] Britain was willing to dodge certain clauses of this agreement and tried to induce Turkey to grant free passage to the Black Sea for British war vessels. [563] Unless the British Navy had access to the Black Sea, Britain could not supply war materials to Poland or protect Romania against attack. [564]

Germany and the Soviet Union were interested in Turkey's maintaining strict neutrality since this would prevent a British-French presence in the Black Sea. In addition, for the Soviet Union, Turkish neutrality eliminated the danger of a confrontation with the Western powers in the Balkans (Romania). [565] If Turkey entered the war, it would be a major positional asset to either side, not to mention the Turkish army of about a million soldiers which protected Turkish national interests and provided the country's internal and external security. [566] Fearing a surprise attack, Turkey had already taken military measures in various parts of the country after the conclusion of the so-called Steel Pact. [567] The British also gave Turkey extra support through an air force mission and the training of Turkish air force personnel in Britain with the aim of boosting Turkish air power in the Aegean and in Thracia. [568]

The Allied powers and the Germans both made major efforts to woo Turkish public opinion, paying columnists to write sympathetic articles and even bribing government officials. [569] According to official correspondence between the German Foreign Minister Ribbentrop and von Papen, the German ambassador

---

(in preparation by the Association of Financial History and the Principality of Liechtenstein).

[561] NARA, RG 38 370/13/22/02 File: Foreign Economic Development: U.S. Division of Military Economics, 1940 Box 597

[562] Zehra Onder, Die türkische Aussenpolitik im Zweiten Weltkrieg. In: Mathias Bernath (ed.) Südosteuropäische Arbeiten Vol. 73 (Munich, 1977), p. 13

[563] Ibid., p. 24

[564] Ibid., p. 23

[565] Ibid., p. 28

[566] Altemur Kiliç, Turkey and the World. (Washington, D.C., 1959), p. 110

[567] Op. cit., p. 23

[568] Ibid.

[569] NARA, RG 38 370/13/22/02 File: Foreign Economic Development: U.S. Division of Military Economics, 1940 Box 597cf. B. Rubin, Istanbul Intrigues. (Istanbul, 2002)

in Turkey, Germany dispatched the sum of five million Reichsmarks in 1942 to support its sympathizers in Turkey. [570]

Between 1941 and 1942, Turkey moved closer to Germany again, not because it had rediscovered its affection, but to safeguard provisions for its people. Increased Turkish contacts with the Axis naturally provoked doubts of Turkish loyalty in the Western camp. None of Allies were particularly concerned with where else neutral Turkey could obtain essential goods. The Allies themselves were not willing or able to guarantee supplies for Turkey's basic needs. For the Turkish government, continuing trade with Germany was – as in the Swiss case – not a question of loyalty but a question of the country's right to secure essential goods needed by its population regardless of where they came from. But Turkey remained closer to the Allied powers, fulfilling its treaty obligations and not granting German forces permission to cross Turkish territory. At one point, Turkey gave such permission, but rescinded it two weeks later – before it could be used. [571]

In order to maintain its neutral status, the Turkish government signed another agreement with Germany on June 18, 1941, providing for a ten-year period of friendship and economic co-operation. This Turkish-German agreement confirmed the integrity of the Turkish borders and the mutual understanding that no hostile action, either direct or indirect, would be undertaken one against the other. The Germans promised to keep their troops 20 miles from the Bulgarian-Turkish border, and – in contrast with his behavior so far – Hitler kept his promise. [572]

Turkey undertook to supply Germany with certain food stuffs and raw materials in exchange for goods Turkey itself needed. German deliveries to Turkey even included – perhaps foolishly for the Germans – steel and war materials which Turkey used to strengthen its defenses against Germany. [573] All in all, notwithstanding minor decreases, Germany remained an important trading partner for Turkey until 1944.

After the spring of 1941, Turkey became what some called the Western powers' spoiled child in their economic war against Germany. Preferential treatment was based on Turkey's importance for the British position in the eastern Mediterranean and the Middle East, as well as on Churchill's personal attempts to draw Turkey into the war on the British side. Even though Turkey declared the 1940 Tripartite Treaty invalid, insofar as France could no longer fulfill its obligations, special treatment provisions for Turkey did not change. [574]

---

[570] Öner Günçavdı and Ertuğrul Tokdemir, "The Second World War And Capital Market Development In a Neutral Country: The Case of Turkey," in: Joseph Jung, Herbert R. Reginbogin and Robert U. Vogler (ed.), Financial Markets of Neutral Countries during the Second World War (in preparation by the Association of Financial History and the Principality of Liechtenstein).

[571] Christian Leitz, Nazi Germany and Neutral Europe During the Second World War. (Manchester, 2000), p. 92

[572] Eizenstat (1998), p. 113

[573] Öner Günçavdı and Ertuğrul Tokdemir, "The Second World War And Capital Market Development In a Neutral Country: The Case of Turkey," in: Joseph Jung, Herbert R. Reginbogin und Robert U. Vogler (ed.), Financial Markets of Neutral Countries during the Second World War (in preparation by the Association of Financial History and the Principality of Liechtenstein).

[574] J.R.M. Butler, "The History of the Second World War", in: United Kingdom Military Series, Grand Strategy. Bd. II September 1939 – June 1941. (London,1958), p. 301 and Sir Llewellyn Woodward, British Foreign Policy in the Second World War. (London, 1962), pp. 13-14, 127

Referring to its neutrality, the Turkish government had always said that it would keep up its political and economic relations with Germany and in 1942 signed a credit agreement with Germany for 100 million Reichsmarks ($35 million) to finance military goods supplied by Krupp. [575] It is perhaps ironic that the defenses of Turkey, Russia, Spain and Switzerland were strengthened by German deliveries and that in the event of an attack, as in Russia or in the violation of the Swiss border, Germany would be facing its own weapons.

Chrome Ore

Even before the outbreak of the war, Turkey had attached major importance to its relations to the USA, and when the United States entered the war, these relations were given new impetus. According to the Lend Lease Agreement introduced in 1941, the American government granted Turkey military support amounting to US$45 million. [576] However, considerably more effort than just purchase option programs for chrome ore and other strategic goods were needed from the Allies to decrease or indeed stop German-Turkish trade.

In October 1943, the Turkish government signed a further agreement with Germany in which Turkey undertook to supply Germany with 135,000 tons of chrome ore in 1944. Apart from the Allied purchase options, it is estimated that Turkey supplied Germany with 44,000 tons in 1943 and as much as 8,000 tons of chrome ore in the first month of 1944 alone. [577]

Again the Allied powers were angry, but neither they nor Turkey were aware at the time of the critical role of Turkish chrome ore in Germany's war production. On November 10, 1943, German Minister for Armament and Ammunition Albert Speer reported in a memo to Hitler the results of a recent inventory of metal alloys. His memo ended with the words:

"Chrome ore is the element with lowest stocks. This is particularly serious since chrome ore is indispensable for a highly developed armament industry. If supplies from Turkey were to be cut off, our existing stocks of chrome ore would only last 5-6 months. After that, the production of planes, tanks, motor vehicles, tank shells, submarines, and nearly the entire spectrum of artillery would have to be ceased within a period of one to three months because by then the stocks still in the distribution channels would be used up." [578]

According to Speer's statement, the war would have ended in approximately 10 months after the loss of the Balkans if the chrome supply were to be cut off. [579] Does this mean that the Turkish deliveries of chrome ore helped prolong World War II? In Speer's opinion the answer would be yes.

---

and 129

[575] E. Bisbee, The New Turks Pioneers of the Republic 1920–1950. (Philadelphia, 1951), p. 193

[576] Öner Günçavdı and Ertuğrul Tokdemir, "The Second World War And Capital Market Development In a Neutral Country: The Case of Turkey," in: Joseph Jung, Herbert R. Reginbogin and Robert U. Vogler (ed.), Financial Markets of Neutral Countries during the Second World War (in preparation by Association of Financial History and the Principality of Liechtenstein).

[577] Eizenstat (1998), p. 125

[578] Ibid., pp. 125-126

[579] Walter Hofer, "Wer hat wann den Zweiten Weltkrieg verlängert? Kritisches zur merkwürdigen These einer Kriegsverlängerung durch die Schweiz," in: Kenneth Angst (ed.), Der Zweite Weltkrieg und die Schweiz. (Zurich, 1997), p. 113

In the spring of 1944 Turkey proclaimed that it would cease chrome ore trade with Germany, and in June announced an export reduction of 50% for various other goods. As in other neutral countries this change of opinion was the result of Allied pressure. On April 14 the Turkish Foreign Minister received a letter from the US and British ambassadors containing critical demands that trade with Germany be wound down. If Turkey did not yield, the letter threatened that blockade measures which the two governments had already applied to other neutral countries would also be applied to Turkey. [580] The wording of the letter implied that, because of Turkey's geopolitical importance and potential as a war ally, neutral Turkey had so far been exempted from blockade measures.

However, neither the Allies nor the Axis were ever absolute and unyielding in their demands on Turkey. While Turkey tried to maintain a balance, the Germans and the Allied powers were both using a wide range of official and unofficial measures to pull Turkey into the war. No less than seventeen foreign secret-service agencies operated in Turkey during the war. Nothing and no one was out of bounds. An attempted attack on Franz von Papen, the German ambassador in Turkey, on February 24, 1942, led to a diplomatic crisis between Turkey and the Soviet Union. [581]

Treatment of Non-Moslems

Notwithstanding the Turkish president's efforts to maintain formal neutrality, he faced groups within and even outside of his own country which had reasons of their own to destabilize the country's neutrality and push this land of the earlier Ottoman Empire toward joining one side or the other. He was not always successful in following specific self-imposed policies by curbing the influence of political, ideological, anti-secularist or irredentist opinions. There were always doubts about the government's resolve and true intentions in the face of internal tensions.

K. Alemdar points out that German pressure on Turkey increased considerably in 1942 and that the government yielded by discharging 26 Jews who had worked for Anadolu Ajansı, the state-owned Turkish news agency. [582]

Some members of government were sympathetic to a broad definition of a Turkish empire. Prime Minister Saraçoğlu and Numen Menemencioğlu, Secretary General at the Foreign Ministry and Foreign Minister after 1942, as well as Fevzi Czkmak, chief of the general staff, were so keen to exert Turkish authority over Turks living abroad that in the end President İnönü had to force them to relinquish their posts. [583]

Government measures also created inflation which resulted in rampant black markets and speculation. German firms in Turkey profited from these black mar-

---

[580] op. cit., p. 125

[581] Robert Denniston, Churchill's Secret War: Diplomatic Decrypts, the Foreign Office and Turkey, 1942-1944. (London, 1997), p. 50-68; cf. B. Rubin, Istanbul Intrigues. (Istanbul, 2002)

[582] Öner Günçavdı and Ertuğrul Tokdemir, "The Second World War And Capital Market Development In a Neutral Country. The Case of Turkey," in: Joseph Jung, Herbert R. Reginbogin and Robert U. Vogler (ed.), Financial Markets of Neutral Countries during the Second World War (in preparation by the Association of Financial History and the Principality of Liechtenstein).

[583] Christian Leitz, Nazi Germany and Neutral Europe During the Second World War. (Manchester, 2000), p. 96-97

kets which sprang up as a consequence of war and restrictions imposed by the authorities. In the early years of the war the Turkish government, led by Prime Minister Refik Saydam, attempted to clamp down on such illegitimate trading by introducing allocation programs. Government controls over economic activity were increased in both domestic and foreign trade. [584]

However these interventions – intended to fight shortages of goods and curb black market activities – were largely unsuccessful. In fact the whole program came to an abrupt end when Prime Minister Saydam died in 1942. The following government, led by Rüştü Saraçoğlu, relied on the market's power of self-regulation and, soon after coming to power, eliminated all price controls and allocations. In this economic climate, a new tax law, the so-called Varlık Vergisi, was passed which introduced a tax on capital for the rich who did not pay any other taxes. The new law also included measures subtly aimed at decreasing the longstanding dominance of non-Moslems in Turkish business life. [585]

Even before the beginning of the war, non-Moslems had been subject to attacks in Turkish society. European anti-Semitism of the 1930s was picked up by some political groups in Turkey. For example, in 1934 a newspaper appealed for a boycott of Jewish merchants in Thracia, who were said to be exploiting 'poor Turkish peasants'. This was the old but still effective tactic of persecuting unwanted minorities by claiming they were oppressing a disadvantaged domestic group. But agitations playing to paranoia and economic distress were easy to employ – contrary to one's best belief – and often successful – then, today or as a thousand of years ago. Calculated diatribes against the Jews were followed by the organization of so-called justified spontaneous public outrage in three locations in Turkey and orchestrated public indignation forced some ten thousand of the thirty thousand Jews living in the area to move to the relative safety of Istanbul. [586]

Many Turks also raised protests against Turkish tax laws. According to Istanbul's Finance Minister Faik Ökte, the newly introduced taxes were extremely unfair and highly discriminatory. Those who could not manage to pay them were banished to work camps in Aşkale, a snow-bound town in Erzurum in eastern Turkey. These facilities were not gulags or concentration camps. Internees were not put to hard labor and some were even allowed to travel to Istanbul to deal with personal matters. Nevertheless, imprisonment for non-payment of taxes remained a sore point and a rallying cry.

The financial consequences of non-payment of taxes could be severe. The government could seize and sell, sometimes at very disadvantageous prices, the delinquent's property – houses, apartments, shops, etc. as well as personal valuables. Owners of foreign companies were also expected to pay. American-owned businesses were exempt from tax but not those owned by Germans. This perceived injustice against Germany outraged the Nazis. After the German embassy in Turkey exerted sufficient pressure, the total tax burden on Germans was reduced to 3 million Turkish liras. The Varlık Vergisi tax was only levied for two years, but brought some 315 million Turkish liras into government coffers – including

---

[584] op.cit.

[585] Ibid.

[586] Ibid.

116 million from non-Moslems, 115.5 million from Moslems and 33 million from foreign nationals. [587]

Notwithstanding positive short-term effects for the government, the long-term repercussions of this draconian tax policy were disastrous. Turkish banks with a large number of non-Moslem customers were considerably affected. For example, the Bank of Saloniki lost 42% of its customers after the introduction of the tax. [588] Moreover, there was a drastic reduction in the number of non-Moslem entrepreneurs who had major textile manufacturing companies in Turkey and the lingering affect of the measures even dampened non-Moslem investment after the war ended. [589]

Esther Benbassa and Aron Rodrigue in their *The Jews of the Balkans* and William Weicker in his *Ottomans, Turks, and the Jewish policy: a History of the Jews of Turkey* agree that the Jewish population in particular suffered under these measures. Although the Varlik Vergisi capital tax targeted not only Jews but all non-Moslems, there was a comparatively high number of Jews among the 1,400 people sent to the work camps in Askale for being unwilling or unable to pay the taxes. [590] Both books deal with the atmosphere before and after the adoption of the law in 1942 and reach the conclusion that its passage was the result of a significant level of anti-foreign and anti-Jewish sentiment. However, this rather 'structural' Anti-Semitism in the years between 1920 and 1945 was in no way comparable to the extreme measures undertaken by the Axis powers. [591] For this speaks the fact that Turkey allowed tens of thousands of mainly Jewish people to pass through Turkey on their way to Palestine. [592]

Turkish Gold

Along with Portugal, Spain, Romania, Hungary and Slovakia, Turkey too was a net recipient of German gold, albeit to a much lesser extent. It was estimated that the Turkish central bank received gold worth US$ 10 million from the Deutsche Reichsbank, both via the SNB (Swiss National Bank) and directly from the Deutsche Reichsbank.

The only official transaction of looted gold which could be traced to the Turkish government was a purchase of Belgian gold worth $3.4 million. Documents coming from the Reichsbank and the Prussian mint show that 249 ingots of Belgian gold were confiscated by the Germans, recast and sent to the Turkish central

---

[587] Ibid.

[588] Ibid.

[589] Z. Y. Hershlag, Turkey: Challenge of Growth. (Leiden, 1968); cf. E. C. Clark, "The Turkish Varlık Vergisi Reconsidered", in: Middle Eastern Studies Vol. 8, No. 2 (1972), p. 214

[590] Esther Benbassa and Aron Rodrigue, The Jews of the Balkans (Oxford 1995), pp 159-198; William Weicker, ttomans, Turks, and the Jewish policy: a history of the Jews of Turkey. (1992), pp. 250-251

[591] Cf. various representations: Stamford J. Shaw, Turkey and the Holocaust. (New York, 1993); Ira Hirschmann, Lifeline to a Promised Land (1963), p. 137ff; Dina Porat, The Blue and Yellow Stars of David (Cambridge 1990) and Dalia Ofer's article, "The activities of the Jewish Agency delegation in Istanbul, 1943" in "Rescue Attempts during the Holocaust: Proceedings of the Second Yad Vashem Historical Conference", April 1974

[592] Stamford J. Shaw, Turkey and the Holocaust. (New York, 1993)

bank in March 1943. [593] At the beginning of the war Turkey and Switzerland were the only European countries which had not imposed wholesale state restrictions on private trading in gold. [594] However, as the war continued German banks in Turkey got involved in gold transactions, which proved to be an extremely profitable business. The Istanbul branch of the Deutsche Bank (DBI) in particular dealt with gold transactions between Istanbul and Zurich on behalf of its customers. The DBI also cashed convertible Reichsmark checks issued by diplomats. When the Turkish market began to reject these checks, the DBI sent them to Zurich to exchange them for Swiss francs. These Swiss francs were then used to buy gold which in turn was transported to Istanbul. It was openly sold on the free market and the equivalent amount of Turkish lira, after deduction of sizeable commissions, was then credited to the accounts of German diplomats and other issuers of Reichsmark checks. [595]

At the end of the war, the books of the Deutsche Bank Istanbul showed that it had sold an overall amount of 4,967 kilograms of gold between April 23, 1942, and July 31, 1944. [596] 83.5% of this gold came from the Deutsche Reichsbank, the remainder from purchases in Zurich. The overall value of the gold sold on the Istanbul gold market was said to be $5.6 million. [597]

Towards the end of World War II, the United States also directed its attention to German gold passing to Turkey. There were two categories: gold bought by the government and put in its financial institutions, and gold bought on the flourishing Turkish gold market in private transactions.

It was almost impossible to estimate the total value of such transactions during World War II because the majority of German gold transactions took place through Turkish private banks and individual buyers. Estimates concerning the amount of gold transferred to Turkey were between $10 and $15 million. On March 28, 1946, the USA, Britain and France presented Turkey with a formal proposal concerning the return of looted gold. Although the Allied powers, at that point the de facto government of Germany, had claimed all German assets abroad, *this* proposal refrained from dealing with the return of other German assets in Turkey. Such assets were first estimated to total $51.2 million. Later, after additional calculations, the estimate was raised to $71 million. [598] In private conversations some Turkish government officials confirmed that German assets in Turkey were even higher than estimated by the Allied powers, but that Turkey was not about to pay what it considered reparations to the Allied powers. [599]

Allied efforts undertaken in 1946 to reach an agreement with Turkey concerning the return of gold and German assets were never pursued vigorously. America became concerned about the world-wide dramatically worsened chrome ore situ-

---

[593] Eizenstat (1998), p. 128

[594] Unabhängige Expertenkommission Schweiz – Zweiter Weltkrieg UEK (ed.) Die Schweiz und die Goldtransaktionen im Zweiten Weltkrieg. (Zurich, 2002), p. 121

[595] A. Barkai, et al., The Deutsche Bank and its Gold Transactions during the Second World War. (Munich, 1998), p.31-33

[596] Harold James, Die Deutsche Bank im Dritten Reich. (Munich, 2003), p. 171

[597] op.cit.

[598] Eizenstat (1998), p. 133

[599] Ibid., p. 137

ation in the summer of 1946 and moved to cement relations with Turkey with a friendship agreement which contained provisions on the supply of chrome ore. [600] A further reason for the lack of pressure was the developing relationship between the western Allies and Turkey following the Soviet Union's 1946 repetition of its 1945 demand to be included in the administration of the Turkish Straits controlling access to the Black Sea. The United States immediately rejected the Russian demand and in September 1946 gained French and British support for a massive military and economic assistance program to Turkey. [601]

In their final attempt to conclude an agreement with Turkey over its wartime activities, the Allied powers *confirmed* that because Turkey had declared war on Germany in February 1945, it had technically not been neutral. The Allies could justify renouncing their claims to German assets in Turkey in exchange for a satisfactory agreement concerning gold. The USA was still seeking the return of Belgian gold valued at $3.4 million as well as $400,000 in gold debited in Switzerland against the Ribbentrop account and sent to Turkey. But there was only silence on the part of the Turks. Finally, the Allies made Turkey what they termed a bargain offer whereby Turkey would pay just $1 million into the international gold pool.

But Turkey had not reacted to previous advances nor did it budge on the so-called bargain offer and another proposal after July 1947. [602] Further attempts by the governments of Britain, France and the United States to persuade the Turkish government to yield to their demands on gold fell flat, too, until the three powers had to admit on August 1, 1953, that their efforts had been to no avail. [603]

There never was any agreement between Turkey and the Allies, either for the return of looted gold or on the use of liquidated German assets in Turkey to aid victims of National Socialism. [604]

VICHY FRANCE – THE ANOMALY

People on various sides have expressed the opinion that all neutral European countries collaborated with Hitler's Germany during World War II. Such charges of collaboration by governments in certain cases may be valid, but it is important not to look at these actions apart from what was actually happening during the war and the situation in which neutrals found themselves. Neutrals were more often than not engaged in a life or death struggle against infinitely more powerful opponents to maintain their economies, their sovereignty and political systems. The only western country which can – with considerable justification – be called a collaborator of Nazi Germany was Vichy France. The defeated but unoccupied part of France was actually classified by Britain as an enemy state and included in blockade measures. What did the Vichy government do to be labeled a collaborator?

---

[600] David A. Alvarez, Bureaucracy and Cold War Diplomacy: The United States and Turkey, 1943-1946. (Thessaloniki, 1980), p. 87
[601] op. cit., p. 135
[602] Ibid., p. 138
[603] Ibid.
[604] Ibid.

After the Germans had occupied a number of neutral countries – Norway, Denmark, Holland, Belgium and Luxemburg – the American ambassador in France William C. Bullit vigorously supported the French government's request to buy American destroyers and also sympathized with the French wish that America should enter the war against Nazi Germany. Bullit conveyed an urgent French request to the American president for the dispatch of squadrons of war planes to France immediately and later replace them by those ordered as early as 1938. Roosevelt agreed to send some planes but rejected all other requests made by Bullit. [605]

France indeed had placed a major order for planes with the Americans in 1938, an order which in early 1940 was worth $425 million. The French wanted the most advanced planes and their cash order for $425 million allowed American airplane manufacturers to quadruple their production capacity. [606] However, when the Germans launched their attack on May 10, 1940, only 10% of the ordered planes had actually arrived in France. [607] While the lightning German invasion prompted Roosevelt to deliver a few more planes, he was not prepared to support France with military intervention or to confront the pervasive anti-war mood in Congress and in America generally. [608]

Against this extremely tense background, events moved rapidly. As the French army reeled back even the relationship between Britain and France became increasingly poisonous. The French expected more support from the British and considered even the slightest disengagement as British dereliction of its treaty obligations.

After the French capitulation Hitler decided not to occupy all of France. Instead he permitted the establishment of a government in the city of Vichy, led by Marshall Henri-Philippe Pétain, the French hero of World War I. The government of unoccupied France was to be known as Vichy France controlling two-fifths of the French nation. More importantly, however, Vichy did remain in at least nominal control of the French empire – primarily French colonies in Africa. [609] In 1940, not desiring an extended war in territory he did not choose, Hitler needed peace and quiet in Africa.

By signing the armistice on June 22, 1940, France formally violated its declaration of March 28, in which Britain and France both promised not to sign any armistice or peace treaty without the other partner's agreement. However, the British were in no condition to put France under pressure for this violation. Rather the British hoped that French forces would manage to continue fighting in Europe and overseas. There was also the issue of the French fleet. The possibility that the French navy – then pulled back to the North African coast – might fall into the hands of the Germans was a nightmare for the British. They made the bold

---

[605] FRUS, Vol. I (1940), p. 222.

[606] John McVickar Haight, Jr., American Aid to France, 1938-1940. (New York, 1970).

[607] Frank Costigliola, France and the United States. The Cold War Alliance Since World War II. (New York, 1992), p. 12.

[608] FRUS, Vol. I (1940), p. 250.

[609] Robert O. Paxton, Vichy France: Old Guard and New Order, 1940-1944, (New York, 1972), p. 8.

and unprecedented move of launching an air attack – and largely destroying – the French squadron lying at anchor in Oran. This British attack against the French navy of July 3, 1940, resulted in the loss of the French battleships Dunkerque, Bretagne, Mogador and Provence. The next day the remnants of the French government broke off diplomatic relations with Britain. [610]

Hitler did allow the rump government at Vichy to keep considerable control over France and its colonies. The Germans were not eager to divert resources into administering such a large expanse of enemy territory. The control of France was largely in French hands, with the country divided into the territories occupied by Germany and the unoccupied territories. Shortly after the British sank the French fleet, the National Assembly meeting in Clermont-Ferrand on July 10, 1940, granted power of attorney to the Pétain government by a vote of 569 to 80. Marshall Pétain took on the title of Chef de l'État français and immediately affirmed his cooperation with the National Socialists by instituting proceedings against previous leading statesmen, and on the strength of a law adopted on July 24, 1940 the Pétain government announced the loss of French citizenship for those who had fled abroad after May 10, 1940. [611]

Many French were rendered depressed, cynical and pessimistic by their country's capitulation. However, the Vichy government's representatives went so far as to paint the French defeat as an opportunity for a rebirth of the French nation and a chance to put a quick end to a futile war. Those who championed cooperation with the Nazis argued that this was the only way to save France from the depths to which it had sunk under prior governments. [612] Early on and with considerable fervor, Pétain seemed to welcome his new role as a favorite of the Nazis. In a statement to the American ambassador in France, Bullit, on June 4 – even before the armistice was signed – he said he expected that "...the British, after a very brief resistance, or even without resistance, would make a peace with Hitler which might involve a British government under a British Fascist leader." [613] Obviously the Pétain government had already adapted to the so-called New European Order and expected, according to the rules of *Crowds and Power,* that other democratic nations would soon fall under National Socialist rule.

At this point old antagonisms between France and Britain emerged with a vengeance. The British considered Vichy France to be collaborating with the Nazis and watched it with great suspicion. The French resented what they saw as British hostility to their county. Formal diplomatic relations between Britain and France no longer existed and, although there was no declaration of war between the two, Britain considered Vichy France enemy territory for economic purposes. Virtually all contacts were prohibited and the export of goods to either part of France fell under the Britain's "Trading with the Enemy Act" subject to the British blockade.

---

[610] A. G. Ploetz (Hrg.), Geschichte des Zweiten Weltkrieges. (Würzburg, 1960), p. 146.

[611] Ibid.

[612] NARA, RG 38 370/13/22/02 Entry 98A – Social Conditions France Box 576, Statement of the Morals of the French People (August through December, 1941), p. 6.

[613] FRUS, Vol. I (1940), pp. 238-239 – Bullitt to Cordell Hull.

Nevertheless, in 1940 Britain did hold secret talks with Vichy France in Madrid with the goal of improving relations, but primarily to solve issues such as continuing payments to British and French pensioners living in the other country, and resolving compensation due on British government properties in France and vice versa. The negotiated transfer amounted to some millions of French francs, but Vichy's payment practices were not rigorous and so the British Treasury was obliged to advance funds from time to time to cover the obligations of the French. [614] This was indeed bizarre: One wartime state voluntarily advancing millions to a country under enemy control, to a country therefore with which it had no diplomatic relations and officially considered an enemy state. In modern times Britain's actions were unprecedented!

But Britain advanced these monies for reasons of its own. So-called enemy assets had not yet been subjected to official controls by any British organ tasked with administration of enemy property. Although government plans, both civilian and military, assumed that the war would last for some time, it was not clear how long and the relative calm of the first few months contributed to a business as usual attitude in financial circles which lasted well into 1940. Certain transactions with the enemy were indeed still permitted on the basis of licenses issued by the British Trading with the Enemy Board. Such licenses were then administered through a Swiss intermediary. [615] Although neutral companies were blacklisted for trading with the enemy, property was not (yet) subject to controls.

British banks and financial institutions were asked to be suspicious of financial transactions made by neutral countries in Britain, but the Trading with the Enemy Board had not yet worked out a process for controlling activities suspected of serving enemy interests. While various British agencies tried to obtain information on enemy assets for tax purposes, at this early stage of the war in mid 1940, the controlling body's task consisted in inventories of such property to preserve rights and records for future disposition, rather than for immediate seizure and sale. By and large, property issues between Britain and Vichy France were still managed on a business as usual basis. [616]

Persecution of Jewish Citizens

Although there was an active French résistance and a government in exile led by Charles de Gaulle, the Vichy government *voluntarily and without German pressure* started systematic and legislative persecution of Jewish citizens of France. In view of French history, one might have expected that the principles of liberty, equality and fraternity, so often uttered by voices trembling with emotion, would include all citizens of the French state. Far from it: liberty, equality and fraternity were not applied uniformly to all French citizens. Not only the Jews of France but also Jews who had succeeded in fleeing to France from the east soon felt the full force of unequal treatment.

---

[614] PRO, FO 371/24296

[615] PRO, FO 371/25055 Foreign Office dispatch No. 11 to Basle, January 29, 1940.

[616] Foreign & Commonwealth Office General Services Command (ed.) Historians, LRD, History Notes. British Policy towards Enemy Property during and after the Second World War. No. 13 April 1998, pp. 5-8.

The Vichy government worked hard to keep on Germans' good side. The most notorious of the measures introduced was the 'Statut des juifs' of October 3, 1940. The law embodied strong similarities to the racial laws existing in Germany. It excluded Jews from top positions in government and the civil service, from the military and from all professions which might influence public opinion, such as jobs in teaching, the media, radio, film and theater. In the end, Jews were only allowed to hold subordinate public positions, and then only if they were able to prove that they had fought on the French side in World War I or distinguished themselves in some other way. The law also limited the participation of Jews in the so-called liberal professions. Other laws allowed authorities to strip individuals of French citizenship if it had been acquired after 1927. About 15,000 citizens lost their French nationality in this way. [617] Furthermore, Vichy permitted the incarceration of foreign Jews living in France and legalized the confiscation of Jewish property, again without any pressure exerted by the Germans.

Historian Philippe Burrin, in his book *France under the Germans: Collaboration and Compromise*, comes to the conclusion that a significant percentage – between a sixth and a fifth – of the French population supported collaboration. Not only the Vichy government but also millions of French citizens quickly adapted to the German way of thinking and acted to support German policies. Collaboration between Vichy France and the Germans extended deeply into daily life, including social and business relations, prostitution, cultural and scientific exchange. It also led to the formation of a pro-Nazi, anti-Jewish militia eager to do the Nazis' dirty work for them. [618]

Christopher Browning has stated that there were absolutely no Nazi-German dictates to pass anti-Semitic laws. [619] In the summer of 1940 the Germans, or rather the German military in France, were primarily absorbed with creating a secure base for continuing the war against Britain. It was not until the fall of 1940 that attention shifted from immediate military concerns to longer-term political issues. But in the meantime, France's Vichy government had already moved ahead on its own and established an administrative foundation to facilitate a reliable collaboration with the Nazis.

French Banks – Willing Helpers

Soon after the capitulation of France French banks started confiscating the accounts of their Jewish customers both in German-occupied and in Vichy territory. During the German occupation over one hundred French banks worked in a quasi-collective manner to root out about 80,000 accounts held by roughly 56,400 Jewish customers over 15 years of age. All these identified accounts were "Aryanized" – confiscated – and about 6,000 bank deposit boxes were also blocked. [620] The fig-

---

[617] Michael R. Marrus and Robert O. Paxton, Vichy France and the Jews. (New York, 1981), p. 4-5: cf. David Pryce-Jones, Paris in the Third Reich. A History of the German Occupation, 1940-1944. (New York, 1981), pp. 160-161.

[618] Philippe Burrin, France under the Germans. Collaboration and Compromise. (London, 1997).

[619] Christopher Browning, The Final Solution and the German Foreign Office. (New York, 1978); cf. also Julian Jackson, France: The Dark Years, 1940-1944. (Oxford and New York, 2001).

[620] Mattéoli Commission, Summary of the Work by the Study Mission on the Spoliation of Jews in France. April 17, 2000, pp. 10 and 25 Cf. Commission for the Compensation of Victims of

ures quoted here are based solely on estimates obtained from French banks and there is considerable skepticism as to the accuracy of these numbers. In addition, the figures reported to the government commission only represent the occupied zone, excluding the assets confiscated by French banks in Vichy France. [621]

Richard Weisberg stated to the American House Committee on Banking and Financial Services: "These banks not only followed the law, they made the law." [622] The banks wielded enormous influence by appointing an 'Aryan' administrator for Jewish property and determining fees. They were not forced to do this, but voluntarily implemented anti-Jewish legislation and made considerable profit in the process. [623]

Blind towards Anti-Semitic Legislation . . .

The decision by the United States to establish full diplomatic relations with the government of Vichy France is questionable at best. There was not a word of criticism from the US concerning Vichy's new anti-Semitic legislation. It also seemed to escape American notice how closely the Vichy government was cooperating in furthering the policies of National Socialist Great-Germany. Despite accepting Vichy, America was at the same time quick to judge other neutral countries, declaring out of hand that their trade agreements were synonymous with collaboration with the enemy. The fact that Charles de Gaulle had provided a French alternative – the provisional national committee established in London on June 18, 1940 – was also conveniently ignored.

. . . as were British banks

Immediately after the armistice between Germany and France, the subsidiaries of foreign banks in the occupied zone were controlled by a German general, a Dr. Michel, who was put in charge of civilian affairs in the zone. Michel appointed a military officer, von Falkenhausen, as representative of foreign banks in occupied France. He had been a director with Deutsche Bank before the war and was given the title of Temporary Administrator of Enemy Banks in France. Von Falkenhausen remained in that position only until July 1941 when he was recalled because the Reichsbank came to suspect his favoring the interests of German private banks over those of the German government. He was replaced by Hans Joachim Cäser, who had previously been a legal adviser to the Reichsbank and was a friend of Hjalmar Schacht. Because of his previous higher positions, Cäser was given much more far-reaching authority than his predecessor. [624]

Spoliation of Jews in France. http://www.cisvs.gouv.fr/uk/commission/commission01.htm. and Mattéoli Commission's Final Report, www.ladocfrancaise.gouv.fr.

[621] Michael J. Bazyler, Holocaust Justice. The Battle for Restitution in America's Courts. (New York, 2003), p. 174.

[622] Hearings on Banking and Financial Services, World War II Assets of Holocaust Victims. House of Representatives, September 14, 1999; R. Richard Weisberg, Vichy Law and the Holocaust in France (1997).

[623] Ibid. Cf. also Vivian Grosswald Curran, "Competing Frameworks for Assessing Contemporary Holocaust-Era Claims," in: Fordham International Law Journal. Vol 25 (2001). Section 121.

[624] NARA, RG 131 Box 138 France: Investigation of British Banks – Summary of Report on the Activities of the British Banks Operating in France during the German Occupation, p. 3a.

Joachim Cäser had full control of all British banks on the occupied Channel Islands, as well as of Westminster Foreign Banks, Ltd., Barclays Bank (France) Ltd., Lloyds & National Provincial Foreign Bank, France, Ltd., Banque Canadienne, Crédit Foncier Franco-Canadien, The Royal Bank of Canada (France); Thomas Cook & Sons, Bankers, Banque pour les pays de l'Europe Centrale and Société Parisienne en France. [625]

Cäser permitted British banks to keep their management staffs, which were by that time French – since British citizens had all left France – provided they came to see him every week and informed him about current operations. The banks' staffs were required to present monthly balances and quarterly profit-and-loss accounts to their German overlords. All credit transactions exceeding 200,000 francs likewise had to be reported. [626]

Germany had good reasons not only to tolerate the continued existence of British banks in France, but to promote them. The authorities recognized the financial potential of their properties and subsidiaries and made great efforts to persuade them to continue doing business in France. Speedy, forceful action might have resulted in immobilizing or even destroying bank records of value to the Germans. But bank operations remained intact and so these banks' resources could be used to extend loans to industries producing for Germany and to finance the export of goods supplied to Germany by France. By including foreign banks in the financial program for France, Germany recognized the importance of maintaining strong international banking links which might ultimately serve as a foundation for reestablishing orderly and efficient bank structures in the post-war years. [627] But the most likely important reason to keep these banks happy was the hope that someday after the war was over that the subsidiaries of these banks all over the world would cooperate with Germany on an international scale. [628]

In June 1940, the following British banks were among those subject to the control of the Officer for Civilian Matters: [629]

Barclays Bank (France)

Westminster Foreign Bank Ltd.

Lloyds & National Provincial Foreign Bank (France) Ltd.

Bank of London and South America, Ltd.

The main activities of British banks consisted of extending short-term loans to French exporters who were waiting in the queue for payments from the German clearing bank. Using British banks provided special advantages for borrowers. Since these banks were under the purview and protection of the German administrator, it was not only quicker to obtain loans from them (French banks had extensive bureaucracies and were slower in processing and approving loans). Also transactions made through British banks were hidden from the French Ministry of

---

[625] Ibid., p. 4.
[626] Ibid., p. 2 Draft British Bank in Occupied France.
[627] NARA, RG 131. 230/38/15/06 Box 138 Memo Report of the Activities of the National City Bank of New York (Paris) S.A. during German Occupation of France.
[628] Ibid., p. 1 Draft British Bank in Occupied France.
[629] Ibid.

Finance due to taxation and other purposes. [630] Occasionally, these British banks even granted long-term loans to finance special German war projects.

The Westminster Foreign Bank assisted the German Aerobank in overcoming its shortage of operating capital by depositing French securities worth 50 million francs in the German bank. British banks also supported French companies working for Germany, such as the Société Générale de Bauxite, which was granted a line of credit by Westminster. The Westminster Bank was also generous in the long-term credit sector. It essentially granted a sizeable loan to the German-owned Mittelmeer-Handelsgesellschaft (Mediterranean Trading Society), which was building fortifications along the French Mediterranean coast, by allowing the company to overdraw its accounts – without supplying standard guarantees to the bank. [631]

Barclays granted the Wendel Lims Company loans of between 6 and 16 1/2 million francs so that it could extend its production, a transaction which benefited the Herman W. Göring Steel Works. [632]

Lloyds supported a French armaments company working for Germany by granting loans and also propped up the financially weak Aerobank with securities worth 150 million francs. [633]

British banks also served as safe havens and conduits for German assets. The so-called Treuhand, the German operation responsible for all enemy nationals' property, deposited its confiscated or stolen acquisitions with Barclays and Lloyds. Capital from the occupation tax was deposited with Westminster Bank for the Reichskreditkasse (Reich Credit Bank). These tax funds were later withdrawn to purchase shares in foreign companies. [634]

Willing Obedience

According to the intermediate report by Mattéoli, during World War II the French subsidiaries of two British banks, Barclays and Westminster Foreign Bank Ltd., handed over to the Nazis accounts of French Jews worth about 3.5 billion old French francs, about a half billion pounds sterling at today's prices. The major part of these monies were then deposited by the Germans with the French Caisse des Dépôts et Consignations. [635]

The French management staffs of British banks also disregarded their privacy obligations to their British employers by disclosing the names and accounts of bank customers to the Germans. However, not all British banks under German occupation displayed such subservience. The banks on the Channel Islands, which retained their British staffs, were also subject to Cäser's administration. He visited Jersey in late 1941 and instructed the banks to fill out questionnaires on their overall operations. These general requests were quickly followed by requests for account specifics. When the questionnaires were returned to Cäser, fourteen out of

---

[630] Ibid.

[631] Ibid., p. 3.

[632] Ibid.

[633] Ibid.

[634] Ibid.

[635] www.telegrap.co.uk vom 4. Februar 1999 "Banks Accused Over Nazi Cash," von Susannah Herbert. Documents compiled by Dr. S. D. Stein Stuart.Stein@uwe.ac.uk

twenty questions – including those concerning nationality and information about whether the bank's customers included Jews – were not answered. Cäser phoned the Jersey banks and was informed that it was not British banking practice to register customers' nationalities. After some negotiation, the British said they would complete the questionnaires with the facts known to them. When the corrected documents were returned to Cäser, however, the majority of customers were declared to be British and the nationalities of the remaining few were listed as not known. Thus the British banks on Jersey made it clear they were not distinguishing between Christians, Jews, and Island or mainland dwellers to aid the Nazis in uncovering assets owned by foreign nationals. The German inquiries were essentially refused. Cäser decided not to visit the other Channel Islands or Guernsey and returned to Paris. Later German banking overseers were not so easy to rebuff but at least in this case the British were successful in stonewalling the Germans. [636]

Unfortunately their French colleagues did not display the same backbone. The Mattéoli report and other documents show that between 1940 and 1944 many of the French and British banks in France even anticipated orders issued by the occupiers and by the Vichy regime. The accounts of about 330,000 Jews were plundered with the assistance of British banks in occupied France. [637]

In retrospect it is hard to understand how the French management of those British banks could possibly be so eager to agree with the German perception of race. The banks willingly provided Joachim Cäser with information on the racial composition of their own bank staffs, including unsolicited proposals on what should be done with Jewish employees. Barclays, Westminster and Lloyds in Paris even commissioned studies from their subsidiaries in the unoccupied part of France and passed the results on to German security agencies.

During the war Barclays had 12 subsidiaries in France besides its central office in Paris. Barclays – like the other banks – maintained that it had *no contact* whatsoever with its subsidiaries after the German occupation. But such claims are extremely difficult to accept considering that the Germans rewarded the actions of the French management staff of British banks by arranging that, after February 3, 1941, the subsidiaries:

a) Enjoyed the same rights as French banks,
b) Had telephones put at their disposal for calling the unoccupied territories,
c) Were granted visas for travel to the unoccupied zone – and abroad. [638]

There is considerable evidence to support – and none to refute – the assumption that the representatives of British banks displayed a strong tendency to cooperate with the Germans, not only to fulfill the stated wishes of the German administration but to do more than was requested. Cäser adopted the practice of confirming in writing that the banks had been ordered to grant loans, but the banks themselves never requested such letters. [639]

---

[636] John Wadsworth, Counter Defensive. A Bank in Battle. (London, 1946), pp. 51-52.

[637] op. cit.

[638] NARA, RG 131 Box 138 France: Investigation of British Banks, – Summary of Report on the Activities of the British Banks Operating in France during the German Occupation, p. 3.

[639] Ibid., p. 16 – – Summary of Report on the Activities of the British Banks Operating in France during the German Occupation.

The subservience of these banks ranged from the miniscule to the absurd. They presented all requested reports as ordered and on time. They put up no resistance to supporting the war economy of Germany – the enemy of both France and Britain – with major loans. The representatives of the British subsidiaries saw no problem in providing extensive reports on economic and political conditions in unoccupied France, notwithstanding the fact that in doing so they both violated French law and aided German intelligence services. [640]

Some subsidiaries of American banks also found it much too easy to come to an arrangement with a German dictatorship operating under principles diametrically opposed to those embodied in the American constitution. Subsidiaries of five American banks – Chase National Bank, Morgan et Cie., Guaranty Trust Co. of New York, Bank of the City of New York and American Express – were involved in highly questionable relationships. Chase and Morgan, in particular, cooperated very closely with Nazi Germany and the remaining three started procedures for seizing accounts in line with German requests. In one way or another, the Germans were handed about 100 Jewish accounts by the American banks. Two thirds of these accounts were later returned to their rightful owners or their heirs. [641]

Summing up, it can be said that banks of the democracies – particularly the management of British banks but also of some American banks, both in the occupied French zone and in Vichy France – cooperated with the German occupiers voluntarily and without offering the least resistance. Apart from unsolicited racial cleansing of their own personnel, handing over of Jewish accounts, and passing on information on the unoccupied part of France, they facilitated increases in German war production by granting major loans to their enemy – thereby contributed to prolonging the war.

---

[640] Ibid., p. 2.
[641] Ibid.

CHAPTER III

MIRROR IMAGE

There's an old saying that even if two people do the same thing, it will end up not be the same thing. The United States government condemned trade between neutral European states and Axis powers as collaboration. But US trade with the Axis powers was categorized as "maintaining commercial interests". That is not the same – or is it?

AMERICA'S CONTRADICTORY FINANCE MARKETS

Despite half a century of research and reporting on the events of World War II, scholars have not taken a close look at the role of US finance markets during the wartime period. American actions have escaped scrutiny leveled at others even though American regulation of its financial sector was extremely uneven and at times contradictory. Both the legislation governing the sector and procedures to implement the laws which did exist were ambiguous. American ambivalence became obvious during the course – and purported punishment – of a number of dubious trades and financial transactions which benefited the Third Reich.

A marked divergence between American foreign policy and commercial interests can be observed as early as the 1930s. When Japan attacked Manchuria and Italy annexed Ethiopia (then Abyssinia), violent opposition was voiced in the United States. But protests soon faded, the country reverted to neutral isolationism – and lucrative trade arrangements continued. Congress did adopt a series of neutrality laws which formally gave all countries access to the American market. [642] However, in reality these laws were designed to benefit mainly the rich and more powerful nations.

When war in Europe broke out in 1939, the USA held to formal neutrality although America favored the threatened European democracies. Indeed President Roosevelt's assistance to beleaguered Britain against Hitler's Germany in the form of the Lend-Lease Act was a clear violation of the United States' status as a neutral. [643]

On April 10, 1940, Roosevelt reacted to the German invasion of Denmark and Norway by issuing Executive Order 8389 to freeze assets of citizens resident in countries occupied by Germany. Immediately the question arose as to whether the Trading with the Enemy Act, passed during World War I, and which had served

---

[642] Cf. Walther Hofer and Herbert R. Reginbogin, Hitler, der Westen und die Schweiz. (Zurich, 2001), pp. 575 – 584.

[643] Arthur L. Funk, "American Wartime Relations with Neutral European States: The Case of the United States and Switzerland", in: Les Etats neutres européens et la Seconde Guerre mondiale. Neuchâtel 1985), p. 283.

as the basis of Order 8389, extended to freezing stocks and shares. The Treasury Office helpfully dealt with this thorny issue by issuing General Ruling No. 2 on April 19, 1940, affirming that the Order indeed included stocks and shares. Roosevelt's order in fact was intended as a stop-gap measure until the Trading with the Enemy Act could be amended, as it was on May 7, 1940. Shortly after the invasion of Denmark and Norway, a Department of Foreign Assets Control was established within the Treasury Office. That department had the authority to prohibit United States residents who did not hold a Treasury Office license from doing any foreign currency transactions. [644] This measure, permitted under section 5(b) of the original 1917, Trading with the Enemy Act, was to prevent Nazi access to foreign currency.

However with time Roosevelt's Executive Order 8389 had far-reaching effects on America's politics, monetary policies and on the ways in which the country's financial markets were regulated. Freezing foreign assets was the first step on the road to all-out economic warfare. The regulation of the financial services sector by state intervention and freezes was part of the national program of monitoring 15,000 banks and similar institutions to prevent transactions benefiting the Axis powers. [645] These state control mechanisms had the positive side effect of preventing significant capital withdrawals, ruling out the potential danger of American capital markets being destabilized and weakening the American economy.

The policy of the American Treasury Office and of the State Department during that critical time was ambiguous at best. While the United States officially proclaimed its neutrality, Executive Order 8389 clearly supported Britain and its allies and sought to prevent financial transactions which might benefit the Third Reich and undermine the American economy. At the same time, however, General Licenses for trade with Germany – the a future enemy – were issued because they were considered "to render greater benefit to the US government than they provided to the enemy". [646] It remains unclear who actually profited more from such licenses. In any case, the American government did not prohibit American companies from doing business deals within German-occupied countries, even after the USA had entered the war. In other words: the American government permitted companies to do business with its 'arch – enemy'. [647]

Control of the American financial market was a constant bone of contention between the State Department and the United States Treasury. Assistant Secretary of State for Economic Affairs Dean Acheson wrote: "From top to bottom our [State] Department, except for our corner of it, was against Henry Morgenthau's campaign to apply asset and currency freezes to Axis countries and their victims." [648] While the Treasury campaigned aggressively for a rapid extension of controls, the State Department urged holding back on such controls with equal force. State was worried about the United States' neutral status and didn't want to risk reprisals stemming from precipitous actions on the part of the US govern-

---

[644] Geschichte des FFC, chapter 3, p. 28.

[645] Ibid., chapter 1, p.19.

[646] Ibid. chapter 1, p. 19.

[647] John S. Friedman, "Kodak's Nazi Connections," Nation, March 26, 2001, p. 7.

[648] Dean Acheson, Present at the Creation (New York 1969), p. 23.

ment. [649] The State Department was very concerned about preserving the immunity of US diplomatic pouches. Oddly enough it was not Germany which violated the Executive Order, but Vichy France. That country used diplomatic pouches to circumvent the US capital market and avoid its currency controls. The State Department thought the aggressive measures considered by the Treasury might result in an end to the immunity of diplomatic mail. Although the War Department agreed with the Treasury, the American chiefs of staff did not want to make any changes to the treatment of that privileged mail. For its part, the State Department stressed the high value of intelligence coming from Switzerland via diplomatic pouches and stated: "it is absolutely necessary that the government undertake no action which might lead to reprisals against our (diplomatic) mail." [650]

As a result of this policy disagreement America's finance and production industries continued to serve Hitler and his regime unchecked until, on June 14, 1941, fourteen months after Roosevelt issued the first blockade order, the Treasury Department called for the long-awaited inventory of all foreign assets in the United States. This was to provide a full report not only of all assets of blocked countries, but also of all assets held by all foreign nationals in the United States.

Report TFR-300 produced this inventory and it was the most comprehensive survey to be published since the government started blocking foreign assets in the USA. It was also the first time in US history that such an inventory had been implemented. [651] All types of assets were supposed to be recorded. [652]

On the basis of these assets – one listing discovered in June 1940 and an additional listing in June 1941 – the government could track transfers and the exchanges of assets. Property valued at less than $1,000 did not have to be registered unless the value could not be readily assessed. But even assets whose value was difficult to assess in dollars had to be reported, for example patents and the contents of safe-deposit boxes. [653]

The ruling was another step towards regulation of American capital markets. Financial service organizations, including banks, brokers and insurance agencies, had to report the names of all foreign nationals who had property in the USA and list properties in which the named persons had an interest. Banks had to report the names of foreign nationals for whom they held securities, as well as the names of recipients of all outstanding bills of exchange, including foreign nation-

---

[649] Geschichte des FFC, chapter 5, p. 101.

[650] Ibid.

[651] The alphabetical index on the TFR-300 reports, (series C-1), and the TFR-300 Report Correspondence were legally destroyed in 1987, after the NARA had assessed them as disposable and their destruction had been approved by the Justice Department. The results of the census were published by the Treasury Department in 1945 in the Census of Foreign-Owned Assets in the United States. On July 14, 1941, the total value of foreign assets in the United States amounted to $12,738,700,000.

[652] "Geschichte des FFC", item 4, p. 20: The following assets needed to be reported: bullion, currency and deposits; domestic and foreign securities; drafts, acceptances, letters of credit, promissory notes, debits and contracts; miscellaneous personal property such as bills of lading, commodity options, merchandise for business use, machinery, jewelry, objects of art; real estate and mortgages; patents, trademarks, copyrights, franchises; estates and trusts; partnerships and insurance policies and annuities.

[653] Ibid., pp. 20–21.

als who were named as beneficiaries of letters of credit. Insurance companies had to report retirement accounts, pensions, as well as claims and debts pertaining to insurance policies. Brokers had to report balances, securities and investment profits belonging to foreign nationals. The rule was extremely comprehensive. All assets, whether real estate or cash, in any form whatsoever in the USA, had to be reported by a whole range of responsible financial institutions. [654] The reporting was to give the government complete visibility into the financial affairs of foreign nationals so that whatever controls were established would be effective.

As a result of this unprecedented order of June 14, 1941, and the USA's subsequent entry into the war on December 7, 1941, the Nazis had considerable difficulty in using assets in the US and routing payments through American financial institutions.

It was only long after the war ended that Americans came to assess the actions of American businesses during the Nazi period. Eventually the government issued a report containing the names of American companies which had continued to trade with the Nazis before and during World War II and who profited from such dealings. The report included well-known names -Chase National Bank, Standard Oil of New Jersey, Texaco, IBM, ITT, the Ford Motor Co., General Motors. [655]

FORD MOTOR COMPANY / GENERAL MOTORS / STANDARD OIL OF NEW JERSEY

During World War II Ford tolerated the use of forced and slave labor in the Ford plant in Cologne, Germany. [656] These laborers were civilians from eastern European countries and the former Soviet Union who had been deported to Germany, as well as contingents of Jewish prisoners who could be requested from the German military by private companies. [657] Although this fact was known, it was not until 1974 that the American public learned about what could be termed collaboration with the enemy by Ford Motor Company and General Motors. The government subcommittee report reads as follows:

"Due to their concentrated economic power over motor vehicle production in both Allied and Axis territories, the Big Three inevitably became major factors in the preparations and progress of the war. In Germany, for example, [as the U.S. was a neutral country] General Motors and Ford became an integral part of the Nazi war efforts. GM's plants in Germany

[654] Ibid., pp. 21–22.

[655] Charles Higham, Trading with the Enemy: An Expose of the Nazi-American Money Plot 1933-1940. (New York, 1983); Walther Hofer and Herbert R. Reginbogin, Hitler, der Westen und die Schweiz. (Zurich, 2001).

[656] In this study, concepts such as forced labor, slave labor, or the NS concept of foreign labor to be used in the Reich (Reichseinsatz) can be found in various forms, in legal, political, moral and historically descriptive forms and they are alternately used in debates. Cf. Florian Freund and Bertrand Perz, Die Zahlenentwicklung der ausländischen Zwangsarbeiter und Zwangsarbeiterinnen auf dem Gebiet der Republik Österreich 1939-1945. (Vienna, 2000) www.historikerkommission.gv.at/pdf/Zahlen_pdf.pdf

[657] Simon Reich, Nachforschungen von Ford zur Beurteilung der Aktivitäten ihrer Tochtergesellschaft während des Nationalsozialismus. December 6, 2001. http.//media.ford.com [called Ford Works Report in the following].

built thousands of aircraft propulsion systems for the Luftwaffe at the same time that its American plants produced aircraft engines for the U.S. Army Air Corps...Due to their multinational dominance of motor vehicle production, GM and Ford became the principal suppliers for the forces of fascism as well as for the forces of democracy." [658]

In 1939 Ford and General Motors together controlled over 70% of the German market. At the beginning of the war both companies retooled into war production in order to fulfill the demands of the German Wehrmacht. [659] The USA headquarters of both companies were informed about the activities of their German subsidiaries. They never showed any intention to divest themselves of their German subsidiaries or their shares in these operations. [660] Documents in Russian archives show that Ford decided to keep its majority stake in the Cologne Ford plant and to support the continued involvement of US companies in German enterprises. [661] American managers justified their attitude by saying that withdrawing American investment would create 'a politically unfavorable image'. [662]

On March 26, 1942, a committee established by Congress directed harsh criticism at Standard Oil of New Jersey because this company had given the German Navy details of the process for manufacturing synthetic rubber while withholding such information from the United States and the British military.

Researchers also quoted correspondence between Standard Oil and the German IG Farben conglomerate concerning a secret trade agreement concluded between these two concerns intended to maintain a modus vivendi relationship throughout the war – whether the USA entered the war or not. Senator Harry Truman, chairman of the specially established Defense Investigating Committee, publicly condemned this arrangement as "treason" and "a crime", while an Assistant US Attorney General considered the agreement as a trick for continuing an illicit relationship during the war. [663]

On September 22, 1939, when the death machines of World War II had already started rolling, German IG Farben and Standard Oil concluded the so-called Hague Memorandum wherein the two companies agreed to maintain communications even if the USA entered the war. IG Farben sold several patents and blocks of shares to Standard Oil in The Hague, or rather entrusted them to Standard Oil for safekeeping. Both concerns had concluded a special agreement which permitted IG Farben to buy back its shares and patents as soon as this could be done without

[658] Bradford C. Snell, American Ground Transport: A Proposal for Restructuring the Automobile, Truck, Bus and Rail Industries. Committee of the Judiciary Subcommittee on Antitrust and Monopoly, United States Senate 16-24 (1974) in: Hearings before a Subcommittee of the Senate Committee on the Industrial Reorganization Act, 93rd Congress 2nd Session (1974), Part 4A p. A-22.

[659] Michael Dobbs, Ford and GM Scrutinized for Alleged Nazi Collaboration, Washington Post, November 30, 1998. p. A1.

[660] Ibid.

[661] RGVA, Bestand 700-1-85, Effektenhandel zwischen Fa. Otto Wolff und der Schweiz und mit weiterem Ausland., p. 444-445; cf. Walther Hofer and Herbert R. Reginbogin, Hitler, der Westen und die Schweiz. (Zurich, 2001).

[662] Ibid.,p. 442.

[663] Edwin Black, IBM and the Holocaust. (New York, 2002), p. 429.

risk, i.e. after the end of the war. The patent for the production of synthetic rubber led to ludicrous developments over American rubber supplies.

According to the Hague Memorandum, Standard Oil received the patents for synthetic rubber (Buna) from IG Farben but initially was not provided with the technical know-how to produce the product. Of course the German government had banned the transfer of such critical information. However, there was not, as it turned out, enough time for formal licensing procedures between the end of development in Germany and the outbreak of the war. But Standard Oil did indeed own the process rights and developed sufficient knowledge to duplicate the IG Farben process for producing synthetic rubber. Assuming the increased demand for rubber in America due to war-related developments could not be met by deliveries to the US from the Far East, Standard Oil offered to sell the process to the American government's armaments planners. However the Roosevelt administration rejected Standard Oil's offer, because that administration a) was not very pro-industry and b) perhaps believed that Standard Oil was profiteering, and c) in 1939/1940 did not foresee that an adequate supply of rubber might indeed become a serious problem for the US.

It was only after the collapse of France that American planners became aware that it might be smart to start caring about US demand for rubber. But the newly earned wisdom did not help in time to develop and implement a long-term supply solution. In an endless tug-of-war orders were made for runner in all different directions, for example to Standard Oil and Dow Chemical. Orders were placed, reduced, increased again as swamped government planners sought to assess and allocate supply against demand. In this way the bureaucrats had succeeded in creating a severe rubber supply shortage which – after the USA entered the war – became in fact an existential problem for the armaments industry. But still chaotic and often contradictory wartime orders flowing through a complex bureaucracy continued to cause problems. In addition, anti-trust measures implemented by American judicial authorities resulted in Standard Oil and IG Farben both being accused of undermining US war preparations. But it was the anti-industry attitudes of Roosevelt's economic administration which was responsible for this rubber circus. Only in 1942, when the government managed to create a Rubber Director with broad authority did it become possible to pursue a coherent rubber policy. Within a short time, the foundation for a vast expansion of the American synthetic rubber industry was created.

But relations between Standard Oil and IG Farben Deutschland were indeed excellent. As Hitler came into power the two companies also shared technology for producing synthetic petrol from coal. The production of synthetic petrol was absolutely indispensable for the German war machine. In 1934 German domestic production only amounted to about 30,000 tons of natural petroleum derivatives and less than 300,000 tons of synthetic petrol. Remaining requirements had to be imported. With the process obtained from Standard Oil of New Jersey for manufacturing synthetic petrol, production could be successively stepped up in Germany. By 1944 German output had risen to a total of 6.5 million tons. 85% of this output – 5.5 million tons – consisted of synthetic oil whose production was made possible by the use of oil hydration patents and associated technology obtained from Standard Oil. [664] With this transfer the output of synthetic oil products in Germany could be increased by millions of tons.

There were further examples of such collaboration. In 1935 Standard Oil and General Motors provided Germany with technology to produce lead-tetraethyl and liquid ethyl used as anti-knock agents in aircraft and automobile engines to increase engine efficiency and prolong engine life. [665] Without such additives it was impossible to build a modern, motorized army. In 1977 Albert Speer told American lawyer Braddford Snell that Hitler would never have conducted the invasion of Poland without the synthetic fuel technology provided by General Motors. [666] "General Motors was far more important to the Nazi war machine than Switzerland." [667] Bradford Snell, who had been doing research on the history of the world's biggest automobile producers for two decades, came to the following conclusions regarding the American automobile industry: "GM was an integral part of the German war effort.... In certain instances, American managers of both GM and Ford went along with the conversion of their German plants to military production at a time when the US government documents show they were resisting calls by the Roosevelt administration to step up military production in their plants at home." [668] "The Nazis could have invaded Poland and Russia without Switzerland. They could not have done so without General Motors." [669]

A committee presented the following confiscated German documents to the Senate of the United States: "The fact that since the beginning of the war we could produce lead-tetraethyl is entirely due to the circumstances that shortly before the Americans had presented us with production plants complete with experimental knowledge." "Without lead tetraethyl," the war document adds, "the present method of warfare would be unthinkable." [670]

CHASE NATIONAL BANK

In 2002 Chase National Bank, later Chase Manhattan Bank merged with J.P. Morgan to become one of the world's biggest banks under the name of J.P. Morgan Chase & Co. At the time of the Japanese attack on Pearl Harbor on December 7, 1941, Chase National Bank was already among the select circle of the richest and most powerful financial institutions in the United States. When Germany took control of France in 1940, Chase was one of the five American banks with subsidiaries in Paris and other parts of France.

---

[664] Antony Sutton, Wall Street and the Rise of Hitler, (London, 1976), p. 22.

[665] Ibid., p. 73.

[666] Michael Dobbs, "Ford and GM Scrutinized for Alleged Nazi Collaboration" in: Washington Post, November 30, 1998., p. A01.

[667] Ibid.

[668] Ibid.

[669] Ibid.

[670] In Hearings before a Subcommittee of the Senate Committee on Military Affairs on the Elimination of German Resources for War, 79th Congress 2nd Session (1946), pt. 10 especially at 1305-1306. Cf. also, Hearings before a Subcommittee of the Senate Committee on the Industrial Reorganization Act, 93rd Congress 2nd Session (1974), Part 4A p. A-22.

During the entire course of World War II, the Chase Bank in Paris partici-pated in the German embassy's finance activities – with the full knowledge of the bank's New York headquarters. Executives of the Chase Bank in France, Carlos Niedermann in Paris and Albert Bertrand and colleagues in the subsidiaries in Vichy France, seemed to be in full support of German hegemony in Europe. Like the Pétain government in Vichy, they sought to prove their loyalty to the Germans by, among other things, pushing ahead with restrictions against Jewish property. Apparently they were inspired by the same so-called pre-emptive obedience as Vichy authorities. Anticipating a Nazi decree which would prohibit withdrawals of Jewish funds from their banks, they refused – on their own initiative and be-fore such a decree were issued – to release monies in bank accounts held by their Jewish customers. [671]

Six months after the USA entered into the war, Albert Bertrand wrote a letter, dated June 5, 1942, to the New York headquarters, informing Joseph J. Larkin, vice-president for Europe, that Niedermann was continuing to work with German authorities. On June 16 Bertrand wrote that Niedermann was in the process of pulling savings accounts, securities and general records of all Chase subsidiaries in France back into Chase's Paris branch. By May 1943 the assets accumulating in Chase's Paris branch had practically doubled. The Germans watched the efforts of this American bank with great pleasure and gave it 15 million francs to cover its operating costs in wartime France. In the meantime Bertrand, with the con-sent of vice-president Larkin, transferred securities and large amounts of money throughout 1942 from Vichy France to Germany and – in co-operation with Emil Puhl of the Reichsbank – to other German-occupied countries. [672]

Both managers of Chase Manhattan Bank cultivated friendships with promi-nent Nazis and developed potential opportunities of doing business with the Third Reich. A report of the US Federal Reserve published after an investigation of the practices of the Chase Bank Paris in April 1945 stated that the New York Chase headquarters had been informed about the questionable activities of its Paris sub-sidiary but had done nothing to stop them. The same conclusion was reached in a report of the Treasury Department which stated that New York knew about Nie-dermann's activities, at least until late 1942 – in other words until well after the United States had entered into the war. [673]

THE REMIGRANT MARK PROGRAM

The US government repeatedly accused the Swiss government of allowing and even supporting operations between its banks and Germany. Leveling such ac-cusations against Switzerland reveals a glaring double standard. The USA itself did not take any legal steps to stop its own conglomerates from trading with Nazi

---

[671] Charles Higham, Trading with the Enemy: An Expose of the Nazi-American Money Plot 1933-1940. (New York, 1983); Walther Hofer and Herbert R. Reginbogin, Hitler, der Westen und die Schweiz. (Zurich, 2001).

[672] Ibid., p. 26.

[673] Michael J. Bazyler, Holocaust Justice. The Battle for Restitution in America's Courts. (New York, 2003), p. 187-188.

Germany. Indeed, Chase National Bank continued to do business with the German occupiers with the full knowledge of the US government. [674]

In 1939 alone Germany imported food stuffs, raw materials such as lead, copper, aluminum, oil and finished products worth 197 million Reichsmarks from America while German exports to the USA totaled only 124 million Reichsmarks. American dollars were urgently needed to finance not only this trade deficit but other pressing needs of the Reich. Finding new ways to acquire dollars was critical for Germany. The Reich's Ministry of Economy, led by the creative and resourceful Hjalmar Schacht, experimented with various methods. He tried using one of his subsidiaries – the German Foreign Currency Office - [675] to obtain dollars. A partial solution to the problem was the creation of the Remigrant Mark (Rückwanderer-Mark) which was first tried out in 1935 and fully legalized after 1936. With assistance of Chase Manhattan, the Remigrant Mark program was successful in bringing millions of dollars to the coffers of the Third Reich. The program sought to lure Germans resident in the United States back to Germany with generous financial offers which – after 1936 were financed by confiscated Jewish property. Chase Bank in the United States was an active participant in the Remigrant program, selling marks for dollars to Germans who were prepared to return to Germany on a temporary or permanent basis. This currency program operated until June 14, 1941, when the United States froze German assets.

Recently declassified documents give a detailed picture of the way the Nazi regime financed the resettlement of Germans returning from the USA. The Reichsbank offered German remigrants a premium exchange rate of 4.10 Reichsmarks per dollar as against the real market exchange rate of about 2.48 Reichsmarks. Documents and statements made to the Federal Grand Jury show that Chase National Bank, J. Henry Schroder Banking Corporation, Robert C. Mayer & Co., New York Overseas Corporation and the German Trade and Economic Service were authorized by the German Foreign Currency Office to handle the Remigrant Mark program. The co-operation of the New York financial institutions in the Remigrant Mark business violated the Neutrality Act, the Johnson Act, the Espionage Act of 1917 and the Foreign Agents Registration Act of 1938. [676]

The banks named were issued permits by the Berlin Foreign Currency Office to exchange US dollars for Reichsmarks at this extraordinary high exchange rate for persons intending to resettle in Germany. Additionally, persons participating in the program could obtain a permit to remigrate to Germany from the Foreign Exchange Office. But Commissions were paid only to the above named New York institutions by the German Gold Discount Bank, a subsidiary of the Reichsbank in Berlin. The entire remigrant operation was under the control of the German government – the Reich's Ministry of Economy and Office for Foreign Currency Regulation.

---

[674] Cf. Norman J.W. Goda, "Banking on Hitler: Chase National Bank and the Rückwanderer Mark Scheme, 1936-1941," in: Richard Breitman et al., Y.S. Intelligence and the Nazis. (Washington, D.C., 2004).

[675] Cf. Norman J.W. Goda, "Banking on Hitler: Chase National Bank and the Rückwanderer Mark Scheme, 1936-1941," in: Richard Breitman et al., Y.S. Intelligence and the Nazis. (Washington, D.C., 2004).

[676] Ibid., p. 189.

In the period between October 1940 and the point at which German assets were frozen in June of 1941, the US Justice Department could have taken steps against the remigrant system. Such action might not have netted the FBI and the Justice Department with the names of real subversives, but it would have hindered Germany from acquiring considerable amounts of US dollars. This is aside from the troubling issue of the commissions paid to Chase Bank and others, who profited from an operation clearly helpful to the Reich. [677]

It was not until July 1941 that the Defense Department finally reported that the Remigrant Mark program had become one of the most important sources of foreign currency for the Germans, enabling them to finance subversive activities such as espionage and propaganda in the United States – and elsewhere. [678]

Chase National Bank's management processed 4,588 of the total of 10,115 remigrant applications and received $8,993,181 for its services. [679] For Chase at that time $8 million was not a major sum of money. When asked by the Foreign Exchange Control in Berlin why the bank got involved in this minor business at all, a member of the Chase board of executives, Kuhlmann, more or less repeated a statement made previously to the Federal Grand Jury: "Chase National Bank had to be able to handle any business as long as the business pertained to foreign matters." [680] For relatively paltry commissions – and on the poor excuse that it concerned foreign matters – a major bank in a democratic state violated the law and collaborated with a murderous dictatorship.

Two employees of the Chase National Bank, Carl Weiss and Leo Kelly, did not approve of their management's actions. Without knowledge of Alfred W. Barth, who was in charge of Chase's foreign department, or other executives, Weiss and Kelly co-operated with the FBI to blow a whistle on these activities. It was absolutely necessary to get possession of original documents and so Weiss, an Assistant Cashier in the foreign department, advised the FBI to have a court issue a subpoena to Chase National Bank ordering the presentation of documents pertaining to remigrant transactions of a particular individual. The subpoena was only to contain the name of the person charged with the offense, not the number, date or amount of money charged in connection with the remigration application. It was thought a request for such details would alert Chase directors to the fact that the bank's records had been under scrutiny. [681]

When an indictment was imminent Chase hired one of the country's best lawyers, John D. Cahill. He told the FBI he knew that Chase employees had violated bank privacy rules by releasing information to the FBI and other agencies, and that he would disclose this in the course of a trial. Thereby, both the sources and legal (but not to be revealed) methods of the FBI and the Army Intelligence would have been compromised. Cahill's move threatened FBI Director

---

[677] Ibid.

[678] Ibid., p. 187.

[679] NARA, RG 65-230/86/07 02.3-4.5 Box 96 – Federal Bureau of Investigation .

[680] op. cit., p.137.

[681] NARA, RG 65 657267 Section 80 Box 96 1 of 1 65/230/8607 01-45 correspondence P. E. Foxworth, Assistant Director to Edgar Hoover, Director of FBI July 9, 1942 regarding German Funds.

Edgar Hoover's expectation that only information provided by summoned witnesses and not knowledge obtained by the secret service would be used in criminal prosecution. The Department of Justice decided that no FBI agent must be put in a position of having to make a public statement. In spite of Hoover's committed efforts to bring Chase National Bank to account for its actions, the case tailed off. [682]

J. P. MORGAN

Morgan et Cie. (J.P. Morgan's subsidiary in France) was another American bank which continued to operate in Paris under the German occupation. The company offered its services to both Nazi and Vichy bureaucrats, initiated anti-Semitic employment purges and emphasized the fact that none of its partners was Jewish. Nazi Germany rewarded the bank's actions by classifying J.P. Morgan as a so-called "international aryan organization". [683]

Among the five American banks in Paris, Chase Bank and Morgan et Cie. were the banks which cooperated most closely with Nazi-Germany, doing so with the full knowledge of their headquarters. Three other subsidiaries of American banks – Guaranty Trust Company, National City Bank of New York, S.A. and the American Express Company – preferred to go into liquidation rather than open their doors to the Nazis. While the collaborating banks, Chase and Morgan, were allowed to retain their stocks and shares, the other three dropouts had their remaining assets confiscated by the German Trust and Auditing Office (Treuhand- und Revisionsstelle). [684]

KODAK

Based on documents in the National Archives in College Park, Maryland, John S. Friedman wrote an article for the 'Nation' on March 26, 2001, titled "Kodak's Nazi Connections." In it Friedman detailed how Kodak subsidiaries continued to do business with Nazi Germany even after America entered the war. US authorities did not order the company to cease such trading, but permitted Kodak to continue in order "not to endanger the company's market position." [685]

During 1942 and 1943 Kodak's Swiss branch was supplied with photographic materials by Kodak plants in Germany, Hungary and occupied France. Kodak, like Ford, used slave labor in its factories on German territory. [686] In March 1942 more than three months after the US entered the war against Germany, the US Secretary of State received a note from the US embassy in Madrid recommending that import licenses for German supplies be issued to Kodak. Depriving the company of German materials would create serious difficulties for Kodak. The note went on to say that cutting off Kodak from Germany would destroy Kodak's

---

[682] op. cit., p. 193.

[683] Ibid., p. 187.

[684] NARA, RG 131 230/28/15/06 Box 138 – Memorandum for the Files "French Branches of the Guaranty Trust Company during the German Occupation of February 20, 1946."

[685] John S. Friedman, "Kodak's Nazi Connections," Nation, March 26, 2001, p. 7.

[686] Ibid.

position in the Spanish market. If Kodak could not supply Spanish demand, then the company's German and Italian competitors would take over Kodak's market share. This would result in a strengthening of the competition and put Kodak at a long-term disadvantage. Kodak would be hard pressed to regain Spanish markets after the war. [687]

In 1943 the American embassy in London referred to Kodak's considerable purchases from enemy territory. In November of the same year, a US Vice Consul in Switzerland, reporting a conversation with a Kodak manager in Switzerland, stated: "The idea that he helped the enemy does not seem to have occurred to him ... I pointed out to him that our only interest is directed at cutting our enemies off from any advantage, notwithstanding possible disadvantages that American commercial interests may suffer." [688]

In London, Kodak's lawyer explained to the British government in 1943 that because of its supplies from plants in Germany, France and Hungary, Kodak could serve more customers – substantially more, than if they had obtained their products from Britain and America alone.

IBM

In contrast with other American companies, IBM did not come under fire for allegedly collaborating with Nazi Germany during and immediately after the war. It was only decades later at the turn of the century that IBM had to face the accusation of being an accomplice of the Nazis in the context of the Holocaust. With the publication of his book *IBM and the Holocaust* in 2001, Edwin Black charged that IBM had supported the racial war and profited from this involvement. [689] Because IBM helped to organize Hitler's administration – including activities related to the Holocaust – IBM New York via its European subsidiaries headquartered in Geneva had been a so-called accomplice to the murder of European minorities such as Jews, Roma and Sinti. Dehomag (Deutsche Hollorith – Maschinen G.m.b.H.), the German subsidiary of IBM New York, praised the speed, precision and reliability of IBM machines in its publications. These machines were able to do bookkeeping and classification tasks and were used by the Germans for normal government record keeping but also in the concentration camps.

Perpetration of crimes against humanity to the extent practiced by the Nazis required considerable bureaucratic organization. So the charge that IBM machines helped facilitate the logistics of mass murder for the Germans does not seem unreasonable. [690] IBM also made money by selling similar machines in the United States and the British Empire.

Interestingly, IBM did not challenge Black's assertion but instead attacked his methods. In addition, IBM was not ready to disclose its business transactions

---

[687] Ibid.

[688] Ibid.

[689] Edwin Black, IBM and the Holocaust. (New York, 2002), p. 9.

[690] Gerichtsurteil Réf. C/1761/2002 von Genf, 11. Juni 2004 zwischen Gypsy International Recognition and Compensation Action (GIRCA) vs. International Business Machines Corporation (IBM).

during World War II. However, Werner Lier, IBM manager for Europe with head-quarters in Geneva during the war, made statements to an American investigator looking at the actions of the Geneva office. According to Lier the Geneva sub-sidiary was not autonomous but only a clearing office which implemented deci-sions made by IBM New York. On April 29, 1942, Lier, in the context of opera-tions of IBM Geneva, said to the American consul in Geneva: "You will readily understand," explained Lier, "that this office is a clearing office between the lo-cal organizations in the various countries and the New York Headquarters." [691] He added that all decisions had to be made by IBM New York. The Geneva office's tasks were purely administrative, such as monitoring business and bookkeeping. "If, for example, local subsidiaries request machines or materials from our plants in the USA, these orders first go to us and we pass them on to the New York headquarters who then supply the local branches directly." [692] The tasks of IBM Geneva also included monitoring the financial transactions of eastern European IBM subsidiaries. [693]

While IBM Geneva was carrying out these tasks, the city was – and still is – the headquarters of the International Committee of the Red Cross which was sup-plied with state-of-the-art alpha-numeric tabulator technology by IBM's president, Thomas J. Watson. Thanks to the sophisticated technology of these machines, the Red Cross was able to cope with organizing an enormous amount of data on pris-oners of war all over the world. [694]

In a 2004 judgment concerning a Roma claim for compensation for victims of World War II, and the use of IBM technology, the Swiss judge proclaimed: "In view of what we have seen, IBM complicity through material and intellectual as-sistance to the Nazis' criminal acts during World War II provided by their Geneva subsidiary cannot be ruled out." [695]

Presently, the role played by punch card tabulator technology during World War II is still being examined. It is an undisputable fact, however, that as early as 1933 Nazi bureaucrats and statisticians were seeking to develop a comprehen-sive data system – with the assistance of tabulator technology – in which racial and other vital characteristics of all citizens could be stored. While the decision to pursue the final solution was in no way influenced by the availability of highly developed calculators and tabulators, there are definite clues that Hollerith ma-chines helped rationalize the management of concentration camps which were an important element in the Nazi program of extermination through work. [696] How-

---

[691] Edwin Black, "IBM and the Holocaust," Jewish Times of July 18, 2004.

[692] Ibid.

[693] Wirtschaftsarchiv Baden-Württemberg, Stuttgart Bestand 95, Bu 141 – Memo of January 2, 1940; Re: general issues / machines from Poland of January 3, 1940; preparation for visit by Mr. Schotte on December 12,1939, and letter from Dehomag to J.W. Schotte IBM in Geneva of January 18, 1940.

[694] Archive of the Red Cross in Geneva – ACICR G AM/A; ACICR, C, G2 WA.

[695] Court judgment Réf. C/1761/2002 of Geneva, June 11, 2004 on Gypsy International Recog-nition and Compensation Action (GIRCA) vs. International Business Machines Corporation (IBM).

[696] Sybil Milton and David Martin Luebke, "Locating the Victim: An Overview of Census Taking, Tabulation Technology and Persecution in Nazi Germany," in: IEEE Annals of the History of

ever, Black was unable to prove that punch cards could be used in concentration camps for locating prisoners because the machines he cited as being able to locate Jews by name could only register numbers, not names. [697] In the spring of 1942, Dehomag was still testing two alphanumeric tabulator models, one of which used type bars, the other a rotating printing mechanism. [698]

According to some historians, the use of punch cards in concentration camps might be a telling example of the so-called industrialization of SS persecution. However, perhaps a more important contribution of IBM technology to the Third Reich was in less visible applications of punch cards – factory production, administration of the German army and in national resource and production controls for the Ministry for Armaments and Ammunition.

Other historians, such as Sybil Milton and David Martin Lübke in their essay *Locating the Victim: An Overview of Census Taking, Tabulation Technology and Persecution in Nazi Germany*, do not doubt that the racially motivated and efficient persecution of victim groups practiced by the Germans needed precise classifications and extensive cooperation between government departments. The system also relied on highly developed technical procedures for locating those groups, using criteria of age, profession, and racial characteristics. [699]

In support of this thesis the two historians demonstrate how numerous administrative tools – including two national censuses, a system for residence registration and various specific race-related data bases – were used for locating groups which were finally destined for deportation and murder. They also looked at the possible role Hollerith tabulation technology might have played in this process. Patterns in the deportation of Jews from Germany indicate that there is a high probability that census data supported this activity.

Notwithstanding Black's sometimes problematic methodologies, his book caused a controversy on the role of IBM in World War II and on the possible involvement of IBM technology in the implementation of the final solution in Eastern Europe. Dehomag was always portrayed as a company which, as a consequence of German efforts at self-sufficiency in the 1930s, was cut off from the outside world and had little if any access to the latest developments in research and production. However, recent research has shown that while Dehomag in Germany produced and sold numeric machines exclusively, IBM New York produced and marketed alphanumeric machines. So as early as 1937 the FDR Social Security Administration used alphanumeric punch card registers i.e. machines processing names as well as numbers for administering contributions and payments for old age pensions.

Was there a link between these IBM operations? Recent research has unearthed documents proving that alphanumerical technology from New York was available in the eastern European territories controlled by Germany, technology

Computing vol. 16, No. 3 (1994), p.25-39.

[697] Edwin Black, IBM and the Holocaust. (New York, 2002), p. 59.

[698] Wirtschaftsarchiv Baden-Württemberg, Stuttgart. Bestand 95. Br. 112 – Report for members of the supervisory board (Bericht für die Mitglieder unseres Aufsichtrates) of May 28, 1942.

[699] Sybil Milton and David Martin Luebke, "Locating the Victim: An Overview of Census Taking, Tabulation Technology and Persecution in Nazi Germany," in: IEEE Annals of the History of Computing vol. 16, No. 3 (1994).

which might have been used by the Nazis for finding names and numbers of potential victims.

In addition, these recently discovered documents show that the IBM New York headquarters permitted its subsidiaries in the eastern European territories to exchange American alphanumeric equipment for purely numeric models of German Dehomag. What happened to the higher value alphanumeric versions has not yet been ascertained. But Black's assertion that IBM alphanumeric machines enabled the Nazis to target the Jews by name gained back some credibility after it was proven that as early as 1940/1941 the Nazis in Eastern Europe had access to IBM alphanumeric equipment as a result of contracts between IBM New York and Dehomag. [700]

Unless the Dehomag archives and those of the German Ministry of Trade and Industry are found, many questions may remain unanswered. But the proven degree of cooperation between IBM New York and Nazi Germany adds another name to the list of American companies which continued to do business with Nazi Germany during the war.

BANK FOR INTERNATIONAL SETTLEMENTS (BIS)

Among the trade and financial organizations collaborating with Nazi Germany, the Bank for International Settlements (BIS) stands out. BIS had its headquarters in Basel, but was – and still is – not subject to Swiss law. This unique bank was headed by the American Thomas H. McKittrick, a New York banker, and during World War II supported the Deutsche Reichsbank in implementing German gold policy. The usefulness of the BIS for Nazi Germany was first recognized when McKittrick, whose country was at war with the Axis powers, was re-elected for an additional term of office in 1942 with Nazi Germany's tacit agreement. At that point the US Treasury Department was beginning to suspect that the BIS was moving assets to neutral countries to circumvent controls on such transfers by the US government. It was feared that these assets could fall into the hands of the Axis powers. [701]

Tensions arose when, in late 1942, McKittrick traveled from Switzerland to New York to meet with the current director of the Federal Reserve Bank and his predecessor, Leon Fraser. [702]

Back in July 1942 the Treasury had refused a request by BIS to transfer $1 million from its New York account to the Swiss National Bank. According to correspondence between an Assistant Secretary of State and the then US ambassador in Switzerland, Leland Harrison, it was feared that the Axis powers might well gain control of the Bank for International Settlements and thus come into con-

---

[700] op. cit. Br 108 – IBM New York & European Offices Geneva Switzerland from Harrison Chuacey in Berlin to Dehomag, dated January 24, 1941; Additional Agreement, dated January 17, 1941 – IBM New York to IBM Prague "parts of machines of either American or German origin...will be supplied by the IBM New York to the IBM Prague....[Even]...in view of the present circumstances...."

[701] Eizenstat (1997), p. 189.

[702] Arthur J. Smith, Jr., Hitler's Gold. (Oxford, 1989). S. 54; Charles Higham, Trading with the Enemy: An Expose of the Nazi-American Money Plot 1933-1940. (New York, 1983), p. 11.

trol of these assets. Later that year when Treasury was informed of an impending gold transfer to Portugal by the BIS commissioned by the Bank of France, Treasury only offered the laconic comment that the entire matter was outside its control. [703] After his arrival in the USA, McKittrick's unusual position led to considerable controversy both within and outside Congress. The question of why an American had to remain president of a bank which was promoting the machinations of the Axis powers became the subject of heated discussion. Why then, despite well founded doubts about McKittrick's role, did Secretary Morgenthau not try to force the American BIS president to stay in New York by confiscating his passport? Such an action would have prevented McKittrick returning to Europe and giving Emil Puhl of the Reichsbank an overview of current opinion and financial problems in the USA? [704] The far-reaching influence of Nazi Germany on BIS business was well known to the leadership of the United States. Nevertheless McKittrick was not prevented from returning to Switzerland. BIS collaboration with the Third Reich continued – and on the basis of current knowledge was tolerated by the Americans.

Later on an attempt was made to justify the US position on the BIS by citing a "highly anomalous situation in time of war." [705] The 1997 Eizenstat Report contains a clue that in February 1941 Paul Hechler, a German banker who worked as BIS Assistant General Manager, declared to representatives of the US Treasury in Berlin that the leadership of the bank was determined to keep the BIS alive as a center for future international financial cooperation. That leadership unanimously agreed on the necessity of keeping McKittrick in office to maintain the connection with the United States. [706] Other researchers such as Arthur L. Smith, Jr. and Charles Higham, referring to scientists such as Carroll Quigley or Anthony C. Sutton, who bluntly calls the BIS "a vast and ambitious system of cooperation and international alliance for world control." [707] Its purpose, was "... nothing less than to create a world system of financial control, in private hands, able to dominate the political system of each country and the economy of the world as a whole." [708] Contributions by Gian Trepp and Marc-André Charguéraud also portray a bank dominated by special interests and purport to show how the bank's American president served the interests of the Third Reich. [709] But even today, there is no final or complete assessment of America's financial and business connections with the BIS and Nazi Germany.

The Bank for International Settlement was founded in May 1930. Its primary task was to help solve payment problems stemming from Germany's inability to

---

[703] op. cit., p. 190.
[704] Ibid.
     op-cit., p. 55
[705] Anthony C. Sutton, Wall Street and the Rise of Hitler. (Sudbury, 1976), S. 28, See also Henry H. Schloss, The Bank for International Settlements. (Amsterdam, 1958).
[706] op.cit., p. 189
[707] op. cit., p. 27.
[708] Carroll Quigley, Tragedy and Hope. (New York, 1966), p. 324.
[709] Gian Trepp, Die Bank für Internationalen Zahlungsausgleich im Zweiten Weltkrieg: Bankgeschäfte mit dem Feind. Von Hitlers Europabank zum Instrument des Marschallplans. (Zurich, 1993); Marc-André Charguéraud, Le Banquier américain de Hitler. (Geneva, 2004).

make reparation payments for World War I as demanded by the Versailles Treaty. In addition the BIS was to be at the disposal of European and non-European central banks for coordinating financial relations and other services.

The BIS was never a bank in the conventional sense. It did not hold deposits outright, but instead maintained offices and conference rooms and administered central bank accounts. From 1938/1939 when Germany took control of Austrian and Czech gold reserves, the BIS, led by Dutchman Johann Beyen between 1936 and 1939, accommodated itself increasingly to the wishes of the Third Reich.

In the following years, as the Germans continued to expropriate the gold reserves of occupied countries, they also took over the voting rights of those national banks in the BIS. In 1939 Johann Beyen stepped down to take a post with Unilever in the Netherlands and McKittrick took office as BIS's new president. In accordance with the BIS's own rules for gold operations and accepted international law based on the 1907 Hague Convention on Land Warfare, BIS acknowledged the legality not only of the confiscation of state assets by a victorious power but also the transfer of the BIS voting rights of the vanquished to Germany. In the face of violent criticism in Europe and the United States, Germany also confiscated private assets in occupied countries. As a consequence of German actions, the BIS – having given legal recognition to German claims – over time became a loyal manager for the *illicit* transfer of 13.5 tons of looted gold from Germany and German-occupied countries. [710]

In the territories it occupied Germany acted as legal government, installed German managers in top positions in the central banks, and instructed the BIS on how to handle their gold. The BIS, led by McKittrick, recognized these new relationships and admitted to following explicit German orders in these matters. By routing gold through BIS accounts in accordance with elaborate chains of instructions from the Germans, gold could be essentially laundered and its ultimate source concealed. The BIS in Basel did not actually store gold. Rather for physical safekeeping it used the facilities of the Swiss National Bank in Bern and occasionally in Zurich. Dependence on an elaborate system of physical transfer required ever closer cooperation between all the banks involved, in spite of a certain aversion the Swiss National Bank had against the BIS. [711]

In the spring of 1940 Germany occupied France, Belgium and the Netherlands. The Bank of France had been considered a safe haven and therefore was commissioned by Belgium and Luxemburg to guard those countries' gold reserves. However, expecting the occupation by the Germans, the Bank of France succeeded in the eleventh hour in shifting the Belgian gold reserves to Dakar in North Africa. Strangely enough, Polish gold reserves also ended up in Dakar. According to a verbal agreement between the Bank of Poland and the Bank of England, Polish gold was entrusted to the French Admiralty to be transported

---

[710] Cf... Piet Clemens, Bank for International Settlements During the Second World War, December 2, 1997, in: Nazi Gold – The London Conference 2nd – 4th December 1997. (London, 1998), pp. 3 and 15

[711] Gian Trepp, Die Bank für Internationalen Zahlungsausgleich im Zweiten Weltkrieg: Bankgeschäfte mit dem Feind. Von Hitlers Europabank zum Instrument des Marschallplans. (Zurich, 1993), p. 66.

to the United States by warship. However, at the last moment it was rerouted to Dakar. [712]

Luxemburg's gold was still in France when the Germans marched in and was handed over to the Reichsbank's representatives. [713] Dakar was not to be a safe haven for Belgian gold either. Marshall Pétain, bowing to German demands, hurried to give the order to hand the Belgian gold over to the Nazis. But the physical transfer proved difficult. In 1940 a route was worked out for the transport of 240 tons of the Belgian gold which ran thousands of miles through West Africa. Due to rising logistical problems only in late May 1942 did the Germans finally get their hands on the Belgian gold. [714] They also tried to seize the Polish gold, but their efforts failed when the Americans succeeded in occupying Dakar in 1942. [715]

After the German invasion of the Netherlands, Dutch gold reserves were successively transferred to the Reichsbank and kept in Germany until 1944. The Germans were to maintain that this gold was in fact German gold from the pre-war period. To establish this fiction, the Reichsbank melted and recast the Dutch gold, marking it with the Prussian mint stamp for 1939. In this way Germany could furnish proof – required by the BIS – that the gold had been cast and marked before 1940. The same procedure was followed with Belgian gold. The Reichsbank used the gold confiscated from the central banks of occupied countries to buy foreign currency and continue interest payments due for World War I reparations.

The Reichsbank's Emil Puhl, though otherwise a realist, was still able to assure the BIS and McKittrick with a straight face that the Reichsbank fully intended to rectify these unusual dispositions and that eventually new international agreements would restore the seized assets of the occupied countries. The BIS board led by Ernst Weber, at the same time president of the Swiss National Bank, accepted Puhl's vague explanations and his assurances to the Belgians that they would get their gold back after the war. In any case the BIS put enough faith in these promises by the vice-president of the Reichsbank to permit the Germans to claim the Belgian gold in the Belgian's BIS account. [716]

Meanwhile voices for the liquidation of the BIS were getting louder. To counter criticism and no doubt to secure its role in post-war reconstruction, the BIS made every effort to portray its actions in as positive a light as possible. US State Department's economic expert Eleanor Lansing Dulles preserved a word-by-word account of a one-hour conversation she had with McKittrick on February 4, 1943. In the course of this conversation McKittrick emphasized the bank's policy of neutrality and gave great weight to Germany's promises to restore the assets of occupied nations by international agreements. [717]

---

[712] Arthur J. Smith, Jr., Hitler's Gold. (Oxford, 1989), p. 9.

[713] Ibid., p. 11.

[714] Ibid., p. 21.

[715] Ibid.

[716] NARA, RG 56, Entry 69A4707, Box 8 Interrogation of Emil Puhl, November 27, 1945, 9:30-10:15 a.m., Section 10, p. 3.

[717] NARA, RG 59, Decimal file 1940-1944, 462.00 R296BIS/2-543, Box 1415 – Memorandum "Interview with President McKittrick" from Eleanor Dulles to L. Pasvolsky and L. Stinebower, State Department, February 5, 1943, p. 7.

McKittrick also pointed out during this exchange that the BIS was punctilious in following instructions. In 1940 and 1941, for instance, the BIS was confronted with conflicting instructions for gold transfers. In May 1940 the BIS received two separate – and different – sets of instructions covering the movement of the property of the Bank of Norway – one set from Oslo (German controlled) and one from London. With no clear instructions, the BIS saw fit to reject both. In July 1940, the Baltic states – Estonia. Latvia and Lithuania – instructed the BIS to put their gold at the disposal of the Soviet Union's state bank. Since the USSR had given BIS no explicit instructions, BIS rejected the orders. In July 1941, after the German occupation of these states, the BIS again refused to move their assets unless the countries and the respective central banks provided detailed explanations. [718]

It was only in July 1944 at the Bretton Woods Conference in the USA that an attempt was made to checkmate the seemingly uncontrollable BIS. The Norwegian delegation presented a resolution demanding the liquidation of the BIS as soon as possible and the establishment of a fact-finding committee to investigate the bank's activities during the war. [719] US Treasury Secretary Henry Morgenthau criticized the handling of looted property by financial institutions and in particular came down hard on the BIS and its former president Johann Beyen, who as a matter of fact was taking part in the Bretton Woods conference as head of the Dutch delegation. The American delegation drafted a resolution requesting all neutral countries " ... to halt the disposition or transfer of looted gold within their jurisdictions." [720] However, attempts to liquidate the BIS met resistance from a small but powerful group: Dean Acheson, representative of the US State Department and head of the American delegation, maintained that such actions ought rather to be postponed until the end of the war. [721] The general manager of the BIS, Auboin, was under the impression that conference delegates' resentment of his bank arose merely from ignorance about the true nature of the bank and its activities during the war. [722]

Meanwhile Beyen and Auboin had set out to gain the support of influential American bankers who were reluctant to accept any action against the BIS and did everything in their power to block the Norwegian motion. One of these bankers was Leon Fraser, president of the First National Bank of Manhattan and a former BIS president. He smiled at the accusation that the Germans exerted excessive influence on the bank, expressing the opinion that hostility against the BIS must be politically motivated and perhaps instigated by President Roosevelt himself. Fraser even went so far as to swear an oath in front of the Congressional Hearing on BIS operations and to defend the BIS as the only logical choice for reconstruction efforts in post-war years. One week after his statement, Fraser committed

---

[718] NARA RG 84, Entry 2056, Box 27, File 851 Report "The Bank for International Settlements-Wartime Activities and Present Position," M.A. Kriz, Foreign Research Division, Federal Reserve System, 1947, p. 13. NARA Nonrecord Reference Materials of the Federal Reserve System, Federal Reserve Bank of New York Documents Related to Nazi Assets, Box 1,

[719] Arthur J. Smith, Jr., Hitler's Gold. (Oxford, 1989), p. 58.

[720] Ibid., p. 59.

[721] Eizenstat (1997), p. 199.

[722] Roger Auboin, "The Bank for International Settlements, 1930-1955," in: Essays in International Finance. (Princeton, 1955), p. 17.

suicide. [723] The Bank for International Settlements continued to exist after the war – and to date, no resolution demanding a formal investigation of its activities during World War II has had a chance of passing in any government arena. [724]

---

[723] NARA, RG 65 Entry A1 136A Box 12 Washington, October 26, 1945 Newspaper Article.
[724] op.cit.

CHAPTER IV

CONCLUSION

In assessing exactly where and how Swiss neutrality differed from that of other neutral countries during World War II, it is obvious that there have been heated exchanges between critics and defenders of Switzerland. The main points of disagreement were as follows: violation of neutrality, border and refugee controls, and economic and financial links with Germany. Those who disapprove of Swiss behavior accuse Switzerland of a whole list of sins. For inexplicable reasons, of all the neutral countries Switzerland has been singled out as the main offender and subjected to grave accusations that Swiss financial credits extended to Germany assisted the National Socialist regime in reaching its goals and contributed to prolonging the war. This accusation begged to be substantiated. Within the limited scope of the present study, the previous chapters have examined the behavior of the other neutral countries during World War II in some detail, and sought to compare such behaviors with those of Switzerland to determine whether the accusation leveled at Switzerland – that it was the main offender – was correct or not.

PROVISIONS FOR WAR

When comparing the role of Switzerland, which was surrounded by Axis powers during the era of National Socialism and Fascism, with that of other neutral countries, there are some similarities, and many differences. Without doubt Switzerland during World War II was unique in the way it integrated its military, political-diplomatic, economic and spiritual defenses in order to safeguard its independence.

The world economic crisis of the 1930s with its concomitant bankruptcies and high unemployment had major negative consequences for Switzerland. When the country's very independence came under threat, the government, the parliament as well as employers' and employees' associations recognized the necessity of avoiding destructive exchanges and confrontations which would undermine national unity.

Thanks to a defense loan accepted by a large majority of citizens, the Swiss considerably increased their military preparedness while at the same time seeking to defuse social and economic issues to achieve the highest possible level of unity and cooperation. To this common end, the otherwise quarrelling bourgeois and social-democratic political parties, as well as the vast majority of the Swiss people, came together and supported programs to strengthen the country's defenses and its determination to defend itself – both towards internal and external threats.

A wide range of measures were aimed at placing the economy on a wartime footing which, in case war actually broke out, had to guarantee the supply of essential goods both to private households and to industry, as well to provide for a considerable increase in land put under agricultural cultivation.

It must be assumed that the symbolic effect of such programs, together with the 1939 National Exhibition, contributed greatly to a unified national awareness. This was particularly important in a country where language loyalties might easily contribute to dissension. Indeed, as had been shown during World War I, German and the French speaking parts of Switzerland tended to sympathize with Germany and France respectively. In 1939, however, the entire population rallied as one around the banner of neutrality. [725]

DETERMINATION TO RESIST

When Allied and Axis pressure on Switzerland increased during World War II, with both sides trying to swing the country over to their side, Switzerland at least had an army and a fierce shared determination to defend the country. Moreover, in case of an attack, the Swiss were prepared to destroy the important transit routes through the Alps that linked Germany and Italy.

There is no evidence or documentation of any other European neutral prepared and willing to put up a prolonged military defense. *Sweden* had a well equipped army, but preferred to let its soldiers remain in their barracks for the sake of keeping the peace. *Spain's* army was even ready to be deployed in support of the Third Reich. *Portugal* gave no indication that it was prepared to defend itself. *Turkey* – the much courted jewel on the Bosporus – never experienced a situation when it had to demonstrate the fighting power of its considerable contingent of about 1 million soldiers.

Switzerland was the only European neutral country which was both prepared and willing to oppose the German colossus with all its military strength – even at the risk of a likely defeat.

The defensive effect of Switzerland's military readiness should not be rashly dismissed out of hand. From a strategic point of view Switzerland was a small island in a sea of Axis domination during the war years and, in turning down Axis demands, faced economic and military reprisals and even possibly an invasion. But its potential to affect Axis war plans cannot be underestimated. Compared with the size and military strength of Germany and Italy, the capacity of the Swiss army to resist may have been little more than a thorn, but some thorns can indeed create an inflammation and make it much more difficult for aggressors to accomplish their goals. For example, Swiss destruction of the transit routes through the Alps would have had severe repercussions to both Germany and Italy.

---

[725] Neville Wylie, "Switzerland: A Neutral of Distinction?," in: European Neutrals and Non-Belligerents During the Second World War. (Cambridge, 2002), p. 532; Christoph Graf, "Die Schweiz in den 1930er Jahren. Bericht über ein Forschungsseminar," in: Schweizerisches Bundesarchiv Bern (ed.), Studien und Quellen. No. 9 (1983), pp. 127-142.

Handling Neutrality

In spite of all its difficulties with Germany's so-called New European Order, Switzerland never failed to emphasize the importance of its neutrality in its negotiations both with the Third Reich and the Allied Powers – before and after the French defeat in summer 1940 and right through to the end of the war.

However, other neutral countries were not nearly so active in defending their neutrality. The term neutral could most fittingly be applied to *Turkey*. But Turkey never was required to defend its neutrality against opposition. The country was never really threatened since its resources were important to both the Axis and the Allies. Although in ideological terms Turkey had little affinity with Germany, the Turkish War Minister nevertheless described his country's foreign policy as an "alliance with Britain and a friendship with Germany." [726]

Spain was a dictatorship whose leader, General Francisco Franco Bahamonde, had strong ideological sympathies with National Socialism, sympathies which brought him very close to entering the war on the side of the Axis. Although Franco ultimately kept his country out of the war, he nevertheless implemented programs that essentially amounted to collaboration with Hitler's Germany, including the supply of secret service information via Spanish embassies in London and Washington until 1944. Spain's so-called neutrality did not last long after the hour of its declaration, and thereafter Spain was more inactive than neutral. Only when the defeat of the Axis Powers was unmistakably clear did Franco move towards supporting the winners, once again demonstrating the moral flexibility he had shown when he first declared Spanish neutrality. But Franco's Fascist leanings continued even then. On May 8, 1945, after the German defeat, Franco extended his regrets to the no longer existing Hitler regime, and the Spanish press praised the German army's valiant fighting spirit. In Spain the horrors of the Holocaust were played down as an entirely unavoidable and understandable consequence of the disorganization caused by the war. [727] Franco was a friend beyond the grave indeed.

Portugal was governed by Antonio de Oliveira Salazar. When war broke out, Salazar quickly declared Portuguese neutrality, although he saw the action primarily as an economic move. In violation of its neutrality, Portugal allowed Britain, and later on also the USA, to establish military bases on the Azores. And Portugal's Salazar – like Franco – expressed public regrets about the German defeat and Hitler's death.

The *United States of America* clearly violated its declared neutrality. Long before entering the war, the USA became a "non-combatant country," doing a nominal amount of trade with Germany while in reality generously supporting Britain with the Lend Lease Act. Supposedly neutral America – at Churchill's request – supplied Britain with 50 destroyers for escort duty and several US ships were involved in direct combat with German vessels.

---

[726] Neville Wylie, Britain, Switzerland and the Second World War. (Oxford and New York, 2003), p. 357.

[727] Paul Preston, "Franco and Hitler: The Myth of Hendaye 1940," in: Contemporary European History. No. 1 (1992), pp.1-2.

Sweden's Prime Minister, Per Albin Hansson, sought to keep his country out of the war at all costs. But the costs were high indeed. At the beginning of the war, Sweden had the honest intention of maintaining its neutrality, but Swedish neutrality was quickly cut down to miniature size when this irritated the Nazis. Because of its prime minister's iron determination to stick with his no-war decision, Sweden was forced into wide-ranging co-operation with Nazi Germany during the entire war in blatant and ongoing violations in particular giving permission to allow German troops to cross Swedish territory was a severe offense of Sweden's neutrality.

With considerable justification, Switzerland can be said to have been be the only neutral country, which can be proved to have been prepared at all times to defend its long tradition of neutrality in all areas.

BLOCKADE ISSUES

Throughout the war, Switzerland and to a large part also Sweden was effectively surrounded by the Third Reich and had no choice but to trade with Germany. But Sweden retained at least limited access to the oceans and shipping links to the Soviet Union thanks to its long coastline. Trade with the Allies was only possible with the Third Reich's permission. With few geographic constraints, Spain and Portugal could maintain economic links with both warring parties, and Turkey was never forced to hold blockade negotiations.

Continuation of supplies to the Swiss economy depended on difficult, ongoing negotiations with both Allied and Axis powers over the terms of import and export. Such negotiations, held against far reaching German demands and an every sharper blockade enforced by both sides required the Swiss to make their way along a tight rope balancing economic issues and the rights of Swiss neutrality. The challenge was obtaining supplies of coal, iron, food and other necessary goods imported from the spheres of influence of the warring countries.

The other neutrals, with the exception of Turkey, were also subject to the rules of their own negotiated blockade agreements. However Sweden had a supplemental agreement with Britain, which allowed her to procure goods from outside the Allied blockade – even though the British realized that such goods might pass to Germany. Yet the same issue, namely the possibility that Swiss imports might somehow be transferred through to Germany, led to almost hysterical Allied reactions in blockade negotiations with Switzerland. England, in its single concession to flexibility with its blockade, allowed Switzerland to build up but a two-month stock of provisions. Neither Spain nor Portugal seems to have been hit by the level of blockade restrictions applied to Switzerland. One cannot avoid the conclusions that there were two standards and not only in the blockade – one for Switzerland and another for the rest of the neutrals.

Gold Trade

Switzerland has been much criticized for its trade in gold and foreign currency. [728] However, other facts are seldom mentioned. The USA had unlawfully blocked all Swiss gold and foreign currency reserves on June 14, 1941. American trusts and the subsidiaries of both US and British banks in France made substantial investments which contributed to the establishment of Germany's New European Order (whether with or without the knowledge of their home offices still needs to be ascertained). American banks, even in the USA, supported various German financial projects in violation of American law. The US itself accepted foreign gold without ascertaining its origin. Was this not engaging in gold trade for profit? Yet the Allied powers accused the neutral countries – and particularly Switzerland – of doing what America did. What's more, contrary to official accounts, until the introduction of form TFR-300 on June 14, 1941, capital markets in the United States were not so thoroughly regulated as to prevent US financial institutions from fulfilling orders from their German customers either directly or via intermediaries.

The American accusation – that gold was traded without consideration of its origin and that profits were made in these transactions – could be made against *all* neutral countries and also against the USA itself. But no European country *except Switzerland* had financial institutions active in virtually all international markets *and* the most coveted European currency. Is it any wonder, then, that the volume of gold transactions and resulting profits were higher in Switzerland? Even had the Swiss banks been able to limit such trading, is not the chief raison d'être of any financial center the buying and selling of gold and trading with foreign currencies? Should Switzerland, as some moralists seem to demand, have simply closed down its financial centers and thereby endangered the country's important means of provision allowing it to survive?

Accusation of Prolonging the War

Switzerland is often singled out for having supplied war materials to Germany and thereby faced with the heavy accusation of having prolonged the war. Yet such criticisms hardly ever mention the activities of other European neutrals – Spain, Portugal, Sweden and Turkey – who all supplied Hitler's war industry with in some cases considerable amounts of both raw materials and finished products. Strangely enough, German imports of Spanish/Portuguese tungsten, Turkish chromium ore and ball bearings and iron ore from Sweden have never been mentioned in the same accusatory tone as the small amounts of war materials supplied by Switzerland. Yet tungsten, chromium ore, ball bearings and iron ore were all indispensable for German armament production. Had such supplies been stopped, or even significantly restricted, Germany would have been forced to end the war at a much earlier date.

In a larger perspective, arms supplied by neutral countries to the Third Reich amounted to very little compared with Germany's own armament production. This also applies to Swiss arms exports, which were of such a small amount com-

---

[728] Eizenstat (1997), p. iii.

pared with German production that even the critical Bergier Commission came to the conclusion that "neither the arms supplied nor the financing of strategic raw materials had . . . a detectable effect on the duration of the war." [729] So Switzerland did *not* contribute to prolonging the war by its supplies. The Commission's report concludes the accusation that Swiss loans prolonged the war were likewise without substance.

WAR PROFITS

Switzerland is accused of having profited from the war. Indeed, Switzerland's economic relations with Axis powers caused Swiss industry to look for innovative solutions to problems which in turn led to new forms of organization and new products. These technological advances, combined with undamaged production facilities and a strong presence in the German market, certainly gave Switzerland an advantageous position in the post-war years. [730]

In this context, however, Portugal, Spain, Turkey and Sweden – as well as subsidiaries of US companies – also made considerable profits. It seems almost absurd to accuse only Switzerland of war profiteering.

REFUNDING

Nazi Germany used gold seized from conquered countries to purchase arms and raw materials, as well as goods and services from neutral countries. This raises the question of the legality of using this gold. According to Detlev Vagts, professor at Harvard Law School, the legality of such use is debatable. The point in question is whether the Hague Convention of October 18, 1907 permits victors to take the state gold reserves of conquered countries and whether the neutral countries were good faith buyers of this gold. [731]

The interpretation of the legitimacy of demands for the return of such gold was dealt with – or allowed to lapse – after the war ended. Portugal and Turkey, for instance, were particularly important to the West in the context of the looming Cold War. The West's overriding concern with the struggle against communism allowed Turkey to avoid the return of any German gold after the war years.

Meanwhile, the American military's need for Portugal's strategic Azores resulted in the original $50 million claim against that country to be reduced to about $4.4 million, with negotiations finally being broken off a full fourteen years after the end of the war. Sweden also got off lightly – refunding only 13.2 tons of the 59.7 tons of Nazi gold. Switzerland, however, was committed by the Washington Agreement of 1946 to refund 250 million Swiss francs. Again one cannot help asking: had Switzerland been a member of the United Nations, or had something like the Azores or occupied an important geopolitical position, would Cold War considerations have induced the Allies to demand an equally small repayment

---

[729] Bergier Report, p. 544.

[730] Ibid., p. 546.

[731] Detlev F. Vagts, "Neutrality Law in World War II," in: Cardozo Law Review. Vol. 20 No. 2, December 1998, p. 471.

from Switzerland? This question will never be answered, but it raises questions about justice and reasons of state.

REFUGEES

The issues of refugees and border policies are very complex and have been subjected to considerable comparative international study. For Switzerland, with its humanitarian traditions, this was a very difficult chapter in its history. Yet the Swiss have been accused of knowing about the existence of the extermination camps when they made the decision to close their borders. This accusation, too, will most probably never be definitively laid to rest. But there certainly were other countries aware of mass killings in Germany which took no action. By not responding, they allowed incredible suffering. So perhaps some credit should be given to the Swiss leadership for taking in hundreds of thousands of people and offering them safe refuge in Switzerland. Again, strangely enough, it is Switzerland which is singled out as the primary culprit in the matter of refugees. How did other neutral states deal with this matter?

Spain's refugee and transit policies were decidedly limited. Between 1942 and 1944, Franco, according to estimates made by historian Haim Avni, offered a safe haven in Spain to only about 7,500 refugees. Requirements for obtaining a Spanish visa were very restrictive and Spanish bureaucracy was extremely creative in producing nightmare scenarios for people trying to escape Nazi rule. On the other hand, Franco did help Jews of Spanish origin in various European countries. Haim Avni estimates that between 20 and 30 thousand refugees were given transit documents allowing them to cross Spanish territory on their way to Portugal. Nonetheless, refugees from France who tried to cross the Spanish border illegally were interned in the concentration camp of Miranda de Ebro and subsequently extradited to Vichy France and in some cases also to Germany. Severin Hochberg, Senior Historian of the United States Holocaust Museum calls Haim Avni the best qualified expert on this topic whose estimates was thoroughly researched and should be seen as reliable. [732] Strangely enough, the Bergier Commission quotes Avni's name, but then refers to another researcher, Belot, who estimated the number of Jewish transit refugees through Spain at about 100,000, [733] i.e. more then three times Avni's estimate. It is peculiar that the Bergier Commission decided to use the much higher transit figure. Was the higher number more useful when comparing Switzerland to a dictatorial state? If so, then Avni's 20 to 30 thousand would not do.

Portugal was not willing to give a permanent home to any refugees, but issued transit visas to many refugees allowing them to pass through Lisbon to overseas destinations. The same applies to *Turkey,* which permitted Jewish refugees a transit through its territories to Palestine.

---

[732] E-mail and telephone communication with Severin Hochberg.
[733] Bergier Report, p. 171; Avni Haim, Spain, the Jews and Franco. (Philadelphia, 1982); Robert Belox, Aux frontières de la liberté: Vichy, Madrid, Alger, Londres, S'évader de France sous l'occupation. (Paris, 1988) Pour une histoire du XX siècle.

In view of the persecution in neighboring countries, *Sweden* changed what had been a lockout policy in 1943, and thereafter showed exemplary commitment to saving and harboring many thousands of refugees. Just as Switzerland, Sweden served as a protective power for other states' interests and used this function to save lives. During the war years, Sweden acted as a representative for 28 countries and held 114 official protection mandates.

The *United States*, though huge, showed very little generosity towards refugees. The first US official position against such undesirables was to deny their existence and relevance to the USA. Unfortunately, that meant the problem did not go away and there were calls for international efforts. But even this action could not hide the facts that in the late fall of 1941, the USA still had no refugee policy. The generally adopted practice was to ignore the problem. For Washington bureaucrats, the word refugee was synonymous with alien, and the Pentagon suspected them as being secret agents. Both definitions sufficed for keeping the doors locked. Far too many self-satisfied Americans whose ancestors had themselves been refugees – often for religious reasons – now saw a refugee as one more person who had to be fed, was out of work, would provoke anti-Semitism, likely bring in un-American ideologies or open the US to an uncontrollable flood of unwashed foreigners. [734] Between 1942 and 1945, the USA allowed a total of only 21,000 refugees to enter the US legally and permanently. [735] That is a small number indeed for a country whose banknotes are inscribed with the words "In God We Trust."

Switzerland was never in a position to prevent the National-Socialists from exterminating the Jews of Europe. But the Swiss did put a few obstacles in the Nazis' way. Since Switzerland acted as representative for interests of other states during the war, Swiss diplomats were able to combine such activities with Switzerland's status as a neutral to save many Jewish lives. The achievements of Swiss diplomat Carl Lutz, to cite just one example, were legend. The humanitarian efforts of the International Committee of the Red Cross (ICRC), [736] which under the Geneva Convention on Prisoners of War of 1929 technically took on the implementation of such representative duties, also saved many lives. [737] During World War II, Switzerland represented the interests of some 43 nations, including the United States of America and Britain.

Maybe the Swiss government did not use all imaginable means to save people seeking refuge in Switzerland, but it is an undeniable fact that small, encircled

---

[734] Bat-Ami Zucker, In Search of Refuge. Jews and US Consuls in Nazi Germany 1933-1941. (London/Portland, 2001), p. 59.

[735] David S. Wyman, The Abandonment of the Jews: America and the Holocaust 1941-1945 (New York, 1998), p. 136. These quotations are all on page 136 of this book published in 1998: Between Pearl Harbor and the end of the war, about 21,000 refugees, mostly Jews, entered the United States from Europe. This number corresponds to 10% of the quota legally available in these years for people from countries occupied by the Axis powers. Wyman does not quote a precise number of Jewish refugees for this period.

[736] Meir Wagner, The Righteous of Switzerland: Heroes of the Holocaust. (New Jersey, 2001), p. xii.

[737] Detlev F. Vagts, "Neutrality Law in World War II," in: Cardozo Law Review. Vol. 20 No. 2 December 1998 p. 475.

Switzerland took in 320,000 refugees. Current research gives that number – which is 30,000 higher than the long-quoted figure of 291,000 refugees. The increase certainly includes more Jewish refugees. Thus the accusation that Switzerland was an accomplice in genocide and mass murder, and that its policies assisted the Nazis in achieving their goals verges on slander.

WAS SWITZERLAND A COUNTRY OF COLLABORATORS AND PROFIT-MONGERS?

The demands of survival and security in a state of national crisis or war often outweigh the commitment to international humanitarian principles and civil liberties. During the Second World War Japanese-Americans were interned for which the US Congress apologized long after the war was over. In 1995 Switzerland's President Kaspar Villiger apologized to the country's Jewish community for its treatment of Jewish refugees during the war and its refusal to accept more into the country. [738] The implications of these lapses in humanity and civil liberties on the part of governments and in some cases its people too is the belief that during times of national security civil liberties, freedoms and humanity are subservient when the safety of the people becomes the supreme law of the land even when it leads to cooperation with Germany. The concessions made by the Swiss government and Swiss private business community to the Axis powers were necessary: Switzerland's economic and political survival depended on such cooperation and in fact "constituted an element of resistance to the clutches of the powerful German neighbor and represented a component of national defense strategy." [739] Businesses saw the opportunity to make a profit while the Federal state viewed their actions as a condition for survival.

Swiss conduct during World War II is not free of moral reproach, but on the whole Switzerland was in compliance with the rules of neutrality and international law as they were understood. According to Jean-François Bergier of the ICE Commission, "there were no instances at all in which our research revealed any cooperation that may have been based on ideological motivation or some type of sympathy for the Nazi regime either on the part of our public institutions or on that of Swiss companies." [740] However, at the same time according to Bergier, the neutrality preached was often not legitimate and cited several examples such as the shipments of war materials, improper control of the train route between Germany and Italy, and the Swiss government's issuance of a credit line to Germany. [741] There were certainly lapses in upholding Swiss neutrality, though some of them leaned in favor of the Allies. The impression of collaborating with the Axis powers, however, continues through the half-truth statements of the Bergier Commission like Switzerland outspokenly collaborated with Germany in support

---

[738] Stuart E. Eizenstat, Imperfect Justice: Looted Assets, Slave Labor, and the Unfinished Business of World War II (New York, 2003), p. 48

[739] See Jean-François Bergier, Introductory Address, ICE Press Conference, (Mar. 22, 2002), available at http://www.uek.ch/en/index.htm

[740] Ibid.

[741] Ibid.

of the Holocaust when the Swiss "...handed over apprehended refugees directly to their persecutors, assisting the National Socialists in achieving their goals," [742] while providing refuge for tens of thousands of Jews and other perople. It is to the great detriment of the Bergier Commission's work that the climate of opinion at the times were not always taken fully into account especially in the area of purchasing and selling gold. The issue of survival following the global economic crisis of the Great Depression and Great Slump in the early 30s was vividly in the minds of many leaders as World War II had erupted in 1939 and clearly was of a higher priority than business ethics. So some important decision makers in the USA thought such as Dexter White, head of the Division of Monetary Research at the United States Treasury Department, it was entirely proper to acquire gold without asking about its origin.

Still there are key questions which must be posed not only to Switzerland but to all countries as well in regard to collaborating with a rogue nation: should a state committed to moral principles really remain silent if a murderous totalitarian regime threatens and violates peace, liberty and even the physical existence of countries and whole peoples not only beyond but within its borders? Is it right to insist on the continuation of a formal neutrality and thereby continue negotiating with a criminal regime which abandons all human virtues like Nazis Germany especially when the war was already coming to end? Is there merit that at time of war voices can be silenced or modulated and citizens of a democratic country can be detained without charge or suspension of the *habeas corpus*? One is reminded of the Latin maxim, *inter arma silent leges*: In time of war, the laws are silent.

Cut off during World War II, Switzerland attempted through many and difficult negotiations with both sides to insure its survival. It was forced to engage in a battle for food production to feed its population as well as plan and pay for costly defense measures all which required financial revenue stemming from an economy dependent on revenue from successful and profitable businesses. In addition Switzerland was limited in its ability to voice its opinion or ask questions let alone make major demands. The only alternative to neutrality – which was never neutrality of its peoples' spirit in favor of democracy – would have been, against all reason, a declaration of war against the Axis. Switzerland was isolated, had no outside help, and had to rely on itself.

It is easier to make objective judgments about history when that history lies further in the past and there are fewer emotional connections. The events which confronted Switzerland, other neutrals and the United States occurred just sixty years ago. That is a relatively short period and in between lays a major watershed in research, science and in our understanding of democracy and human rights. Yet the current predisposition to condemn actions of that period comes from a closeness which is more apparent than real. In other words, since members of our families were active in those times and because we are very familiar with the period, it is easy for historians to think that those decades were shaped like our own and overlook ways in which they differed profoundly from our own. We may see it as "yesterday" but the people of those times, in many areas of their lives,

---

[742] Bergier Report, p. 172

oriented their lives according to principles very different from those of today's society.

In a letter written by Winston Churchill to Foreign Secretary Anthony Eden in December 1944, Churchill refers to Switzerland: "Of all the neutrals, Switzerland has the greatest right to distinction.... What does it matter whether she has been able to give us the commercial advantage we desire or has given too many to the Germans...? She has been a democratic state, standing for freedom in self-defense...and largely on our side." [743] So one may indeed be justified in judging Switzerland as a leader, but as a leader in maintaining the legitimacy of neutrality, as guaranteed by the states of Europe since 1815 and upheld in two World Wars.

---

[743] Winston Churchill, The Second World War: Triumph and Tragedy. (London, 1953), p. 712

BIBLIOGRAPHY

ARCHIVES AND UNPUBLISHED SOURCES

Archives of the Committee of the International Red Cross:
  ACICR, G AM/A; ACICR, C, G2 WA
Franklin D. Roosevelt Library, New York:
  Henry A. Wallace Collection, President's Secretary's File
Militärisches Bundesarchiv Freiburg:
  BA / MA RW19/440
Princeton University:
  Seely Mudd Library. Harry Dexter White Collection
Public Record Office, London:
  FO 371/22935, FO 371/23174, FO 371/24296, FO 371/24532, FO 371/25055
Swiss Federal Archives, Berne:
  E 1004-1 Bundesratsprotokoll 6,M, October 24 and 30, 1939; November 14 and
  28, 1939; December 11 and 27, 1939; February 24 and 27, 1940 and May 21,
  1940;1/Vol. 400 August 12, 194; 7110 EVD 1967/32; 7110 EVD 1973/134 Vol. 14
  7110 EVD 1973/134 Vol. 15; 7110 EVD 1973/134 Vol. 16; BA E2001
Swiss National Bank, Zurich:
  Report by Victor Gautier "Voyage à Lisbonne et à Madrid du 12 au 26 octobre."
Special Archives, Moscow:
  Documentation 700-1-85
United States National Archives and Records Administration (NARA):
  Record Group RG 38; RG 56; RG 59; RG 65; RG 131; RG 165
Wirtschaftsarchiv Baden-Württemberg, Stuttgart
  Documentation 95: book 112; book 141

PUBLISHED SOURCES

Amtliche Sammlung eidgenössischer Gesetzeserlasse (Swiss official Collection of Federal Acts), "Verordnung über die Handhabung der Neutralität vom 14. April 1939"

Akten zur Deutschen Auswärtigen Politik 1918-1945 (ADAP), Series D (1937-1941), Vols. 9-12 und Series E (1941-1945) Vols. 3-9

Bonjour, Edgar, Geschichte der Schweizerischen Neutralität. Vier Jahrhunderte eidgenössischer Aussenpolitik: Vols.7-9. (Basel, 1974-1976)

Commission for the Compensation of Victims of Spoliation of Jews in France: http://www.cisvs.gouv.fr/uk/commission/commission01.htm.

Commission of Research on Gold Transactions between Portuguese and German Authorities during the Period between 1936 and 1945

Commission of Jewish Assets in Sweden at the time of the Second World War (ed.), The Nazigold and the Swedish Riksbank – Interim Report August, 1998

Commission on Jewish Assets in Sweden at the time of the Second World War (ed.), Sweden and the Nazi Gold. (Conference paper presented at the London Conference on Nazi Gold, December 2-4, 1997)

Convention Respecting the Rights and Duties of Neutral Powers and Persons in Case of War on Land (Hague V). October 18, 1907, 36 Stat. 2310, 1 Bevans 654

Department of Commerce (Hal Lary and Associates), "The United States in World Economy" (Washington, D.C., 1943)

Diplomatische Dokumente der Schweiz (Swiss Diplomatic Documents) 1934-1949, Vols. 11 – 17 (Zurich, 1997-1999)

Documents on British Foreign Policy 1919-1939, (London 1947-1961)

Dokumente zur Deutschlandpolitik. Vol. 3 (Frankfurt am Main. 1988/1989)

Eidgenössische Zentralstelle für Kriegswirtschaft (ed.), Die Schweizerische Kriegswirtschaft 1939-1948. Bericht des Eidgenössischen Volkswirtschafts-Departementes (Bern, 1950)

Foreign & Commonwealth Office General Services Command (ed.): Historians, LRD, History Notes. British Policy towards Enemy Property during and after the Second World War. Number 13, April, 1998.

Foreign Relations of the United States Diplomatic Papers (FRUS), 1939-1946 (Washington, D.C., 1956 – 1967)

Freund, Florian und Bertrand Perz, Die Zahlenentwicklung der ausländischen Zwangsarbeiter und Zwangsarbeiterinnen auf dem Gebiet der Republik Österreich 1939-1945. (Vienna, 2000) www.historikerkommission.gv.at/pdf/Zahlen_pdf.pdf

Gerichtsurteil (Verdict) Réf. C/1761/2002 of Geneva June 11, 2004 between Gypsy International Recognition and Compensation Action (GIRCA) vs. International Business Machines Corporation (IBM)

Handbuch der schweizerischen Aussenpolitik. (Bern. 1975)

Hearings Before the Committee on Banking and Financial Services, House of Representatives, December 11, 1996; June 25, 1997; September 14, 1999

Hearings Before a Subcommittee of the Senate Committee on Military Affairs on the Elimination of German Resources for War, 79th Congress 2nd Session (1946)

Hearings Before a Subcommitte of the Senate Judicial Committee on the Industrial Reorganization Act, 93rd Congress 2nd Session (1974), Part 4A p. A-22 Bradford C. Snell American Ground Transport: A Proposal for Restructuring the Automobile, Truck, Bus and Rail Industries. Committee of the Judiciary Subcommittee on Antitrust and Monopoly, United States Senate 16-24 (1974)

Matteoli, Jean, Summary of the Work by the Study Mission on the Spoliation of Jews in France: Mattéoli Commission's Final Report, www.ladocfrancaise.gouv.fr. April 17, 2000

Morgenthau, Henry, Morgenthau Diaries. (New York, 1967)

Presidential Advisory Commission on Holocaust Assets in the United States and Staff Report – Findings and Recommendation (Washington, D.C., 2001)

El presidente de la Comisión de Investigación de las Transacciones de Oro Procedentes del III Reich durante la II Guerra dated April 8, 1998

Schweizerische Handelsstatistik, Jahresbericht 1945 (Swiss Trade Statistics, annual Report 1945) Eidgenössische Oberzolldirektion (ed.) part 2 (Bern, 1946)

Slaney, William S., US and Allied Efforts to Recover and Restore Gold and Other Assets Stolen or Hidden by Germany During World War II. Preliminary Study. Coordinated by Stuart E. Eizenstat. Undersecretary of Commerce and International Trade. (Washington, D.C., May, 1997)

Slaney, William, S., US and Allied Wartime and Postwar Relations and Negotiations with Argentina, Portugal, Spain, Sweden, and Turkey on Looted Gold and German External Assets and US Concerns about the Fate of the Wartime Ustasha Treasury. (June, 1998)

Speer, Albert, Erinnerungen. (Frankfurt/Main, 1969)

Statistisches Jahrbuch der Schweiz (Swiss Statistical Yearbook) 1945, Eidgenössisches Statistisches Amt. (Bern, 1946)

United States Department of State, Documents on German Foreign Policy. Series D. Vol. IX (Washington, D.C. 1949-1957)

United States Statutes at Large, 73rd Congress, 2nd Session

NEWSPAPERS AND PERIODICALS

Bitterli, Urs, "Humanitärer Auftrag und politische Ambition: Paul Stauffers neues Buch über Carl J. Burckhardt," in: Neue Zürcher Zeitung dated September 1, 1998, p. 13

Dobbs, Michael, Ford and GM Scrutinized for Alledged Nazi Collaboration, Washington Post, November 30, 1998

Ertel, Manfred, "Braunes Netzwerk im Norden in: Hitler's Krieg: Sechs Jahre, die die Welt erschüttern", in: Der Spiegel No. 2/2005

Frenkel, Max, "Die Flüchtlingspolitik in rechtlicher Sicht: Juristisches Lehrstück für historische Arbeit," in: Neue Zürcher Zeitung (NZZ), December 11/12, 1999 Nr. 289, p. 91

Friedman, John S., "Kodak's Nazi Connections," Nation, March 26, 2001

Herbert, Susannah, www.telegrap.co.uk dated February 4, 1999 "Banks Accused Over Nazi Cash," von Documents compiled by Dr. S. D. Stein. www.Stuart.Stein@uwe.ac.uk

Hofer, Walther, "Warum die Schweiz verschont blieb" in: Schweizer Illustrierte (September 18, 1989), pp. 133-138

Jost, Hans-Ulrich, "Die Schweiz im Zielkonflikt zwischen Neutralität, Solidarität und legitimem Egoismus" in: Tages-Anzeiger dated May 15, 1997

Keller, Max, "Eine unglaubliche Verwechslung" "Die Schuldzuweisung an Heinrich Rothmund für den J-Stempel beruht auf einem fatalen Irrtum." in: Schweizerzeit, publication No. 19 dated September 14, 1998

Koehler, Andrea, Neue Zürcher Zeitung (NZZ), "Der 'Aufbau' am Ende? Dated April 15, 2004

Lambelet, Jean-Christian, "Die Schweiz und die Flüchtlinge zur Zeit des Nationalsozialismus," in: Schweizer Monatshefte, March (2000) pp. 7-15

Müller, F.F., Stockholm und der J-Stempel, Neue Zücher Zeitung (NZZ), January 3, 2000

Neue Zürcher Zeitung, "Das Schicksal der Juden in Polen." dated June 20, 1943

Neue Zürcher Zeitung (NZZ), "Das Reduit auf den Weltmeeren. Ausstellung zur Schweizer Handelsflotte," at the Schweizerisches Landesmuseum in Prangins, January 2004.

Rauber, Urs, "Von Kooperation zum Widerstand: Der Schweizerische Israelitische Gemeindebund und die Flüchtlingspolitik von 1938 bis 1942" in Neue Zürcher Zeitung dated March 15, 2000, No. 63, p. 16

Rauber, Urs, "Rettungshafen St. Gallen. Der Ostschweizer Kanton nahm mehr Nazi-Flüchtlinge auf als bisher angenommen," in: Neue Zürcher Zeitung (NZZ am Sonntag) dated September 18, 2005, p. 81

Tanner, Jakob, "Der Frage der Kriegsverlängerung nachgehen," in : Basler Zeitung dated May 21, 1997

US News and Reports, June 23, 1996

von Salis, J.R., "Kriegsende in Europa," in: Neue Schweizer Rundschau, 13 1945/1946, pp. 67-88

The David Wyman Institute for Holocaust Studies, "History Channel Distorted FDR's Response to the Holocaust." www.wymaninstitute.org

BOOKS AND ARTICLES

Aalders, Gerard und Cees Wiebes, Die Kunst der Tarnung. Die geheime Kollaboration neutraler Staaten mit der deutschen Kriegsindustrie. Der Fall Schweden. (Frankfurt/Main, 1994)

Acheson, Dean, Present at the Creation: My Years in the State Department. (New York, 1969)

Åkerrén, Bengt, "Schweden als Schutzmacht," in: Rudolf L. Bindschedler et al. (ed.) Schwedische und schweizerische Neutralität im Zweiten Weltkrieg. (Basel, 1985)

Alemdar, K, "Anadolu Ajansi'na Alman Baskisi," in: Tarih ve Toplum. Ocak, No. 37 (1987)

Altrichter, Helmut und Josef Becker (ed.), Kriegsausbruch 1939 Beteiligte, Betroffene, Neutrale. (Munich, 1989)

Angermann, Erich, Die Vereinigten Stataten von Amerika. Vol. 7 (Munich, 1975)

Arbeitskreis Gelebte Geschichte, Erpresste Schweiz (Stäfa, 2002)

Arbeitskreis Gelebte Geschichte, Wir ziehen Bilanz (Stäfa, 2005)

Aström, Sveker, Swedish Neutrality: "Credibility through Commitment and Consistency," in: Bengt Sundelius (Hrg.), The Committed Neutral; Sweden's Foreign Policy. (Boulder, 1989)

Auboin, Roger, "The Bank for International Settlements, 1930-1955," in: Essays in International Finance. (Princeton, 1955)

Auer, Felix, Das Schlachtfeld von Thun oder Dichtung und Wahrheit bei Jean Ziegler, (Stäfa, 1997)

Avni, Haim, Spain, the Jews and Franco (1982)

Bartolini, Stefano, "The Membership of Mass Parties: The Social Democratic Experience, 1889-1978," in: Hans Daalder und Peter Mair (ed.), Western European Party Systems. (London, 1983)

Bauer, Yehuda, "Anmerkungen zum 'Auschwitz Bericht' von Rudolf Vrba," in: Dietrich Bracher et al (ed.), Vierteljahrshefte für Zeitgeschichte. Volume 2 (Munich, 1997), pp. 297-307

Bauer, Yahuda, American Jewry and the Holocaust. The American Jewish Joint Distribution Committee 1939-1945. (Detroit, 1981)

Bauer, Yehuda, Jews for Sale? Nazi-Jewish Negotiations 1933-1945. (New Haven, 1994)

Bazyler, Michael J., Holocaust Justice. The Battle for Restitution in America's Courts. (New York, 2003)

Bazyler, Michael J. and Amber J. Fitzgerald, "Trading with the Enemy: Holocaust Restitution, The United States Government and American Industry", in: Brookings Journal of International Law. Vol. 28:3, 2004 www.brooklaw.edu/students/journals/bjil/bjil28iii_bazyler.pdf

Belot, Robert, Aux frontières de la liberté: Vichy, Madrid, Alger, Londres, s'évader de France sous l'occupation. (Paris, 1998) Pour une histoire du XX siècle

Benbassa, Esther und Aron Rodrigue, The Jews of the Balkans (Oxford l995)

Bernecker, Walther L,. "Neutralität wider Willen. Spaniens verhinderter Kriegseintritt," in: Helmut Altrichter und Josef Becker (ed.) Kriegsausbruch 1939. Beteiligte, Betroffene, Neutrale. (Munich 1989)

Bickel, Wilhelm, Die Volkswirtschaft der Schweiz. Entwicklung und Struktur. (Aarau, 1973)

Bindschedler, Rudolf L. et al., Schwedische und schweizcrische Neutralität im Zweiten Weltkrieg. (Basel, 1985)

Bisbee, E., The New Turks Pioneers of the Republic 1920–1950. (Philadelphia, 1951)

Black, Edwin, IBM and the Holocaust. (New York, 2002)

Boelcke, Willi A. (ed.), Deutschlands Rüstung im Zweiten Weltkrieg. Hitlers Konferenzen mit Albert Speer 1942-1945. (Frankfurt am Main, 1969)

Boelcke, Willi A., Deutschland als Welthandelsmarkt, 1930-1945 (Stuttgart, 1994)

Boelcke, Willi A., Die "europäische Wirtschaftspolitik des Nationalsozialismus," in: Historische Mitteilungen 5 (1992) pp. 194-232

Bolliger, Kurt, "Die Neutralitätswahrung im Luftraum," in: Rudolf L. Bindschedler et al. (ed.), Schwedische und schweizerische Neutralität im Zweiten Weltkrieg. (Basel, 1985)

Bondo, Michael D., The Gold Standard and Related Regimes. Collected Essays. (Cambridge, 1999), Bond, Brian, France and Belgium, 1939-1940. (London, 1965)

Bonjour, Edgar, Geschichte der Schweizerischen Neutralität. Vier Jahrhunderte eidgenössischer Aussenpolitik. Vols. 1-6 (Basel, 1967)

Botur, André, "Privatversicherung im Dritten Reich. Zur Schadensabwicklung nach der Reichskristallnacht unter dem Einfluss nationalsozialistischer Rassen- und Versicherungspolitik," in: Berliner juristische Universitätenschriften, Reihe Zivilrecht, Vol. 6 (Berlin, 1995)

Bosshard, Felix, Der Gotthardvertrag von 1909, Ein Beitrag zur schweizerischen Innen- und Aussenpolitik vor Ausbruch des Ersten Weltkrieges. Dissertation. (Zurich, 1973)

Bourgeois, Daniel, Le Troisième Reich et la Suisse, 1933-1941. (Neuchâtel, 1974)

Bourgeois, Daniel, Das Geschäft mit Hitler-Deutschland. Schweizer Wirtschaft und das Dritte Reich. (Zurich, 2000)

Bower, Tom, Blood Money: The Swiss, the Nazis and the Looted Billions. (London, 1997)

Bower, Tom, Blind Eye to Murder: Britain, America and the Purging of Nazi Germany – A Pledge Betrayed. (London, 1981)

Boyce, Robert W.D., British Capitalism at the Crossroads 1919-1932: A Study in Political, Economic and International Relations. (Cambridge, 1987)

Braunschweig, Pierre-Th., Secret Channel to Berlin: The Masson-Schellenberg Connection and Swiss Intelligence in World War II (Casemate Publishers, Pennsylvania, 2004)

Breitman, Richard und Alan M. Kraut, American refugee policy and European Jewry, 1933-1945. (Bloomington, 1987)

Breitman, Richard, Staatsgeheimnisse. Die Verbrechen der Nazis – von den Alliierten toleriert. (Munich 1999)

Browning, Christopher, The Final Solution and the German Foreign Office. (New York, 1978)

Brügel, Johann Wolfgang, "Dahlerus als Zwischenträger nach Kriegsausbruch," in: Historische Zeitschrift No. 228 (1979), pp. 70-97

Bucher, Rudolf, Zwischen Verrat und Menschlichkeit. Erlebnisse eines Schweizer Arztes an der deutsch-russischen Front 1941/1942. (Frauenfeld, 1967)

Burdick, Charles B., "Moro": The Resupply of German Submarines in Spain 1939-1942," in: Central European History. No. 3 (1970), pp. 256-284

Burrin, Philippe, France under the Germans. Collaboration and Compromise. (London, 1997)

Butler, J.R.M., "The History of the Second World War", in: United Kingdom Military Series, Grand Strategy. Vol. II September 1939 – June 1941. (London, 1958)

Cabrera, Mercedes and Fernando del Rey, "Spanish Entrepreneurs in the Era of Fascism. From the Primo de Rivera Dictatorship to the Franco Dictatorship (1923-1945)." Paper read at the conference held on November 26/27th 2002 by The Society for European Business History e.V. – SEBH on Enterprises in the Period of Fascism in Europe

Cain, P.J. und A.G. Hopkins, British Imperialism: Crisis and Destruction 1914-1990. Vol. 2, (London/New York, 1993)

Cain, P.J., "Gentlemanly Imperialism at Work: the Bank of England, Canada, and the

Sterling Area, 1932-1936," in: Economic History Review, Vol.XLIX, No. 2 (London, 1996)

Cairns, J.C., "Great Britain and the Fall of France: A Study in Allied Disunity," in: Journal of Modern History. Vol. xxvii No. 4 (1955)

Carlsson, Sten, "Die schwedische Neutralität – Eine historische Übersicht," in: Rudolf L. Bindschedler et al. (ed.), Schwedische und schweizerische Neutralität im Zweiten Weltkrieg. (Basel, 1985)

Caruana, L. und H. Rockhoff, "A Wolfram in Sheep's Clothing: Economic Warfare in Spain, 1940-1944," in: The Journal of Economic History, No. 63 Part 1 (2003), pp. 100-126

Cattani, Alfred, Hitlers Schatten über Europa: Brennpunkte der Zeitgeschichte 1933-1945. (Zurich, 1995)

Chapman, Guy, Why France Collapsed. (London, 1968)

Charguéraud, Marc-André, La Suisse présumée coupable, (Lausanne, 2001) pp. 33-42

Charguéraud, Marc-André, Le Banquier américain de Hitler. (Geneva, 2004)

Chenaux, Jean-Philippe, et al., Les Conditions de la Survie. La Suisse, la Deuxième Guerre mondiale et la crise des années 90. (Lausanne)

Chevallaz, Georges-André, Le défi de la neutralité; diplomatie et défense de la Suisse 1939-1945. (Vevey, 1995)

Churchill, Winston S., The Second World War: Their Finest Hour. vol. II (Boston, 1949)

Clark, E. C., "The Turkish Varlık Vergisi Reconsidered", in: Middle Eastern Studies Vol. 8, No. 2 (1972)

Clarke, S.V.O., Central Bank Cooperation, 1924-1931. (New York, 1967)

Clement, Piet, The Bank for International Settlements During the Second World War. in: Nazi Gold – The London Conference 2nd – 4th December 1997. (London, 1998)

Coogan, John W., The End of Neutrality. The United States, Britain, and Maritime Rights 1899-1915 (Ithaca, 1981)

Costigliola, Frank, France and the United States. The Cold War Alliance Since World War II. (New,York, 1992)

Cross, Ira, Domestic and Foreign Exchange. (London, 1923)

Crouch, Colin, "Inflation and the Political Organization of Economic Interests," in: Fred Hirsch and John H. Goldthorpe, The Political Economy of Inflation. (Cambridge, 1978)

Curran, Vivian Grosswald, "Competing Frameworks for Assessing Contemporary Holocaust-Era Claims," in: Fordham International Law Journal. Vol. 25 (2001). Section 121

Davidson, Lawrence, "The State Department & Zionism 1917-1945: A Reevaluation," in: Middle East Policy, Vol. VII, No. 1, October, 1999

Das Deutsche Reich und der Zweite Weltkrieg. (Stuttgart, 1987)

Denniston, Robert, Churchill's Secret War: Diplomatic Decrypts, the Foreign Office and Turkey, 1942-1944. (London, 1997)

Deringil, Selim, "The Preservation of Turkey's Neutrality During the Second World War: 1940", in: Middle Eastern Studies, vol. 18 (1982), pp. 30–53

Dougherty, James J., The Politics of Wartime Aid: American Economic Assistance to France and French North Africa 1940-1946. (Westport, 1978),

Dulles, Foster Rhea, Amerikas Weg zur Weltmacht 1898 – 1956. (Stuttgart, 1957)

Durrer, Marco, Die schweizerisch-amerikanischen Finanzbeziehungen im Zweiten Weltkrieg: Von der Blockierung der schweizerischen Guthaben in den USA über die "Safehaven"-Politik zum Washington Abkommen 1941-1946. (Bern und Stuttgart, 1984)

Eichengreen, Barry, (ed.), The Gold Standard in Theory and History. (New York, 1985)

Eichengreen, Barry, Golden Fetters: The Gold Standard and the Great Depression, 1919-1939. (New York and Oxford, 1992)

Ellis, L.F., The War in France and Flanders, 1939-1940. (London, 1953)

Erdman, Paul, Swiss-American Economic Relations: Their Evolution in an Era of Crisis. (Tübingen, 1959)

Ernst, Alfred, "Die Bereitschaft und Abwehrkraft Norwegens, Dänemarks und der Schweiz in deutscher Sicht," in: Neutrale Kleinstaaten im Zweiten Weltkrieg. (Münsingen, 1973)

Ernst, Alfred, Die Konzeption der schweizerischen Landesverteidigung 1815 – 1966. (Frauenfeld/Stuttgart, 1971)

Favez, Jean-Claude, Une Mission Impossible? Le CICR, les déportations et les camps de concentration nazie. (Lausanne, 1998)

Favez, Jean-Claude, The Red Cross and the Holocaust. (Cambridge/New York, 1999)

Feis, Herbert, The Spanish Story. Franco and the Nations at War. (New York, 1966)

Feldman Gerald D., "Die Deutsche Bank vom Ersten Weltkrieg bis zur Weltwirtschaftskrise 1914-1933," in: Lothar Gall et al., Die Deutsche Bank 1870-1995. (Munich, 1995), pp. 138-314

Fink, Juerg, Die Schweiz aus der Sicht des Dritten Reiches 1933-1945. (Zurich, 1985)

Finkelstein, Norman G., The Holocaust Industry: Reflections on the Exploitation of Jewish Suffering. (New York, 2000)

Fior, Michel, Die Schweiz und das Gold der Reichsbank. Was wusste die Schweizerische Nationalbank? (Zurich, 1997)

Fisher, Irving, The Stock Market Crash and After. (New York, 1930)

Fitzgerald, E. V. K., "ECLA and the Theory of Import Substituting Industrialization in Latin America," in: Enrigue Cardenas, José Antonio Ocampo, and Rosemary Thorp (ed.), An Economic History of Twentieth Century Latin America, Vol. III (New York, 2000)

Flückiger, Pierre, Les réfugiés civils et la frontière genevoise durant la Deuxième Guerre Mondiale, Archives de Genève sous la direction de Catherine Santschi. (Geneva 2000)

Forbes, Neil, "Doing Business with the Nazis: Britain and Germany in the 1930s," in: Society for European History Fourth Annual Workshop: The Management of Political Risk in Dictatorial Environments: European Foreign Investment: 1918-1980. (Paris, March 21/22, 2002)

Forster, Gilles, Transit ferroviaire à travers la Suisse 1939 – 1945. (Zurich, 2001)

Frech, Stefan, Die deutsche Kriegswirtschaft und die Schweiz 1943-1945. Bedeutung der Schweiz als Handelspartnerin und Warenlieferantin. (Bern, 1998)

Fritz, Martin, "Wirtschaftliche Neutralität während des Zweiten Weltkrieges," in: Rudolf L. Bindschedler et al. (ed.), Schwedische und schweizerische Neutralität im Zweiten Weltkrieg. (Basel, 1985)

Fritz, Martin, German Steel and Swedish Iron Ore 1939–1945. (Göteborg, 1974)

Funk, Arthur L., "American Wartime Relations with Neutral European States: The Case of the United States and Switzerland", in: Les Etats neutres européens et la Seconde Guerre Mondiale. Neuchâtel 1985)

Gabriel, Jürg Martin, The American Conception of Neutrality After 1941. (Basingstoke, 1988)

Gabriel, Jürg Martin, Sackgasse Neutralität. (Zurich, 1997)

Gauchmann, Lothar, Der Zweite Weltkrieg. Kriegführung und Politik. (Munich, 1967)

Goda, Norman J.W., "Banking on Hitler: Chase National Bank and the Rückwanderer Mark Scheme, 1936-1941," in: Richard Breitman et al., Y.S. Intelligence and the Nazis. (Washington, D.C., 2004)

Gregory, Theodor Emanuel, The Gold Standard and Its Future. (London, 1932)

Grossman, Alexander, Nur das Gewissen. Carl Lutz und seine Budapester Aktion. (Wald, 1987)

Günçavdı, Öner und Ertuğrul Tokdemir, "The Second World War And Capital Market Development In a Neutral Country: The Case of Turkey," in: Verein für Finanzgeschichte – Schweiz und Liechtenstein. (Zurich, 2006)

Hafner, Georg, Bundesrat Walther Stampfli (1884-1965). (Olten, 1986)

Haight, John McVickar Jr., American Aid to France, 1938-1940. (New York, 1970)

Haim, Avni, Spain, the Jews and Franco. (Philadelphia, 1982)

Hedberg, Peter und Mats Larsson, "Banks, Financial Markets and the Swedish State During the Second World War," in: Verein für Finanzgeschichte -Schweiz und Liechtenstein. (Zurich, 2006)

Heiniger, Markus, Dreizehn Gründe. Warum die Schweiz im Zweiten Weltkrieg nicht erobert wurde. (Zurich, 1989)

Hernandez-Sandoica, Elena und Enrique Moradiellos, "Spain and the Second World War, 1939-1945," in: Neville Wylie (ed.), European Neutrals and Non-Belligerents During the Second World War. (Cambridge, 2002)

Heuberger, Max, Die Strukturwandlungen des schweizerischen Aussenhandels in den Jahren 1938 bis 1949. (Basel, 1955)

Hirsch, Peter, Er nannte sich Peter Suvara. Stäfa 1991; Keller, Stefan, Grüningers Fall. Geschichten von Flucht und Hilfe. (Zurich, 1993)

Hirschmann, Ira, Lifeline to a Promised Land (1963)

Hofer,Walther, Neutraler Kleinstaat im europäischen Konfliktfeld: Die Schweiz," in Helmut Altrichter und Josef Becker (ed.), Kriegsausbruch 1939: Beteiligte, Betroffene, Neutrale. (Munich, 1989)

Hofer, Walther and Herbert R. Reginbogin, Hitler, der Westen und die Schweiz. (Zurich, 2003)

Hofer, Walther, "Wer hat wann den Zweiten Weltkrieg verlängert? Kritisches zur merkwürdigen These einer Kriegsverlängerung durch die Schweiz," in: Kenneth Angst (ed.), Der Zweite Weltkrieg und die Schweiz. (Zurich, 1997)

Hofer, Walther, Die Diktatur Hitlers bis zum Beginn des Zweiten Weltkrieges. (Konstanz, 1960)

Hofer, Walther, "Neutralität im totalen Krieg," in: Mächte und Kräfte im 20. Jahrhundert. (Zurich, 1985)

Hofer, Walther, "Gestaltung der diplomatischen Beziehungen der Schweiz zu neuen oder untergegangenen Staaten sowie zu Staaten mit grundlegenden Systemänderungen," in: Rudolf L. Bindschedler et al. (ed.), Schwedische und schweizerische Neutralität im Zweiten Weltkrieg. (Basel, 1985)

Homberger, Heinrich, "Die Schweiz in der internationalen Wirtschaft," in: Aussenwirtschaft (AS). (Bern, 1949)

Horne, A., To Lose a Battle (New York, 1969)

Hotz, Jean, "Handelsabteilung und Handelspolitik in der Kriegszeit," in: Die Schweizerische Kriegswirtschaft 1939-1948. Bericht des Eidgenössischen Volkswirtschafts-Departementes. (Bern, 1950)

Hübinette, Tobias und Klaus Böhme, Den svenska nationalsocialismen: medlemmar och sympatisörer, 1931-1945. (Stockholm, 2002)

Hug, Peter, Schweizerische Rüstungsindustrie und Kriegsmaterialhandel zur Zeit des Nationalsozialismus. Unabhängige Expertenkommission Schweiz – Zweiter Weltkrieg UEK (ed.), Vols. 11/1and 11/2 (Zurich, 2002)

Hull, Cordell, The Memoirs of Codell Hull, Vol. II (London, 1948)

Inglin, Oswald, Der stille Krieg. Der Wirtschaftskrieg zwischen Grossbritannien und der Schweiz im Zweiten Weltkrieg. (Zurich, 1991)

Iriye, Akira, The Cambridge History of American Foreign Relations – The Globalizing of America, 1913–1945. Vol. III. (New York, 1993)

Jacobson, Max, The Diplomacy of the Winter War. (Cambridge, 1961)

Jackson, Gabriel, Spanish Republic and the Civil War, 1931–1939. (New York, 1976)

Jackson, Julian, France: The Dark Years, 1940-1944. (Oxford and New York, 2001)

Johnson D., "Britain and France 1940," in: Trans. Royal Historical Society. Vol. xxii (1972), pp. 142-146

Johnson, Griffeth, The Treasury and Monetary Policy 1933 – 1938 (Cambridge, 1939)

Jost, Adam, Die Haltung der Schweiz gegenüber dem nationalsozialistischen Deutschland im Jahre 1940. Dissertation (Berlin, 1972)

Jost, Hans Ulrich, Politik und Wirtschaft im Krieg: Die Schweiz 1938-1948. (Zürich, 1998), p. 148

Jost, Hans-Ulrich, "Bedrohung und Enge (1914-1945)," in: Geschichte der Schweiz und der Schweizer. (Basel, 1986)

Jung, Joseph, From Schweizerische Kreditanstalt to Credit Suisse Group – The History of a Bank. (Zurich, 2000)

Jung, Joseph (ed.), Zwischen Bundeshaus und Paradeplatz. Die Banken der Credit Suisse Group im Zweiten Weltkrieg. (Zurich, 2001)

Kaderli, Rudolph J. und Edwin Zimmermann, Handbuch des Bank-, Geld- und Börsenwesens der Schweiz. (Thun, 1947)

Kamber, Peter, Schüsse auf die Befreier. (Zurich, 1993)

Kaestli, Tobias, Selbstbezogenheit und Offenheit. Die Schweiz in der Welt des 20. Jahrhunderts. Zur politischen Geschichte eines neutralen Kleinstaats. (Zurich. 2005)

Karsh, Efraim, Neutrality and Small States. (London, 1988)

Keller H., und F. T. Wahlen, "Sektion für landwirtschaftliche Produktion und Hauswirtschaft," in: Die Schweizerische Kriegswirtschaft 1939/1948. Bericht des Eidgenössischen Volkswirtschaftsdepartementes. Die Eidgenössische Zentralstelle für Kriegswirtschaft (ed.), (Bern, 1950), pp. 257-298

Keller, Max, Das Ende der J-Stempel-Saga, Schriftenreihe Pro Libertate No. 11 (Bern, 1999)

Keller, Stefan, Grüningers Fall. Geschichten von Flucht und Hilfe. (Zurich, 1993)

Kimball, Warren F., Churchill and Roosevelt: The Complete Correspondence, Vol. I. (London, 1985)

Kimche, Jon., Spying for Peace: General Guisan and Swiss Neutrality. (London, 1961)

Kindleberger, Charles, The World in Depression, 1929-1939. (Berkeley, 1973)

Kinz, Diane B., The Battle for Britain's Gold Standard in 1931. (London, 1987)

Kleinfeld, Gerald R. und Lewis A. Tambs, Hitler's Spanish Legion. The Blue Division. (Carbondale, 1979)

Kleisel, Jean-Daniel, Electricité suisse et Troisième Reich. Unabhängige Expertenkommission Schweiz – Zweiter Weltkrieg (ed.) Vol. 5 (Lausanne, 2001)

Koblik, Steven, "Sweden's Attempt to Aid the Jews, 1939-1945" in: Scandinavian Studies, 56 (1984)

Kreis, Georg, Auf den Spuren von La Charité. Die schweizerische Armeeführung im Spannungsfeld des deutsch-französischen Gegensatzes 1936-1941. (Basel, 1976)

Kreis, Georg, "Das verpasste Rendezvous mit der Geschichte," in: Schweizerische Zeitschrift für Geschichte. Vol. 54 No. 3 (2004)

Kreis, Georg, Die Rückkehr des J-Stempels, zur Geschichte einer schwierigen Vergangenheitsbewältigung. (Zurich, 2000)

Kreis, Georg, Switzerland and the Second World War. (London/Portland, 2000)

Kreis, Georg, "Die schweizerische Flüchtlingspolitik der Jahre 1933-1945," in: schweizerische Zeitschrift für Geschichte, No. 4 (1997), pp. 552-579

Kreidler, Eugen, Die Eisenbahnen im Machtbereich der Achsenmächte während des

Zweiten Weltkrieges. Einsatz und Leistung für die Wehrmacht und Kriegswirtschaft. (Frankfurt/Zurich, 1975)

Krummenacher-Schoell, Joerg, Flüchtiges Glück: Die Flüchtlinge im Grenzkanton St. Gallen zur Zeit des Nationalsozialismus. (Zurich, 2005)

Kubitschek, Christian, Die wirtschaftliche Situation der Schweiz im Zweiten Weltkrieg. Beiträge zur Wirtschafts- und Sozialgeschichte. Vol. 7 (Weiden, 1994)

Kurz, Hans Rudolf, Dokumente des Aktivdienstes. (Frauenfeld, 1965)

Kurz, H.R., Operationsplanung Schweiz. Die Rolle der Schweizer Armee in zwei Weltkriegen. (Thun, 1974)

Lambelet, Jean-Christian, Evaluation critique du rapport Bergier sur "La Suisse et les réfugiés à l'époque du national-socialisme" et nouvelle analyse de la question. (Lausanne, 2000)

Lambelet, Jean-Christian, Le Mobbing d'un petit pays: Onze thèses sur la Suisse pendant la Deuxième Guerre Mondiale. (Lausanne, 1999)

Langer, William L. und S. Everett Gleason, The Challenge to Isolation 1937-1940. (London, 1952)

Lasserre, André, Frontières et camps: Le Refuge en Suisse de 1933 à 1945. (Lausanne, 1995)

LeBor, Adam, Hitler's Secret Bankers: The Myth of Swiss Neutrality during the Holocaust. (London, 2000)

Leitz, Christian, "Nazi Germany's Intervention in the Spanish Civil War and the Foundation of Hisma/Rowak," in: Paul Preston and Ann L. Mackenzie (ed.), The Republic Besieged; Civil War in Spain 1936-1939. (Edinbourgh, 1996), pp. 53-86

Leitz, Christian, Nazi Germany and Neutral Europe During the Second World War. (Manchester, 2000)

Leitz, Christian, Economic Relations between Nazi Germany and Franco's Spain, 1936-1945. (Oxford, 1996)

Leitz, Christian, " 'More Carrot than Stick,' British Economic Warfare and Spain, 1942-1944" in: Twentieth Century British History. No. 9 (1998)

Leitz, Christian, "Nazi Germany's Struggle for Spanish Wolfram during the Second World War," in: European History Quarterly. No. 25 (1995)

Levine, Paul, Swedish Neutrality During the Second World War: "Tactical Success or Moral Compromise?," in: Neville Wylie (ed.), European Neutrals and Non-Belligerents during the Second World War. (Cambridge, 2002)

Levine, Paul A., From Indifference to Activism: Swedish Diplomacy and the Holocaust 1938-1944. (Uppsala, 1996)

Linder, Wolf, "Entwicklung, Strukturen und Funktionen des Wirtschafts- und Sozialstaats in der Schweiz," in: Alois Riklin (ed.), Handbuch Politisches System der Schweiz. Vol. I. (Bern, 1983)

Lindgren, H., Bank, Investmentbolag, Bankfirma. Stockholms Enskilda Bank 1924 – 1945. (Stockholm, 1988)

Linke, Horst Guenther (ed.), "Quellen zu den Deutsch-Sowjetischen Beziehungen 1917-1945. (Darmstadt, 1998)

Lipschitz, Chaim U., Franco, the Jews, and the Holocaust (1984)

Lööw, Helene, Nazismen i Sverige 1924 – 1979: pionjärerna, partierna, propagandan. (Ordfront, 2004)

Lönnroth, Erik, "Sweden's Ambiguous Neutrality," in: Scandinavian Journal of History. No. 2 (1977)

Loepfe, Willi, Geschäfte in spannungsgeladener Zeit. Finanz- und Handelsbeziehungen zwischen der Schweiz und Deutschland 1923 bis 1946. (Weinfelden, 2006)

Logue, John, "The Legacy of Swedish Neutrality," in Bengt Sundelius (ed.), The Committed Neutral: Sweden's Foreign Policy. (Boulder, 1989)

Loudon, Louise, Whitehall and the Jews, 1933-1948: British Immigration Policy, Jewish Refugees and the Holocaust (Cambridge, 2000)

Louca, Antonio und Ansgar Schäfer, "Portugal and the Nazi Gold: The 'Lisbon Connection' in the Sales of Looted Gold by the Third Reich." http//www.yad.vashem.org.il/download/about_holocaust/studies/louca_full.pdf

Ludwig, Carl, Die Flüchtlingspolitik der Schweiz seit 1933 zur Gegenwart. (Bern, 1957)

Ludwig, Carl, La politique pratiquée par la Suisse à l'égard des réfugiés au cours des années 1939 à 1955. (Berne, 1957)

Lutzhöft, Hans-Jürgen, Deutsche Militärpolitik und schwedische Neutralität 1939-1942. (Neumünster, 1981)

Lüönd, Karl, Spionage und Landesverrat in der Schweiz, 2 Vols. (Zurich, 1997)

Lukauskas, Arvid, The Political Economy of Financial Deregulation: The Case of Spain. (Pennsylvania, 1992)

Maissen, Thomas, Verweigerte Erinnerung: Nachrichtenlose Vermögen und Schweizer Weltkriegsdebatte 1989-2004. (Zurich, 2005)

Marcuzzo, Maria Cristina und Annalisa Rosselli, Ricard and the Gold Standard. (Bologna, 1986)

Marguerat, Philippe, "La Suisse et la Neutralité dans le domaine économique pendant la seconde guerre mondiale 1940 – fin 1944," in: Louis-Edouard Roulet und Roland Blättler (ed.), Les Etats neutres européens et la seconde guerre mondiale. (Neuchâtel, 1985)

Marguerat, Philippe, Or allemand, BNS et dissuasion 1940-1944.

Marrus, Michael R und Robert O. Paxton, Vichy France and the Jews. (New York, 1981)

Marrus, Michael R., Some Measures of Justice: The Holocaust Era Restitution Campaign of the 1990s. (Not published)

Martin, Bernd, "Deutschland und die neutralen Staaten Europas im zweiten Weltkrieg," in: Louis-Edouard Roulet und Roland Blätter (ed.), Les Etats neutres européens et la seconde guerre mondiale. (Neuchâtel, 1985)

Matson, Robert W., Neutrality and Navicerts. Britain, the United States, and the Economic Warfare, 1939-1940. (New York/London, 1994)

Matt, Alphons, Einer aus dem Dunkeln. Die Befreiung des Konzentrationslagers Mauthausen durch den Bankbeamten H. (Zurich, 1988)

Medlicott, W.M, The Economic Blockade, 2 Vols. (London, 1952 und 1959)

Meyer, Frederick Victor, Britain, the Sterling Area and Europe.(Cambridge, 1952)

Militärgeschichtliches Forschungsamt (ed.), Das Dritte Reich und der Zweite Weltkrieg. (Stuttgart, 1979 – 1997)

Milton, Sybil und David Martin Luebke, "Locating the Victim: An Overview of Census Taking, Tabulation Technology and Persecution in Nazi Germany," in: IEEE Annals of the History of Computing Vol. 16, No. 3 (1994), pp. 25-39

Milward, Alan S., "Could Sweden Have Stopped the Second World War?" in: The Scandinavian Economic History Review 15 (1967), pp. 127-138

Millman, Brock, "Credit and Supply in Turkish Foreign Policy and the Tripartite Alliance of October 1939: A Note," in: International History Review. Vol. XVI (1994)

Morrison, Samuel Eliot und Henry Steele Commager, The Growth of the American Republic. (New York, 1962)

Müller, Rolf-Dieter, "Von der Wirtschaftsallianz zum kolonialen Ausbeutungskrieg," in: Das Deutsche Reich und der Zweite Weltkrieg. (Stuttgart, 1983) von Muralt, Peter Leonhard, Die Schweiz als Schutzmacht. (Dissertation) (Basel, 1947)

Newton, Ronald, Nazi Menace in Argentina, 1931-1947. (Stanford, 1995)

Ochsner, Richard, "Transit von Truppen, Einzelpersonen, Kriegsmaterial und zivilen Gebrauchgütern zugunsten einer Kriegspartei durch das neutrale Land," in: Rudolf L.

Bindschedler et al. (ed.), Schwedische und schweizerische Neutralität im Zweiten Weltkrieg. (Basel, 1985)

Ofer, Dalia, "The activities of the Jewish Agency delegation in Istambul, l943" in "Rescue Attempts during the Holocaust: Proceedings of the Second Yad Vashem Historical Conference, April l974

Olsson, Ulf, "Stockholms Enskilda Bank and the Bosch Group, 1939-1950," in: Banking & Enterprise. No I (Stockholm, 1998)

Olsson, Sven-Olof, German Coal and Swedish Fuel 1939-1945. (Goeteborg, 1975)

Orvik, Nils, The Decline of Neutrality, 1914-1941, (London, 1971)

Overy, R. J., War and Economy in the Third Reich. (Oxford, 1994)

Paxton, Robert O., Vichy France: Old Guard and New Order, 1940-1944, (New York, 1972)

Payne, Stanley G., The Franco Regime, 1939-1975. (Madison, 1975)

Perrenoud, Marc, "Banques et diplomatie suisse à la fin de la Deuxième Guerre mondiale. Politique de neutralité et relations financières internationales," in: Studien und Quellen. 13/14 (Bern, 1987/88)

Perrenoud, Marc, "Aspects de la politique financière et du mouvement ouvrier en Suisse dans les années 1930," in: Gerald Arletaz (ed.), Die Finanzen des Bundes im 20. Jahrhundert. (Bern, 2000)

Perrey, Hans-Juergen, Der Russlandausschuss der deutschen Wirtschaft. (Munich, 1985)

Picard, Jacques, Die Schweiz und die Juden, 1933-1945. Schweizerischer Antisemitismus, jüdische Abwehr und internationale Migrations- und Flüchtlingspolitik (Zurich, 1997)

Ploetz, A. G. (ed.), Geschichte des Zweiten Weltkrieges. (Würzburg, 1960)

Plumpe, Gottfried, Die I.G. Farbenindustrie AG – Wirtschaft, Technik und Politik 1904 – 1945. (Berlin, 1988)

Porat, Dina, The Blue and Yellow Stars of David (Cambridge l990)

Preston, Paul, A Biography. (London, 1995)

Preston, Paul, A Concise History of the Spanish Civil War. (London, 1996)

Preston, Paul, "Franco and Hitler: The Myth of Hendaye 1940," in: Contemporary European History. No. 1 (1992)

Pryce-Jones, David, Paris in the Third Reich. A History of the German Occupation, 1940-1944. (New York, 1981)

Quigley, Carroll, Tragedy and Hope. (New York, 1966)

Reginbogin, Herbert R., "The Financial Market of America During World War II," in: Verein für Finanzgeschichte Schweiz und Fürstentum Liechtenstein (ed.), Financial Markets of Neutral Countries During World War II. (Zurich, 2006)

Reich, Simon, Nachforschungen von Ford zur Beurteilung der Aktivitäten ihrer Tochtergesellschaften während des Nationalsozialismus. December 6, 2001. http.//www.media.ford.com

Rickmann, Greg J., Swiss Banks and Jewish Souls. (New Brunswick and London, 1999)

Rings, Werner, Raubgold aus Deutschland. Die "Golddrehscheibe" Schweiz im Zweiten Weltkrieg. (Zurich, 1985)

Rings, Werner, Schweiz im Krieg 1933-1945. (Zurich, 1997)

Roesch, Werner, Bedrohte Schweiz. Die Operationsplanungen gegen die Schweiz im Sommer/Herbst 1940 und die Abwehrbereitschaft der Armee im Oktober 1940. (Frauenfeld, 1986)

Rosas, Fernando, "Portuguese Neutrality in the Second World War," in: Neville Wylie (ed.), European Neutrals and Non-Belligerents During the Second World War. (Cambridge, 2002)

Roth, Karl Heinz, "Wirtschaftliche Vorbereitung auf das Kriegsende und Nachkriegsplanung," in: Dietrich Eichholtz, Geschichte der deutschen Kriegswirtschaft, 1939-1945. Vol. III (1943-1945). (Berlin, 1996)

Rubin, B., Istanbul Intrigues. (Istanbul, 2002)

Ruffieux, Roland, La Suisse de l'entre-deux-guerres. (Lausanne, 1974)

Ruhl, Klaus-Joerg, Spanien im Zweiten Weltkrieg. Franco, die Falange und das 'Dritte Reich'. (Hamburg, 1975)

Saul, E., Visas for Life, EDA, (Bern, 1998)

Schaffner, Hans, Eidgenössische Zentralstelle für Kriegswirtschaft (ed.), Die Schweizerische Kriegswirtschaft 1939/1948. (Bern, 1950)

Schiemann, Catherine, Neutralität in Krieg und Frieden. Die Aussenpolitik der Vereinigten Staaten gegenüber der Schweiz 1941-1949. (Zurich, 1991)

Schindler, Dietrich, "Dauernde Neutralität", in A. Riklin/H.Haug/H.C.Binswanger (ed.), Handbuch der schweizerischen Aussenpolitik. (Bern, 1975), pp. 159-180

Schloss, Henry H., The Bank for International Settlements. (Amsterdam, 1958)

Schreiber, Gerhard, "Die politische und militärische Entwicklung im Mittelmeerraum 1939/40," in: Das Deutsche Reich und der Zweite Weltkrieg. Vol. 3 part 1 (Stuttgart, 1984)

Schwarz, Urs, Vom Sturm umbrandet. Wie die Schweiz den Zweiten Weltkrieg überlebte. (Frauenfeld, 1981)

Schwarz, Urs, The Eye of the Hurricane: Switzerland in World War II. (Boulder, 1980)

Senn, Hans, "Die Schweizer Armee stand bereit," in: Kenneth Angst, (ed.), Der Zweite Weltkrieg und die Schweiz. (Zurich, 1997), p. 87

Senn, Hans, Der Schweizerische Generalstab, Vol. VII: Anfänge einer Dissuasionsstrategie während des Zweiten Weltkrieges. (Basel, 1995)

Shaw, Stamford J., Turkey and the Holocaust. (New York, 1993)

Shirer, William, The Collapse of the Third Republic: An Enquiry into the Fall of France in 1940. (New York, 1969)

Silberschmidt, Max, Der Aufstieg der Vereinigten Staaten von Amerika zur Weltmacht. (Aarau, 1941)

Simmons, Beth A., Who Adjusts: Domestic Sources of Foreign Economic Policy During the Interwar Years. (Princeton, 1994)

Slaney, William S., US and Allied Efforts to Recover and Restore Gold and Other Assets Stolen or Hidden by Germany During World War II. Preliminary Study. Coordinated by Stuart E. Eizenstat. Undersecretary of Commerce and International Trade. (Washington, D.C., May, 1997)

Slaney, William, S., US and Allied Wartime and Postwar Relations and Negotiations with Argentina, Portugal, Spain, Sweden, and Turkey on Looted Gold and German External Assets and US Concerns about the Fate of the Wartime Ustasha Treasury. (June, 1998)

Smith Jr., Arthur L., Hitler's Gold. (Oxford, 1989)

Smyth, Denis, Diplomacy and Strategy of Survival: British Policy and Franco's Spain., 1940-1941 (Cambridge, 1986), p.2; Neville Wylie, Britain, Switzerland and the Second World War. (Oxford and New York, 2003)

Stadler, Peter, Epochen der Schweizergeschichte. (Zurich, 2003)

Stamm, Luzi et al. (ed.), Dignity and Coolness. (Lenzburg, 2004)

Stauffer, Paul, Sechs furchtbare Jahre ... "Auf den Spuren Carl J. Burckhardts durch den Zweiten Weltkrieg. (Zurich, 1998)

Stauffer, Paul, Zwischen Hofmannsthal und Hitler. Carl J. Burckhardt. Facetten einer gewöhnlichen Existenz. (Zurich, 1991)

Stauffer, Paul, Polen, Juden, Schweizer. (Zurich 2004)

Steiner, Max, "Die Verschiebungen der schweizerischen Aussenhandelsstruktur während des Zweiten Weltkrieges. Dissertation, (Zurich, 1950)

Stoessinger, John G., Why Nations go to War. (Belmont, 2005)

Stone, Glyn, The Oldest Ally: Britain and the Portuguese Connection, 1936-1941. (Rochester, 1994)

Sutton, Antony, Wall Street and the Rise of Hitler, (London, 1976)

Tanner, Jakob, Bundeshaushalt, Währung und Kriegswirtschaft. Eine finanz-soziologische Analyse der Schweiz zwischen 1938 und 1953. (Zurich, 1986)

Tanner, Jakob, "Switzerland's International Financial Relations, 1931-1950," in: Georg Kreis (ed.), Switzerland and the Second World War. (London and Portland, 2000)

Temin, Peter, "Transmission of the Great Depression." In: Journal of Economic Perspectives No. 7 (1993), pp. 87-102

Theo, Tschuy, Carl Lutz und die Juden von Budapest. (Zurich, 1995)

Thomas, R. T., Britain and Vichy. The Dilemma of Anglo-French Relations 1940-1942. (London, 1979)

Thürer, Daniel, "Zur Neutralität der Schweiz im Zweiten Weltkrieg und den daraus zu ziehenden Lehren," in Bernhard Ehrenzeller et al. (ed.), Der Verfassungsstaat vor neuen Herausforderungen: Laudatio for Yvo Hangartner. (St. Gallen. 1998)

Tortella, Gabriel, "The Spanish Financial Sector During The Second World War," in: Verein für Finanzgeschichte Schweiz und Fürstentum Liechtenstein (ed.), Financial Markets of Neutral Countries During World War II. (Zurich, 2006)

Toynbee, Arnold und Veronica M. Toynbee (ed.), The War and the Neutrals, In: Survey of International Affairs 1939-1941. (London und New York, 1956)

Trepp, Gian, Die Bank für Internationalen Zahlungsausgleich im Zweiten Weltkrieg: Bankgeschäfte mit dem Feind. Von Hitlers Europabank zum Instrument des Marschallplans. (Zurich, 1993)

Uhlig, Christine, Petra Barthelmess, Mario Koenig und Peter Pfaffenroth, Tarnung, Transfer, Transit. Die Schweiz als Drehscheibe verdeckter deutscher Operationen (1939-1952), in: Unabhängige Expertenkommission Schweiz-Zweiter Weltkrieg (ed.), Vol. 9. (Zurich, 2002)

Unabhängige Expertenkommission Schweiz – Zweiter Weltkrieg, Die Schweiz und die Flüchtlinge zur Zeit des Nationalsozialismus. – UEK-Flüchtlingsbericht. (Bern, 1999)

Unabhängige Expertenkommission Schweiz – Zweiter Weltkrieg (ed.), Die Schweiz und die Goldtransaktionen im Zweiten Weltkrieg. Vol. 16 (Zurich, 2001)

Unabhängige Expertenkommission Schweiz – Zweiter Weltkrieg (ed.), Die Schweiz und die Flüchtlinge zur Zeit des Nationalsozialismus. Vol. 17. (Zurich, 2001)

Unabhängige Expertenkommission Schweiz – Zweiter Weltkrieg (ed.), Die Schweiz, der Nationalsozialismus und der Zweite Weltkrieg: Schlussbericht. (Zurich, 2001)

United States Holocaust Memorial Museum (ed.), The Holocaust. (Washington, 1994)

Urner, Klaus, Let's Swallow Switzerland. Hitler's Plans against the Swiss Confederation. Lexington Books, (Maryland 2001)

Urner, Klaus, "Neutralität und Wirtschaftskrieg: Zur schweizerischen Aussenhandelspolitik 1939-1945," in: Rudolf L. Bindschedler et al. (ed.), Schwedische und schweizerische Neutralität im Zweiten Weltkrieg. (Basel, 1985)

Vagts, Detlev F., "Neutrality Law in World War II," in: Cardozo Law Review. Vol. 20 No. 2 December 1998

Valerio, Nuno, "The Portuguese Capital Market During World War II," in: Verein für Finanzgeschichte Schweiz und Fürstentum Liechtenstein (ed.), Financial Markets of Neutral Countries During World War II. (Zurich, 2006)

Vaudaux, Adolph, Blockade und Gegenblockade. Handelspolitische Sicherung der schweizerischen Ein- und Ausfuhr im Zweiten Weltkrieg. (Basel, 1948)

Vetsch, Christian, Aufmarsch gegen die Schweiz. Der deutsche "Fall Gelb". Irreführung der Schweizer Armee 1939-1940. (Olten, 1973)

Vieli, Paul, 'Das Rechtssystem der Clearingverträge', Lecture presented on May 27, 1934 at the Schweizerische Vereinigung für internationales Recht, Publication No. 32.

Vogler, Robert, Die Wirtschaftsverhandlungen der Schweiz zwischen der Schweiz und Deutschland 1940 und 1941. Basel / Frankfurt am Main, 1997)

Vogler, Robert, "The Genesis of Swiss Banking Secrecy: Political and Economic Environment," in: Financial History Review. Vol. 8 Part 1 (Cambridge, 2001)

Vogler, Robert, "Das Schweizer Bankgeheimnis: Entstehung, Bedeutung, Mythos," in: Beiträge zur Finanzgeschichte. Publication No. 7 (Zurich, 2005) von Castelmur, Linus, Schweizerisch-Allierte Finanzbeziehungen im Übergang vom Zweiten Weltkrieg zum Kalten Krieg: Die deutschen Guthaben in der Schweiz zwischen Zwangsliquidierung und Freigabe (1945-1952). (Zurich, 1992)

Vrba, Rudolf, "Die missachtete Warnung. Betrachtungen über den Auschwitz-Bericht 1944," in: Dietrich Bracher et al (ed.), Vierteljahreshefte für Zeitgeschichte. Brochure 1 (Munich, 1996), pp. 1-24

Wadsworth, John, Counter Defensive. A Bank in Battle. (London, 1946)

Wagner, Meir, The Righteous of Switzerland: Heroes of the Holocaust. (New Jersey, 2001)

Waibel, Wilhelm J., Schatten am Hohentwiel. Zwangsarbeiter und Kriegsgefangene in Singen am Hohentwiel. (Konstanz, 1997)

Weicker, William, Ottomans, Turks, and the Jewish policy: a history of the Jews of Turkey. (1992)

Weinberg, Gerhard, A World at Arms: A Global History of World War II. (New York, 1994)

Weisberg, R. Richard, Vichy Law and the Holocaust in France. (1997)

Wheeler, Douglas L., "The Price of Neutrality; Portugal, the Wolfram Question and World War II," in: Luso-Brazilian Review, Vol. XXIII, part II (1986)

White, Harry, The French International Accounts. 1880-1913. (Cambridge, 1933)

Widmer, Sigmund, Geschichte der Schweiz. (Zurich, 1973)

Wilkins, Mira, "Swiss Investments in the United States 1914 – 1945," in: Switzerland and the Great Powers. (Geneva, 1999)

Wittmann, Klaus, Schwedens Wirtschaftsbeziehungen zum Dritten Reich. 1933-1945. (Munich, 1978)

Woodward, Sir Llewellyn, British Foreign Policy in the Second World War. (London, 1962)

Wright, G., "Ambassador Bullitt and the Fall of France," in: World Politics. Vol.X, No. 1 (1957)

Wylie, Neville, Britain, Switzerland and the Second World War. (Oxford and New York, 2003)

Wylie, Neville, "Switzerland: a neutral of distinction?," in: Neville Wylie, European Neutrals and Non-Belligerents during the Second World War. (Cambridge, 2002)

Wylie, Neville, "The Swiss Franc and British Policy Towards Switzerland 1939-1945," in: Sebastions Guex (ed.), Switzerland and the Great Powers 1914-1945. (Geneva 1999), pp. 461-480

Wyman, David, The Abandonment of the Jews. (New York, 1998)

Wyman, David, Das unerwünschte Volk, Amerika und die Vernichtung der europäischen Juden. (Munich, 1986)

Ziegler, Jean, The Swiss, the Gold and the Dead. (New York, 1998)

ABBREVIATIONS

ACICR	Archives du Comité international de la Croix-Rouge (Archives of the Committee of the International Red Cross)
ADAP	Akten zur Deutschen Auswärtigen Politik (Records on German Foreign Policy)
AfZ	Archiv für Zeitgeschichte (Archives for Contemporary History)
AG	Aktiengesellschaft (Corporation, Joint-stock company)
AHV	Alters- und Hinterbliebenenversicherung (Old-Age Pensions and Survivors' Insurance)
BA – MA	Deutsches Bundesarchiv – Militärarchiv (German Federal Archives – Military Archives)
BArch	Bundesarchiv Berlin (Federal Archives Berlin)
BCB	Basel Commercial Bank
BHB	Basler Handelsbank (Basel Commercial Bank, BCB)
DDS	Diplomatische Dokumente der Schweiz (Swiss Diplomatic Documents)
EIBA	Eidgenössische Bank (Federal Bank)
EJPD	Eidgenössisches Justiz- und Polizeidepartement (Federal Department of Justice and Police)
EPD	Eidgenössisches Politisches Departement (Federal Political Department), today: Eidgenössisches Departement für Ausswärtige Angelegenheiten (EDA)
EVD	Eidgenössisches Volkswirtschaftsdepartement (Federal Department of Economic Affairs)
Gestapo	Geheime Staatspolizei (Secret State Police)
IKRK/ICRC	Internationales Komitee vom Roten Kreuz (International Committee of the Red Cross)
kg	kilogram
KZ	Konzentrationslager (Concentration camp)
NARA	National Archives and Records Administration (United States National Archives)
NS	National Socialist
NSDAP	Nationalsozialistische Deutsche Arbeiterpartei (National Socialist German Workers' Party)
PCHA	Presidential Advisory Commission on Holocaust Assets
OSS	Office of Strategic Services (predecessor of the Central Intelligence Agency)
RM	Reichsmark
RGVA	Russisches Staatliches Militärarchiv (Russian Military State Archives)

SBG	Schweizerische Bankgesellschaft (Union Bank of Switzerland, today integrated into UBS)
SBV	Schweizerischer Bankverein (Swiss Bank Corporation today integrated into UBS)
SIG	Schweizerischer Israelitischer Gemeindebund (Swiss Federation of Jewish Communities, SFJC)
SKA	Schweizerische Kreditanstalt (Credit Suisse, CS)
SNB	Swiss National Bank
SS	Schutzstaffel der NSDAP (Protective Squadron of the NSDAP, Blackshirts)
SVB	Swiss Volksbank
UEK	Independent Commission of Experts, Switzerland – Second World War (also known as Bergier–Commission)
VSIA	Verband Schweizerischer Israelitischer Armenpflege (Association of Swiss Jewish Poor Relief); later: VSJF
VSJF	Verband Schweizerischer Jüdischer Flüchtlingshilfen (Association of Swiss Jewish Welfare and Refugee Relief); earlier: VSIA
WJC	World Jewish Congress

INDEX

226